lonely planet

D0609975

Discover
India

Throughout this book, we use these icons to highlight special recommendations:

 The Best...
Lists for everything from bars to wildlife – to make sure you don't miss out

 Don't Miss
A must-see – don't go home until you've been there

Local Knowledge Local experts reveal their top picks and secret highlights

Detour
Special places a little off the beaten track

If you like...
Lesser-known alternatives to world-famous attractions

These icons help you quickly identify reviews in the text and on the map:

 Sights

 Eating

 Drinking

 Sleeping

 Information

This edition written and researched by
Abigail Hole,
Michael Benanav, Lindsay Brown, Mark Elliott,
Katja Gaskell, Kate James, Amy Karafin,
Anirban Mahapatra, Bradley Mayhew, Daniel McCrohan,
John Noble, Kevin Raub, Sarina Singh

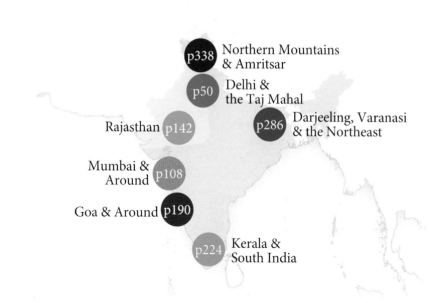

Contents

Plan Your Trip   On the Road

●●●

Delhi & the Taj Mahal   50

●●●

Mumbai (Bombay) & Around   108

Contents

On the Road

This is India

Bamboozling. No other word better captures the enigma that is India. With its ability to inspire, frustrate, thrill and confound all at once, India presents an extraordinary spectrum of encounters for the traveller. From rural serenity to big-city swirls of colour, from dizzyingly intricate carved temples to musicians playing ragas in the desert, from harlequin-bright elephants to gourmet restaurants in stylish cities, India will jostle your entire being, and no matter where you go or what you do, it's a place that fires the imagination and stirs the soul like nowhere else on Earth.

India is arguably the world's most multidimensional nation.

Even a fleeting visit there could encompass snow-dusted mountains, sun-washed beaches, lantern-lit villages and software-supremo cities. For those seeking spiritual sustenance, India has sacrosanct sites and thought-provoking philosophies galore. For those in search of a different kind of nourishment – you're about to jump on board one of the wildest culinary trips of your life! Frying, simmering, sizzling, kneading and flipping a deliciously diverse variety of regional dishes, feasting your way through the subcontinent is certainly one hell of a ride. History buffs will stumble upon gems from the past almost everywhere – from grand vestiges of former empires serenely peering over swarming streets, to crumbling fortresses looming high above plunging ravines. Meanwhile, aficionados of the great outdoors can paddle in the shimmering waters of one of many beautiful beaches, scout for big jungle cats on blood-pumping wildlife safaris or simply inhale pine-scented air on meditative forest walks.

With such a feast of opportunities, you're bound to find many more things to fascinate in this astounding, confounding country.

And even on a short trip you can go surprisingly in-depth and experience a remarkable range of wonders.

> India fires the imagination and stirs the soul like nowhere else.

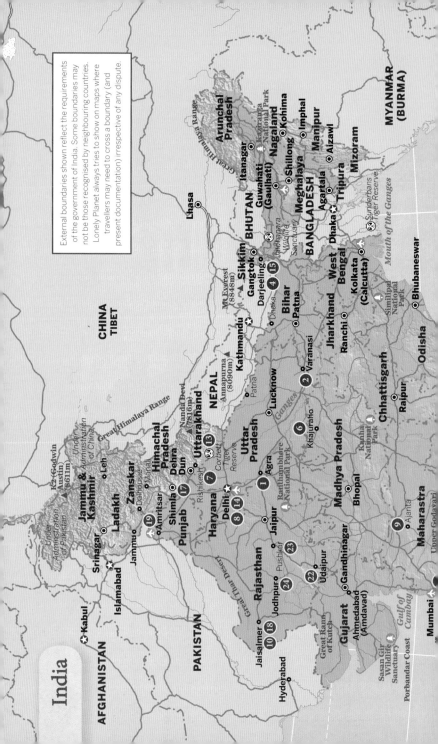

India

External boundaries shown reflect the requirements of the government of India. Some boundaries may not be those recognised by neighbouring countries. Lonely Planet always tries to show on maps where travellers may need to cross a boundary (and present documentation) irrespective of any dispute.

AFGHANISTAN

Kabul

Islamabad

PAKISTAN

Under Administration of Pakistan

K2 Godwin Austin (8611m)

Jammu & Kashmir

Srinagar

Jammu

Ladakh

Leh

Under Administration of China

CHINA

TIBET

Lhasa

Great Himalaya Range

Zanskar

Manali

Dalhousie

Himachal Pradesh

Shimla

Amritsar

Punjab

Dehra Dun

Rishikesh

Nanda Devi (7816m)

Corbett Tiger Reserve

Uttarakhand

Mt Everest (8848m)

NEPAL

Annapurna (8090m)

Kathmandu

Patna

Great Thar Desert

Jaisalmer

Jodhpur

Rajasthan

Pushkar

Haryana

Delhi

Jaipur

Agra

Ranthambhore National Park

Uttar Pradesh

Lucknow

Ganges

Varanasi

Khajuraho

Madhya Pradesh

Bhopal

Patna

Great Himalaya Range

Arunachal Pradesh

Itanagar

Namdapha National Park

BHUTAN

Guwahati (Gauhati)

Shillong

Nagaland

Kohima

Imphal

Manipur

Aizawl

Mizoram

Meghalaya

Agartala

Tripura

Sikkim

Gangtok

Darjeeling

Dheka

Bihar

BANGLADESH

Dhaka

Jaldhapara Wildlife Sanctuary

Sunderbans Tiger Reserve

Jharkhand

Ranchi

West Bengal

Kolkata (Calcutta)

Mouth of the Ganges

Similipal National Park

Chhattisgarh

Raipur

Odisha

Bhubaneswar

MYANMAR (BURMA)

Kanha National Park

Ajanta

Maharastra

Upper Godavari

Mumbai

Gandhinagar

Gujarat

Ahmedabad (Amdavad)

Udaipur

Sasan Gir Wildlife Sanctuary

Porbandar Coast

Great Rann of Kutch

Gulf of Cambay

Hyderabad

Nanda Devi

Leh

25
Top Experiences

1. Taj Mahal
2. Varanasi
3. Kerala Backwaters
4. Darjeeling
5. Hampi
6. Khajuraho
7. Yoga, Rishikesh
8. Delhi
9. Ajanta Caves
10. Camel Safaris, Jaisalmer
11. Puducherry
12. Architecture, Mumbai
13. Corbett Tiger Reserve
14. Markets, Delhi
15. Himalayan Mountains & Monasteries
16. Sri Meenakshi Temple, Madurai
17. Shimla Toy Train
18. Jaisalmer Fort
19. Golden Temple, Amritsar
20. Goan Beaches
21. Kochi
22. Udaipur
23. Pushkar Camel Fair
24. Mehrangarh Fort, Jodhpur
25. Tea & Spice Plantations, Kerala

ELEVATION

6000m
5000m
4000m
3000m
2000m
1000m
0

0   500 km
0   250 miles

Arabian Sea

Andaman Sea

Bay Of Bengal

Indian Ocean

Lakshadweep Sea

Gulf Of Mannar

Konkan Hills
Panaji (Panjim)
Goa
Karnataka
Hyderabad
Andhra Pradesh
Eastern Ghats
Bengaluru (Bangalore)
Hampi
Indira Gandhi (Annamalai) Wildlife Sanctuary
Lakshadweep Islands
Western Ghats
Kerala
Kochi (Cochin)
Thiruvananthapuram (Trivandrum)
Kovalam
Periyar Wildlife Sanctuary
Madurai
Tamil Nadu
Trichy (Tiruchirappalli)
Puducherry (Pondicherry)
Chennai (Madras)
Andaman Islands
Nicobar Islands
SRI LANKA
Colombo

25 India's Top Experiences

Taj Mahal

Don't let fears of tour buses or hordes of visitors make you think you can skip the Taj – you can't. Even on a crowded, hot day, this world wonder (p99) is still the 'Crown of Palaces', a monument to love whose very walls seem to resound with the emperor Shah Jahan's adoration of his beloved Mumtaz Mahal, the 'Gem of the Palace'. The marble mausoleum is inlaid with calligraphy, precious and semiprecious stones, and intricate flower designs representing paradise.

1

2

Holy Varanasi

Everyone in Varanasi (p319) seems to be dying or praying or hustling or cremating someone, or swimming or laundering or washing buffaloes in the sewage-saturated Ganges. The godde river will clean away your sins and help you escape from that tedious life-and-death cycle – a Varanasi is *the* place to take a sacred dip. So take a deep breath, put on a big smile for the ev present touts, go to the holy water and get your karma in order. Sunrise prayer ritual by the Ganges

Backwaters of Kerala

It's unusual to find a place as gorgeous as Kerala's back-waters (p230): 900km of interconnected rivers, lakes and lagoons lined with tropical flora. And if you do, there likely won't be a way to experience it that's as peaceful and intimate as a few days on a teak-and-palm-thatch houseboat. Float along the water – maybe as the sun sets behind the palms, maybe while eating to-die-for Keralan seafood, maybe as you fall asleep under a twinkling sky – and forget about life on land for a while.

The Best...
Beaches

PALOLEM
Nodding palms, beach huts on stilts and white sands – this is one of Goa's loveliest spots. (p218)

VARKALA
Dramatic russet sea cliffs drop down to a broad sandy beach that hosts a mix of Hindu priests, back-packers and local volleyball enthusiasts. (p243)

GIRGUAM CHOWPATTY
This jostling, colourful beach is a favoured spot for an evening stroll and a serve of *bhelpuri* (fried dough with rice, lentils and spices). (p121)

BENAULIM BEACH
A beautifully unspoilt stretch of South Goa sand, with good facilities and less of a scene than some other resorts. (p215)

The Best...
Forts

JAISALMER
A grand sandcastle of a fort, rearing out of the desert; once a stop on the ancient camel trade routes. (p183)

MEHRANGARH
Awesome fortress towering over Jodhpur, protruding out of a great rocky escarpment. (p177)

AGRA FORT
With the Taj Mahal overshadowing it, it's easy to overlook one of the finest Mughal forts in India. (p103)

AMBER FORT
Mighty, pale yellow and pink sandstone and white marble fortress outside Jaipur. (p167)

KUMBALGARH
A breathtakingly imposing, isolated fortress in the hills – the journey there is almost as amazing as arriving. (p181)

MARTIN HUGHES/LONELY PLANET IMAGES ©

Alluring Darjeeling

Up in a tippy-top nook of India's far northeast is storied Darjeeling (p310). It's no longer a romantic mountain hideaway, but the allure remains. Undulating hills of bulbous tea shrubs are pruned by women in colourful dresses; the majestic Himalaya peek through puffy clouds as the sun climbs out from behind the mountains; and little alleys wend their way through mountain mist, past clotheslines and monasteries. Ride the 'toy train' and drink it all in – the tea and the town's legendary enchantment.

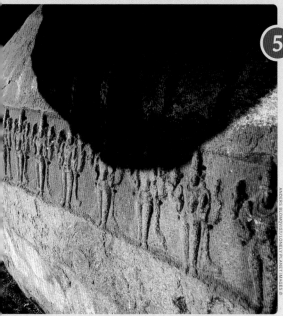

ANDERS BLOMQVIST/LONELY PLANET IMAGES ©

Dreamy Hampi

The surreal rockscape of Hampi (p222) was once the cosmopolitan capital of a powerful Hindu empire. The glorious ruins of its temples and royal structures join sublimely with the terrain: giant rocks balance on pedestals near an ancient elephant stable; temples tuck into crevices between boulders; boats float by rice paddies near a giant bathtub fit for a queen. Watching the sunset's rosy glow over the dreamy landscape, you might just forget what planet you're on.

Sexy Khajuraho

Are the sensuous statues on the temples of Khajuraho (p330) the Kamasutra, Tantric examples for initiates or allegories for the faithful? They're definitely naughty fun, with hot nymphs, a nine-person orgy and even men getting it on with horses. Once the titillation passes, you'll be pleasantly absorbed by the exquisite carving of these thousand-year-old temples and the magical feeling of 11th-century India.

Yoga in Rishikesh

Where better to do the downward dog than in the self-styled 'Yoga Capital of the World'? Rishikesh (p352) has a beautiful setting, surrounded by forested hills and cut through by th fast-flowing Ganges. There are masses of ashrams and all kinds of yoga, meditation classe and alternative therapies, from laughing yoga to crystal healing.

Delhi

India's capital has had several incarnations over the past few thousand years, which partly explains why there's so much going on here. Dust, noise and chaos aside, Delhi (p64) is full of stunning architecture, culture (its residents come from all over the country), good food and even better shopping. The Mughal legacy is one of its biggest attractions: Old Delhi is all crumbling splendour, with the majestic Jama Masjid, the massive Red Fort and other monuments of the historic Mughal capital adorning the old city like royal jewels. Jama Masjid (p65)

The Best...
Temples

SRI MEENAKSHI, MADURAI
Abode of a triple-breasted, fish-eyed goddess, a pinnacle of South Indian temple architecture. (p282)

SHORE TEMPLE, MAMALLAPURAM
A magnificent masterpiece of rock-cut elegance overlooking the sea. (p271)

KHAJURAHO
The erotic carvings of Khajuraho's World Heritage–listed temples are among the finest sacred art in the world. (p330)

AKSHARDHAM TEMPLE, DELHI
A sumptuous, salmon-coloured sandstone temple, with an interior of white marble. (p83)

LOTUS TEMPLE, DELHI
The Lotus Temple's minimalist, furled petals make it one of Delhi's most soothing sights. (p72)

Caves of Ajanta

They may have been ascetics, but the 2nd-century-BC mon[...] who created the Ajanta caves (p139) had an eye for the dramatic. The 30 rock-cut forest grottoes punctuate the side of [...] horseshoe-shaped cliff, and originally had individual staircases leading down to the river. The architecture and toweri[...] stupas made these caves inspiring places in which to medita[...] and live, but the real bling came centuries later, in the form o[...] exquisite carvings and paintings depicting Buddha's former lives. Makes living in a cave look pretty good.

The Best...
Views

10 Camel Safaris

Live out a maharaja fantasy and take a desert safari around Jaisalmer (p187). You'll lollop through rolling deserts atop the tall, goofy animals, camp out among dunes under star-packed skies and visit remote villages where desert dwellers' clothes flicker like flames against the landscape, gaggles of children run out to see you and musicians sing about local life.

Puducherry Savoir Faire

A little pocket of France in Tamil Nadu? *Pourquoi pas?* In this former French colony (p275), yellow houses line cobblestone streets, grand cathedrals are adorned with architectural frou-frou and the croissants are the real deal. But Puducherry's also a Tamil town – with all the history, temples and hustle and bustle that go along with that – and a classic retreat town, too, with the Sri Aurobindo Ashram at its heart. Turns out that yoga, *pain au chocolat,* Hindu gods and colonial-era architecture make for an atmospheric melange. Notre Dame de Anges (p278)

PAUL HARDING/LONELY PLANET IMAGES ©

Mumbai's Architectural Visions

Mumbai (p120) has always absorbed everything in her midst and made them her own. The architectural result is a heady mix of buildings with countless influences. The art deco and modern towers are flashy, but it's the eclectic Victorian-era structures – the neo-Gothic, Indo-Saracenic and Venetian Gothic hodgepodge – that have come to define Mumbai and make her the flamboyant beauty that she is. All those spires, gables, arches and onion dom make for a pleasant walk through the city's past. Chhatrapati Shivaji Terminus (p121)

Tiger-spotting

You have to be lucky to spot a tiger in India, but it can be done. Try Corbett Tiger Reserve (p357), near Ramnagar. It's one of India's mo exciting experiences to stea through the undergrowth, surrounded by birds and buterflies, in search of a tiger. And even if you don't catch sight of one, the other wildl will prove a breathtaking distraction.

Delhi's Markets

Shopaholics: be careful not to lose control. No interest in shopping? Get in touch with your consumerist side. Delhi (p88) is one of the world's finest places to shop, and its markets – Old Delhi, Khan Market or the specialty bazaars – have something you want, guaranteed (though you may not have known this beforehand). The range of technicolour saris, glittering gold and silver bling, mounds of rainbow vermilion, aromatic fresh spices, stainless-steel head massagers, bangles and bobby pins, heaping piles of fruit and marigold and coconut offerings is simply astounding.

The Best...
Places for Crafts

JAIPUR
Rajasthan's capital of artisanship, with a glittering array of textiles, leatherwork, jewellery and gems. (p163)

DELHI
All the riches of India are gathered in Delhi, which has artworks and crafts from all over the country, as well as a Crafts Museum. (p88)

KASHMIR
Kashmiri crafts are particularly known for dazzling carpets and rugs, and jewel-like painted papier mâché. (p375)

MAMALLAPURAM, TAMIL NADU
Good place to buy stone carvings, where artisans chink away at pieces with their chisels on the street. (p270)

The Best...
Places for Food

DELHI
Dine on almost any international flavour in India's capital, with remarkably good food ranging from streetside stalls to creative-cuisine restaurants. (p60)

KERALA
With a long coastline, endless spice plantations and coconut groves, the fragrant cuisine of Kerala is refreshingly delicious. (p234)

GOA
Famous for fresh fish curries, often served on a banana leaf, Goan cuisine is perfumed with many influences brought by traders from overseas. (p198)

MUMBAI
One of India's great gastro centres, where a cornucopia of flavours from all over the country collides with international trends and tastebuds. (p116)

(ABOVE) RICHARD I'ANSON/LONELY PLANET IMAGES © (RIGHT) DAVID ELSE/LONELY PLANET IMAGES ©

Himalayan Mountains & Monasteries

Up north, where the air is cooler and crisper, quaint hill stations give way to snow-topped peaks. Here, the cultural influences came not by coasts but via mountain passes. Tibetan Buddhism thrives, and multilayered monasteries emerge from the forest or steep cliffs as vividly and poetically as the sun rises over golden Khangchendzonga (p310). Weathered prayer flags on forest paths blow in the wind, the sound of monks chanting reverberates in meditation halls, and locals bring offerings and make merit, all in the shadow of the mighty Himalaya. Buddhist monastery, Ladakh

Madurai's Sri Meenakshi Temple

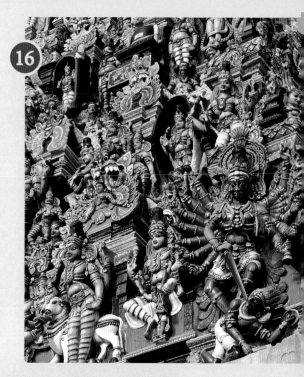

A 6-hectare complex enclosed by 12 tall *gopurams* (gateway towers), covered in a multi-coloured stucco frenzy of thousands of deities, mythical creatures and monsters, Sri Meenakshi (p282) is the pinnacle of South Indian temple architecture. It's an inspirational dedication to Shiva, a work of utmost splendour that's an onslaught on the senses. Within is a hive of activity, with tranquil tanks and dramatic halls, and one of India's key places to experience the vibrant wonder of religious life.

Shimla Toy Train

India's quintessential journey is still the train ride, and one of the prettiest and quaintest journeys to be found in India is the narrow-gauge train trip (p362) between Kalka and Shimla. This enchanting journey through the hills offers breathtaking views and has a back-in-time gentleness that makes it the ideal way to reach one of India's loveliest hill stations.

IMAGEBROKER/JOCHEN TACK

Jaisalmer's Desert Mirage

Rising up like a sandcastle from the deserts of Rajasthan, the 'Land of Kings', Jaisalmer's 12th-century citadel (p183) looks more like something from a dream than reality. The enormous golden sandstone fort, with its crenellated ramparts and undulating towers, is a fantastical structure, even while camouflaged against the desert sand. Inside, an ornate royal palace, fairy-tale *havelis* (mansions), intricately carved Jain temples and narrow lanes conspire to create the world's best place to get lost. Musician at entrance to Jaisalmer Fort

The Best...
Unesco World Heritage Sites

ELLORA CAVES
The epitome of ancient Indian rock-cut architecture, chipped out laboriously over five centuries by generations of Buddhist, Hindu and Jain monks. (p137)

AJANTA CAVES
These ancient, secluded caverns guard a hoard of unparalleled artistic treasures. (p139)

KHAJURAHO
Khajuraho's temples are carved with exquisite skill and eye-popping erotic detail. (p330)

QUTB MINAR
One of Delhi's finest sights, its architecture reflects different cultural building styles over hundreds of years. (p96)

HAMPI
An incredible collection of 15th- and 16th-century temples just a short trip from Goa. (p222)

The Best...
Quiet Retreats

HOUSEBOAT, SRINAGAR
Kick back with a stay on a 1930s-style houseboat on beautiful Dal Lake, where there's little to do but relax and meander around the waterways by gondola. (p377)

BACKWATERS, KERALA
There are few things more relaxing than travelling through the 900km network of waterways fringing Kerala's coast. (p230)

SHIMLA, HIMACHAL PRADESH
An engaging blend of hilltop holiday town and Indian city, surrounded by rolling landscapes of green, reached via toy train. (p359)

MUNNAR, KERALA
Relax in a homestay at a remote tea plantation near this Kerala hill station. (p252)

Amritsar's Golden Temple

The Sikhs' holiest of shrines, the Golden Temple (p386) is a magical place designed for people of all religions to worship. Seeming to float atop a glistening pool named for the 'nectar of immortality', the temple is a gorgeous structure, made even more so by its extreme goldness (the lotus-shaped dome is gilded in the real thing). Even when crowded with happy pilgrims, the temple is peaceful, with birds singing outside and the lake gently lapping against the godly abode.

MICHAEL GEBICKI/LONELY PLANET IMAGES ©

Goan Beaches

(20) There might be no better place in the world to be lazy than on one of Goa's spectacular beaches (p194). With palm-tree groves on one side of the white sands and gently lapping waves on the other, the best of the beaches live up to your image of a tropical paradise. But it's not an undiscovered one: the sands are also peppered with fellow travellers and beach-shack restaurants. Goa's treasures are for social creatures and fans of creature comforts who like their seafood fresh and their holidays easy. Palolem Beach, Goa

ANDERS BLOMQVIST/LONELY PLANET IMAGES ©

Kochi

Be beguiled in the ancient Keralan port of Kochi (p256). The district of Fort Cochin displays a tantalising cocktail of influences, from the rambling Dutch, British and Portuguese villas to the cantilevered Chinese fishing nets still in use off the promenade, from the overgrown foreign cemeteries to the ancient synagogue, tiled in hand-painted Cantonese tiles. It's a laid-back place to wander and breathe in the living history of this historic, atmospheric spice port.

Udaipur

On your honeymoon? No? Well, make as if you are and indulge in the storybook romance o Udaipur (p170), a town seemingly sculpted from faded lace and built around several beaut lakes, framed by pale blue hills. It's a great place to laze on sun-bleached rooftops, kick bac and read some good books, explore the city's fascinating shops and labyrinthine palace an have a cream tea at the Gallery Restaurant. Jagdish Temple (p171), Udaipur

Pushkar Camel Fair

India knows how to throw a good festival. It has been perfecting religious celebrations and fanfare for, oh, a few millennia. It usually starts with the far-off sound of the trumpets, then the drums and, before you know it, there's a mass of humanity, fine traditional regalia, chariots and decorated camels and elephants. And arguably the most epic festival of them all is Pushkar's Camel Fair (p168), when thousands of camels and horses are gathered to be bought and sold, and pilgrims descend to bathe in the holy town's petal-shaped lake.

23

The Best...
Festivals

PUSHKAR CAMEL FAIR
Around 200,000 people converge annually on picturesque Pushkar, bringing with them some 50,000 camels, horses and cattle. (p168)

DIWALI
One of the prettiest places during Diwali is Jaisalmer, whose golden-stone old city streets are lit up by oil lamps and fireworks. (p183)

HOLI
India's most exuberant festival is best experienced in small-town Rajasthan, where the streets turn polychrome under fistfuls of paint. (p43 & p413)

ONAM
A Kerala harvest festival celebrated in August and September, when houses are decorated with flowers and the 10-day celebrations culminate in huge family dinners.

Mehrangarh Fort, Jodhpur

India is full of incredible, fantastical forts, but one of the mo[st]
memorable you will see is Mehrangarh (p177), which tower[s]
over the blue city of Jodhpur like an illustration from the
Brothers Grimm. It seems to grow out of the rock face, with
imposing walls shooting skywards from the cliff on which it
stands. The architecture is half solid fortress, half delicate
palace.

The Best...
Animal
Experiences

RANTHAMBHORE NATIONAL PARK
With 1334 sq km of wild
jungle hemmed in by rocky
ridges, and the amazing
10th-century Ranthamb-
hore Fort, this is a fantastic
place for spotting tigers.
(p168)

CORBETT TIGER RESERVE
This legendary park has
175 tigers, though spotting
them can take time as
they're neither baited nor
tracked. (p357)

CAMEL SAFARI, JAISALMER
Trekking around by camel
is the most evocative and
fun way to sample Thar
Desert life. (p187)

SUNDERBANS TIGER RESERVE
A 2585-sq-km reserve
with one of the world's
largest concentrations of
tigers, surprisingly close
to Kolkata. (p311)

25

Kerala's Tea & Spice Plantations

The southern state of Kerala is famous for its beaches and backwaters, but one of the region's highlights is its lush plantations in the hills, such as around Munnar (p252). Travel inland and you'll discover more shades of green than you thought could possibly exist, with endless rolling clumps of tea, brilliantly bright rice paddies, spiky ginger plantations, and field after field of coffee, cardamom and pepper.

India's Top Itineraries

Delhi to Jaipur The Golden Triangle

5 DAYS

This is the classic, awe-inspiring route: you can discover the many different sides of Delhi, before visiting India's most famous monument, the Taj Mahal, taking a side trip to the deserted town of Fatehpur Sikri, then heading to the pink city of Jaipur, before returning to Delhi.

❶ Delhi (p64)

Explore the capital's highlights, from its buzzing restaurants and astounding shops to the medieval old city with its **Jama Masjid**, and from the imposing carcass of the **Red Fort** to the sprawling serenity of **Qutb Minar**, the **Lotus Temple** and **Humayun's tomb**.

DELHI ➲ AGRA

🚊 **Two hours** The fastest train is the twice-daily (except Friday) *Shatabdi Express* from New Delhi station. The slower *Taj Express* takes a still respectable three hours. 🚌 **Four hours** 🚌 **Five hours** AC and non-AC buses run regularly between Delhi and Agra's Idgah bus stand.

❷ Taj Mahal (p99)

Rabindranath Tagore described it as 'a teardrop on the cheek of eternity', Rudyard Kipling as 'the embodiment of all things pure', while its creator, Emperor Shah Jahan, said it made 'the sun and the moon shed tears from their eyes'. This epic monument to love actually lives up to all the hype. Try to visit in the early morning or book onto one of the sought-after moonlight visits.

A carved gate at the Qutb Minar complex
DAMIEN SIMONIS/LONELY PLANET IMAGES ©

AGRA ➲ FATEHPUR SIKRI

🚌 **One hour** Bus from Agra's Idgah bus stand, every 30 minutes. 🚌 **One hour** It's around 40km southwest by road.

❸ Fatehpur Sikri (p105)

The short-lived capital of the Mughal empire in the 16th century, the magnificent fortified ancient city of **Fatehpur Sikri**, 40km southwest of Agra, is a well-preserved and atmospheric Unesco World Heritage Site. The city was an Indo-Islamic masterpiece, but erected in an area that suffered from water shortages and so was abandoned shortly after Emperor Akbar's death.

AGRA ➲ JAIPUR

🚊 **Five hours** Easily the best way to reach Jaipur, with a daily train in the early morning. 🚌 **Five to six hours** It's around 230km from Agra to Jaipur.

❹ Jaipur (p156)

The dusky, grubby pink city glitters with bazaars and centres around its sprawling **City Palace** as well as the **Hawa Mahal** – a honeycomb-like palace. Outside the city is the majestic **Amber Fort**, which you can reach on the back of a painted elephant.

5 DAYS

Mumbai to Palolem
A Scud Around the South

This trip will immerse you in the mixed-up rhythms of Mumbai – financial and film industry centre, fashion capital and home of one of Asia's largest slums – before you head south to relax on the white-sand beaches of Goa, eat delicious seafood and explore this fascinating region's culture.

ARABIAN SEA

1 MUMBAI (BOMBAY)

2 PANAJI (PANJIM)

3 PALOLEM

① Mumbai (Bombay; p120)

Enjoy eating in some of India's best restaurants, browsing in some of its most fantastical bazaars, admiring the grandiose frilliness of Mumbai's colonial-era architecture, strolling on **Girguam Chowpatty** eating *kulfi* (ice cream) and taking the boat out to **Elephanta Island** with its rock-cut temples.

MUMBAI ⟶ PANAJI

✈ **45 minutes** Take a flight from Mumbai south to Goa's diminutive airport, Dabolim, 29km south of Panaji, take a taxi to the state capital. 🚆 **10½ hours** Take an overnight train from Mumbai's CST station, arriving at Karmali (Old Goa), a short taxi ride from Panaji, at around 9.40am.

② Panaji (p202)

Discover the Portuguese-flavoured old quarters of the Goan capital, **Panaji** (Panjim), lingering over lunch at one of its ravishing restaurants and enjoying a tranquil boat trip on the Mandovi River. Take a day trip to **Old Goa**, once the ecclesiastical wonder of the Eastern world, a lovely place to wander and discover elegantly crumbling grand cathedrals, vestiges of its former splendour.

PANAJI ⟶ PALOLEM

🚗 **Two hours** It's a short drive southwards to Palolem; it's an even shorter taxi ride from Palolem to Dabolim Airport for your return journey. 🚆 **1½ hours** Take the train from Karmali (Old Goa) south to Cancona, from where it's a short autorickshaw or taxi ride to Palolem.

③ Palolem (p218)

Formerly Goa's best-kept secret, **Palolem** is the perfect place to end your trip and relax for a few days, with a stunning crescent beach. There's not much nightlife, but it's ideal for chilling out, basking in the sunshine, swimming in limpid seas, and choosing from the variety of yoga, massages and therapies on offer.

Girguam Chowpatty beach, Mumbai
CHRISTER FREDRIKSSON/LONELY PLANET IMAGES ©

10 DAYS

Delhi to Amritsar
Gold & Kings

Start with the Indian capital, then head to the Taj Mahal. Your trip into the 'Land of the Kings' will then take in tiger spotting at Ranthambhore, lazing in Udaipur, exploring the blue city of Jodhpur and visiting Sikhism's holiest shrine, the majestic Golden Temple.

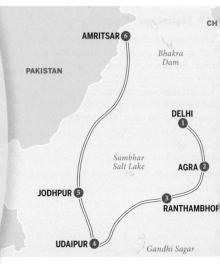

AMRITSAR 6

Bhakra Dam

CH

PAKISTAN

DELHI 1

Sambhar Salt Lake

AGRA 2

JODHPUR 5

3

RANTHAMBHO

UDAIPUR 4

Gandhi Sagar

1 Delhi (p64)

Starting your trip in Delhi, be sure to visit some of its major sights: **Qutb Minar**, **Humayun's tomb** and the **Red Fort**. Nor will you want to miss exploring its government emporiums and eating at some of best restaurants in India, or sampling the city's delicious street food.

DELHI → AGRA

🚆 **Two hours** The fastest train is the twice daily (except Friday) Shatabdi Express from New Delhi station. The slower Taj Express takes a still respectable three hours. 🚗 **Four hours** 🚌 **Five hours** AC and non-AC buses run regularly between Delhi and Agra's Idgah bus stand.

2 Agra (p99)

Make an early start to see the **Taj Mahal**, one of the wonders of the world, followed by a lazy lunch in Agra before visiting the magnificent Mughal **Agra Fort**.

AGRA → RANTHAMBHORE

🚗 **Five to six hours** It's around 250km drive from Agra to Ranthambhore. 🚆 **4½ hours** There are a couple of trains from Agra Fort station to Sawai Madhopur (for Ranthambhore), but they leave very early in the morning. An overnight train takes almost six hours.

3 Ranthambhore (p168)

Visit **Ranthambhore National Park**, 1334 sq km of wild jungle scrub, hemmed in by rocky ridges and dotted by ruined chhatris, temples, and a spectacularly overgrown 10th-century fort. The main reason people come here is to spot tigers; if you're determined to spot one, make time for a few safaris into the park, which will increase your chances.

Palace attendant at Mehrangarh Fort, Jodhpur
IZZET KERIBAR/LONELY PLANET IMAGES ©

RANTHAMHORE → UDAIPUR

🚆 **7½ hours** There's a handy overnight train, the Mewar Express, from Sawai Madhopur to Udaipur, which leaves at 11.50pm and arrives at 7.30am. 🚗 **Six to seven hours** It's a 380km journey by car southwestwards to Udaipur.

4 Udaipur (p170)

Relax in what is perhaps India's most romantic city, framed by ancient Aravalli hills and ranged around the glassy waters of Lake Pichola. You can visit its impressive **City Palace**, go boating on the lake and explore the **Old City**, perhaps even staying in the **Lake Palace**, which seems to float at the centre of the lake.

UDAIPUR → JODHPUR

🚗 **Six to seven hours** The easiest way to get between Udaipur and Jodhpur is by hiring a car and driver, as there is no direct train line between the two cities.

5 Jodhpur (p177)

Towered over by the mighty fortress of **Mehrangarh**, the blue town of Jodhpur stretches out, a jumble of pale-painted houses – from the bird's-eye viewpoint of the fort, it looks like a fantastical, cubist painting. Visit here to climb up to the fort-palace and explore its tangle of bazaars.

JODHPUR → AMRITSAR

✈ **Five to seven hours** You'll have to fly to Amritsar via Delhi, but the journey will be well worth it.

6 Amritsar (p387)

Amritsar is home to Sikhism's holiest site, the beautiful **Golden Temple**, a place with a potent atmosphere of spirituality and a soul-soothing sense of splendour. It's a fascinating and unforgettable sight, and the perfect place to end your trip.

10 DAYS

Chennai to Goa
Southern Temples, Waterways & Beaches

This itinerary takes in many southern highlights, travelling from the ancient temple town of Mamallapuram to the historic port of Kochi, floating around Kerala's beautiful waterways, visiting the laid-back resort of Varkala and finishing up with a touch of Goan hedonism.

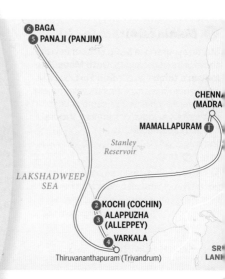

⑥ BAGA
⑤ PANAJI (PANJIM)

CHENN
(MADRA

MAMALLAPURAM ①

Stanley Reservoir

LAKSHADWEEP SEA

② KOCHI (COCHIN)
ALAPPUZHA
③ (ALLEPPEY)

④ VARKALA

Thiruvananthapuram (Trivandrum)

SR
LAN

① Mamallapuram (p270)

Make your way directly from Chennai to the fascinating temple town of **Mamal-lapuram** (Mahabalipuram), which is only two hours' drive from the Tamil Nadu capital. Here, its collection of exquisite temples and carvings include the **Shore Temple**, a fist of rock-cut elegance that symbolises the heights of Pallava architecture.

MAMALLAPURAM ➲ KOCHI

✈ **Three to four hours** It's a two-hour drive from Mamallapuram to Chennai airport, from where the flight to Kochi (Cochin) is only one hour.

② Kochi (Cochin; p256)

Soak in 500 years of colonial history and stay in one of Fort Cochin's beautiful heritage hotels. This is a town that's a living homage to a vibrant past, with its **giant fishing nets** from China, a 400-year-old **synagogue**, fantastic **Kerala Folklore Museum**, ancient mosques and Portuguese-era mansions.

KOCHI ➲ ALAPPUZHA

🚊 **1½ hours** Regular trains run from Ernakulam (Kochi) to Alappuzha. 🚌 **1½ hours** It's also a short journey via road.

③ Alappuzha (p245)

Alappuzha (Alleppey) is the gateway to **Kerala's fabled backwaters**, a network of lakes and canals, lined by lush vegetation and waterside villages. It's one of India's most magical experiences to take an overnight houseboat and sleep on the water under the stars, or to explore the waterways and get up close to the fascinating village life along the water's edge via canoe.

A Kathakali dancer (p261) in make-up and costume
KIMBERLEY COOLE/LONELY PLANET IMAGES ©

ALAPPUZHA ➲ VARKALA

🚊 **Two hours** There are three daily trains to Varkala – the station is a rickshaw or taxi ride away from the beach. 🚌 **Two to 2½ hours** It's around 115km from Alappuzha to Varkala.

④ Varkala (p243)

Hindu place of pilgrimage and laid-back resort, **Varkala** stretches out along the coast on the edge of some stunningly dramatic, russet-streaked sea cliffs. It's a great place to kick back for a day or two, resting up at its small-scale resorts and guesthouses and indulging in some **ayurvedic treatments**.

VARKALA ➲ PANAJI

✈ **Six to seven hours** From Varkala, take a taxi to Trivandrum airport (one hour), from where you can take a flight to Kochi (45 minutes) and then on to Dabolim Airport (3½ hours) in Goa. From the airport, take a taxi northwards to Goa's laid-back capital, Panaji.

⑤ Panaji (p202)

The relaxing city of **Panaji** is a great place to dine, wander, take boat trips along the **Mandovi River**, and take a day trip to explore the picturesque, colonial-era churches of **Old Goa**.

PANAJI ➲ BAGA

🚌 **45 minutes** It's a short hop from the capital to Baga. 🚌 **45 minutes** There are plenty of buses making the trip.

⑥ Baga (p208)

Finish your southern sojourn with some party action and delicious waterside restaurants in the lively resort of **Baga**, perhaps fitting in a visit to **Anjuna's** famous flea market, a short distance to the north.

Kolkata to Alappuzha
A Taste of North & South

Taking two weeks, you can see a surprising amount via a few canny domestic flights, visiting some of the most breathtaking cities and rural places in the north and south of India.

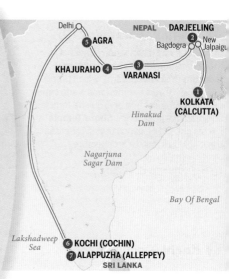

Delhi
NEPAL **DARJEELING**
❺ AGRA
Bagdogra ❷ New Jalpaigu
KHAJURAHO ❹
❸ **VARANASI**
❶ **KOLKATA (CALCUTTA)**
Hinakud Dam
Nagarjuna Sagar Dam
Bay Of Bengal
Lakshadweep Sea
❻ **KOCHI (COCHIN)**
❼ **ALAPPUZHA (ALLEPPEY)**
SRI LANKA

❶ **Kolkata** (Calcutta; p298)

Explore the vibrant, clattering, stimulating city of Kolkata, with its faded colonial-era architecture and excellent Bengali restaurants.

KOLKATA ➲ DARJEELING

✈ **Three to four hours** Fly from Kolkata to Bagdogra, 90km away – on arrival, take a pre-arranged taxi for the last part of the journey.

❷ **Darjeeling** (p310)

Gorgeously green, Darjeeling is one of India's best-loved hill stations, reachable via a narrow gauge toy train that hauls up the hills through wonderful vistas (you can take it on a joy ride). The town itself is surrounded by jagged snow-capped mountains, and is the ideal place to relax, trek into the hills, visit tea plantations and sip the best possible cup of Darjeeling.

DARJEELING ➲ VARANASI

🚃 **15½ hours** There's a Wednesday direct overnight train from New Jalpaiguri, around 12km south of Darjeeling, which leaves at 6.30pm and arrives in Varanasi at 10am, but other days of the week there

are many trains to Mughlai Sarai Junction, from where it's a short 30- to 40-minute train ride to Varanasi.

❸ **Varanasi** (p319)

Varanasi is one of the most blindingly colorful, unrelentingly chaotic and unapologetically indiscreet places on earth. It's one of Hinduism's seven holy cities. Pilgrims come to the ghats lining the River Ganges here to wash away a lifetime of sins in the sacred waters or to cremate their loved ones. It's a remarkable place to experience, particularly by taking an early-morning boat trip along the Ganges.

VARANASI ➲ KHAJURAHO

🚃 **12 hours** There's an overnight train from Varanasi to Khajuraho, which leaves at 5.30pm daily.

❹ **Khajuraho** (p330)

With exquisitely fine carving, the temples of Khajuraho are one of India's most extraordinary sights, swathed as they are in ancient erotica.

Village children play in a canoe in the Keralan backwaters
MARK DAFFEY/LONELY PLANET IMAGES ©

Synagogue, take a trip to the Kerala Heritage Museum, and eat at some splendid restaurants.

KOCHI ➲ ALAPPUZHA

🚃 **1½ hours** There are regular trains from Kochi (Ernakulam) to Alappuzha 🚗 **1½ hours** It's around 50km from Kochi to Alappuzha by road.

7 Alappuzha (p245)

Head to the main gateway of backwaters to explore the network of waterways that fringe the coast and trickle inland. You can stay overnight on a houseboat or take a canoe trip, ferry boat or village tour to explore the canals, ending your epic journey on a serene, high note.

KHAJURAHO ➲ AGRA

🚃 **8½ hours** There's a useful direct train to Agra at 6pm on Mondays, Wednesdays and Saturdays.

5 Agra (p99)

Now is your chance to visit the Taj Mahal, India's most iconic sight, an exquisite tomb made of semi-translucent white marble, carved with flowers and inlaid with thousands of semiprecious stones in beautiful patterns. It will not disappoint, a perfect exercise in symmetry, and in the afternoon you can visit the impressive Mughal Agra Fort.

AGRA ➲ KOCHI

✈ **Four to five hours** Fly to Delhi (one hour), then take a connecting flight south to Kochi (three hours).

6 Kochi (p256)

Head for **Fort Cochin**, where you can stay in a cosy, characterful guesthouse, a homestay or a delightful heritage hotel, visit **Jew Town** and the ancient **Pardesi**

India Month by Month

Top Events

⊛ **Carnival**, January or February

⊛ **Trekking**, May–June and September–October

⊛ **Ganesh Chaturthi**, August or September

⊛ **Navratri**, September or October

⊛ **Diwali (Festival of Lights)**, October or November

📅 January

⊛ Republic Day (Free India)

Republic Day commemorates the founding of the Republic of India on 26 January 1950; the biggest celebrations are in Delhi, which holds a huge military parade along Rajpath and the Beating of the Retreat ceremony three days later.

⊛ Kite Festival (Sankranti)

Sankranti, the Hindu festival marking the sun's passage into Capricorn, is celebrated in many ways across India – from banana-giving to dips in the Ganges to cockfights. But it's the mass kite-flying in Uttar Pradesh and Maharashtra that steals the show.

⊛ Pongal (Southern Harvest)

The Tamil festival of Pongal marks the end of the harvest season. Southern families prepare pots of *pongal* (rice, sugar, dhal and milk), symbolic of prosperity and abundance, then feed it to decorated cows.

⊛ Vasant Panchami

Hindus dress in yellow and place books, musical instruments and other educational objects in front of idols of Saraswati, the goddess of learning, to receive her blessing. As it follows the Indian lunar calendar, it can also fall in February.

📅 February

⊛ The Prophet Mohammed's Birthday

The Islamic festival of Eid-Milad-un-Nabi celebrates the birth of the Prophet Mohammed with prayers and processions, especially in Jammu and Kashmir. It occurs during the third month of the Islamic calendar: around 4 February (2012), 24 January (2013) and 13 January (2014).

(left) February Skiing the Northern Slopes

Losar (Tibetan New Year)

Tantric Buddhists all over India – particularly in Himachal Pradesh and Ladakh – celebrate for 15 days, with the most important festivities during the first three. Losar is usually in February or March, though dates can vary between regions.

Skiing the Northern Slopes

Jammu and Kashmir (when peaceful), Himachal Pradesh and Uttarakhand have fine skiing and snowboarding for all levels (at some of the ski world's lowest costs). Snow season tends to be January to March, with February a safe bet.

Carnival in Goa

The four-day party kicking off Lent is particularly big in Goa. Sabado Gordo, Fat Saturday, starts it off with parades of elaborate floats and costumed dancers, and the revelry continues with street parties, concerts and general merrymaking.

March

Holi

One of North India's most ecstatic festivals; Hindus celebrate the beginning of spring according to the lunar calendar (either February or March) by throwing coloured water and *gulal* (powder) at anyone within range. Bonfires held the night before symbolise the death of the demoness Holika.

Wildlife-watching

When the weather warms up, water sources dry out and animals have to venture into the open to find refreshment – your chance to spot elephants, deer and, if you're lucky, tigers and leopards. Visit www.sanctuaryasia.com for detailed info.

Rama's Birthday

During Ramanavami, which lasts anywhere from one to nine days, Hindus celebrate the birth of Rama with processions, music, fasting and feasting, readings and enactments of scenes from the Ramayana and, at some temples, ceremonial weddings of Rama and Sita idols.

April

Mahavir's Birthday

Mahavir Jayanti commemorates the birth of Jainism's 24th and most important *tirthankar* (teacher and enlightened being). Temples are decorated and visited, Mahavir statues are given ritual baths, processions are held and offerings are given to the poor. It can also fall in March.

May

Buddha's Birthday

Commemorating Buddha's birth, nirvana (enlightenment) and parinirvana (total liberation from the cycle of existence, or passing away), Buddha Jayanti is quiet but moving: devotees dress simply, eat vegetarian food, listen to dharma talks and visit monasteries or temples.

Trekking

May and June, the months preceding the rains in the northern mountains, are surprisingly good times for trekking, with sunshine and temperate weather. Try trekking tour operators in Himachal Pradesh, Jammu & Kashmir and Uttarakhand.

July

Naag Panchami

This Hindu snake festival is dedicated to Ananta, the coiled serpent Vishnu rested upon between universes. Women return to their family homes to fast, while snakes are venerated as totems against flooding and other evils. Falls in July or August.

ceremonies (the biggest one is in Delhi), parades and patriotic cultural programs.

🎇 Pateti (Parsi New Year)

Parsis celebrate Pateti, the Zoroastrian new year, especially in Mumbai. Houses are cleaned and decorated with flowers and *rangoli* (chalk pictures), families dress up and eat special fish dishes and sweets, and offerings are made at the Fire Temple.

🎇 Eid al-Fitr

Muslims celebrate the end of Ramadan with three days of festivities, beginning 30 days after the start of the fast. Prayers, shopping, gift-giving and, for women and girls, *mehndi* (henna designs) may all be part of the celebrations.

📅 September

🎇 Ganesh Chaturthi

Hindus celebrate the birthday of Ganesh, the elephant-headed god, with verve, particularly in Mumbai. Clay idols of Ganesh are paraded through the streets before being ceremonially immersed in rivers, tanks (reservoirs) or the sea. Ganesh Chaturthi may also be in August.

🎇 Durga Puja

The conquest of good over evil, exemplified by the goddess Durga's victory over the buffalo-headed demon Mahishasura, is celebrated, particularly in Kolkata, where images of Durga are displayed then ritually immersed in rivers and water tanks.

🎇 Raksha Bandhan

Women fix amulets known as *rakhis* to the wrists of brothers and close male friends to protect them in the coming year. Brothers reciprocate with gifts and promises to take care of their sisters.

🎇 Ramadan (Ramazan)

Thirty days of dawn-to-dusk fasting mark the ninth month of the Islamic calendar. Muslims traditionally turn their attention to Allah, with a focus on prayer and purification. Ramadan begins around 20 July (2012), 9 July (2013) and 28 June (2014).

📅 August

🎇 Independence Day (15 August)

This public holiday marks the anniversary of India's independence from Britain in 1947. Celebrations are a countrywide expression of patriotism, with flag-hoisting

📅 October

🎇 Gandhi's Birthday (2 October)

A solemn national celebration of Mohandas Gandhi's birth, with prayer meetings at his cremation site in Delhi. Schools and businesses close for the day.

🎇 Navratri

This Hindu 'Festival of Nine Nights' celebrates the goddess Durga in all her incarnations. Special dances are performed, and the goddesses Lakshmi and Saraswati are also celebrated. Festivities are particularly vibrant in Gujarat and Maharashtra. Navratri sometimes falls in September.

🎇 Diwali (Festival of Lights)

In October or November, Hindus celebrate Diwali for five days, giving gifts, lighting fireworks, and burning oil lamps or hanging lanterns to lead Lord Rama home from exile. One of India's prettiest festivals.

🎇 Eid al-Adha

Muslims commemorate Ibrahim's readiness to sacrifice his son to God by slaughtering a goat or sheep and sharing it with family, the community and the poor. Upcoming

celebrations fall around 26 October (2012), 15 October (2013) and 4 October (2014).

🗓 November

🎇 Muharram

A month of remembrance when Shiite Muslims commemorate the martyrdom of the Prophet Mohammed's grandson Imam with beautiful processions. It begins around 15 November (2012), 4 November (2013) and 25 October (2014).

🗓 December

🎇 Christmas Day (25 December)

Indian Christians celebrate the birth of Jesus. The festivities are especially big in Goa and Kerala, with musical events, elaborate decorations and special Masses, while Mumbai's Catholic neighbourhoods become festivals of lights.

Far left: October Diwali
Left: March Holi

Get Inspired

📖 Books

○ **Ramayana** (1973) RK Narayan's condensed, novelistic retelling of the ancient classic.

○ **India's Struggle for Independence** (1989) Bipan Chandra expertly chronicles the history of India from 1857 to 1947.

○ **A Fine Balance** (1995) A moving and tragic Mumbai story by Rohinton Mistry.

○ **White Mughals** (2002) William Dalrymple tells the true story of a British soldier who married an Indian princess.

○ **The God of Small Things** (1997) Vibrant, beautiful novel by Arundhati Roy, set in Kerala.

🎞 Films

○ **Gandhi** (1982) Hugely popular biographical film about the Great Soul.

○ **Lagaan** (2001) Critically acclaimed historical drama (with songs).

○ **Devdas** (2002) Lush Bollywood treat starring Aishwarya Rai.

○ **Fire** (1996) **Earth** (1998) **Water** (2005) Deepa Mehta's acclaimed trilogy.

○ **Sholay** (1975) An action-adventure classic, one of the highest-grossing Indian films.

🎵 Music

○ **Hare Rama Hare Krishna** (1971) Film soundtrack with fantastic 'Dum Maro Dum'.

○ **The Sounds of India** (1968) Legendary sitar player Ravi Shankar's finest.

○ **A Morning Raga/An Evening Raga** (1968) Beautiful raga played by virtuoso Ravi Shankar and tabla player Alla Rakha.

○ **Chaudhvin Ka Chand** (1960) Film music by Shankar with vocals by Asha Bhosle.

○ **Pakeezah** (1972) Sumptuous film soundtrack by Ghulam Mohammed and Naushad Ali.

🖱 Websites

○ **Lonely Planet** (www. lonelyplanet.com) Country profile, accommodation information and the Thorn Tree forums.

○ **Times of India** (www .timesofindia.com) India's largest English-language newspaper.

○ **Events in India** (www. eventsinindia.com) What's on where and when.

○ **Art India** (www.artindia .net) About India's vibrant performing-arts scene.

🕐 Short on time?

This list will give you an instant insight into the country.

Read RK Narayan's novel *Ramayana* gives the low-down on the great epic.

Watch *Gandhi,* directed by Richard Attenborough, about the nation's favourite son.

Listen Ravi Shankar's *The Sounds of India* is a seminal sitar album.

Log on Incredible India (www. incredibleindia.org) is the tourist board's useful site.

Hawa Mahal palace (p157), Jaipur

(LEFT) KRZYSZTOF DYDYNSKI /LONELY PLANET IMAGES ©; (ABOVE) APRIL MACIBORKA/LONELY PLANET IMAGES ©

Need to Know

Currency
Indian rupees (₹)

Language
Hindi and English
(plus local languages)

ATMs
Most urban centres have
ATMS; carry cash as back-up.

Credit Cards
MasterCard and Visa
widely accepted.

Visas
Six-month tourist visa valid
from date of issue (not
date of arrival).

Mobile Phones
Use local networks to avoid
expensive roaming costs.

Wi-Fi
In most upmarket hotels
and some restaurants in
major cities.

Internet Access
Internet cafes in cities and
towns; few in rural areas.

Driving
Affordable car-with-driver hire
lets you avoid dealing with
hair-raising road conditions.

Tipping
Restaurants usually add
service charges (tipping more
is optional). Tip drivers for long
trips; tip porters around ₹50.

When to Go

Leh
GO Jul–Sep

Delhi
GO Nov–Mar

Kolkata (Calcutta)
GO Nov–Mar

Mumbai (Bombay)
GO Nov–Feb

Kochi (Cochin)
GO Nov–Mar

- Desert, dry climate
- Mild to hot summers, cold winters
- Tropical climate, rain year-round
- Tropical climate, wet & dry seasons
- Warm to hot summers, mild winters

High Season
(Dec-Mar)

o Pleasant
weather, mostly.
Peak crowds
and prices. Pre-
book flights and
accommodation.

o In December and
January northern
cities can get cold,
bitterly so in the far
north.

Shoulder Season
(Jul-Nov)

o July to early
September is the
prime time to visit
Ladakh.

o Southeast coast
(and southern
Kerala) experiences
heavy rain any time
from October to
early December.

Low Season
(Apr-Jun)

o April to June
can be unbearably
hot. Hotels prices
competitive.

o June's southern
monsoons sweep
up north (except
Ladakh) by July.
Fatiguing humidity.

o Beat the heat by
fleeing to the hills.

Advance Planning

o **One to two months before** Check your passport is valid for at
least six months, and apply for a visa.

o **Six weeks before** Seek advice regarding the necessary
vaccinations, and obtain malaria tablets if necessary.

o **One week before** Get travel insurance and ensure it will cover you
for any activities you want to do.

Your Daily Budget

Budget less than ₹1000
- Stay at cheap guesthouses with shared bathrooms, or hostels.
- Eat at roadside stalls or basic restaurants.
- Travel by train and bus, and occasionally autorickshaw.

Midrange ₹1000 to ₹5000
- Good accommodation (with private bathrooms) and restaurants.
- Travel by train, autorickshaw and taxi.

Top End more than ₹5000
- Sleep and dine like royalty in a restored palace.
- Hire a car and driver, but take the train for romance and an autorickshaw for adventure!

Exchange Rates

Australia	A$1	₹48
Canada	C$1	₹46
Euro zone	€1	₹64
Japan	¥100	₹55
New Zealand	NZ$1	₹37
UK	UK£1	₹73
US	US$1	₹45

For current exchange rates see www.xe.com

What to Bring
- **Non-revealing clothes** Covering up will win locals' respect; essential when visiting holy sites.
- **Money belt** A well-concealed belt for valuables.
- **Sunscreen & sunglasses** To be sure of good UV protection, bring them from home.
- **Tampons** Usually found only in big (or touristy) towns, though sanitary pads are widely available.
- **Mosquito repellent** Especially for malarial areas.
- **Water bottle** Use water-purification tablets or filters.
- **Sleeping sheet** If you're unsure about hotel linen or taking overnight train journeys.

Arriving in India
Ask if your hotel can arrange an airport pickup.

∘ Delhi

Taxi Prepaid taxi booths at the airport

Metro Airport Metro runs to central New Delhi Railway; from there take a prepaid autorickshaw

∘ Mumbai

Taxi Prepaid taxi booths at the airport

∘ Chennai

Train MRTS train is cheapest way to the centre

Taxi & autorickshaw Catch from prepaid booths

∘ Kolkata

Taxi Prepaid fixed-price taxis available from the airport; very few after 10pm (when it costs more)

Bus Half-hourly AC buses from the airport

Getting Around
- **Rail** Reliable; especially recommended for overnight journeys.
- **Car** Easiest and safest to hire a car and driver. Advisable not to travel on the roads at night.
- **Air** Quick and efficient for long distances; numerous airlines have competitive prices.
- **Bus** From sleek AC coaches to decrepit vehicles. Take only if most convenient.
- **Rickshaws** The easiest way to zip around towns; mostly motorised.

Accommodation
- **Government-owned & tourist bungalows** Usually mid-priced, some heritage properties.
- **Homestays/B&Bs** Family-run, small-scale places, from basic to grand.
- **Top-end & heritage hotels** From modern five-star chains to glorious palaces and forts.

Be Forewarned
- **Touts** Use recommended guides – ask other travellers or at the local tourist office.
- **Taxi & rickshaw drivers** Disregard 'it's no good/closed/burnt down': they'll try to take you to places that pay them commission.
- **Gem scams** If a gem deal seems too good to be true, *it is*.
- **Clean water** Drink bottled or purify your own.

Delhi & the Taj Mahal

Medieval mayhem, the New India, stately maiden aunt: India's capital could capture your heart. Yes, it's aggravating, polluted and hectic, but hey – nobody's perfect.

This seething metropolis, where many people start or end their trip, is punctuated with vestiges of lost empires. Ancient forts, tombs and temple complexes freckle the suburbs. Old Delhi was once the capital of Islamic India. The British built New Delhi, with its exaggerated avenues. And even-newer Delhi features utopian malls linked by potholed roads. There are also magnificent museums, temples, mosques, a busy cultural scene, some of the subcontinent's finest food, and all the riches of India twinkle in Delhi's emporiums. Plus it's an easy trip from here to some of the Mughal empire's most flabbergastingly beautiful monuments: wonder of the world the Taj Mahal, Agra Fort and the deserted city of Fatehpur Sikri.

Humayun's Tomb (p73)

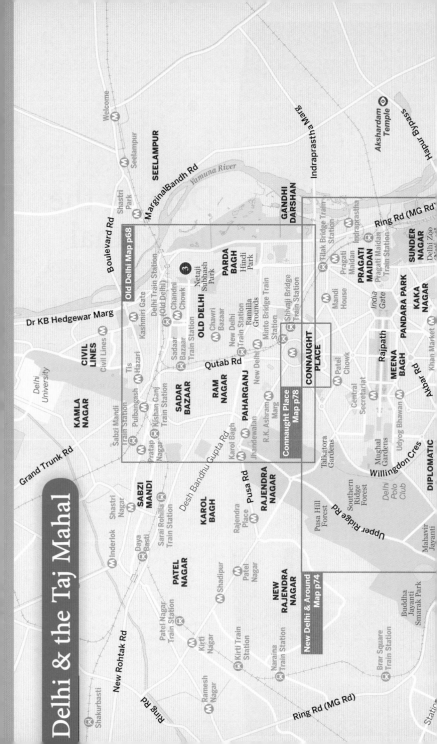

Delhi & the Taj Mahal

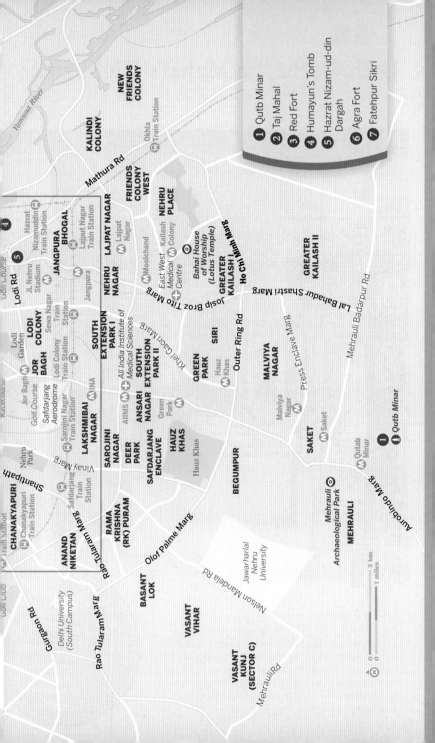

Delhi & the Taj Mahal's Highlights

① Qutb Minar

One of Delhi's most spectacular sights, the ruins of Qutb Minar date from the onset of Islamic rule in India. Not only is the site a beautiful place to wander, but it's fascinating to see the political and religious historical developments of the time through the adaptations of its architecture. Above: Sandstone pillars at the Qutb Minar complex; Top Right: Alai Minar; Bottom Right: Qutb Minar minaret

Need to Know

AVOID Weekends, when it's crowded. **EAT** Pack a picnic, or eat in nearby Saket. **QUTB MINAR METRO** Several km from the site; take a rickshaw for around ₹50. **For more, see p96.**

Local Knowledge

Qutb Minar Don't Miss List

DILLIWALA SUREKHA NARAIN PROVIDES WALKING TOURS AROUND DELHI SIGHTS, INCLUDING QUTB MINAR, WITH DELHI METRO WALKS

1 QUWWAT-UL-ISLAM MOSQUE

In 1192 AD, Muhammad Ghori from Afghanistan defeated Prithviraj Chauhan, a Hindu and Rajput ruler, and left his slave, Qutbuddin Aibak, to establish the Qutb complex. Aibak demolished around 27 Hindu temples and built a mosque (known as Quwwat-Ul-Islam or Might of Islam), using the remains. The result is an intriguing blend of Hindu and Islamic elements. The Hindu elements include conical domes with supporting pillars and beams. At the far end, you will see Islamic ideas in the form of corbelled arches.

2 QUTB MINAR

This victory tower was established in 1199, and is the tallest stone tower in India: 72.5m high with 379 steps leading to five storeys. On each floor you can see details of stalactite corbelling and arabesque Islamic decoration with floral and geometrical patterns and calligraphy of Quranic verses.

3 ALAI DARWAZA & ALAI MINAR

Alauddin Khilji, the invader who founded the second city of Delhi, added the Alai Darwaza – a stunning gateway in arabesque decoration – in 1311 by beautifully blending red sandstone and marble to create a southern entrance to the Qutb Minar.

4 TOMB OF IMAM ZAMIM

Next to the Alai Darwaza, this Lodhi-style square tomb has 12 pillars with beautiful red sandstone lattice work. Inside you see how a circle has been converted to a dome (circular structure) with the help of squinches. The marble sculpture of a small pen box on the lid of the tomb shows that this is the tomb of a man.

5 TOMB OF ALTAMISH

At the far end of the complex is the stunning square tomb of Iltutmish, which has no Hindu features, and combines the Islamic practices of arabesque floral and geometrical patterns in sandstone and marble with a large pen sculpture on a male tomb, decorative prayer niche, and calligraphy from the Quran.

Taj Mahal

A building that gleams, its perfection like something from a dream, the Taj Mahal will exceed all your expectations, however high they are. This was the pinnacle of Mughal architecture, and the building has not been diminished by age or any of the surrounding commerciality. Definitely make time to come here.

Need to Know

TAKE Cameras, small bags, water bottles, mini torch. **CAN'T TAKE** Food, big bags, cigarettes, lighters, phone chargers, loose batteries, laptops. **CLOSED** Fridays. **For more, see p99.**

The Taj Mahal Don't Miss List

HISTORIAN AND WRITER DR NEVILLE SMITH'S FAMILY HAS LIVED IN AGRA FOR OVER FOUR GENERATIONS

1 PERFECT SYMMETRY

There is a perfect balance of parts and structures to the left and right of an imaginary middle line cut through the building's centre. You see the same number of turrets, cupolas, pavilions and other designs on the left and right of the central dome, as well as on the left and right of the main structure.

2 MATHEMATICAL ACCURACY

If you stand in front of the main tomb in the Cenotaph Chamber and look straight towards the main gateway due south, you will find that the tomb aligns with the middle of the gateway. There is not even a few millimetres difference. That such accuracy was achieved, without the technical instruments of today, says much about the architectural and engineering skills of the builders.

3 OPTICAL ILLUSION

The Quranic verses on the mausoleum do not appear to decrease in size as they go up to the base of the main dome, which would be the case if they were chiselled in equal size and placed in their grooves. The letters were increased in size along with the grooves in which they were to be inserted, so that a person looking at them from the ground would see them as equal in size and the optical effect of their tapering to the top would be avoided.

4 ARCHITECTURAL SYMBOLISM

The Taj can be seen as conceptualising the feminine grace of Mumtaz Mahal. The dome has been likened to the head of a woman and its base as her neck, around which the marble inlay gives the appearance of Mumtaz Mahal arrayed in all her finery.

5 LANDSCAPING INNOVATION

Unlike other Mughal and, indeed, Muslim garden tombs, which all have the Charbagh plan (a tomb set in the centre of a garden with waterways radiating from the tomb), the Taj has been placed at the northen end of a garden. Shah Jahan broke away from the typical Muslim garden tomb for better scenic effect, so the edifice dominates the garden, instead of being dominated by it.

Red Fort

The Red Fort (p65) is awash with splendour, a sandstone queen bee overlooking the Old Delhi hive. Surrounded by magnificent red walls, the remaining buildings might be a shadow of their former selves, but it's still possible to imagine the glories of the imperial court; the battered structures, and grounds dotted with British-built barracks, resonate with Delhi's tumultuous history.

Humayun's Tomb

Desperate for a little piece of tranquillity amid the hubbub and traffic of Delhi? This great Mughal tomb (p73) was the inspiration for and forerunner of the Taj Mahal. Built for the second Mughal emperor, it is also one of the most serene places in the capital, surrounded by manicured Mughal gardens.

HUW JONES/LONELY PLANET IMAGES ©

Hazrat Nizam-ud-din Dargah ⑤

To experience one of Delhi's most mystical religious events, head to the vibrant marble shrine (p77) of the Sufi saint Hazrat Nizam-ud-din at sunset on Thursdays, to hear *qawwali* singers and musicians perform. The area is a tangle of streets centred on the shrine, which is thronged with pilgrims making offerings, burning incense and listening to the music.

Agra Fort ⑥

With its neighbour the Taj Mahal garnering all the glory, it's easy to overlook that Agra Fort (p103) is perhaps India's finest Mughal fort. Originally constructed purely as a military fortification, it was transformed into an exquisite palace, which later became Shah Jahan's gilded cage after his son Aurangzeb seized power.

Fatehpur Sikri ⑦

Stand in awe beside immense Mughal monuments in the ruined city of Fatehpur Sikri (p105). You can almost glimpse the ghosts of the great empire in its beautifully sculpted mosques, tombs and palaces. It's remarkably preserved because it was never rebuilt or reinvented; the city was deserted after Emperor Akbar's death, when severe water shortages made the settlement untenable.

Delhi & the Taj Mahal's Best...

Wining & Dining

○ **Bukhara** (p84) Small menu, big reputation: regarded as Delhi's finest

○ **Karim's** (p82) Old-school Mughlai cuisine in the heart of the Old City

○ **Saravana Bhavan** (p83) Delhi's best dosas, in canteen-style surroundings

○ **Monsoon** (p84) Imaginative, creative Indian cooking

○ **Andhra Pradesh Bhawan Canteen** (p84) Tasty, cheap South Indian thalis

○ **Indian Accent** (p79) Creative new Indian cuisine at its finest

Shopping

○ **Chandni Chowk** (p71) Crazy, glittering bazaars

○ **Khadi Gramodyog Bhawan** (p89) Khadi (homespun cloth) clothing

○ **Khan Market** (p89) Exclusive enclave for clothes, homewares and books

○ **Central Cottage Industries Emporium** (p88) Aladdin's cave of handicrafts

○ **State Emporiums** (p88) Regional handicraft centres

Views

○ **Jama Masjid** (p105) Climb the minaret for vistas over Old Delhi

○ **Taj Mahal** (p99) Enter the compound: up close and personal

○ **North Bank of Yamuna River** (p99) See the reflection of the Taj

○ **Rooftop cafe in Taj Ganj** (p103) Sip a drink at sunset

○ **Agra Fort** (p103) Climb the tower where Shah Jahan was imprisoned

○ **Fatehpur Sikri** (p105) Find a vantage point as the sun sets

Need to Know

Places to Chill

o **Sunset at Delhi's India Gate** (p72) Everyone gathers to wander and eat ice cream

o **Humayun's Tomb** (p73) Graceful Mughal tomb, set in serene symmetrical gardens

o **Lodi Garden** (p72) Delhi's loveliest escape, dotted by crumbling tombs

o **Lotus Temple** (p72) For people of all religions, this petal-shaped temple is designed for quiet meditation

ADVANCE PLANNING

o **Two months before** Get your visa

o **Six weeks before** Have any vaccinations

o **One month before** Book long train journeys online

o **A few days before** Book to see the Taj by moonlight (full moon only)

GETTING AROUND

o **Delhi Metro** The quickest way to get around the city

o **Trains to Agra** The fastest trains from Delhi take only two hours

o **Fatehpur Sikri** Buses from Agra take one hour

o **Taxi hire** Straightforward in all major towns; reckon on around ₹1800 per day

BE FOREWARNED

o **Commission** Rickshaw and taxi drivers try to take you to local hotels/shops to gain a cut

o **Tourist Office** The Government Tourist Office in Delhi is on Janpath; don't believe anyone who tells you otherwise

o **Recommendations** Ask fellow travellers or at an official tourist office for guide or tour recommendations

RESOURCES

o **Delhi Tourism** (www.delhitourism.nic.in) Sights, accommodation and practical information

o **Times City** (www.timescity.com/delhi) Restaurant and bar reviews from the *India Times*

o **Delhi Metro Rail** (www.delhimetrorail.com) Official site with timetables and travel planner

o **The Delhi Walla** (www.thedelhiwalla.com) An offbeat view of Delhi by local journalist Mayank Austen Soofi

o **Eat & Dust** (www.eatanddust.com) 'Food Aventures in India' blog written by food writer and cook Pamela Timms; particularly good on street food

Left: The Diwan-i-Kas, Fatehpur Sikri (p105);
Above: Shopkeeper on Chandni Chowk (p71).

(LEFT) TIM MAKINS/LONELY PLANET IMAGES ©;
(ABOVE) RICHARD I'ANSON/LONELY PLANET IMAGES ©

Old Delhi Walking Tour

This loop visits Old Delhi's major bazaars and monuments. It's hectic walking through the crowds: if it gets too much, hail a cycle-rickshaw to glide through the mayhem.

WALK FACTS
- **Start** Red Fort
- **Finish** Fatehpur Mosque
- **Distance** 2.5km
- **Duration** Three hours

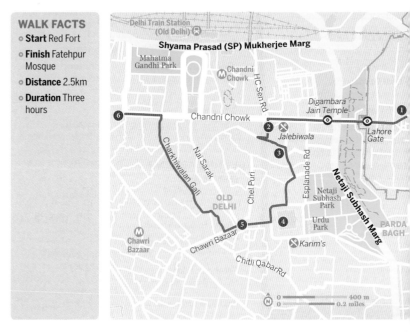

1 Red Fort

Start your walk outside the Red Fort, looking up at Lahore Gate and the walls of the Red Fort stretching out on either side of you. Then turn your back on the fort and start down Chandni Chowk. Crossing the frantic road, the first thing you will see on your left is Digambara Jain Temple. It contains a bird hospital, reflecting the Jain philosophy of the preservation of all life.

2 Sisganj Gurdwara

Continuing to walk down Chandni Chowk, you'll next pass the Jalebiwala on your left, where there's always a crowd of people waiting for the next freshly fried batch of sweet squiggles. On your left you'll see

the Sisganj Gurdwara, a permanently thronged Sikh temple. It commemorates the martyrdom of Sikh Guru Tegh Bahadur, who was beheaded by the Mughals on this spot in 1675.

3 Kinari Bazaar

Just after the temple, dive left into one of the narrow lanes that snake off the main drag (the one just before the famous sweet shop of Ghantewala). First you'll find a delicious cluster of hole-in-the-wall restaurants, where you can eat a freshly fried *paratha* (bread) stuffed with vegetables and cheese, the perfect snack. Then the lane meets busy Kinari Bazaar – turn left onto the bazaar. This market stocks verything you might need for a wedding: arlands, grooms' turbans, bridal jewellery nd decorations.

④ Jama Masjid

ollow Kinari Bazaar until the junction with Dariba Kalan Rd, then turn right, following it until you meet another junction, whereupon ou should turn right and follow the lane ound a short distance until it opens out o look onto Jama Masjid. It's a surprise to ee the imposing building, reached via tall lights of steps. To take a bird's-eye view ver where you've been walking, enter and climb the minaret.

⑤ Chawri Bazaar

f you haven't eaten lunch yet, you might vant to stop at Karim's on the south side of the Jama Masjid, famous for its delicious Mughlai cuisine. Otherwise, take the street eading west from the great mosque, Chawri Bazaar. This is piled high with paper products, from greeting cards to wallpaper, but lso specialises in brass and copper items. Around 200m along here take the lane on he right, Charkhiwalan Gali, and follow the azaar lane straight until you hit the juncion with Chandni Chowk.

⑥ Fatehpur Mosque

The western end of Chandni Chowk is marked by the mid-17th-century Fatehpuri Masjid, named after one of Shah Jahan's vives. It offers a striking tranquillity after he craziness of the street. After the 1857 First War of Independence the mosque was sold to a Hindu merchant, who used it as a varehouse, but it was later returned to local Muslims.

Delhi in...

TWO DAYS

On day one, acclimatise gently at tranquil sites such as the **National Museum**, **Gandhi Smriti** and **Humayun's tomb**. In the evening head to **Hazrat Nizam-ud-din Dargah** to hear the Sufis sing *qawwalis*.

On day two, follow our Old Delhi Walking Tour, launching into the Old City's action-packed **bazaars**.

FOUR DAYS

The first day, wander around **Qutb Minar** and **Mehrauli** before some meditation at the **Bahai House of Worship**. In the evening, watch the mesmerising **Dances of India**, then kick back at a bar.

On day two, ramble around Old Delhi's **Red Fort**, then launch into the Old City's **bazaars** and visit the mighty **Jama Masjid**. Day three, visit some of the sights of New and South Delhi, including **Humayun's Tomb**, then take an autorickshaw to **Connaught Place** for a bite to eat.

On day four, wonder at the glories in the laid-back **Crafts Museum** and finish off around **Connaught Place** to explore the hassle-free, treasure-trove government **emporiums**.

Painting of Mahatma Gandhi, Gandhi Smriti (p81)

Discover Delhi & the Taj Mahal

At a Glance

- **Delhi** (p64) India's multi-layered capital is like many cities in one, and a feast for all the senses.

- **Taj Mahal** (p99) Mughal emperor Shah Jahan's monument to love is a wonder of the world.

- **Fatehpur Sikri** (p105) An evocative, beautifully preserved ghost town, this was a short-lived Mughal capital.

DELHI

 Sights

Most sights in Delhi are easily accessible via metro. Note that many places are closed on Monday.

Old Delhi

Medieval-seeming Old Delhi is a crazy hubbub that bombards the senses. Set aside at least half a day to do this fascinating area justice. All of the following attractions feature on Map p68.

The old walled city of **Shahjahanabad** stretches west from the Red Fort. It was at one time surrounded by a sturdy defensive wall, only fragments of which now exist. The **Kashmiri Gate**, to the north, was the scene of desperate fighting when the British retook Delhi during the 1857 First War of Independence (Indian Uprising). Close to here is the **Nicholson Cemetery** (☉8am-6pm summer, 9am-5pm winter), a 3-hectare forgotten corner of Delhi. It's named after John Nicholson, who died in 1857 and is buried here amid a sea of British graves that hint at fascinating stories. At the time he was described as the 'Hero of Delhi' but author William Dalrymple calls him an 'imperial psychopath' in *The Last Mughal*. Northwest of here is the British-erected **Mutiny Memorial**, dedicated to the soldiers who died during the Uprising. Near the monument is an **Ashoka Pillar**; like the one in Firoz Shah Kotla, it was brought here by Firoz Shah.

Busy shopping bazaar at night, Delhi
CHRISTER FREDRIKSSON/LONELY PLANET IMAGES ©

TIM MAKINS/LONELY PLANET IMAGES ©

Don't Miss **Jama Masjid**

India's largest mosque can hold a mind-blowing 25,000 people. Towering over Old Delhi, the 'Friday Mosque' was Shah Jahan's final architectural opus, built between 1644 and 1658. It has three gateways, four angle towers and two minarets standing 40m high, and is constructed of alternating vertical strips of red sandstone and white marble. You can enter from gate 1 or 3.

For an extra charge you can climb the 121 steps up the narrow southern minaret (notices say that unaccompanied women are not permitted) for incredible views. From the top of the minaret, you can see one of the features that architect Edwin Lutyens incorporated into his design of New Delhi – the Jama Masjid, Connaught Place and Sansad Bhavan (Parliament House) are sited in a direct line.

You should remove your shoes at the top of the stairs. There's no charge to enter the mosque, but the camera charge is required even if you don't want to use your camera.

THINGS YOU NEED TO KNOW

Map p68; camera/video each ₹200, tower ₹100; ⊙non-Muslims 8am-30min before sunset, minaret 9am-5.30pm; MChandni Chowk

---

RED FORT (LAL QILA) Fort
Indian/foreigner ₹10/250, video ₹25, combined museum ticket ₹5; ⊙9am-6pm Tue-Sun; MChandni Chowk) This massive fort is a sandstone shadow of its former self; but it's the best place in Delhi to imagine the Mughal city's sometime splendour. It dates from the peak of the dynasty's power, a time of unparalleled pomp: of eunuchs, ceremonial elephants, palanquins, and buildings lined with precious stones.

The 2km-long walls of the fort vary in height from 18m on the river side to 33m on the city side. Shah Jahan constructed the fort between 1638 and 1648, but never completely moved his capital from Agra to his new city of Shahjahanabad, because he was deposed and imprisoned in Agra Fort by his son Aurangzeb.

Mughal reign from Delhi was short; Aurangzeb was the first and last great Mughal emperor to rule from here.

65

● ● ●
Red Fort

Highlights

The main entrance to the Red Fort is through Lahore Gate **1** – the bastion in front of it was built by Aurangzeb for increased security. You can still see bullet marks from 1857 on the gate.

Walk through the Chatta Chowk (Covered Bazaar), which once sold silks and jewellery to the nobility; beyond it lies Naubat Khana **2**, a russet-red building, also known as Hathi Pol (Elephant Gate) because visitors used to dismount from their elephants or horses here as a sign of respect. From here it's straight on to the Diwan-i-Am **3**, the Hall of Public Audiences. Behind this are the private palaces, the Khas Mahal **4** and the Diwan-i-Khas **5**. Entry to this Hall of Private Audiences, the fort's most expensive building, was only permitted to the highest official of state. Nearby is the Moti Masjid (Pearl Mosque) **6** and south is the Mumtaz Mahal **7**, housing the Museum of Archaeology, or you can head north, where the Red Fort gardens are dotted by palatial pavilions and old British barracks. Here you'll find the *baoli* **8**, a spookily deserted water tank. Another five minutes' walk – across a road, then a railway bridge – brings you to the island fortress of Salimgarh **9**.

Salimgarh
Salimgarh is the 16th-century fort built by Salim Shah Sur. It was constructed on an island of the Yamuna River and only recently opened to the public. It is still partly used by the Indian army.

Chatta Chowk

Lahore Gate
Lahore Gate is particularly significant, as it was here that Jawaharlal raised the first tricolour flag of independent India in 1947.

Naubat Khana
The Naubat Khana (Drum House) is carved in floral designs and featured musicians playing in the upper gallery. It housed Hathi Pol (Elephant Gate), where visitors dismounted from their horse or elephant.

TOP TIPS

To avoid crowds, get here early or late in the day; avoid weekends and public holidays.

An atmospheric way to see the Red Fort is by night; you can visit after dark if you attend the nightly Sound-&-Light Show.

Baoli

The Red Fort step well is seldom visited and is a hauntingly deserted place, even more so when you consider its chambers were used as cells by the British from August 1942.

Moti Masjid

The Moti Masjid (Pearl Mosque) was built by Aurangzeb in 1662 for his personal use. The domes were originally covered in copper, but the copper was removed and sold by the British.

Diwan-i-Khas

This was the most expensive building in the fort, consisting of white marble decorated with inlay work of cornelian and other stones. The screens overlooking what was once the river (now the ring road) were filled with coloured glass.

Baidon Pavilion

Zafar Mahal

Hammam

⑤

⑥

④

Rang Mahal

Mumtaz Mahal

⑦

③

②

Pit Stop

To refuel, head to Paratha Gali Wali, a food-stall-lined lane off Chandni Chowk noted for its many varieties of freshly made *paratha* (traditional flat bread).

←NORTH

Delhi Gate

Diwan-i-Am

These red sandstone columns were once covered in shell plaster, as polished and smooth as ivory, and in hot weather heavy red curtains were hung around the columns to block out the sun. It's believed the panels behind the marble throne were created by Florentine jeweller Austin de Bordeaux.

Khas Mahal

Most spectacular in the Emperor's private apartments is a beautiful marble screen at the northern end of the rooms; the 'Scales of Justice' are carved above it, suspended over a crescent, surrounded by stars and clouds.

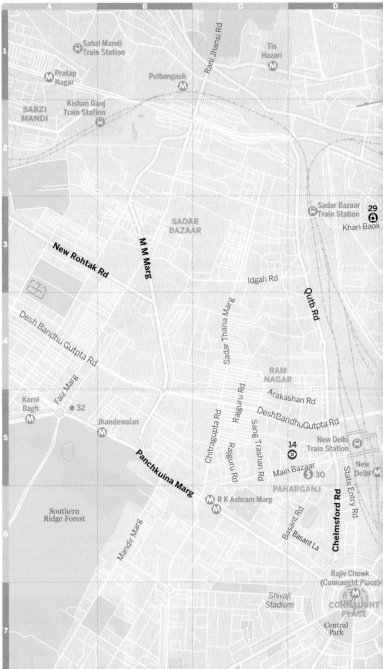

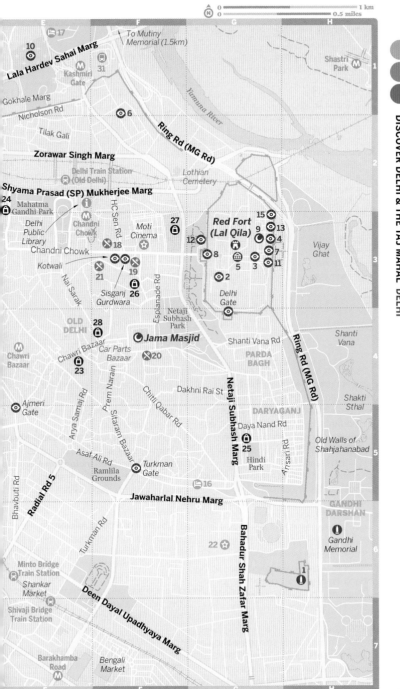

Old Delhi

Subsequent rulers, sapped by civil war, were unable to maintain the fort properly, and slums within the walls were thronged with impoverished imperial descendants. By the 19th century it was already much dilapidated. Following the 1857 First War of Independence, the British cleared all but the most important buildings to make way for ugly barracks and army offices.

The 10m-deep moat, which has been dry since 1857, was originally crossed on creaky wooden drawbridges, replaced with stone bridges in 1811.

Since Independence many landmark political speeches have taken place at the fort and every year on Independence Day (15 August) it hosts the prime minister's address to the nation.

LAHORE GATE
The fort's main gate is so named because it faces towards Lahore, now in Pakistan. You enter the fort through here and immediately find yourself in the vaulted arcade known as the **Chatta Chowk** (Covered Bazaar). The tourist-trap arcade once sold rather more exclusive items to the royal household – silks, jewellery and gold.

The arcade leads to the **Naubat Khana** (Drum House), where musicians used to perform. There's an **Indian War Memorial Museum** upstairs, full of fearsome weaponry and phallic shells.

DIWAN-I-AM
In the **Hall of Public Audiences** the emperor would hear disputes from his subjects. Many of the precious stones set above the emperor's throne were looted following the First War of Independence. The hall was restored following a directive by Lord Curzon, the viceroy of India between 1898 and 1905.

DIWAN-I-KHAS
The white marble **Hall of Private Audiences** was the luxurious chamber where the emperor would hold private meetings. The centrepiece was once the magnifi-

ent solid-gold and jewel-studded Peacock Throne, looted from India by Persia's Nadir Shah in 1739. In 1760 the Marathas removed the hall's silver ceiling.

ROYAL BATHS

Next to the Diwan-i-Khas are the hammams (baths) – three large rooms surmounted by domes, with a fountain in the centre – one of which was set up as a sauna. The floors were once inlaid with pietra dura (marble inlay work) and the rooms were illuminated through stained-glass roof panels.

SHAHI BURJ

This modest, three-storey, octagonal tower to the northeastern edge of the fort was once Shah Jahan's private working area. From here, cooling water, known as the nahr-i-bihisht (river of paradise), used to flow south through the Royal Baths, the Diwan-i-Khas, the Khas Mahal and on to the Rang Mahal.

MOTI MASJID

The small, enclosed, marble **Pearl Mosque** is next to the baths. Its outer walls are oriented exactly in symmetry with the rest of the fort, while the inner walls are slightly askew, so that the mosque is correctly orientated to Mecca.

OTHER FEATURES

The **Khas Mahal**, south of the Diwan-i-Khas, was the emperor's private palace. It was divided into rooms for worship, sleeping and living, with carved walls and painted ceilings.

The **Rang Mahal** (Palace of Colour), further south again, took its name from its vividly painted interior, now long gone. This was the residence of the emperor's chief wife and is where he dined. On the floor in the centre there's an exquisitely

carved marble lotus; the water flowing along the channel from the Shahi Burj would end up here.

SOUND-&-LIGHT SHOW

Each evening (except Monday) this one-hour **show (admission ₹60; ⏱in English 7.30pm Nov-Jan, 9pm May-Aug, 8.30pm rest of year)** gives Red Fort history the coloured-spotlight and portentous-voice-over treatment. It's great to see the fort by night, though the history lesson is a tad ponderous. Tickets are available from the fort's ticket kiosk. Bring mosquito repellent.

CHANDNI CHOWK   Area

Old Delhi's backbone is the madcap Chandni Chowk ('moonlight place'), a wide avenue thronged by crowds, hawkers and rickshaws. In the time of Shah Jahan, a canal ran down its centre, lined by peepal and neem trees – at night the waters reflected the moon, hence the name. Tiny bazaar-crammed lanes snake off the broadway-like clogged arteries.

Old man outside a Hindu temple
GETTY CITY COMMISSION/LONELY PLANET IMAGES ©

New Delhi & Around

All of the attractions in this section feature on Map p74.

RAJPATH Area

Rajpath (Kingsway) is the imposing approach to New Delhi. It hosts the huge Republic Day parade every 26 January and the Beating of the Retreat on 29 January.

Raj-appointed English architect Edwin Lutyens constructed New Delhi between 1914 and 1931, when the British moved their capital here from Calcutta. His designs were intended to spell out in stone the might of the British empire – but a mere 16 years later, the British were out on their ear. New Delhi became the powerhouse of the new Republic.

At the western end of Rajpath is the official residence of the president of India, the **Rashtrapati Bhavan** (President's House), built in 1929. Pre-Independence, this 340-room palace was the viceroy's residence. At the time of Mountbatten, India's last viceroy, the number of servants employed here was staggering. There were 418 gardeners alone, 50 of whom were boys employed to chase away birds.

Rashtrapati Bhavan is flanked by the mirror-image, dome-crowned North and South **Secretariat buildings**, housing government ministries, which have over 1000 rooms between them. The three buildings sit upon a small rise, known as Raisina Hill.

At Rajpath's eastern end is **India Gate**. This 42m-high stone memorial arch, designed by Lutyens, pays tribute to around 90,000 Indian army soldiers who died in WWI, the Northwest Frontier operations of the same time and the 1919 Anglo-Afghan War.

NATIONAL MUSEUM Museum
(☏23019272; www.nationalmuseum india. gov.in; Janpath; Indian ₹10, foreigner incl English, French or German audio guide ₹300, Hindi audio guide ₹150, camera Indian/foreigner ₹20/300; ⊙10am-5pm Tue-Sun; Ⓜ Central Secretariat) An overview of India's last 5000 years, this is a splendid museum. Exhibits include rare relics from the Harappan Civilisation, including some fascinating mundane items such as tweezers and hairpins from around 2700 BC, Central Asian antiquities including many artefacts from the Silk Route, a mesmerising collection of jewel-bright miniature paintings, exquisite old coins including pure gold examples from the 1st century, woodcarving, textiles, musical instruments, and Indus jewellery made from shells and bones.

Connaught Place Area

New Delhi's colonnaded heart is commercial centre **Connaught Place** (CP; Map p78), named after George V's uncle, who visited in 1921. Streets radiate from the central circle, divided into blocks and devoted to shops, restaurants, hotels and offices.

Touts are especially rampant in Connaught Place.

JANTAR MANTAR Historic Site
(Map p78; Sansad Marg; Indian/foreigner ₹5/100 ⊙9am-dusk; Ⓜ Patel Chowk) 'Jantar Mantar' may mean the equivalent to 'abracadabra' in Hindi, but the site was constructed in 1725 for scientific purposes – it's the earliest of Maharaja Jai Singh II's five

TIM MAKINS/LONELY PLANET IMAGES ©

Don't Miss **Humayun's Tomb**

This is Delhi's most sublime sight, and the one the Obamas were taken to visit when they were in town. A beautiful example of early Mughal architecture, this tomb was built in the mid-16th century by Haji Begum, the Persian-born senior wife of the second Mughal emperor, Humayun. The tomb brought Persian style to Delhi, but the two-tone combination of red sandstone and white marble is entirely local, showing the complementary merging of the cultures. Elements in its design – a squat building with high arched entrances that let in light, topped by a bulbous dome and surrounded by 12 hectares of formal gardens – were to be refined over the years to eventually create the magnificence of Agra's Taj Mahal (p99).

THINGS YOU NEED TO KNOW

Map p74; Indian/foreigner ₹10/250, video ₹25; ⊙dawn-dusk; Ⓜ JLN Stadium

bservatories. It's dominated by a huge undial and houses other instruments lotting the course of heavenly bodies.

 **Activities**

matrra Spa Spa
Map p74; ☎24122921; www.amatrraspa.com; shok Hotel, Chanakyapuri; ⊙9am-10pm; ⚑Racecourse) The most legendarily luxurious of ll Delhi's luxury spas, Amatrra is the A-list place be pampered. There's a cover charge of ₹1000 or nonguests; massages, such as 'Asian Blend',

cost from ₹3000, and there are many other treatments, like 'Sparkle Body Scrub' (₹3500).

 Courses

Tannie Baig Cooking
(☎9899555704; baig.murad@gmail.com; 2hr lesson ₹3200; Ⓜ Hauz Khas) The elegant Tannie Baig has written 16 cookery books. A two-hour cooking lesson sounds pricey, but it's a flat rate for up to five people. If you stay at her guesthouse, lessons are half price.

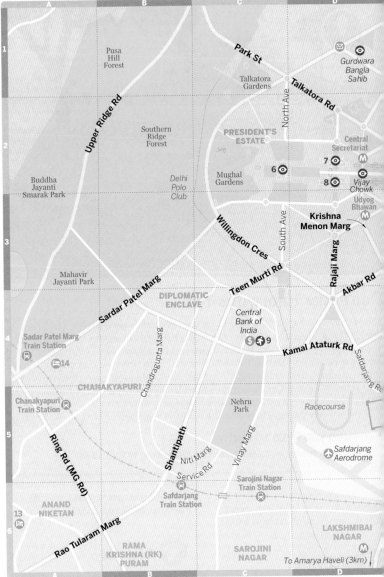

Tours

Delhi is a spread-out city so taking a tour makes sense, although you can feel rushed at some sites. Avoid Monday when many sites are shut. Admission fees and camera/video charges aren't included in tour prices below, and rates are per person. Book several days in advance as minimum numbers may be required. India Tourism Delhi (p91) can arrange multilin-

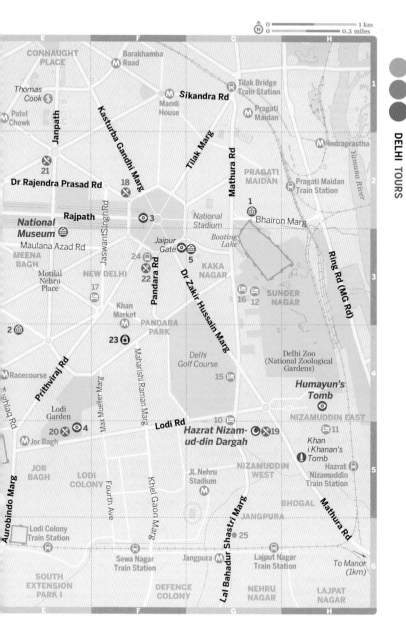

ual, government-approved guides (from 150/300 per half-/full day).

ELHIBYCYCLE   Cycling
(9811723720; www.delhibycycle.com; ₹1250;
6.45-10am) Run by Jack Leenaars, a

journalist from the Netherlands, this is a fantastic way to see Delhi. There's the Shah Jahan Tour around the back lanes and bazaars of Old Delhi, and the Raj Tour around New Delhi.

New Delhi & Around

Top Sights
- Hazrat Nizam-ud-din Dargah G5
- Humayun's Tomb H4
- National Museum E3

Sights
- 1 Crafts Museum G2
- 2 Gandhi Smriti E4
- 3 India Gate F2
- 4 Lodi Garden E5
- 5 National Gallery of Modern Art G3
- 6 Rashtrapati Bhavan C2
- 7 Secretariat (North Block) D2
- 8 Secretariat (South Block) D2

Activities, Courses & Tours
- 9 Amatrra Spa C4

Sleeping
- 10 Aman New Delhi G4
- 11 Brnineteen H5
- 12 Devna G3
- 13 Inn at Delhi A6
- 14 ITC Maurya A4
- 15 Oberoi G4
- 16 Shervani G3
- 17 Taj Mahal F3

Eating
- Amici .... (see 23)
- 18 Andhra Bhawan Pradesh Canteen F2
- Bukhara .... (see 14)
- Gulati .... (see 22)
- 19 Karim's G5
- Khan Chacha .... (see 23)
- 20 Lodi Garden Restaurant E5
- Mamagoto .... (see 23)
- 21 Monsoon E2
- 22 Pandara Market F3
- Pindi .... (see 22)

Drinking
- Café Oz .... (see 23)
- Café Turtle .... (see 23)

Shopping
- Anand Stationers .... (see 23)
- Anokhi (Branch) .... (see 23)
- Bahri Sons .... (see 23)
- Fabindia .... (see 23)
- Full Circle Bookstore .... (see 23)
- Good Earth .... (see 23)
- 23 Khan Market F4
- Silverline .... (see 23)

Transport
- 24 Bikaner House F3
- 25 Metropole Tourist Service G6

SALAAM BAALAK TRUST Walking
(23584164, 9910099348; www.salaambaalaktrust.com; Gali Chandiwali, Paharganj; suggested donation ₹200; M RK Ashram Marg) This charitable organisation offers two-hour 'street walks' with a twist – your guide is a former (Trust-trained) street child, who will show you firsthand what life is like for inner-city homeless kids. The money goes to the Trust to assist children on the streets.

DELHI TOURISM & TRANSPORT DEVELOPMENT CORPORATION Bus Tours
(DTTDC; delhitourism.nic.in) Baba Kharak Singh Marg (off Map p78; 23363607; 7am-9pm); international airport (25675609; 8am-9pm) New Delhi (9am to 2pm) and Old Delhi (2.15pm to 5.15pm) AC tours cost ₹310. Also runs the new AC **Hop-on, Hop-off (HOHO) Bus Service** (1280; ₹300; every 30min, 7.30am-8pm Tue-Sun), which passes by all Delhi's major sights. Same-day trips to Agra (₹1100 AC) run thrice-weekly while three-day tours of Agra and Jaipur (₹6350, via rail) operate twice weekly.

Sleeping

It's wise to book in advance, as Delhi's most salubrious places can fill up in a flash, leaving new arrivals easy prey for commission sharks. Most hotels offer pick-up from the airport with advance notice.

Midrange prices have rocketed upwards over recent years, so homestays are becoming an attractive alternative. For details of government-approved places contact India Tourism Delhi, or

ANDERS BLOMQVIST/LONELY PLANET IMAGES ©

Don't Miss **Hazrat Nizam-ud-din Dargah**

Amid a tangle of alleys, attracting hordes of devotees, is the vibrant marble shrine of the Muslim Sufi saint Nizam-ud-din Chishti. He died in 1325, aged 92, but the mausoleum has been revamped several times, and dates from 1562. It's one of Delhi's most extraordinary pleasures to experience the buzz around the site and hear Sufis sing *qawwali* (devotional songs) at around sunset, just after evening prayers on Thursdays and feast days.

THINGS YOU NEED TO KNOW
Map p74; ⏱24hr

check www.incredibleindianhomes.com and www.mahindrahomestays.com.

Hotels with a minimum tariff of ₹1000 charge 12.5% luxury tax and some also whack on a service charge (5% to 10%). Taxes aren't included in this chapter unless indicated and all rooms have private bathrooms unless otherwise stated. Most hotels have a noon checkout and luggage storage is usually possible (sometimes for a small charge).

It's a good idea to call or email ahead to confirm your booking 24 hours before you arrive.

Old Delhi

Few foreign tourists stay in teeming Old Delhi – those who do will probably attract a bit of innocuous attention.

MAIDENS HOTEL　　　　Hotel $$$
(Map p68; ☎23975464; www.maidens
hotel.com; Sham Nath Marg; r from ₹15,000;
✳@☎; Ⓜ Civil Lines) Set in a 3.2-hectare garden, Maidens is a graceful wedding cake, built in 1903. Lutyens stayed here while supervising the building of New Delhi. The high-ceilinged rooms are traditional, old-fashioned, well equipped and some have good views.

Connaught Place

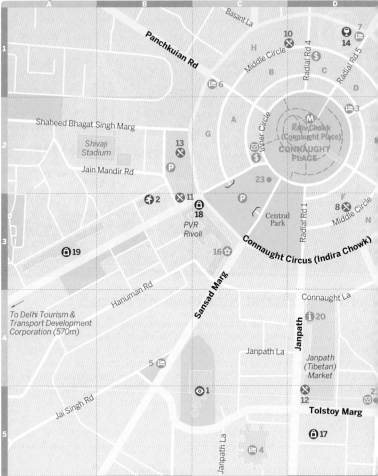

HOTEL BROADWAY Hotel **$$**
(Map p68; ☎43663600; www.hotelbroadway
delhi.com/; 4/15 Asaf Ali Rd; s/d incl breakfast
₹2495/4495; ❄@; MNew Delhi) Semiluxuri-
ous Broadway, between the old and new
cities, has some rooms with views over
Old Delhi. Room standards vary (some
are sleek and smart), so look at a few.
Nos 44 and 46 have been kitschly kitted
out by French designer Catherine Lévy,
as has the Chor Bizarre restaurant, and
there's the atmospheric, if divey, 'Thugs'
bar upstairs.

New Delhi & Around

Connaught Place properties are unbeat-
ably central, but you pay a premium for
the location. These listings feature on
Map p78 and are close to metro stop Rajiv
Chowk.

IMPERIAL Hotel **$$$**
(☎23341234; www.theimperialindia.com;
Janpath; s/d ₹15,000/17,500; ❄@🛜🏊) The
inimitable, Raj-era Imperial marries Victorian colonial classicism with gilded art
deco, houses an impressive collection of

breezily chic restaurant, and a great poolside bar.

HOTEL PALACE HEIGHTS　Hotel　$$$
(☎ 43582610; www.hotelpalaceheights.com; 26-28 D-Block; s/d ₹6500/7000; ❄ @ ☎) Connaught Place's most accessibly priced boutique hotel has sleek rooms with gleaming white linen, black lamp-shades and caramel padded headboards. There's an excellent restaurant and 24-hour room service.

RADISSON BLU MARINA　Hotel　$$$
(☎ 46909090; www.radissonblu.com/marina hotel-newdelhi; 59 G-Block; superior/deluxe ₹7000/7500; ❄ @ ☎) The Radisson's up-date of the old Hotel Marina is CP's flashest hotel, with stylish all-mod-con rooms, two restaurants and the cool **Connaught** bar.

YORK HOTEL　Hotel　$$$
(☎ 23415769; www.hotelyorkindia.com; K-Block; s/d ₹3800/4300; ❄ @) The York's rooms are good-sized and smartly refurbished in neutral colours, with wood-panelled floors and satiny bedcovers. Try to avoid the noisy, street-facing rooms.

South Delhi

AMAN NEW DELHI　Hotel　$$$
(Map p74; ☎ 43633333; www.amanresorts.com; Lodi Rd; d from US$600; ❄ @ ☎ ⛭; Ⓜ JLN Stadium) India's lushest chain runs this glamorous haven close to Lodi Garden. It's Delhi's finest hotel, with rooms and suites around an exquisite courtyard, and modern contemporary design merging with traditional elements, such as *jali* (covered lattice) screens.

17th- and 18th-century paintings, and has hosted everyone from princesses to pop stars. The high-ceilinged rooms have it all, from French linen and puffy pillows to marble baths and finely crafted furniture. There's a great bar, **1911**, which is perfect for High Tea.

PARK　Hotel　$$$
(☎ 23744000; www.theparkhotels.com; 15 Parliament St; s/d from ₹12,000/14,000; ❄ @ ☎ ⛭) Conran-designed, with lots of modern flair, and has a smashing spa,

MANOR　Hotel　$$$
(☎ 26925151; www.themanordelhi.com; 77 Friends Colony (West); d incl breakfast from ₹8500; ❄ @) If you're looking for a more intimate alternative to Delhi's opulent five stars, this 16-room boutique hotel is it. Off Mathura Rd, set amid manicured lawns, the renovated bungalow combines contemporary luxury with caramel-hued elegance that seems from another era. The restaurant, Indian Accent, is superb, and lush lawns and a sun-warmed terrace complete the picture.

Connaught Place

Young boys swimming in a pond along the Rajpath (p72)

BNINETEEN Guesthouse $$$

(Map p74; 41825500; www.bnineteen.com; B-19 Nizamuddin East; d from ₹7500; ❄ @) A secluded place located in fascinating Nizamuddin East, this guesthouse offers fabulous views over Humayun's tomb from the rooftop. It's a gorgeous place that shows an architect's touch: the rooms are spacious and cool, and great for long-stayers, with a state-of-the-art shared kitchen on each floor.

AMARYA HAVELI Guesthouse $$$

(off Map p74; 41759267; www.amarya group.com; Hauz Khas Enclave; s/d ₹6500/6900; ❄ @; M Hauz Khas) The French owners of Amarya Haveli have created a haven in Hauz Khas, a boutique place that is funkily furnished with Indian artefacts, carved furniture and textiles, and has an appealing roof terrace swathed in pink and orange. They also opened in 2010 the even-more-chic **Amarya Villa** (D-179 Defence Colony; M Lajpat Nagar), with slightly more expensive rooms (same contact details).

ITC MAURYA Hotel $$$

(Map p74; 26112233; www.starwoodhotels. com; Sardar Patel Marg; s/d ₹13,500/15,000; ❄ @ 🖥 🏊) This is where the Obamas stayed when they were in town in 2010. In the diplomatic enclave, it offers all creature comforts, and excellent service. Luxuriate in high thread counts and dine at a clutch of sterling restaurants, including **Bukhara**.

Oberoi Hotel $$$

(Map p74; 23890606; www.oberoihotels. com; Dr Zakir Hussain Marg; s/d ₹12,000/13,500 ❄ @ 🖥 🏊; M Khan Market) Superlative, contemporary rooms with views over Humayun's tomb, the pool or golf course.

Taj Mahal Hotel $$$

(Map p74; 23026162; www.tajhotels.com; Man Singh Rd; s/d ₹13,200/14,400; ❄ @ 🖥 🏊; M Khan Market) The Taj pulls out all the stops, with high-brow Indian artwork, Persian rugs, glossy silk furnishings and manicured lawns.

If You Like…
Museums

If you like the National Museum (p72), Delhi has many other fascinating museums that will pique your interest.

1 **INDIRA GANDHI SMRITI**
(23010094; 1 Safdarjang Rd; admission free; ⊙9.30am-4.45pm Tue-Sun; M Racecourse) The former residence of Indira Gandhi is now a fascinating museum, displaying artefacts, photos and personal belongings.

2 **GANDHI SMRITI**
(Map p74; 23012843; 5 Tees January Marg; admission free, camera/video free/prohibited; ⊙10am-1.30pm & 2-5pm Tue-Sun, closed every 2nd Sat of month; M Racecourse) This poignant museum occupies the house where Mahatma Gandhi was shot dead by a Hindu zealot on 30 January 1948.

3 **CRAFTS MUSEUM**
(Map p74; 23371641; Bhairon Marg; admission free; ⊙10am-5pm Tue-Sun; M Pragati Maidan) This tree-shaded treasure trove of a museum contains more than 20,000 exhibits from around India. Artisans on-site demonstrate their skills.

4 **NATIONAL GALLERY OF MODERN ART**
(Map p74; 23382835; ngmaindia.gov.in; Jaipur House; Indian/foreigner ₹10/150; ⊙10am-5pm Tue-Sun; M Khan Market) This fantastic gallery includes all the great modern Indian masters, such as FN Souza and MF Husain.

Sunder Nagar

Posh Sunder Nagar has some comfortable guesthouses, both on Map p74.

Devna Guesthouse $$$
(24355047; www.newdelhiboutiqueinns.com; 10 Sunder Nagar; d ₹5500; ❄) Fronted by a pretty garden, gloriously pretty Devna is one of Delhi's most charismatic choices, with four curio- and antique-furnished rooms. Those opening onto the terrace upstairs are the best.

Hawker on Chandni Chowk selling almond-flavoured biscuits

GREG ELMS/LONELY PLANET IMAGES ©

Shervani Guesthouse **$$$**
(☎42501000; www.shervanihotels.com;
11 Sunder Nagar; s/d incl breakfast ₹7000/7500;
❄ @) Sleek Shervani is Sunder Nagar's
smartest place to stay. The rooms have
parquet wooden floors, LCD TVs and
cocoa-brown furniture.

Airport Area

INN AT DELHI Homestay **$$**
(Map p74; ☎24113234; www.innatdelhi.com;
s/d ₹3500/4500; ❄ @ ☎) Between the
city and the airport, in a smart area close
to the diplomatic enclave, this is a good
choice for single women. Your hosts are
a professional couple, the rooms are spacious and comfortable and, upstairs, one
has an impressive wooden carved bed
from Rajasthan.

RADISSON HOTEL Hotel **$$$**
(☎26779191; www.radisson.com/newdelhiin;
National Hwy 8; s/d from ₹11,500/12,500;
❄ @ ☎ ☀) Radisson's rooms are
business-hotel comfortable. But oh,
what a joy to lie down on soft linen and
orthopaedic beds after a long-haul flight.
On-site are Chinese, kebab and Italian
restaurants.

 Eating

Delhiites love to eat, and visitors will
find plenty of delicious options, ranging
from ramshackle stalls serving delicious
kebabs to top-of-the-range temples of
excellence.

Most midrange and all upmarket
restaurants charge a service tax of
around 10%, while drinks taxes can
suck a further 20% (alcoholic) or 12.5%
(nonalcoholic) from your moneybelt.
Taxes haven't been included in this
chapter unless indicated.

Telephone numbers have been
provided for restaurants where
reservations are recommended.

North Delhi

OLD DELHI

The following eateries are featured on
Map p68 unless otherwise stated.

KARIM'S Mughlai **$**
(mains ₹27-110; ⏱7am-midnight) Old Delhi
(Ⓜ Chawri Bazaar); Nizamuddin West (Map p74;
168/2 Jha House Basti) Down a lane across

from the Jama Masjid's south gate (No 1), legendary Karim's has been delighting Delhiites with divine Mughlai cuisine since 1913. The chefs prepare brutally good (predominantly nonveg) fare: try the *burrah* (marinated mutton) kebab.

HALDIRAM'S Fast Food **$$**
(mains ₹50-140; ⏱9.30am-10.30pm) Old Delhi (Chandni Chowk; Ⓜ Chandni Chowk); Connaught Place (Map p78; 6 L-Block; Ⓜ Rajiv Chowk) A clean, bright cafeteria-sweet shop, this is a handy spot for a top-notch thali (₹156), snacking on *choley bhature* (₹68) and other morsels, some tasty South Indian cuisine, *namkin* (savouries) and *mithai* (sweets) on the dash. Try the *soan papadi* (flaky sweet with almond and pistachio).

CHOR BIZARRE Kashmiri **$$**
(☏23273821; Hotel Broadway, 4/15 Asaf Ali Rd; mains ₹240-500; ⏱7.30-10.30am, noon-3.30pm & 7.30-11.30pm; Ⓜ New Delhi) A dim-lit, atmospheric place, filled with eccentric clutter, Chor Bizarre (meaning 'thieves market') offers particularly delicious Kashmiri cuisine. It's popular with tourists and locals

PARATHA WALI GALI Street Food **$**
(parathas ₹15-35; Ⓜ Chandni Chowk) Head to this foodstall-lined (some with seating) lane off Chandni Chowk for delectable *parathas* (traditional flat bread) fresh off the *tawa* (hotplate). Stuffed varieties include *aloo* (potato), *mooli* (white radish), smashed pappadams and crushed *badam* (almond), all served with a splodge of tangy pickles.

JALEBIWALA Street Food **$**
(Dariba Corner, Chandni Chowk; jalebis per kg ₹250; Ⓜ Chandni Chowk) Calories schmalories! Century-old Jalebiwala does Delhi's – if not India's – finest *jalebis* (deep-fried, syrupy 'squiggles'), so pig out and worry about your waistline tomorrow.

New Delhi & Around

CONNAUGHT PLACE AREA

The following eateries appear on Map p78, unless otherwise indicated, and are

Detour:
Akshardham Temple

The Hindu Swaminarayan Group's controversially ostentatious **Akshardham Temple** (Map p52; www.akshardham.com; Noida turning, National Hwy 24; ⏱9am-6pm Tue-Sun Oct-Mar, 10am-7pm Tue-Sun Apr-Sep; Ⓜ Akshardham), on the outskirts of Delhi, has something of a Disney feel. Inaugurated in 2005, it's made of salmon-coloured sandstone with an interior carved from white marble in giddying detail. It contains around 20,000 carved deities.

Allow at least half a day to do it justice (weekdays are less crowded) as there's lots to see, including a boat ride through 10,000 years of Indian history, elaborate animatronics telling stories of the life of Swaminarayan, and musical fountains.

closest to Metro Rajiv Chowk, unless otherwise stated.

SARAVANA BHAVAN South Indian **$**
(mains ₹55-120; ⏱8am-10.30pm) Connaught Place (Map p78; 15 P-Block); Janpath (Map p78; 46 Janpath); Karol Bagh (8/54 Desh Bandhu Gupta Rd; Ⓜ Karol Bagh) Massively popular, Tamil Saravana has a fast-food feel, but food is by no means junk: dosas, *idlis* (fermented rice cakes) and other southern specialities, accompanied by delectable coconut chutneys. Inventive sweets include cucumber-seed *ladoos* (sweet balls). Finish with a South Indian coffee.

RAJDHANI Indian **$$**
(1/90 P-Block; thalis from ₹125-249; ⏱noon-3.30pm & 7-11pm) Opposite PVR Rivoli Cinema, this pristine, nicely decorated two-level place serves up excellent-value delicious vegetarian Gujarati and Rajasthani thalis to grateful local and foreign punters.

NIZAM'S KATHI KABAB   Fast Food   **$**
(5 H-Block; kebabs ₹110-150) This takeaway eatery has some seating and creates masterful kebabs and *kathi* rolls (kebab wrapped in *paratha*). It's always busy with kebab-loving hoards.

ANDHRA PRADESH BHAWAN CANTEEN   South Indian   **$**
(Map p74; 1 Ashoka Rd; veg thalis ₹80; ☺noon-3pm; ⓜPatel Chowk) A hallowed bargain: tasty unlimited South Indian thalis at cheap-as-chips prices; non-veg is also available. It's canteen-style, delicious and hugely popular.

CHINESE   Chinese   **$$$**
(☎65398888; 14/15 F-Block; mains ₹300-1200; ☺lunch & dinner) Popular with Chinese diplomats, here the Hunan chef serves up authentic cuisine, such as Hunan smoked lamb or *gong boa ji ding* (chicken with onion, chilli, peanut and hot garlic sauce) in a wow-factor calligraphy-decorated interior.

DIPLOMATIC ENCLAVE & CHANAKYAPURI AREA

BUKHARA   North Indian   **$$$**
(Map p74; ☎26112233; ITC Maurya, Sadar Patel Marg; mains ₹600-800; ☺lunch & dinner; ❄) Considered Delhi's best restaurant, this rustic place serves Northwest Frontier-style cuisine. Its tandoor and dhal are particularly renowned. Clinton and Obama have eaten here. Reservations are essential (taken between 7pm and 8pm).

MONSOON   Indian   **$$$**
(Map p74; ☎23710101; Le Meridien, Janpath; mains around ₹600-1000; ❄; ⓜPatel Chowk) With waterfall plate-glass windows, this is a wow-factor restaurant for sampling some creative Indian cuisine, with sensationally presented, taste-sensation dishes such as *millefeuille* of sole with mint chutney and sumptuous pistachio *kulfi* (ice cream) to finish off.

LODI COLONY & PANDARA MARKET

The eateries below feature on Map p74.

Left: Morning yoga practice at the Lodi Garden (p72);
Below: Bronze statue of Lord Shiva, National Museum (p72)

LODI GARDEN RESTAURANT
Mediterranean **$$$**

(Lodi Rd; mains ₹395-895; ⊙lunch & dinner;
M Jor Bagh) In an elegant garden shaded
by trees hung with lanterns, and with
a fountain made out of watering cans,
beside Lodi Garden. The menu and
clientele are remarkably non-Indian, but
it's good for Mediterranean and Lebanese
cuisine (think lamb chops with mint and
tamarind, and herb-crusted Manali trout).
Brunch (₹1399) is available at weekends.

PANDARA MARKET
Indian **$$$**

(M Khan Market) This market has a little
horseshoe of restaurants popular among
'late birds' – most are open daily from
noon to 1am or 2am. Highlights: **Pindi**
(mains ₹130-370), serving tasty Mughlai
Punjabi food since 1948, it's famous for
its butter chicken, but also try *kashmiri
kebab* and *shahi paneer* (cottage cheese
in rich cashew sauce); and **Gulati** (mains
₹140-480), which has a North Indian focus
amid beige-and-mirrored decor, serving

delicious *tangri kebab* (charcoal-grilled
chicken drumsticks) and *dum aloo*
(stuffed potatoes).

South Delhi

KHAN & SUNDER NAGAR MARKETS

If you're shopping at the **Khan** (M Khan
Market) or Sunder Nagar Markets, there are
some great places to top up your tank.

AMICI
Italian **$$$**

(Map p74; Khan Market; mains ₹300-400;
⊙lunch & dinner) This sleek, calm jewel of a
cafe serves up splendid pizzas and tasty
burgers. It has soothing biscuit-coloured
walls and a palpable sense of style. The
only thing missing is the booze licence.

KHAN CHACHA
Middle Eastern **$$**

(Map p74; Khan Market; snacks ₹110-160;
⊙noon-11pm) Chacha has gone chichi,
prices have doubled and it's lost something of its charm in the process. But all is

Vegetable shopping at an evening bazaar

CHRISTER FREDRIKSSON/LONELY PLANET IMAGES ©

not lost! It still turns out pretty lipsmacking roti-wrapped mutton/chicken/paneer. There's now plentiful seating, under nail-formed lamps that look like torture implements.

MAMAGOTO   Asian Fusion **$$$**
(Map p74; ☎45166060; 1st fl, Middle Lane, Khan Market; mains ₹325-500; ⏱12.30pm-12.30am) The name means 'to play with food' in Japanese, the decor is prettily kitsch and the food fun – a meal can span snow peas and green bean salad, lamb sticky rice, and date rolls with vanilla ice cream.

🍷 Drinking

Whether it's cappuccino and pastries for breakfast, or beer and kebabs for supper, Delhi's cool cafes and buzzing bars deliver.

Cafes

CAFÉ TURTLE   Cafe
Greater Kailash Part I (N-Block); Khan Market (Map p74; 2nd fl, Full Circle Bookstore; ⏱9.30am-9.30pm; Ⓜ Khan Market) This bookish, boho

cafe ticks all the boxes when you're in the mood for coffee and gateau (the 'gooey chocolate cake' is a triumph). Food ranges from Lucknow mint wraps to bucatini with arrabiata.

Café Oz   Cafe
(Map p74; Khan Market; ⏱9am-midnight; Ⓜ Khan Market) A busy Australian cafe, this has reasonable food and Delhi's best coffee, including flat whites.

Bars & Nightclubs

Most Delhi bars double up as both restaurants and nightclubs. The scene might not be huge, but as the sun goes down, the party starts, particularly from Wednesday to Saturday night. A smart-casual dress code (no shorts, vests or flip-flops) applies at most places.

The fancier bars are overflowing with domestic and foreign booze, but taxes can pack a nasty punch (alcoholic/nonalcoholic 20%/12.5%); taxes aren't included here unless stated. Most bars have two-for-one happy hours from around noon till 8pm or on certain days.

CONNAUGHT PLACE AREA

The following venues are located on Map p78, close to Metro Rajiv Chowk, and most have happy hours during the daytime.

1911 — Bar

(Imperial Hotel, Janpath) Named after the year in which Delhi was proclaimed British India's capital, this is the ultimate neocolonial treat. Sip cocktails overlooked by oil-painted Maharajas (drinks ₹650 plus).

AQUA — Bar

(Park Hotel, 15 Parliament St; ☺11am-1am) A chic poolside bar, this see-and-be-seen place is perfect after visiting Jantar Mantar or shopping in Connaught Place. There's seating overlooking the pool, or white-clad, curtained daybeds on which to lounge. A Kingfisher costs ₹225, and you can munch on mezze, kebabs or Lebanese snacks.

@LIVE — Live Music

(12 K-Block) Intimate and smart without being formal, @live has a cool gimmick: a live jukebox. The band plays from 8.30pm, and you choose songs from a menu including the Bee Gees, Bob Dylan and Sir Cliff. The band mightn't be the most dynamic you've seen, but they're great, and it's a fun night out (food's good too).

24/7 — Bar

(Lalit Hotel, Maharaja Rajit Singh Marg; ☺24hr) Every now and again, a 24-hour bar comes in extremely handy. This is at the Lalit hotel, so if you're hankering after a Martini at 5am you can drink it somewhere defiantly unseedy.

 **Entertainment**

To access Delhi's dynamic arts scene, check the local listings published in *Delhi Diary*, *First City* or *Time Out Delhi*. October and March is the 'season', with happenings (often free) nightly.

Old Delhi's Bazaars

Old Delhi's **bazaars** (Map p68; Ⓜ Chandni Chowk) are a head-spinning assault on the senses: an aromatic muddle of flowers, urine, incense, chai, fumes and frying food. They're busiest (and best avoided) on Monday and Friday and during other afternoons. Come at around 11.30am, when most shops have opened and the jostling is bearable.

For silver jewellery (some gold) head for **Dariba Kalan**, near the Sisganj Gurdwara. Nearby **Kinari Bazaar** (literally 'trimmings market') is famous for *zari* (gold-thread weaving) and *zardozi* (gold embroidery), and is the place to head for your bridal trousseau. The **cloth market** sells swathes of uncut material and linen, while electrical gadgets are the speciality of **Lajpat Rai Market**. **Chowri Bazaar** is the wholesale paper and greeting-card market. Nearby, **Nai Sarak** deals in wholesale stationery, books and saris.

Near the Fatehpuri Masjid, on Khari Baoli, is the nose-numbing **Spice Market**, ablaze with powdery piles of scarlet-red chilli powder and burnt-orange turmeric, as well as pickles, tea and nuts. As it's a wholesale market, spices here rarely come hermetically sealed.

The **Daryaganj Book Market**, north of Delhi Gate, is a bookworm's delight (Sunday afternoons).

ATTIC Cultural Program
(Map p78; ☎23746050; www.theatticdelhi.
org; 36 Regal Bldg; Ⓜ Rajiv Chowk) Small arts
space, with regular free classical concerts
and talks. There are also explorations of
forgotten foods and 'food meditation'
(where participants eat in silence and then
have a discussion) – these sessions cost
₹100 and should be booked in advance.

DANCES OF INDIA Dance
(Map p68; ☎26234689; Parsi Anjuman Hall,
Bahadur Shah Zafar Marg; ₹400; ⊙6.45pm) A
one-hour performance of regional dances
that includes Bharata Natyam (Tamil
dance), Kathakali, bhangra and Manipuri.

🛍 Shopping

From bamboozling bazaars to *bijoux*
boutiques, Delhi is a fantastic place to
shop. There's an astounding array of
wonderful stuff: handicrafts, textiles,
clothing, carpets, jewellery and a kaleidoscope of saris.

Away from the emporiums and other
fixed-price shops, put on your haggle hat.
Many taxi and autorickshaw drivers earn
commissions (via your inflated purchase
price) and may not take you to the most
reputable stores, either, making it best to
decline their shopping suggestions.

For dependable art gallery
recommendations (many of which sell
exhibits), check *First City* and *Time Out*.

Connaught Place
CENTRAL COTTAGE INDUSTRIES
EMPORIUM Handicrafts
(Map p78; ☎23326790; Janpath; Ⓜ Rajiv Chowk)
This government-run, fixed-price multilevel Aladdin's cave of India-wide handicrafts
is a great place to shop: woodcarvings, sil-
verware, jewellery, pottery, papier mâché,
brassware, textiles (including shawls),
beauty products and heaps more.

STATE EMPORIUMS Handicrafts
(Map p78; Baba Kharak Singh Marg; ⊙11am-7pm
Mon-Sat; Ⓜ Rajiv Chowk) These neighbouring
state government emporiums showcase

Left: Two men playing traditional Indian musical instruments;
Below: Henna artwork, called *mehndi*, on a woman's hand
(LEFT) MICHAEL COYNE/LONELY PLANET IMAGES ©; (BELOW) RICHARD I'ANSON/LONELY PLANET IMAGES ©

products from different states, from Rajasthan to Bihar. Set aside several hours for these fabulous shops.

THE SHOP Clothing & Homewares
(Map p78; 10 Regal Bldg, Sansad Marg; ⏰9.30am-7pm Mon-Sat; Ⓜ Rajiv Chowk) Lovely homewares and clothes (including children's clothes) from all over India in this chic boutique, with reasonable fixed prices.

✎ Khadi Gramodyog Bhawan
Handicrafts
(Map p78; Regal Bldg, Sansad Marg; ⏰10.30am-7.15pm Mon-Sat; Ⓜ Rajiv Chowk) Best known for its excellent *khadi* (homespun cloth) clothing, including good-value shawls, but also worth a visit for its handmade paper, incense, spices, henna and lovely natural soaps.

South Delhi

KHAN MARKET
Market
(Map p74; ⏰around 10.30am-8pm Mon-Sat; Ⓜ Khan Market) Favoured by expats and Delhi's elite, the boutiques in this enclave are devoted to fashion, books, homewares and gourmet groceries. For handmade paperware check out **Anand Stationers**. For a fantastic range of English-language fiction and nonfiction head to **Full Circle Bookstore** and **Bahri Sons**. There's a Tardis-like branch of **Fabindia** for clothes and home textiles, clothing store **Anokhi**, wow-factor homewares store **Good Earth** (featuring London-style prices) and the excellent **Silverline**, which does attractive, reasonable silver and gold jewellery.

ℹ Information

Dangers & Annoyances

SCAMS First-time visitors especially should be on their guard against Delhi's touts and tricksters, who are remarkably inventive in their schemes to part tourists from their cash. Touts buzz around tourist honeypots such as Connaught Place, Paharganj, Karol Bagh and the New Delhi train station. These oh-so-helpful fellows will try to cart you off to shops, travel agencies or 'official' tourist offices, where they earn commissions at your expense.

However, if you follow a policy of ignoring them or politely refusing any 'assistance', the scammers won't impinge on your trip. If you do get drawn into a 'tourist office' or 'information centre', first bear in mind that the *real* official India Tourism office *does not* offer packages – their staff will instead refer you to a list of recommended agencies, also available on their website (www.incredibleindia.org).

Think twice before parting with any money. Since 2010, it is now a criminal offence for travel agencies, information centres and individuals to misguide and cheat the public. If you do have problems, seek out the Tourist Police, who have marked jeeps stationed at tourist centres, including the international airport, New Delhi train station and Janpath. You can also call them on ☏100.

HOTEL TOUTS Taxi-wallahs at the international airport frequently act as touts. These sneaky drivers will try to persuade you that your hotel is full, poor value, overbooked, dangerous, burnt down or closed, or even that there are riots in Delhi. Their intention is to take you to a hotel where they'll get some commission. Some will even 'kindly' take you to a 'tourist office' where a colleague will phone your hotel on your behalf, and corroborate the driver's story. In reality, of course, he's talking to his mate in the next room. Alternatively, the driver may claim that he's lost and stop at a travel agency for directions. The agent supposedly dials your hotel and informs you that your room is double-booked, and 'helpfully' finds you another hotel where he'll get commission and you get a high room rate.

Tell persistent taxi drivers that you've paid for your hotel in advance, have recently confirmed the booking or have friends/relatives waiting for you there. If they continue, ask that they stop the car so that you can write down the registration plate number. Just to be sure, call or email to confirm your hotel booking, if possible, 24 hours before check-in.

TRAVEL AGENT TOUTS Be cautious with travel agencies, as many travellers every year report being overcharged and underwhelmed by unscrupulous agents. To avoid grief, ask for traveller recommendations, or ask for a list of recommended agents from the India Tourist office (88 Janpath). *Think twice before parting with your money.* Choose agents who are members of accredited associations such as the Travel Agents Association of India and the Indian Association of Tour Operators. Don't get talked into something

Children heading to school by cycle-rickshaw (p95)

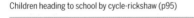

you had no intention of doing prior to the conversation. When booking with a travel agent, talk it over, and then go for a walk, take a little time to think about it and examine the numbers before you go ahead with the deal. Don't be smooth-talked into a hasty decision you might regret later. If you do decide the deal is the right one for you, insist on getting what you've been promised in *writing* – this will be invaluable if you need to lodge a complaint with the tourist office or police.

Be especially careful if booking a multistop trip out of Delhi. Lonely Planet often gets letters from travellers who've paid upfront and then found out there are extra expenses, they've been overcharged or the accommodation is terrible. Some travellers have arranged 'Northern mountains' or 'lake' trips, then later find out that they're headed for Kashmir. Given the number of letters we've received from unhappy travellers, it's also best not to book Kashmir tours or houseboats from Delhi; see the boxed text on p377 for more.

TRAIN STATION TOUTS These touts are at their worst at New Delhi train station. Here they may try to prevent you reaching the upstairs International Tourist Bureau and divert you to a local (overpriced and often unreliable) travel agency. Make the assumption that the office is *never* closed (outside the official opening hours; see p93) and has not shifted. It's still in its regular place on the 1st floor, close to the Paharganj side of the station.

Other swindlers may insist that your ticket needs to be stamped or checked (for a hefty fee) before it is considered valid. Some may try to convince wait-listed passengers that there is a charge to check their reservation status – don't fall for it. Try not to get embroiled in discussion: just politely and firmly make your way to the office. If you're encountering real problems, threaten to fetch or call the tourist police (☎100). Once you are out of the station, avoid an overpriced conveyance by heading for the car park's prepaid autorickshaw booth, but bear in mind that you're in walking distance of Paharganj.

Medical Services

Pharmacies are ubiquitous in most markets.

All India Institute of Medical Sciences (Aiims; ☎26588500; www.aiims.edu; Ansari Nagar; MAIMS)

East West Medical Centre (☎24690429; www.eastwestrescue.com; B-28 Greater Kailash Part I) Opposite N-Block Market; this is one of the

easier options if you have to make an insurance claim.

Money

There are ATMs almost everywhere you look in Delhi. Many travel agents and money changers, including Thomas Cook, can do international money transfers.

Baluja Forex (☎41541523; 4596 Main Bazaar, Paharganj; ☉9am-7.30pm) Does cash advances on MasterCard and Visa.

Central Bank of India (Map p74; ☎26110101; Ashok Hotel, Chanakyapuri; ☉24hr)

Thomas Cook International airport (☎25653439; ☉24hr); Janpath (Map p74; ☎23342171; Hotel Janpath, Janpath; ☉9.30am-7pm Mon-Sat)

Tourist Information

Beware Delhi's many dodgy travel agencies and 'tourist information centres'. Do *not* be fooled – the only official tourist information centre is India Tourism Delhi. Touts may (falsely) claim to be associated with this office.

For Indian regional tourist offices' contact details ask at India Tourism Delhi, or dial directory enquiries on ☎197.

India Tourism Delhi (Government of India; Map p78; ☎23320008/5; www.incredibleindia.org; 88 Janpath; ☉9am-6pm Mon-Fri, to 2pm Sat) gives tourist-related advice as well as a free Delhi map and brochures. Has a list of recommended agencies and bed & breakfasts. Their special branch investigates tourism-related complaints.

❶ Getting There & Away

Delhi is a major international gateway. It's also a centre for domestic travel, with extensive bus, rail and air connections. Delhi's airport can be prone to thick fog in December and January (often disrupting airline schedules), making it wise not to book back-to-back flights during this period.

Air

International and domestic flights all leave from and arrive at the airport's gleaming new Terminal 3. For flight enquiries, call the international airport (☎0124-3376000; www.newdelhiairport.in). At the new Terminal 3 there are 14 'nap & go' rooms with wi-fi, a desk, TV and bed (₹315/hr).

Major Trains from Delhi

DESTINATION	TRAIN NO & NAME	FARE (₹)	DURATION (HR)	FREQUENCY	DEPARTURES & TRAIN STATION
Agra	12280 *Taj Exp*	75/263 (A)	3	1 daily	7.10am HN
	12002A *Bhopal Shatabdi*	370/700 (B)	2	1 daily	6.15am ND
Amritsar	12013 *Shatabdi Exp*	645/1200 (B)	5½	1 daily	4.30pm ND
	12029/12031 *Swarna/ Amritsar Shatabdi*	600/1145 (B)	5½	1 daily	7.20am ND
Chennai	12434 *Chennai Rajdhani*	2075/2700/ 4500 (C)	28	2 weekly	4pm HN
	12622 *Tamil Nadu Exp*	528/1429/ 1960/3322 (D)	33	1 daily	10.30pm ND
Goa (Madgaon)	12432 *Trivndrm Rajdhani*	2035/2615/ 4370 (C)	25½	2 weekly	11am HN
Jaipur	12958 *ADI SJ Rajdani*	605/775/ 1285 (C)	5	6 weekly	7.55pm ND
	12916 Ashram Exp	175/434/ 581/969 (D)	5¾	1 daily	3pm OD
	12015 *Shatabdi Exp*	465/885 (B)	4¾	6 weekly	6.05am ND
Khajuraho	12448 *Nizamuddin-Khajuraho Exp*	269/802 (E)	10¼	3 weekly	8.15pm HN
Mumbai	12952 *Mumbai Rajdhani*	1495/1975/ 3305 (C)	16	1 daily	4.30pm ND
	12954 *Ag Kranti Rajdani Exp*	1495/1975/ 3305 (C)	17¼	1 daily	4.55pm HN
Udaipur	12963 *Mewar Exp*	320/801/1087/ 1821 (D)	12	1 daily	7.05pm HN
Varanasi	12560 *Shivganga Exp*	320/806/ 1095/1805 (D)	13	1 daily	6.45pm ND

Train stations: HN – Hazrat Nizamuddin; ND – New Delhi; OD – Old Delhi
Fares: A – 2nd class/chair car; B – chair car/1st-class AC; C – 3AC/2AC/1st-class AC;
D – sleeper/3AC/2AC/1st-class AC; E – sleeper/3AC

Muslim cleric reads at a mosque

DAMIEN SIMONIS/LONELY PLANET IMAGES ©

For comprehensive details of domestic air routes, see Excel's *Timetable of Air Services Within India* (₹55), available at newsstands. When making reservations request the most direct (quickest) route. Note that airline prices fluctuate and website bookings with some carriers can be markedly cheaper.

DOMESTIC ARRIVALS & DEPARTURES Check-in at the airport for domestic flights is one hour before departure.

DOMESTIC AIRLINES The Air India office (3 Safdarjung Airport; ⏰9.30am-5.30pm) is in South Delhi. To confirm flights dial 📞1407.

Other domestic airlines:

Jagson Airlines (Map p78; 📞23721593; Vandana Bldg, 11 Tolstoy Marg)

Kingfisher Airlines (Map p78; 📞23730238; 42 N-Block, Connaught Place)

INTERNATIONAL ARRIVALS The arrivals hall has 24-hour money-exchange facilities, ATM, prepaid taxi and car-hire counters, a tourist information counter, cafes and bookshops.

INTERNATIONAL DEPARTURES At the check-in counter, ensure you collect tags to attach to hand luggage (mandatory to clear security later).

Bus

Bikaner House (Map p74; 📞23383469; Pandara Rd), near India Gate, operates good state-run buses. These are the best buses for Jaipur (super deluxe/Volvo ₹325/625, six hours, hourly); Udaipur (₹750, 15 hours, one daily); Ajmer (₹400, nine hours, three daily); and Jodhpur (₹500, 11 hours, one daily).

Delhi's main bus station is the **Inter State Bus Terminal** (ISBT; Map p68; 📞23860290; Kashmiri Gate; ⏰24hr), north of the (Old) Delhi train station. It has a 24-hour left-luggage facility (₹14 per bag). This station is chaotic so arrive at least 30 minutes ahead of your departure time.

Train

For foreigners, it's easiest to make ticket bookings at the helpful **International Tourist Bureau** (Map p68; 📞23405156; 1st fl, New Delhi train station; ⏰8am-8pm Mon-Sat, to 2pm Sun). Do *not* believe anyone who tells you it has shifted, closed or burnt down: this is a scam to divert you elsewhere (see p89). There are reportedly railway porters involved in such scams, so stay on your toes and don't let anyone stop you from going to the 1st floor of the *main* building for bookings. When making reservations here, if you are paying in rupees you may have to provide back-up money-exchange certificates (or ATM receipts), so take these with you just in case. You can also pay in travellers cheques: in Thomas Cook US dollars, euros or pounds sterling, Amex US dollars and euros, and US dollars in Barclays cheques. Any change is given in rupees. Bring your passport. When you arrive, complete a reservation form, then wait to check availability at the Tourism Counter in the office. You can then queue to pay for the ticket at one of the other counters.

There are two main stations in Delhi – (Old) Delhi train station (Map p68) in Old Delhi, and New Delhi train station (Map p68) at Paharganj; make sure you know which station serves your destination (New Delhi train station is closer to Connaught Place). If you're departing from the Delhi train station, allow adequate time to meander through Old Delhi's snail-paced traffic.

There's also the Hazrat Nizamuddin train station (Map p74), south of Sunder Nagar, where various trains (usually for southbound destinations) start or finish.

Railway porters should charge around ₹30 per bag.

There are many more destinations and trains than those listed in the boxed text, p92 – check the Indian Railways Website (www.indianrail.gov.

in), consult *Trains at a Glance* (₹45), available at most newsstands, or ask tourist office staff.

❶ Getting Around

The metro system has transformed getting around the city, making it incredibly easy to whizz out to places that were once a long traffic-hampered struggle to reach. Most of Delhi's main sights lie close to a metro station. Local buses get horrendously crowded so the metro, autorickshaws and taxis are desirable alternatives Keep small change handy for fares.

To/From the Airport

Airport-to-city transport is not as straightforward as it should be, due to predatory taxi drivers – see p89. Many international flights arrive at ghastly hours, so it pays to book a hotel in advance and notify it of your arrival time.

PRE-ARRANGED PICK-UPS If you arrange an airport pick-up through a travel agency or hotel, it's more expensive than a prepaid taxi from the airport due to the airport parking fee (up to ₹140) and ₹80 charge for the person collecting you to enter the airport arrivals hall. Sometimes drivers are barred from arrivals for security reasons, in which case most will wait outside Gates 4–6.

A cycle-rickshaw driver

ORIEN HARVEY/LONELY PLANET IMAGES

METRO The new high-speed metro line is the best way to get to/from the airport, and runs between New Delhi train station and Dwarka Sector 21, via Shivaji Stadium, Dhaula Kuan NH8 (Mahipalpur station) and Indira Gandhi International station (Terminal 3). Trains operate every 10 minutes from 5am to 1am.

TAXI There is a Delhi Traffic Police Prepaid Taxi counter (☏ helpline 23010101; www. delhitrafficpolice.nic.in) inside the arrivals building. It costs about ₹310 to Connaught Place, plus a 25% surcharge between 11pm and 5am.

You'll be given a voucher with the destination on it – insist that the driver honours it. Never surrender your voucher until you get to your destination; without that docket the driver won't get paid.

You can also book a prepaid taxi at the Megacabs counter inside the arrivals building at both the international and domestic airports. It costs around ₹600 to the centre, but you get a cleaner, AC car, and you can pay by credit card.

Car

HIRING A CAR & DRIVER Numerous operators offer chauffeur-driven cars. The following companies get positive reports from travellers. Each has an eight-hour, 80km limit per day. All offer tours beyond Delhi (including Rajasthan) but higher charges apply for these. The rates below are only for travel within Delhi. Beware of frauds/touts claiming association with these companies or insisting their offices have closed.

Kumar Tourist Taxi Service (Map p78; ☏ 23415930; kumartaxi@rediffmail.com; 14/1 K-Block, Connaught Place; non-AC/AC per day ₹800/900; ◷ 9am-9pm) Near the York Hotel. Tiny office run by two brothers, Bittoo and Titoo. Their rates are among Delhi's lowest.

Metropole Tourist Service (Map p74; ☏ 24310313; www.metrovista.co.in; 224 Defence Colony Flyover Market; non-AC car per day from ₹850; ◷ 7am-7pm) Under the Defence Flyover Bridge (on the Jangpura side), this is another reliable choice – likewise beware touts pretending to be linked to this office.

Cycle-Rickshaw & Bicycle

Cycle-rickshaws are still in use in parts of Old Delhi, though they have been banned in Chandni Chowk to reduce congestion. Let's hope they're not banned in other areas, as they're the best way to get around Old Delhi – the drivers are wizards at weaving through the crowds. Tips are appreciated for this gruelling work.

Cycle-rickshaws are also banned from the Connaught Place area and New Delhi, but they're handy for commuting between Connaught Place and Paharganj (about ₹30).

The largest range of new and secondhand bicycles for sale can be found at Jhandewalan Cycle Market (Map p68).

Metro

Delhi's marvellous metro (open 6am to around 11pm) has efficient services with arrival/departure announcements in Hindi and English. Two carriages on each train are designated women-only – look for the pink signs on the platform. The trains can get very busy, particularly at peak commuting times (around 9am to 10am and 5pm to 6pm).

Tokens (₹8 to ₹30) are sold at metro stations; there are also one-/three-day (₹70/200) 'tourist cards' for unlimited short-distance travel; or a Smart Card (₹50, refundable when you return it), which can be recharged for amounts from ₹50 to ₹800 – fares are 10% cheaper than paying by token.

For the latest developments (plus route maps) see www.delhimetrorail.com or call ☏ 23417910.

Autorickshaw Rates

To gauge fares vis-à-vis distances, the following list shows one-way (official) rates departing from Janpath's prepaid autorickshaw booth. Taxis charge around double.

DESTINATION	COST (₹)
Bahai House of Worship	100
Humayun's tomb	50
Karol Bagh	50
Old Delhi train station	50
Paharganj	30
Purana Qila	30
Red Fort	50
Defence Colony	65

Radiocab

If you have a local mobile number, you can call a radiocab. These AC cars are clean, efficient and use reliable meters. They charge ₹20 per km. After calling the operator, you'll receive a text with your driver's registration number, then another to confirm arrival time (book 20 to 30 minutes in advance). You can also book online.

Easycabs (🕿43434343; www.easycabs.com)

Megacabs (🕿41414141; www.megacabs.com)

Quickcabs (🕿45333333; www.quickcabs.in)

Taxi & Autorickshaw

All taxis and autorickshaws have meters but they are often 'not working' or drivers refuse to use them (so they can overcharge). If the meter isn't an option, agree on a fare before setting off. If the driver won't agree, look for one who will. From 11pm to 5am there's a 25% surcharge for autorickshaws and taxis.

Otherwise, to avoid shenanigans, catch an autorickshaw from a prepaid booth:

Janpath (Map p78; 88 Janpath; ⊘11am-8.30pm) Outside the India Tourism Delhi office.

New Delhi train station car park (⊘24hr)

Palika Bazaar's Gate No 2 (Map p78; Connaug Place; ⊘11am-7pm)

GREATER DELHI

 Sights

QUTB MINAR   Historic Site
(Map p52; 🕿26643856; Indian/foreigner ₹10/250, video ₹25; ⊘sunrise-sunset; Ⓜ Qutb Minar) The beautiful religious buildings of the Qutb Minar complex form one Delhi's most spectacular sights. They date from the onset of Islamic rule in India, and tell o tumultuous rises and falls in stone. Today on Delhi's outskirts, once these constructions formed the heart of the Muslim city.

The Qutb Minar itself is a mighty, awesome tower of victory, which closely resembles similar Afghan towers, and wa also used as a minaret. Muslim sultan Qutb-ud-din began its construction in 1193, immediately after the defeat of the

GREATER DELHI SIGHTS

last Hindu kingdom in Delhi. It's nearly 73m high and tapers from a 15m-diameter base to a mere 2.5m at the top.

The tower has five distinct storeys, each marked by a projecting balcony. The first three storeys are made of red sandstone, the 4th and 5th storeys are of marble and sandstone. Qutb-ud-din built only to the 1st storey. His successors completed it and then, in 1326 it was struck by lightning. In 1368, Firoz Shah rebuilt the top storeys and added a cupola. An earthquake brought the cupola crashing down in 1803 – it was replaced with another in 1829, later removed.

There's a **Decorative Light Show** (Indian/foreigner ₹20/250; ⏲6.30-8pm) nightly. The Qutb Festival takes place here every October/November.

Be warned that Qutb Minar gets crowded on weekends.

QUWWAT-UL-ISLAM MASJID
At the foot of the Qutb Minar stands the first mosque to be built in India, known as the Might of Islam Mosque. Also constructed in 1193, with various additions over the centuries, this building symbolises in stone the ascendance of one religious power over another. The original mosque was built on the foundations of a Hindu temple, and an inscription over the east gate states that it was built with materials obtained from demolishing '27 idolatrous temples' – it's possible to see many Hindu and Jain elements in the decoration.

Altamish, Qutb-ud-din's son-in-law, surrounded the original mosque with a cloistered court between 1210 and 1220.

IRON PILLAR
This 7m-high pillar stands in the courtyard of the mosque and it was here long before the mosque's construction. A six-line Sanskrit inscription indicates that it was initially erected outside a Vishnu temple, possibly in Bihar, and was raised in memory of Chandragupta II, who ruled from AD 375 to 413.

What the inscription does not tell is how it was made, for the iron in the pillar is of exceptional purity. Scientists have never discovered how the iron, which has not rusted after some 2000 years, could be cast using the technology of the time.

ALAI MINAR

When Ala-ud-din made his additions to the mosque he also conceived a far more ambitious construction program. He aimed to build a second tower of victory, exactly like the Qutb Minar, but twice as high! By the time of his death the tower had reached 27m and no one was willing to continue his overambitious project. The incomplete tower, a solid stack of rubble, stands to the north of the Qutb Minar and the mosque.

OTHER FEATURES

Ala-ud-din's exquisite **Alai Darwaza** gateway is the main entrance to the whole complex. It was built of red sandstone in 1310 and is just southwest of the Qutb Minar. The **tomb of Imam Zamin** is beside the gateway, while the **tomb of Altamish**, who died in 1235, is by the northwestern corner of the mosque. The largely ruined **madrasa of Ala-ud-din** stands at the rear of the complex.

The tomb of Altamish

FREE **MEHRAULI ARCHAELOGICAL PARK**   Historic Park
(Map p52; ⏲dawn-dusk; Ⓜ Qutb Minar)
There's an entrance a few hundred metres to the left of that to Qutb Minar as you face it – walk down a narrow road which leads into the park. It's a rambling forest, once a hunting ground for the Mughals, then a favoured spot of colonial officers. It's dotted by extraordinary monuments, and has an undiscovered feel. The major monuments include **Jamali Kamali** (⏲sunrise-sunset), a mosque, alongside which lies a small building containing two tombs: that of Jamali, a sufi saint, and Kamali, his unknown male friend, obviously important enough to be buried alongside him. Ask the caretaker to unlock the building to see the well-preserved painting within. A short walk from here is the dizzying **Rajon ki Baoli**, a majestic 16th-century step well with an Eicheresque sweeping flight of steps.

ⓘ Getting There & Away

The metro extends to Qutb Minar, but the entrance is a couple of kilometres away along busy, broad roads from the station, so catch a rickshaw (₹30).

UTTAR PRADESH

Agra

◉ Sights

TAJ MAHAL   Historic Building
(Indian/foreigner ₹20/750, video ₹25; ☼dawn-dusk Sat-Thu) Rabindranath Tagore described it as 'a teardrop on the cheek of eternity', Rudyard Kipling as 'the embodiment of all things pure', while its creator, Emperor Shah Jahan, said it made 'the sun and the moon shed tears from their eyes'. Every year, tourists numbering more than twice the population of Agra pass through its gates to catch a once-in-a-lifetime glimpse of what is widely considered the most beautiful building in the world. Few leave disappointed.

The Taj was built by Shah Jahan as a memorial for his third wife, Mumtaz Mahal, who died giving birth to their 14th child in 1631. The death of Mumtaz left the emperor so heartbroken that his hair is said to have turned grey virtually overnight. Construction of the Taj began in the same year and, although the main building is thought to have been built in eight years, the whole complex was not completed until 1653. Not long after it was finished Shah Jahan was overthrown by his son Aurangzeb and imprisoned in Agra Fort where, for the rest of his days, he could only gaze out at his creation through a window. Following his death in 1666, Shah Jahan was buried here alongside Mumtaz.

In total, some 20,000 people from India and Central Asia worked on the building. Specialists were brought in from as far away as Europe to produce the exquisite marble screens and pietra dura (marble inlay work) made with thousands of semiprecious stones.

The Taj was designated a World Heritage Site in 1983 and looks as immaculate today as when it was first constructed – though it underwent a huge restoration project in the early 20th century. In 2002, having been gradually discoloured by city pollution, it was spruced up with an ancient face-pack recipe known as *multani mitti* – a blend of soil, cereal, milk and lime once used by Indian women to beautify their skin. Now only nonpolluting vehicles are allowed within a couple of hundred metres of the building.

Best Times to See the Taj

The Taj is arguably at its most atmospheric at **sunrise**. This is certainly the most comfortable time to visit, with far fewer crowds. **Sunset** is another magical viewing time. You can also view the Taj for five nights around **full moon**. Entry numbers are limited, though, and tickets must be bought a day in advance from the **Archaeological Survey of India office** (☎2227263; www.asi.nic.in; 22 The Mall; Indian/foreigner ₹510/750). See its website for details. Note: this office is known as the Taj Mahal Office by some rickshaw drivers.

One final word of advice: whatever you do, don't plan your trip around seeing the Taj on a Friday, as the whole complex is closed to anyone not attending Friday prayers at the mosque inside the Taj grounds.

INSIDE THE GROUNDS
The Taj Mahal itself stands on a raised marble platform at the northern end of the ornamental gardens, with its back to the Yamuna River. Its raised position means that the backdrop is only sky – a masterstroke of design. Purely decorative 40m-high white **minarets** grace each corner of the platform. After more than three centuries they are not quite perpendicular, but they may have been designed to lean slightly outwards so that in the event of an earthquake they would fall away from the precious Taj. The red sandstone **mosque** to the west is an important

Taj Mahal

Timeline

1631 Emperor Shah Jahan's beloved third wife, Mumtaz Mahal, dies in Buhanpur while giving birth to their 14th child. Her body is initially interred in Buhanpur itself, where Shah Jahan is fighting a military campaign, but is later moved, in a golden casket, to a small building on the banks of the Yamuna River in Agra.

1632 Construction of a permanent mausoleum for Mumtaz Mahal begins.

1633 Mumtaz Mahal is interred in her final resting place, an underground tomb beneath a marble plinth, on top of which the Taj Mahal will be built.

1640 The white-marble mausoleum is completed.

1653 The rest of the Taj Mahal complex is completed.

1658 Emperor Shah Jahan is overthrown by his son Aurangzeb and imprisoned in Agra Fort.

1666 Shah Jahan dies. His body is transported along the Yamuna River and buried underneath the Taj, alongside the tomb of his wife.

1908 Repeatedly damaged and looted after the fall of the Mughal empire, the Taj receives some long-overdue attention as part of a major restoration project ordered by British viceroy Lord Curzon.

1983 The Taj is awarded Unesco World Heritage Site status.

2002 Having been discoloured by pollution in more recent years, the Taj is spruced up with an ancient recipe known as *multani mitti* – a blend of soil, cereal, milk and lime once used by Indian women to beautify their skin.

Today More than three million tourists visit the Taj Mahal each year. That's more than twice the current population of Agra.

Go Barefoot
Help the environment by entering the mausoleum barefoot instead of using the free disposable shoe covers.

Pishtaqs
These huge arched recesses are set into each side of the Taj. They provide depth to the building while their central, latticed marble screens allow patterned light to illuminate the inside of the mausoleum.

Minaret

Entrance

Plinth

Marble Relief Work
Flowering plants, thought to be representations of paradise, are a common theme among the beautifully decorative panels carved onto the white marble.

Be Enlightened
Bring a small torch into the mausoleum to fully appreciate the translucency of the white marble and semiprecious stones.

DANIEL MCCROHAN

Filigree Screen
This stunning screen was carved out of a single piece of marble. It surrounds both cenotaphs, allowing patterned light to fall onto them through its intricately carved *jali* (latticework).

Central Dome
The Taj's famous central dome, topped by a brass finial, represents the vault of heaven, a stark contrast to the material world, which is represented by the square shape of the main structure.

Yamuna River

NORTH →

Pietra Dura
It's believed that 35 different precious and semi-precious stones were used to create the exquisite pietra dura (marble inlay work) found on the inside and outside of the mausoleum walls. Again, floral designs are common.

Calligraphy
The strips of calligraphy surrounding each of the four pishtaqs get larger as they get higher, giving the impression of uniform size when viewed from the ground. There's also calligraphy inside the mausoleum, including on Mumtaz Mahal's cenotaph.

Cenotaphs
The cenotaphs of Mumtaz Mahal and Shah Jahan, decorated with pietra dura inlay work, are actually fake tombs. The real ones are located in an underground vault closed to the public.

JOHN BORTHWICK/LONELY PLANET IMAGE

Don't Miss Taj Museum

Within the Taj complex, on the western side of the gardens, is the small but excellent Taj Museum, housing a number of original Mughal miniature paintings, including a pair of 17th-century ivory portraits of Emperor Shah Jahan and his beloved wife Mumtaz Mahal. Also found here are some very well-preserved gold and silver coins dating from the same period, plus architectural drawings of the Taj and some nifty celadon plates, said to split into pieces or change colour if the food served on them contains poison.

THINGS YOU NEED TO KNOW
admission ₹5; ⊙10am-5pm Sat-Thu

gathering place for Agra's Muslims. The identical building to the east, the **jawab**, was built for symmetry.

The central Taj structure is made of semitranslucent white marble, carved with flowers and inlaid with thousands of semiprecious stones in beautiful patterns. A perfect exercise in symmetry, the four identical faces of the Taj feature impressive vaulted arches embellished with pietra dura scrollwork and quotations from the Quran in a style of calligraphy using inlaid jasper. The whole structure is topped off by four small domes surrounding the famous bulbous central dome.

Directly below the main dome is the **Cenotaph of Mumtaz Mahal**, an elaborate false tomb surrounded by an exquisite perforated marble screen inlaid with dozens of different types of semiprecious stones. Beside it, offsetting the symmetry of the Taj, is the **Cenotaph of Shah Jahan**, who was interred here with little ceremony by his usurping son Aurangzeb in 1666. Light is admitted into the central chamber by finely cut marble screens. The real tombs of Mumtaz Mahal and Shah Jahan are in a locked basement room below the main chamber and cannot be viewed.

AGRA FORT
Fort

ndian/foreigner ₹20/300, video ₹25; ⏱dawn-
usk) With the Taj Mahal overshadowing it,
one can easily forget that Agra has one of
the finest Mughal forts in India. By visiting
the fort and Taj on the same day you get
₹50 reduction in ticket price. Construction of the massive red-sandstone fort,
on the bank of the Yamuna River, was
begun by Emperor Akbar in 1565. Further
additions were made, particularly by his
grandson Shah Jahan, using his favourite
building material – white marble. The fort
was built primarily as a military structure,
but Shah Jahan transformed it into a palace, and later it became his gilded prison
for eight years after his son Aurangzeb
seized power in 1658.

The ear-shaped fort's colossal double
walls rise over 20m in height and measure
2.5km in circumference. The Yamuna River
originally flowed along the straight eastern
edge of the fort, and the emperors had
their own bathing ghats here. It contains a
maze of buildings, forming a city within a
city, including vast underground sections,
though many of the structures were
destroyed over the years by Nadir Shah,
the Marathas, the Jats and finally the
British, who used the fort as a garrison.
Even today, much of the fort is used by the
military and so is off-limits to the general
public.

The **Amar Singh Gate** to the south
is the sole entry point to the fort these
days and where you buy your entrance
ticket. Its dogleg design was meant to
confuse attackers who made it past
the first line of defence – the crocodile-
infested moat.

You can walk here from Taj Ganj, or it's
₹20 to ₹30 in a cycle-rickshaw.

 Eating

Dalmoth is Agra's famous version of
namkin (spicy nibbles). Peitha is a
square sweet made from pumpkin and
glucose that is flavoured with rosewater,
coconut or saffron. You can buy it all over
Agra. From October to March look out

for gajak, a slightly spicy sesame-seed
biscuit strip.

Taj Ganj Area

This lively area directly south of the Taj
has plenty of budget rooftop restaurants,
where menus appear to be carbon copies
of one another. None are licensed but
most will find you a beer if you ask nicely
and drink discreetly.

SANIYA PALACE
HOTEL Multicuisine $$
(mains ₹70-200; ⏱6am-11pm) With cute
tablecloths, dozens of potted plants and
a bamboo pergola for shade, this is the
most pleasant rooftop restaurant in Taj
Ganj. It also has the best rooftop view of
the Taj bar none. Again, it's the usual mix
of Western dishes and Western-friendly
Indian dishes on offer, including set
breakfasts, pizza and pancakes.

ESPHAHAN North Indian $$$
(☎2231515; Oberoi Amar Vilas hotel, Taj East
Gate Rd; mains ₹1000-1400; ⏱dinner) Agra's
best hotel has now opened the doors of
its top-notch Indian restaurant to nonguests. There are only two sittings each
evening, at 7pm and 9.30pm, so booking
a table is essential. The menu is small but
exquisite, specialising in Mughlai cuisine
with unusual offerings such as quail curry.
We couldn't afford the ₹2500-thali, but
it's bound to be extraordinarily good.

Sadar Bazaar

This area offers better quality restaurants and makes a nice change from the
please-all, multicuisine offerings in Taj
Ganj.

LAKSHMI VILAS South Indian $
(Taj Rd; meals ₹40-90; ❄) This no-nonsense,
plainly decorated, nonsmoking restaurant
is the place in Agra to come for afford-
able South Indian fare. Treats include idli
(spongy, round, fermented rice cake),
vada (doughnut-shaped, deep-fried lentil
savoury), uttapam (thick, savoury rice
pancake) and more than 20 varieties of
dosa (large savoury crepe), including a
family special that is 1.2m long! The thali

meal (₹88), served noon to 3.30pm and 7pm to 10.30pm, is very good indeed.

DASAPRAKASH   South Indian **$$**
(☎2363535; 1 Gwalior Rd; meals ₹90-150; ⏱11am-10.45pm; ❄) Highly recommended by locals for consistently good South Indian vegetarian food, Dasaprakash whips up spectacular unlimited thalis (₹100 to ₹225), dosa and a few token continental dishes. The ice-cream desserts (₹90 to ₹125), which take up a whole page of the two-page menu, are another speciality. Comfortable booth seating and wood-lattice screens make for intimate dining.

❶ Getting There & Away

Air

Kingfisher Airlines (☎2400693; www.flykingfisher.com; airport; ⏱10am-5pm) has one daily flight to Delhi (from ₹2000, one hour, 3pm). Agra's Kheria airport is in Indian Air Force territory so you won't get in without your name being on the list of those who have booked flights for that

day. You'll have to purchase your ticket online or over the phone.

Train

Train is easily the quickest way to travel to/from Delhi, Varanasi, Jaipur and Khajuraho (see table, p106). Most trains leave from Agra Cantonment (Cantt) train station (☎2421204), although some go from Agra Fort station.

Express trains are well set up for day trippers to/from Delhi (see table, p106) but trains run to Delhi all day. If you can't reserve a seat, just buy a 'general ticket' for the next train (about ₹60), find a seat in sleeper class then upgrade when the ticket collector comes along. Most of the time, he won't even make you pay any more.

❶ Getting Around

Autorickshaw

Agra's green-and-yellow autorickshaws run on CNG (compressed natural gas) rather than petrol and so are less environmentally destructive. Just outside Agra Cantonment train station is the prepaid autorickshaw booth (⏱24hr),

Left: Vegetable sellers on the bank of the Yamuna River near the Taj Mahal;
Below: Architectural detail, Agra Fort (p103)

(LEFT) MICHAEL GEBICKI/LONELY PLANET IMAGES ©; (BELOW) DAMIEN SIMONIS/LONELY PLANET IMAGES ©

which gives you a good guide
or haggling elsewhere. Note, autos
aren't allowed to go to Fatehpur Sikri. Sample
prices: Taj Mahal ₹50; half-day (four-hour) tour
₹200; full-day (10-hour) tour ₹400.

Taxi

Outside Agra Cantonment train station the
prepaid taxi booth (⊘24hr) gives a good idea
of what taxis should cost. Prices include: Delhi
₹2500; Fatehabad Rd ₹150; Sadar Bazaar ₹70; Taj
Mahal ₹150; half-day (four-hour) tour ₹450; full-
day (eight-hour) tour ₹650.

Fatehpur Sikri

JAMA MASJID   Mosque
This beautiful, immense mosque, completed in 1571, contains elements of Persian
and Indian design. The main entrance, at
the top of a flight of stone steps, is through
the spectacular 54m-high **Buland Darwaza**
(Victory Gate), built to commemorate
Akbar's military victory in Gujarat.

Inside the courtyard of the mosque is
the stunning white-marble **tomb of Shaikh
Salim Chishti**. Completed in 1581, it's
entered through a door made of ebony.
Inside are colourful flower murals; the
canopy is decorated with mother-of-pearl
shell. Just to the east is the red sandstone
tomb of Islam Khan, the final resting place
of Shaikh Salim Chishti's grandson and
one-time governor of Bengal.

On the east wall of the courtyard is a
smaller entrance to the mosque – the
Shahi Darwaza (King's Gate), which leads
to the palace complex.

PALACES & PAVILIONS   Palaces
(Indian/foreigner ₹20/260, video ₹25; ⊘dawn-
dusk) The first palace building entered from
the south is the largest, the **Palace of Jodh
Bai**, once the home of Akbar's Hindu wife,
said to be his favourite. Set around an enormous courtyard, it blends traditional Indian
columns, Islamic cupolas and turquoise-
blue Persian roof tiles.

Just outside, to the left of Jodh Bai's
former kitchen, is the **Palace of the**

Agra Train Services

DELHI–AGRA TRAINS FOR DAY TRIPPERS

TRIP	TRAIN NO & NAME	FARE (₹)	DURATION (HR)	DEPARTURES
New Delhi station–Agra	12002 *Shatabdi Exp*	370/700*	2	6.15am (except Fri)
Agra–New Delhi station	12001 *Shatabdi Exp*	400/745*	2	8.30pm (except Fri)
Hazrat Nizamuddin station–Agra	12280 *Taj Exp*	75/263**	3	7.10am
Agra–Hazrat Nizamuddin station	12279 *Taj Exp*	75/263**	3	6.55pm

*chair/1AC; **2nd/chair

OTHER TRAINS FROM AGRA

DESTINATION	TRAIN NO & NAME	FARE (₹)	DURATION (HR)	DEPARTURES
Jaipur*	14853/14863 *Marudhar Exp*	135/349/474	5	6.15am (except Thu)
Khajuraho	12448 *UP SMPRK KRNTI*	207/526**	8	11.20pm (Tue, Fri, Sun)
Varanasi	13238/13240 *MTJ PNBE Exp*	262/707/969	12	11.30pm

Fares are sleeper/3AC/2AC; *leaves from Agra Fort station; **sleeper/3AC only

Christian Wife. This was used by Akbar's Goan wife Mariam, who gave birth to Jehangir here in 1569. Like many of the buildings in the palace complex, it contains elements of different religions, as befitted Akbar's tolerant religious beliefs. The domed ceiling is Islamic in style, while remnants of a wall painting of the Hindu god Shiva can also be found.

Continuing anticlockwise will bring you to the **Ornamental Pool**. Here, singers and musicians would perform on the platform above the water while Akbar watched from the pavilion in his private quarters, known as **Daulat Khana** (Abode of Fortune). Behind the pavilion is the **Khwabgah** (Dream House), a sleeping area with a huge stone bunk bed.

Heading north from the Ornamental Pool brings you to the most intricately carved structure in the whole complex, the tiny, but elegant **Rumi Sultana**, the palace built for Akbar's Turkish Muslim wife.

Just past Rumi Sultana is **Pachisi Courtyard** where Akbar is said to have played the game *pachisi* (an ancient version of ludo) using slave girls as pieces.

From here you can step down into **Diwan-i-Am** (Hall of Public Audiences), a large courtyard (which is now a garden) where Akbar dispensed justice by orchestrating public executions, said to have been carried out by elephants trampling to death convicted criminals.

The **Diwan-i-Khas** (Hall of Private Audiences), found at the northern end f the Pachisi Courtyard, looks nothing special from the outside, but the interior is dominated by a magnificently carved stone central column. This pillar flares to create a flat-topped plinth linked to the four corners of the room by narrow stone bridges. From this plinth Akbar is believed to have debated with scholars and ministers who stood at the ends of the four bridges.

Next to Diwan-i-Khas is the **Treasury**, which houses secret stone safes in some corners (one has been left with its stone lid open for visitors to see). Sea monsters carved on the ceiling struts were there to protect the fabulous wealth once stored here. The so-called **Astrologer's Kiosk** in front has roof supports carved in a serpentine Jain style.

On one corner of the **Ladies Garden** is the impressive **Panch Mahal**, a pavilion whose five storeys decrease in size until the top one consists of only a tiny kiosk. The lower floor has 84 columns, all different.

Walking past the Palace of the Christian Wife once more will take you west to **Birbal Bhavan**, ornately carved inside and out, and thought to have been the living quarters of one of Akbar's most senior ministers. The **Lower Haramsara**, just to the south, housed the royal stables.

ℹ Information

Dangers & Annoyances

Disregard anyone who gets on the Fatehpur Sikri–Agra bus before the final stop at Idgah bus stand to tell you that you've arrived at the city centre or the Taj Mahal. You haven't. You're still a long rickshaw ride away, and the man trying to tease you off the bus is – surprise, surprise – a rickshaw driver.

ℹ Getting There & Away

Buses run to Agra's Idgah bus stand from the bazaar every half-hour, from 6am to 5.30pm. If you miss those, walk to Agra Gate and wave down a Jaipur–Agra bus on the main road. They run regularly, day and night.

For Bharatpur (₹15, 40 minutes) or Jaipur (₹140, 4½ hours), wave down a westbound bus from Agra Gate.

Trains for Agra Fort Station (₹6, one to two hours) leave Fatehpur Sikri at 4.53am, 10.28am, 2.10pm (to Agra Cantonment station), 3.56pm and 8.17pm. Just buy a 'general' ticket at the station and pile in.

The tomb of Shaikh Salim Chisti (p105), Jama Masjid, Fatehpur Sikri

Mumbai (Bombay) & Around

Mumbai is a beautiful mess, full of dreamers and hard-labourers, actors and gangsters, stray dogs and exotic birds, artists and servants, fisherfolk and *crorepatis* (millionaires) and many, many other people. Peppered among the masses is crumbling architecture in various states of Technicolor dilapidation.

But Mumbai has never stumbled. Today, it's home to the world's most prolific film industry, one of Asia's biggest slums and the largest tropical forest in an urban zone. Between the fantastical buildings and the modern skyscrapers, the fine dining and frenetic streets, the madness and the mayhem, there's a cinematic cityscape set to a playful and addictive raga, dancing to the beat of its own *desi* drum. While you're here, seize the chance to visit the nearby Unesco sites of Ellora and Ajanta, epic cave temples containing some astounding religious art.

Young girls selling toys on Girguam Chowpatty (p121)

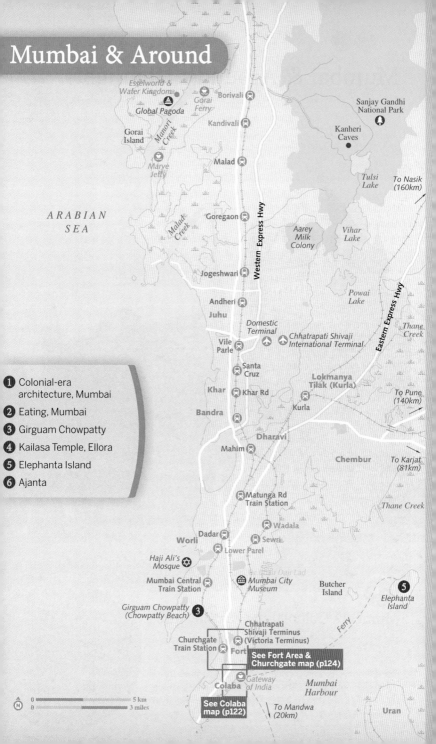

Mumbai & Around

Map legend / key:

1. Colonial-era architecture, Mumbai
2. Eating, Mumbai
3. Girguam Chowpatty
4. Kailasa Temple, Ellora
5. Elephanta Island
6. Ajanta

Map labels:

ARABIAN SEA

Esselworld & Water Kingdom
Global Pagoda
Gorai Island
Manori Creek
Marve Jetty
Gorai Ferry
Borivali
Kandivali
Malad
Malad Creek
Goregaon
Jogeshwari
Andheri
Juhu
Vile Parle
Santa Cruz
Khar
Khar Rd
Bandra
Mahim
Worli
Dadar
Lower Parel
Haji Ali's Mosque
Mumbai Central Train Station
Girguam Chowpatty (Chowpatty Beach) 3
Churchgate Train Station
Fort
Colaba

Sanjay Gandhi National Park
Kanheri Caves
To Nasik (160km)
Tulsi Lake
Aarey Milk Colony
Vihar Lake
Western Express Hwy
Powai Lake
Eastern Express Hwy
Thane Creek
Domestic Terminal
Chhatrapati Shivaji International Terminal
Lokmanya Tilak (Kurla)
To Pune (140km)
Kurla
Dharavi
Chembur
To Karjat (81km)
Thane Creek
Matunga Rd Train Station
Wadala
Sewri
Mani Bhavan Dr Bhau Daji Lad
Mumbai City Museum
Butcher Island
Elephanta Island 5
Chhatrapati Shivaji Terminus (Victoria Terminus)
Ferry
Gateway of India
Mumbai Harbour
To Mandwa (20km)
Uran

See Fort Area & Churchgate map (p124)

See Colaba map (p122)

0 — 5 km
0 — 3 miles

Mumbai & Around's Highlights

1

Mumbai's Colonial-era Architecture

The grandiose frilliness of Mumbai's 19th-century colonial-era architecture (p121) marries well with the larger-than-life feel of the city itself – this place of Bollywood dreams, tumults of people, slick business operations, fashionistas, tycoons, and endless-seeming slums.

Above: Playing cricket in front of the High Court; Top Right: Keneseth Eliyahoo Synagogue; Bottom Right: Victoria Terminus

Need to Know

LOCATION Most of these buildings are clustered around the central Fort area. **TOUR** The best way to see them is to follow our walking tour, or take a guided tour. **For more, see p118.**

Mumbai Don't Miss List

ARCHITECT ABHA BAHL IS
CO-FOUNDER OF THE BOMBAY
HERITAGE WALKS GROUP

1 ST THOMAS' CATHEDRAL, FORT

Standing witness to almost the entire history of the British in Bombay, this was the city's first Anglican church. A 44m Gothic-style clock tower dominates, along with the distinctive stone flying buttresses. Stepping into the large airy cathedral, with its striking stained-glass windows, you are transported back into the 19th century.

2 TOWN HALL

The Town Hall on Horniman Circle is also one of Mumbai's oldest surviving colonial buildings. Built in 1833 to serve the burgeoning port, its grand scale and key location were designed to flaunt British might. Today it houses the members-only Asiatic Library.

3 KENESETH ELIYAHOO SYNAGOGUE, KALA GHODA

On VB Gandhi Marg is an unmistakable blue-painted building, the KE Synagogue, built in 1884 by Jacob Sassoon. Its beautifully maintained ornate interior has wooden balconies resting on carved brackets, the *tebah* (raised platform in the centre of the main prayer room) and a fine *hekhal* (wall niche where the Torah is kept) that faces west, towards Jerusalem.

4 VICTORIA TERMINUS (CHHATRAPATI SHIVAJI TERMINUS)

Perhaps the world's finest railway station, and Mumbai's largest public building. An architectural gem and symbol of the city's prosperity, it's also an engineering marvel with an astounding ensemble of statues, carvings, stained glass and embellishments that took 10 years to complete.

5 BHAU DAJI LAD SANGRAHALAYA (FORMERLY VICTORIA & ALBERT MUSEUM)

Built in 1871 as a near replica of its London namesake, this recently restored museum has a marvellous collection of photographs, books and plans relating to Mumbai's history, as well as maps, clay models and craft objects. The main hall, which features a marble statue of Prince Albert, is dazzlingly ornate, from the Minton flooring up to the carved-iron brackets and railings and brilliantly painted ceiling.

Eating in Mumbai

You can dine like a maharaja at Mumbai's restaurants (p126) – this is one of India's gastro-epicentres, with some superb dining opportunities. You can find cuisine from all over India, from Parsi to South Indian, plus international trends, fusion, street food and more. Street food being made at Crawford Market (p131)

3 Girguam Chowpatty

The favoured place for a late-afternoon amble, a great swathe of sand edged by sparkling (if toxic) sea and backed by the Mumbai skyline (p121). It's fantastic for people-watching while munching on the famous Mumbai *bhelpuri* (fried, savoury rounds of dough). During the Ganesh Chaturthi festival (in August/September) you'll experience glorious colour a mayhem as huge effigies of the elephant god are dunked in the sea. Snacks for sale at Girguam Chowpatty

GREG ELMS/LONELY PLANET IMAGES ©

Kailasa Temple, Ellora

Ellora contains many breathtaking cave temples, beautifully carved. The grandest, however, is Cave 16, the awesome Kailasa Temple (p137). This is the world's largest monolithic sculpture, hewn top to bottom against a rocky slope by 7000 labourers over a 150-year period. Dedicated to Lord Shiva, it is one of the finest pieces of ancient Indian architecture on the subcontinent.

Elephanta Island

This tranquil island and Unesco World Heritage Site (p135) is home to a labyrinth of cave temples carved into the basalt rock. The artwork represents some of the most impressive temple carving in all of India. There's a classical music festival here in February.

Ajanta

Visit the incredible ancient Ajanta temple complex (p139), with its beautiful carvings, paintings and fantastically dramatic and remote setting, and make sure you seek out its most famous and iconic artwork, the Bodhisattva Padmapani, an exquisite, highly decorative wall painting in vivid colours, depicting Bodhisattva dressed as a prince, holding a waterlily, alongside the Buddha himself.

Mumbai & Around's Best...

Wining & Dining

○ **Khyber** (p127) Mouthwatering Punjabi/ North Indian kebabs, biryanis and curries

○ **Indigo** (p126) A gourmet haven serving inventive European cuisine

○ **Five Spice** (p127) Fantastic Indo-Chinese, with chicken, lamb, prawn and veg dishes

○ **Trishna** (p127) Outstanding, intimate seafood restaurant focused on Mangalorean preparations

○ **Brittania** (p127) Going since 1923; this is a Mumbai icon, serving Parsi dishes

Shopping

○ **Merewether Road** (p131) Fabulous small antique and curio shops

○ **World Trade Centre Arcade** (p131) Glittering and colourful crafts in the state government emporiums

○ **Fabindia** (p132) Stylish, original Indian clothes boutique

○ **Shrujan** (p132) Amazing embroidery from Kutch in Gujarat

People-watching

○ **High Court** (p118) See trials in progress at this 19th century building

○ **Girguam Chowpatty** (p121) An early-evening beach stroll: a quintessential Mumbai experience

○ **Victoria Terminus** (p121) Crazy Gothic architecture and Asia's busiest train station

○ **Leopold's Café** (p129) Wobbly fans and a lively atmosphere: a Mumbai travellers' institution

○ **Gateway of India** (p118) Photographers, beggars, touts and tourists create all the hubbub of a bazaar

Pockets of Tranquillity

○ **Global Pagoda** (p123) A haven for Viupassana meditation, built to promote peace

○ **Cruises** (p123) A boat around Mumbai Harbour is a good way to escape the city

○ **Jijamata Udyan** (p121) Home of the City Museum, lush 19th-century gardens

○ **Elephanta Island** (p135) A peaceful place with ancient rock-cut temples

Need to Know

ADVANCE PLANNING

○ **One month before** Book your accommodation; start even earlier if you're travelling over Christmas and New Year

○ **One week before** Book any domestic flights and long-distance train tickets

○ **On arrival** Arrange any long-distance taxi rides via a recommended local agency or your hotel

BE FOREWARNED

○ **Bring directions** Print out a map or some detailed landmark directions for your hotel – many airport taxi drivers don't speak English

○ **Avoid** Would-be guides meeting you at the ferry at Elephanta Island; a guide is included in the price

○ **Touts** Tend to hang around the Gateway of India – keep your wits about you here

○ **Old-style meters** Print out rate conversion charts from the Mumbai Traffic Police (www.trafficpolicemumbai.org/Tariffcard_Auto_taxi_form.htm) in case your taxi or rickshaw has an old-fashioned meter (outside on the left)

GETTING AROUND

○ **Premier taxi** The black-and-yellow cabs are the easiest way to get around the city, and in South Mumbai drivers usually use the meter without prompting

○ **Autorickshaw** Confined to the suburbs north of Mahim Creek

○ **Metro** Mumbai's US$8.17 billion metro project has commenced but is still several years from completion

RESOURCES

○ **Maharashtra Tourism Development Corporation** (www.maharashtratourism.gov.in) Official tourism site

○ **Time Out Mumbai** (www.timeoutmumbai.net) Local listings website/magazine

○ **burrp! Mumbai** (http://mumbai.burrp.com) Local events, activities and services

Left: Mural at Khyber restaurant (p127); e: Sunset at Girguam Chowpatty beach (p121)

Mumbai's Colonial-era Architecture Walking Tour

The grandiose colonial-era architecture of Mumbai is a remarkable feature of the cityscape. Take this stroll to see its most spectacular 19th-century hits.

WALK FACTS

- **Start** Gateway of India
- **Finish** Eros Cinema
- **Distance** 2.5km
- **Duration** 1½ hours

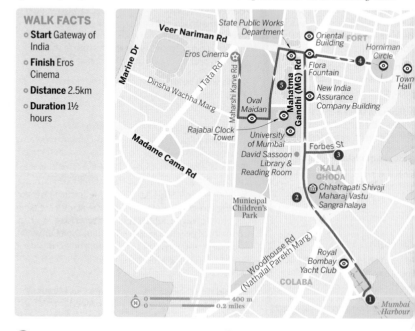

❶ Gateway of India

Starting from the Gateway of India walk up Chhatrapati Shivaji Marg past the members-only colonial relic Royal Bombay Yacht Club on one side and the art deco complex Dhunraj Mahal on the other towards Regal Circle. The car park in the middle of the circle has the best view of the surrounding buildings, including the old Sailors Home, which dates from 1876 and is now the Maharashtra Police Headquarters, the art deco cinema Regal and the old Majestic Hotel, now the Sahakari Bhandar cooperative store.

❷ National Gallery of Modern Art

Continue up MG Rd, past the restored facade of the National Gallery of Modern Art. Opposite is the Chhatrapati Shivaji Maharaj Vastu Sangrahalaya; step into the front gardens to admire this grand building. Back across the road is the 'Romanesque Transitional' Elphinstone College and the David Sassoon Library & Reading Room, where members escape the afternoon heat lazing on planters' chairs on the upper balcony.

3 Keneseth Eliyahoo Synagogue

Cross back over to Forbes St to visit the synagogue before returning to MG Rd and continuing north along the left-hand side to admire the art deco stylings of the New India Assurance Company Building. In a traffic island ahead lies the pretty Flora Fountain, erected in 1869 in honour of Sir Bartle Frere, the Bombay governor responsible for dismantling the fort. From here, there's a nice view to the north of the 1885 Oriental Building.

4 St Thomas' Cathedral

Turn east down Veer Nariman Rd, walking towards St Thomas' Cathedral. Ahead lies the stately Horniman Circle, an arcaded ring of buildings laid out in the 1860s around a circular botanical garden. The circle is overlooked from the east by the neoclassical town hall, which contains the regally decorated members-only Asiatic Society of Bombay Library and Mumbai's State Central Library.

5 High Court

As you retrace your steps back to Flora Fountain, glance to the north at the striking red Bombay Samachar building, home to the oldest continuously published newspaper in India, before continuing west past the Venetian Gothic-style State Public Works Department, now the entrance to the High Court. Turn south on to Bhaurao Patil Marg to see the High Court in full glory and the equally venerable and ornately decorated University of Mumbai. The university's 80m-high Rajabai Clock Tower and the facade of the High Court are best observed from within the Oval Maidan. Turn around to compare the colonial edifices with the row of art deco beauties lining Maharshi Karve (MK) Rd, culminating in the wedding-cake tower of the Eros Cinema.

Mumbai in...

TWO DAYS

In the morning, follow our walking tour, have lunch at a local restaurant, and visit **Haji Ali's Mosque** in the afternoon.

The next day, visit the ornate **Dr Bhau Daji Lad Mumbai City Museum**, then take in a beach sunset at **Girguam Chowpatty** before heading for dinner at one of Mumbai's superb restaurants.

FOUR DAYS

Take a walking tour of Mumbai's colonial-era architecture, then enjoy some excellent lunch before taking it easy in the afternoon. The following day, head out to the **Global Pagoda** and return to visit the museums and galleries of **Kala Ghoda**. In the evening, head out for dinner at **Khyber**, followed by immersion in some local culture by taking in a concert or dance show at the **National Centre for the Performing Arts**. On the third day, you could take a cruise around the bay before hitting the shops.

Another day could be spent visiting the beautiful rock temples on **Elephanta Island**. Then have a leisurely lunch and rest up, ready for a night of avant-garde clubbing at **Bluefrog** in Worli.

A cave temple at Elephanta Island (p135)

Discover Mumbai (Bombay) & Around

MUMBAI (BOMBAY)

 Sights

Mumbai, the capital of Maharashtra state is an island connected by bridges to the mainland. The southernmost peninsula is Colaba, traditionally the travellers' nerve-centre, with most of the major attractions, and directly north of Colaba is the busy commercial area known as Fort, where the old British fort once stood.

Colaba

TAJ MAHAL PALACE, MUMBAI   Landmark

(Map p122) This iconic hotel (p124) is a fairy-tale blend of Islamic and Renaissance styles jostling for prime position among Mumbai's famous landmarks. Facing the harbour, it was built in 1903 by the Parsi industrialist JN Tata, supposedly after he was refused entry to one of the European hotels on account of being 'a native'.

GATEWAY OF INDIA   Monument

(Map p122) This bold basalt arch of colonial triumph faces out to Mumbai Harbour from the tip of Apollo Bunder. Derived from the Islamic styles of 16th-century Gujarat, it was built to commemorate the 1911 royal visit of King George V. It was completed in 1924. See also p118.

Kala Ghoda

'Black Horse', the area between Colaba and Fort, contains most of Mumbai's main galleries and museums alongside a wealth of colonial-era buildings.

Studying in the University of Mumbai library
ANDER BLOMQVIST/LONELY PLANET IMAGES ©

CHHATRAPATI SHIVAJI MAHARAJ VASTU SANGRAHALAYA (PRINCE OF WALES MUSEUM) Museum

(Map p124; www.themuseummumbai.com; Dubash Marg; Indian/foreigner ₹25/300, camera/video ₹200/1000; ⊙10.45am-6pm Tue-Sun) Mumbai's biggest and best museum, this domed behemoth is an intriguing hodgepodge of Islamic, Hindu and British architecture displaying a mix of dusty exhibits from all over India. The museum has undergone a ₹12 million upkeep renovation, which introduced a fascinating new miniature-painting gallery and a new gallery dedicated to Vishnu.

KENESETH ELIYAHOO SYNAGOGUE Synagogue

(Map p124; www.jacobsassoon.org; Dr VB Gandhi Marg; admission free, camera ₹100; ⊙9am-6pm) Built in 1884, this impossibly sky-blue synagogue still functions and is tenderly maintained by the city's dwindling Jewish community (and protected to Baghdad Green Zone levels by Mumbai's finest). See also p119.

Fort Area & Churchgate

CHHATRAPATI SHIVAJI TERMINUS (VICTORIA TERMINUS) Historical Building

(Map p124) Imposing, exuberant and overflowing with people, this is the city's most extravagant Gothic building, the beating heart of its railway network, and an aphorism for colonial India. Designed by Frederick Stevens, it was completed in 1887, 34 years after the first train in India left this site. Today it's the busiest train station in Asia. Officially renamed Chhatrapati Shivaji Terminus (CST) in 1998, it's still better known locally as VT. It was added to the Unesco World Heritage list in 2004.

UNIVERSITY OF MUMBAI (BOMBAY UNIVERSITY) Historical Building

(Map p124) Looking like a 15th-century French-Gothic masterpiece plopped incongruously among Mumbai's palm trees, this university on Bhaurao Patil Marg was designed by Gilbert Scott of London's St Pancras Station fame.

♥ If You Like...
Colonial-era Architecture

If you love Mumbai's sumptuous colonial-era buildings such as Chhatrapati Shivaji, seek out the following fantastic examples in the Fort area, or try our walking tour on p118.

1 HIGH COURT
(Map p124; Eldon Rd) A hive of daily activity, packed with judges, barristers and other cogs in the Indian justice system, the High Court is an elegant 1848 neo-Gothic building. You are permitted (and it is highly recommended) to walk around inside the building and check out the pandemonium and pageantry of public cases that are in progress – just walk right in!

2 ST THOMAS' CATHEDRAL
(Map p124; Veer Nariman Rd; ⊙6.30am-6pm) Recently restored to its former glory, this charming cathedral is the oldest English building standing in Mumbai (construction began in 1672, though it remained unfinished until 1718).

Girguam Chowpatty Area
GIRGUAM CHOWPATTY Beach

(Map p111) Girguam Chowpatty (often referred to as 'Chowpatty Beach' in English, though this means 'Beach Beach' and often confuses locals) remains a favourite evening spot for courting couples, families, political rallies and anyone out to enjoy what passes for fresh air. Eating an evening time *bhelpuri* at the throng of stalls found here is an essential part of the Mumbai experience. Forget about taking a dip: the water is toxic.

Byculla
DR BHAU DAJI LAD MUMBAI CITY MUSEUM Museum

(Map p111; Dr Babasaheb Ambedkar Rd; Indian/foreigner ₹10/100; ⊙10am-5.30pm Thu-Tue) Jijamata Udyan – aka Veermata Jijabai Bhonsle Udyan and formerly named Victoria Gardens – is a lush and sprawling mid-19th-century garden and zoo. It's home to this gorgeous museum, originally

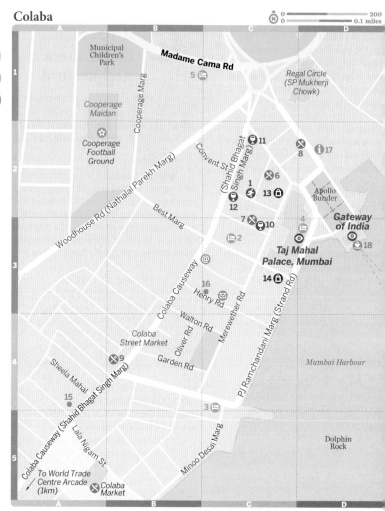

Colaba

built in Renaissance revival style in 1872 as the Victoria & Albert Museum. It reopened in 2007 after an impressive and sensitive four-year renovation. Even the sweet mint-green paint choice was based on historical research. Also restored were the museum's 3500-plus objects from Mumbai's history – clay models of village life, photography and maps, archaeological finds, costumes, a library of books and manuscripts, industrial and agricultural exhibits, and silver, copper, Bidriware, laquerware, weaponry and exquisite pottery, all set against the museum's very distracting, very stunning decor. Skip the zoo.

Mahalaxmi to Worli

HAJI ALI'S MOSQUE Mosque

(Map p111) Floating like a sacred mirage off the coast is this mosque, one of Mumbai's most striking symbols, an exquisite Indo-Islamic shrine. Built in the 19th century on the site of a 15th-century structure, it contains the tomb of the Muslim saint Haji – legend has it that Haji Ali died while on a pilgrimage to Mecca and his casket

DISCOVER MUMBAI (BOMBAY) & AROUND MUMBAI (BOMBAY)

Colaba

iiraculously floated back to this spot. A
ong causeway reaches into the Arabian
ea, providing access to the mosque.

Gorai Island

GLOBAL PAGODA Landmark
(Map p111; www.globalpagoda.org; near Es-
elworld, Gorai Creek; ⊙9am-6pm) Rising up
ke a mirage from polluted Gorai Creek
nd the lush but noisy grounds of the
sselworld and Water Kingdom amuse-
nent parks, the breathtaking structure is
96m-high stupa modelled after Burma's
Shwedagon Pagoda. The dome, which is
esigned to hold 8000 meditators and
ouses relics of Buddha, was built entirely
vithout supports using an ancient tech-
ique of interlocking stones. To get here,
ake the train from Churchgate to Borivali,
hen an autorickshaw (₹28) to the ferry
anding, where the Esselworld ferries (re-
urn ₹35) come and go every 30 minutes.
The last ferry back is at 5.25pm.

Tours

BOMBAY HERITAGE WALKS Walking
(☑23690992; www.bombayheritagewalks.
om) Run by two enthusiastic architects,
as the best city tours. Private two-hour

guided tours are ₹1500 for up to three
people, ₹500 for each additional person.

**REALITY TOURS &
TRAVEL** Dharavi Tour
(Map p122; ☑9820822253; www.realitytours
andtravel.com; 1/26 Akbar House, Nawroji F Rd,
Colaba; short/long tours ₹500/1000) Runs so-
cially-responsible tours of Dharavi (p127).
Enter the office through SSS Corner store
on Nawroji F Rd.

Cruises Cruise
(☑22026364; ⊙9am-7pm) A cruise on Mumbai
Harbour is a good way to escape the city and
a chance to see the Gateway of India as it was
intended. Ferry rides (₹60, 30 minutes) depart
from the Gateway of India.

🛏 Sleeping

You'll need to recalibrate your budget
here: Mumbai has the most expensive accommodation in India. To stay with a local
family, contact the Government of India
tourist office for a list of homes partici-
pating in Mumbai's **paying-guest scheme**
(r & full-board ₹1500-2500; ❄).

A 4% (more common at budget end)
or 10% tax should be added to all prices
listed below unless otherwise stated.

Fort Area & Churchgate

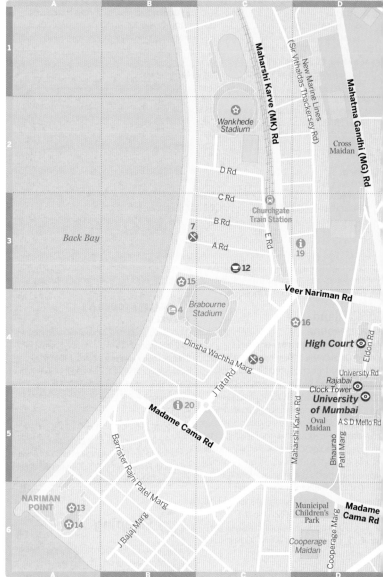

Colaba

TAJ MAHAL PALACE, MUMBAI Heritage Hotel **$$$**
(Map p122; ☎66653366; www.tajhotels.com; Apollo Bunder, Colaba; s/d tower from ₹21,500/23,000,
palace from ₹25,250/26,750; ❄@🤏🏊) The hotel formerly known as the Taj Mahal Palace & Tower debuted its new name and new spaces on Indian Independence Day 2010, the result of a meticulous restoration following the November 2008 terrorist at-

YWCA
Guesthouse **$$**

(Map p122; ☎22025053; www.ywcaic.info; 18 Madame Cama Rd; s/d/tr/q incl breakfast, dinner & taxes ₹2024/3000/4200/6000; ❄@☎) The YWCA presents a frustrating dilemma: It's immaculate and surprisingly good, considering it's a cool ₹1000 cheaper than most in its class. Rates include tax, breakfast, dinner, 'bed tea', free wi-fi *...and a newspaper,* so it's the best value (and location, for that matter) within miles. But there's a trade-off here with a series of unorthodox rules, including the very stubborn policy of not allowing early check-in – even if your room is ready – unless you pay extra.

HOTEL MOTI
Guesthouse **$$**

(Map p122; ☎22025714; hotelmotiinternational @yahoo.co.in; 10 Best Marg; s/d/tr with AC incl tax from ₹1800/2000/3200; ❄@) This travellers' haven occupies the ground floor of a gracefully crumbling, beautiful colonial-era building. Simple rooms have whispers of charm and some nice surprises, like ornate stucco ceilings and Western showers.

SEA SHORE HOTEL
Guesthouse **$**

(Map p122; ☎22874237; 4th fl, Kamal Mansion, Arthur Bunder Rd; s/d without bathroom ₹500/700) In a building housing several budget guesthouses, the Sea Shore will go above and beyond your expectations for the price, mainly due to a spiffy new makeover that has turned ratty plywood walls and shoebox-sized rooms into simple but near hotel-quality accommodation, with communal bathrooms and sinks that approach those of design hotels.

Fort, Churchgate & Marine Drive

SEA GREEN SOUTH HOTEL
Hotel **$$**

(Map p124; ☎22821613; www.seagreensouth. com; 145A Marine Dr; s/d ₹2500/3150; ❄☎) This art deco hotel has spacious but spartan AC rooms, originally built in the 1940s to house British soldiers. Snag a sea-view room – they're the same price – and you've secured top value in this price range (even with the 10% service charge).

...acks that nearly brought this 1903 Mumbai landmark to its knees. But as one of the world's most distinguished hotels, with its sweeping arches, staircases and domes, it as risen again, unstoppably exquisite and efiantly opulent.

Fort Area & Churchgate

⊗ Eating

In this gastro-epicentre a cornucopia of flavours from all over India collides with international trends and tastebuds.

Colaba

INDIGO   Fusion, European $$$
(Map p122; 📞66368980; 4 Mandlik Marg; mains ₹525-945; ◷lunch & dinner) Over a decade in and still a star, Colaba's finest eating option is a gourmet haven serving inventive European cuisine, a long wine list, sleek ambience and a gorgeous roof deck lit with fairy lights. Favourites include excellent kiwi margaritas, tea-grilled quail (₹625), anise-rubbed white salmon (₹725) and inventive takes on traditional cuisine like juniper-berry-cured tandoori chicken (₹625). Its cool quotient has chilled a bit with the focus on the suburbs, but it remains a high-gastronomy favourite.

BADEMIYA   Indian $
(Map p122; Tulloch Rd; meals ₹50-100) If you can walk by this street-stall-on-steroids without coming away with a chicken tikk roll in hand, you are a better person than us. This whole street buzzes nightly with punters from all walks of Mumbai life lining up for spicy, fresh grilled treats.

INDIGO DELICATESSEN   Cafe $$
(Map p122; Pheroze Bldg, Chhatrapati Shivaji Marg; mains ₹245-495; ◷9am-midnight) Indigo's casual and less expensive sister is just as big a draw as the original, with coo tunes, warm decor and massive wooden tables. It has breakfast all day (₹155 to ₹295), casual meals, French press coffee wines (₹300 to ₹690 per glass) and is also a bakery and deli.

Dharavi Slum

Mumbaikars had mixed feelings about the stereotypes in 2008's runaway hit, *Slumdog Millionaire* (released in Hindi as *Slumdog Crorepati*). But slums are very much a part of – some would say the foundation of – Mumbai city life. An astonishing 55% of Mumbai's population lives in shantytowns and slums, and the largest slum in Mumbai (and Asia, for that matter) is Dharavi. Originally inhabited by fisherfolk when the area was still creeks, swamps and islands, it became attractive to migrant workers, from South Mumbai and beyond, when the swamp began to fill in as a result of natural and artificial causes. It now incorporates 1.75 sq km sandwiched between Mumbai's two major railway lines and is home to more than one million people.

Slum tourism is a polarising subject, so you'll have to decide your feelings for yourself. If you opt to visit, **Reality Tours & Travel** (p123) does a fascinating tour, and pours a percentage of profits back into Dharavi, setting up community centres and schools.

THEOBROMA Cafe **$**
(Map p122; Colaba Causeway; confections ₹40-65) Theobroma calls its creations 'food of the gods' – and they ain't lying. Dozens of perfectly executed cakes, tarts and chocolates, as well as sandwiches and breads, go well with the coffee here. The genius pistachio-and-green-cardamom truffle (₹30) or decadent chocolate overload brownie (₹65) should send you straight into a glorious sugar coma.

Kala Ghoda & Fort Area

KHYBER North Indian **$$$**
(Map p124; 40396666; 145 MG Rd, Fort; mains ₹225-450; lunch & dinner) Like Bukhara in Delhi, Khyber is an iconic restaurant the thought of which will spark Pavlovian drooling for years to come. The burnt-orange, Afghan-inspired interiors are a multi-tiered and cavernous maze of moody Mughal royalty art embedded in exposed brick, tasteful antique oil lanterns and urns and railway-trestle ceilings. As mouth-watering Punjabi/North Indian kebabs, biryanis and curries saunter their way to a who's who of Mumbai's elite, your tastebuds will do a happy dance – before the disheartening realisation: too much food, too little space.

FIVE SPICE Indo-Chinese **$$**
(Map p124; 296-A Perin Nariman St, Sangli Bank Bldg, Fort; mains ₹220-275; lunch & dinner) A 30-minute wait is commonplace at this overheated, near-divey Indo-Chinese godsend that's so good, it'll make you downright angry you can't eat Chinese like this at home. The menu is packed with chicken, lamb, prawn and veg dishes, all tantalising, so choosing is an issue.

TRISHNA Seafood **$$$**
(Map p124; 22614991; Sai Baba Marg, Kala Ghoda; mains ₹170-575; lunch & dinner) An outstanding and intimate seafood restaurant focused on Mangalorean preparations. The crab with butter, black pepper and garlic and Hyderabadi fish tikka are house specialities that warrant the hype, while service is underbearing, friendly and helpful.

BRITTANIA Parsi **$$**
(Wakefield House, 11 Sprott Rd, Ballard Eatte; mains ₹100-250; lunch Mon-Sat) The kind of place travellers' tales are made of – this Mumbai icon, and its endearing owner, has been going since 1923. The signature dish is the berry *pulao* (₹250) – spiced and boneless mutton or chicken buried in basmati rice and tart barberries,

Mumbai for Children

Rina Mehta's www.mustformums.com has the Mumbai Mums' Guide, with info on crèches, health care and even kids' salsa classes in the city. *Time Out Mumbai* (₹50) often lists fun things to do with kids.

Little tykes with energy to burn will love the Gorai Island amusement parks, **Esselworld** (www.esselworld.in; adult/child ₹510/380; ◷11am-7pm) and **Water Kingdom** (www.waterkingdom.in; adult/child ₹510/380; ◷11am-7pm). Both are well maintained and have lots of rides, slides and shade. Combined tickets are ₹710/580 (adult/child). Off-season weekday ticket prices are lower. It's a ₹35 ferry ride from Borivali jetty.

The **Bombay Natural History Society** (BNHS; Map p124; ☏22821811; www.bnhs. org; Hornbill House, Dr Salim Ali Chowk, Shaheed Bhagat Singh Rd, Kala Ghodaw) and Sunjoy Monga at **Yuhina Eco-Media** (☏9323995955) often conduct **birdwatching trips** for kids, while **Yoga Sutra** (☏32107067; www.yogasutra.co.in; Chinoy Mansions, Bhulabhai Desai Rd, Cumballa Hill; drop-in classes ₹300) has kids' yoga classes, taught in English.

imported to the tune of 1000kg per year from Iran.

MAHESH LUNCH HOME   Seafood $$$
(Map p124; ☏22023965; 8B Cowasji Patel St, Fort; mains ₹150-600; ◷lunch & dinner) A great place to try Mangalorean seafood in Mumbai. It's renowned for its ladyfish, pomfret, lobster and crabs; the *rawas tikka* (marinated white salmon) and tandoori pomfret are outstanding.

Churchgate
KOH   Thai $$$
(Map p124; ☏39879999; InterContinental Marine Dr; mains ₹495-925; ◷lunch & dinner) India's first signature Thai restaurant is Mumbai's hottest dining destination. Celebrity chef Ian Kittichai works his native cuisine into an international frenzy of flavour that starts with the 'liquid gastronomy', which might be a jasmine and honey martini or a Bloody Mary made with lemongrass-infused vodka and sriracha chilli; from there the envelope is further pushed into revelational dishes like the 12-hour lamb shank Massaman curry – pair it with hot-stone garlic rice – that throws preconceived notions about Thai food to the Mumbai curb.

SAMRAT   South Indian $$
(Map p124; ☏42135401; Prem Ct, J Tata Rd; lunch/dinner thalis ₹220/260; ◷lunch & dinner) If this is your first thali, strap yourself in – the cavalcade of taste and texture will leave you wondering what the hell just happened – *then* they bring the rice. With a dizzying number of concoctable bites, it's as adventurous and diverse as India itself.

Girgaum Chowpatty
NEW KULFI CENTRE   Sweets $
(cnr Chowpatty Seaface & Sardar V Patel Rd; kulfi per 100gm ₹20-40; ◷9am-1.30am) Serves the best *kulfi* (firm-textured ice cream served in killer flavours like pistachio, rose and saffron) you'll have anywhere, which means it will rock your pants off. When you order, the *kulfi* is placed on a betel-nut leaf and then weighed on an ancient scale – which makes it even better.

Cream Centre   Cafe $
(Chowpatty Seaface; mains ₹100-249; ◷lunch & dinner) This sleek and contemporary Indian diner is hugely popular for its pure-veg hodgepodge of Indian, Mexican and Lebanese as well as their extensive menu of sizzling sundaes (₹195 to ₹220), which take 'hot fudge' to the boiling point!

☐ Drinking

Mumbai's lax attitude to alcohol means that there are loads of places to drink – from hole-in-the-wall beer bars and chichi lounges to brash, multilevel superclubs – but the 25% liquor tax means bills can bring sticker shock.

If it's the caffeine buzz you're after, Barista and Café Coffee Day cafes are ubiquitous in Mumbai.

Cafes

☐ KALA GHODA CAFÉ   Cafe
(Map p124; 10 Ropewalk Lane, Fort) Artsy, modern and miniscule, this cafe is a favourite with journalists and other creative types, who come for the organic Arabica and Robusta coffee (from sustainable plantations), organic teas, small bite sandwiches and salads, and charming breakfasts – and then fight for one of the few tables.

MOCHA BAR   Cafe
(⊙10am-1.30am) Churchgate (Map p124; 82 Veer Nariman Rd); Juhu (67 Juhu Tara Rd) This atmospheric Arabian-styled cafe is often filled to the brim with bohemians and students deep in esoteric conversation, Bollywood gossip or just a hookah pipe. Cosy, low-cushioned seating (including some old cinema seats), exotic coffees, shakes and teas, and global comfort cuisine promote an intellectually chilaxed vibe.

Bars

CAFE MONDEGAR   Bar
(Map p122; ☎ 22020591; Metro House, 5A Shahid Bhagat Singh Rd, Colaba) Like Leopold's, 'Mondys' draws a healthy foreign crowd, too, but with a better mix of friendly Indians, who all cosy up together in the much smaller

space, bonding over the excellent jukebox, one of Mumbai's only.

BUSABA   Bar, Lounge
(Map p122; ☎ 22043779; 4 Mandlik Marg) Red walls and contemporary Buddha art give this loungey restaurant-bar a nouveau Tao. It's next to Indigo so gets the same trendy crowd but serves cheaper, more potent cocktails (₹330 to ₹480).

LEOPOLD'S CAFÉ   Bar
(cnr Colaba Causeway & Nawroji F Rd) Love it or hate it, most tourists end up at this Mumbai travellers' institution at one time or another. Around since 1871, Leopold's has wobbly ceiling fans, open-plan seating and a rambunctious atmosphere conducive to swapping tales with random strangers.

☆ Entertainment

The daily English-language tabloid *Mid-Day* incorporates a guide to Mumbai entertainment. Newspapers and *Time Out Mumbai* list events and film screenings,

Cafe Mondegar
ORIEN HARVEY/LONELY PLANET IMAGES ©

Below: Young boys at a watermelon stall, Crawford Market;
Right: Cinema fans queuing under Bollywood film posters

(BELOW) ANDERS BLOMQVIST/LONELY PLANET IMAGES ©; (RIGHT) MICHAEL COYNE/LONELY PLANET IMAGES ©

while www.nh7.in has live music listings.
The cutting-edge **Bombay Elektrik
Projekt** (www.bombayelektrik.com) organises
everything from live DJs to poetry slams
to short film screenings.

Big club nights are (oddly) Wednesday,
as well as the traditional Friday and
Saturday; there's usually a cover charge.
Dress codes apply so don't rock up in
shorts and sandals.

Nightclubs

TRILOGY — Nightclub

(Hotel Sea Princess, Juhu Tara Rd, Juhu; cover
per couple after 11pm ₹1000; ⊙ closed Tue)
Mumbai's newest club at time of writing is
all attitude – rumour has it that they size
up potentials for looks and charge a varying cover accordingly. That bodes well for
those who make it past face patrol. The
tri-level space is gorgeous, highlighted
by a black granite dance floor lit up by
1372 LED cube lights that go off like an

epileptic Lite-Brite in an Indian power surge. The imported
sound system favours house and hip-hop
while the bartenders look imported from
Ed Hardy's employee pool.

VALHALLA — Resto-Lounge

(Map p124; ☎ 67353535; 1st fl, East Wing,
Eros Theatre Bldg, Churchgate) This discreet
resto-lounge caters to Mumbai's bold
and beautiful, who turn up here amid
aubergine walls and baroque aesthetics
on Friday and Saturday club nights when
everywhere else closes (it's unofficially
open until 4am or so). Getting in isn't
easy – you need to call ahead and get on
the list – but if you manage it, you'll rub
elbows with a very high-profile crowd.

Music, Dance & Theatre

BLUEFROG — Live Music

(☎ 6158; www.bluefrog.co.in; D/2 Mathuradas
Mills Compound, NM Joshi Marg, Lower Parel;
admission after 9pm Sun & Tue-Thu ₹300, Fri &
Sat ₹500; ⊙ 7pm-1am Tue-Sun) The most ex-

iting thing to happen to Mumbai's music
scene in a long time, Bluefrog is a concert
space, production studio, restaurant and
one of Mumbai's most happening spaces.
It hosts exceptional local and international acts, and has space-age, orange-
glowing 'pod' seating in the intimate main
room.

NOT JUST JAZZ BY THE BAY Live Music
(Map p124; ☎22851876; 143 Marine Dr; admission weekdays/weekends ₹100/300; ⏰noon-
1.30am) This is the best, and frankly the
only, jazz club in South Mumbai. True to
its name, there are also live pop, blues
and rock performers most nights from
10pm, but Sunday, Monday and Tuesday
are reserved for karaoke. By day, there's a
well-done all-you-can-eat buffet (₹ 325).

**NATIONAL CENTRE FOR THE
PERFORMING ARTS**   Theatre
(NCPA; Map p124; ☎66223737, box office
2824567; www.ncpamumbai.com; cnr Marine
Dr & Sri V Saha Rd, Nariman Point; tickets ₹200-
500; ⏰box office 9am-7pm) Spanning 800

sq metres, this cultural centre is the hub
of Mumbai's music, theatre and dance
scene. In any given week, it might host
Marathi theatre, poetry readings and
art exhibitions, Bihari dance troupes,
ensembles from Europe or Indian classical music.

🔓 Shopping

Mumbai is India's great marketplace, with
some of the best shopping in the country.
You can buy just about anything in the
dense bazaars north of CST. The main areas are **Crawford Market** (fruit and veg),
Mangaldas Market (silk and cloth), **Zaveri
Bazaar** (jewellery), **Bhuleshwar Market**
(fruit and veg) and **Chor Bazaar** (antiques
and furniture). Dhabu St is lined with fine
leather goods and Mutton St specialises
in antiques, reproductions and fine junk.

Various state-government emporiums
sell handicrafts in the **World Trade Centre
Arcade** (off Map p122) near Cuffe Parade.

131

Small **antique and curio shops** (Map p122) line Merewether Rd behind the Taj Mahal Palace. They aren't cheap, but the quality is a step up from the government stores.

FABINDIA
Clothing

(Map p124; Jeroo Bldg, 137 MG Rd, Kala Ghoda) Founded as a means to get traditional fabric artisans' wares to market, Fabindia has all the vibrant colours of the country in its trendy cotton and silk fashions, materials and homewares in a modern-meets-traditional Indian shop.

BOMBAY ELECTRIC
Clothes

(Map p122; www.bombayeletric.in; 1 Reay House, Best Marg, Colaba) Trendy high fashion is the calling at this unisex boutique next to the Taj Mahal Palace hotel. It sources fabrics (for its own hip brand, Gheebutter) and weaved scarfs and jackets from NGOs in Madhya Pradesh and Gujarat; as well as select antiques and handicrafts.

SHRUJAN
Handicrafts

Juhu (Hatkesh Society, 6th North South Rd, JVPD Scheme; ⊘closed Sun); Breach Candy (Sagar Villa, Warden Rd, opposite Navroze Apts; ⊘closed Sun) Selling the intricate embroidery work of women in 114 villages in Kutch, Gujarat, the nonprofit Shrujan aims to help women earn a livelihood while preserving the spectacular embroidery traditions of the area.

❶ Information

Medical Services

Breach Candy Hospital (✆23672888; www.breachcandyhospital.org; 60 Bhulabhai Desai Rd, Breach Candy) Best in Mumbai, if not India.

Money

Akbar Travels Fort (Map p124; ✆22633434; Terminus View, 167/169 Dr Dadabhai Naoroji Rd; ⊘10am-7pm Mon-Fri, to 6pm Sun); Colaba (Map p122; ✆22823434; 30 Alipur Trust Bldg; ⊘10am-7pm)

Thomas Cook (⊘9.30am-6pm Mon-Sat) Fort (Map p124; ✆61603333; 324 Dr Dadabhai Naoroji Rd); Colaba (Map p122; ✆22882517-20; Colaba Causeway)

Laundry being done at a ghat

ORIEN HARVEY/LONELY PLANET IMAGES

Major Nonstop Domestic Flights from Mumbai

DESTINATION	SAMPLE LOWEST ONE-WAY FARE (₹)	DURATION (HR)
Bengaluru	2533	1½
Chennai	3482	1¾
Delhi	3483	2
Goa	2532	1
Hyderabad	2282	1¼
Jaipur	2533	1¾
Kochi	3483	1¾
Kolkata	3882	2¾

Tourist Information

Government of India tourist office (Map p124; ☏22074333; www.incredibleindia.com; 123 Maharshi Karve Rd; ◷8.30am-7pm Mon-Fri, to 2pm Sat) Provides information for the entire country.

Government of India tourist office airport booths domestic (☏26156920; ◷7am-midnight); international (☏26813253; ◷24hr)

Maharashtra Tourism Development Corporation booth (MTDC; Map p122; ☏22841877; Apollo Bunder; ◷8.30am-4pm Tue-Sun & 5.30-8pm weekends) For city bus tours.

MTDC reservation office (Map p124; ☏22841877; www.maharashtratourism.gov.in; Madame Cama Rd, opposite LIC Bldg, Nariman Point; ◷9.45am-5.30pm Mon-Sat) Information on Maharashtra and bookings for MTDC hotels and the *Deccan Odyssey* train package. This is also the only MTDC office that accepts credit cards.

Travel Agencies

Akbar Travels (Map p124; ☏22633434; www.akbartravelsonline.com; Terminus View, 167/169 Dr Dadabhai Naoroji Rd, Fort; ◷10am-7pm Mon-Fri, to 6pm Sun)

Magnum International Travel & Tours (Map p122; ☏61559700; 10 Henry Rd, Colaba; ◷10am-5.30pm Mon-Fri, to 4pm Sat)

ℹ Getting There & Away

Air

AIRPORTS Mumbai is the main international gateway to South India and has the busiest network of domestic flights. **Chhatrapati Shivaji International Airport** (Map p111; ☏domestic 26264000, international 26813000; www.csia.in), about 30km from downtown, has been undergoing a $2 billion modernisation since 2006. At time of writing, the airport comprised three domestic (1A, 1B and 1C) and one international terminal (2A). However, the domestic side is accessed via Vile Parle and is known locally as Santa Cruz airport, while the international, with its entrance 4km away in Andheri, goes locally by Sahar. A free shuttle bus runs between the two every 30 minutes for ticket holders only. By 2014 the shiny new terminal T2 is expected to be open, serving both domestic and international flights, with the existing Santa Cruz terminal being converted to cargo only.

Bus

Private buses are usually more comfortable and simpler to book but can cost significantly more than government buses; they depart from

Dr Anadrao Nair Rd near Mumbai Central train station (Map p111). Fares to popular destinations (like Goa) are up to 75% higher during holiday periods. To check on departure times and current prices, try National CTC (23015652; Dr Anadrao Nair Rd; 7am-10pm), near Mumbai Central train station.

More convenient for Goa and southern destinations are the private buses run by Chandni Travels (Map p124; 22713901) that depart three times a day from in front of Azad Maidan, just south of the Metro cinema. Ticket agents are located near the bus departure point.

Train

Three train systems operate out of Mumbai, but the most important services for travellers are Central Railways and Western Railways. Tickets for either system can be bought from any station, in South Mumbai or the suburbs, that has computerised ticketing.

Central Railways (134), handling services to the east, south, plus a few trains to the north, operates from CST. The reservation centre (Map p124; 139; 8am-8pm Mon-Sat, to 2pm Sun) is around the side of CST where the taxis gather. Foreign tourist-quota tickets (Counter 52) can be bought up to 90 days before travel, but must be paid in foreign currency or with rupees backed by an encashment certificate or ATM

receipt. Indrail passes (boxed text, p445) can also be bought at Counter 52. You can buy nonquota tickets with a Visa or MasterCard at the much faster credit-card counters (10 and 11) for a ₹30 fee. Refunds for Indians and foreigners alike are handled at Counter 8.

Some Central Railways trains depart from Dadar (D), a few stations north of CST, or Churchgate/Lokmanya Tilak (T), 16km north of CST.

Western Railways (131, 132) has services to the north (including Rajasthan and Delhi) from Mumbai Central (MC) train station (23061763, 23073535), usually called Bombay Central. The reservation centre (Map p124; 8am-8pm Mon-Sat, to 2pm Sun), opposite Churchgate train station, has a foreign tourist-quota counter (Counter 14). The same rules apply as at CST station. The credit-card counter is No 6.

🛈 Getting Around

To/From the Airports

INTERNATIONAL The prepaid-taxi booth that is located at the international airport has set fares for every neighbourhood in the city; Colaba, Fort and Marine Dr are AC/non-AC ₹495/395, Bandra West ₹310/260 and Juhu ₹235/190. There's a ₹10 service charge and a charge of ₹10 per bag. The journey to Colaba takes about 45 minutes at

Marine Drive at night

ORIEN HARVEY/LONELY PLANET IMAGES

Detour:
Elephant Island

In the middle of Mumbai Harbour, 9km northeast of the Gateway of India, the rock-cut temples on **Elephanta Island** (http://asi.nic.in/; Indian/foreigner ₹10/250; ⊙caves 9am-5.30pm Tue-Sun) are a Unesco World Heritage Site and worth crossing the waters for.

The temples are thought to have been created between AD 450 and 750, when the island was known as Gharapuri (Place of Caves). The Portuguese renamed it Elephanta because of a large stone elephant near the shore, which collapsed in 1814 and was moved by the British to Mumbai's Jijamata Udyan.

The English-language guide service (free with deluxe boat tickets) is worthwhile; tours depart every hour on the half-hour from the ticket booth. Beware of touts that meet you at the jetty and try to convince you to employ their services – the included English guide will meet you at the entrance to the temples.

Launches (Map p122; economy/deluxe ₹105/130) head to Elephanta Island from the Gateway of India every half-hour from 9am to 3.30pm Tuesday to Sunday. Buy tickets at the booths lining Apollo Bunder. The voyage takes just over an hour. The ferries dock at the end of a concrete pier, from where you can walk (around three minutes) or take the **miniature train** (₹10) to the **stairway** (admission ₹5) leading up to the caves.

night and 1½ to two hours during the day. Tips are not required.

A taxi from South Mumbai to the international airport should be between ₹350 and ₹400 by negotiating a fixed fare beforehand; official baggage charges are ₹10 per bag. Add 25% to the meter charge between midnight and 5am. We love the old-school black-and-yellows, but there are also AC, metered call taxis run by **Meru** (☑44224422; www.merucabs.com), charging ₹20 for the first kilometre and ₹14 per kilometre thereafter (25% more at night).

DOMESTIC Taxis and autorickshaws queue up outside both domestic terminals. The prepaid counter is outside arrivals. A non-AC/AC taxi to Colaba or Fort costs ₹350/400, day or night, plus ₹10 per bag. For Juhu, it's ₹150/200.

Car

Cars are generally hired for an eight-hour day and an 80km maximum, with additional charges if you go over. For an AC car, the best going rate is about ₹1000.

Agents at the Apollo Bunder ticket booths near the Gateway of India can arrange a non-AC Maruti with driver for a half-day of sightseeing for ₹1000

(going as far as Mahalaxmi and Malabar Hill). Regular taxi drivers often accept a similar price.

Taxi & Autorickshaw

Drivers don't always know the names of Mumbai's streets (especially new names) – the best way to find something is by using nearby landmarks. A 2010 fare increase means taxi meters start at ₹16 during the day (₹20 after midnight) for the first 1.6km and ₹10 per kilometre after this (₹12 after midnight). If you get a taxi with the old-fashioned meters, the fare will be roughly 16 times the amount shown.

MAHARASHTRA

Aurangabad
☑0240 / POP 892,400 / ELEV 515M

Aurangabad lay low through most of the tumultuous history of medieval India and only hit the spotlight when the last Mughal emperor, Aurangzeb, made the city his capital from 1653 to 1707. With the emperor's death came the city's rapid decline, but the brief period of glory saw the building of some fascinating monuments, including a Taj Mahal replica (Bibi-qa-Maqbara), that continue to draw a steady trickle of visitors today. But the real reason for traipsing all the way here is because the town is an excellent base for exploring the World Heritage Sites of Ellora and Ajanta.

Sights

BIBI-QA-MAQBARA — Monument
(Indian/foreigner ₹5/100; ⊙dawn-10pm) Built by Aurangzeb's son Azam Khan in 1679 as a mausoleum for his mother Rabia-ud-Daurani, Bibi-qa-Maqbara is widely known as the 'poor man's Taj'. With its four minarets flanking a central onion-domed mausoleum, the white structure bears a striking resemblance to the original Taj Mahal in Agra. However, it is much less grand, and apart from having a few marble adornments, most of the structure is finished in lime mortar.

Tours

Classic Tours (☎2337788; www.classictours.info; MTDC Holiday Resort, Station Rd East) and the **Indian Tourism Development Corporation** (ITDC; ☎2331143) both run daily bus tours to the **Ajanta caves** (₹400; ⊙8am-5.30pm Tue-Sun) and **Ellora caves** (₹270; ⊙9.30am-5.30pm Wed-Mon), which include a guide but don't cover admission fees.

For private tours, try **Ashoka Tours & Travels** (☎9890340816; Hotel Panchavati, Station Rd West), which owns a decent fleet of taxis and can personalise your trip around Aurangabad and to Ajanta and Ellora.

Sleeping

LEMON TREE — Hotel **$$**
(☎6603030; www.lemontreehotels.com; R7/2 Chikalthana, Airport Rd; s/d incl breakfast from ₹3499/4499; ❄☎☎) Fresh as lemonade, this swish, all-new boutique hotel (spread lazily around what we thought was the best swimming pool in the Deccan)

makes you want to stay back in Aurangabad even after you're done sightseeing.

HOTEL PANCHAVATI — Hotel **$**
(☎2328755; www.hotelpanchavati.com; Station Rd West; s/d ₹525/625, with AC ₹775/900; ❄) This place is fast establishing itself as one of the more reputed hotels in Aurangabad (quite a turnaround from the days when it took some serious stick from travellers). Generally packed to the gills with guests, it offers a range of compact but thoughtfully appointed rooms, with comfortable beds and patterned rugs on the floor that match the upholstery and pastel wall shades.

Eating

CHINA TOWN — Chinese **$$**
(Hotel Amarpreet, Jalna Rd; mains ₹180-200) For a place like Aurangabad, this in-house restaurant at Hotel Amarpreet tosses up Chinese dishes of a surprisingly fine quality. A good range of noodles is on offer, which goes extremely well with the numerous chicken and lamb preparations all presented appetisingly in the restaurant's well-dressed interiors.

SWAD VEG RESTAURANT — Indian **$**
(Kanchan Chamber, Station Rd East; mains ₹70-80) This place has come a long way since its formative years, and now offers a fantastic range of Indian snacks and staples – plus a few pizzas, ice creams and shakes – in its prim and clean basement premises.

ⓘ Getting There & Away

Air

The airport is 10km east of town. En route are the offices of Indian Airlines (☎2485241; Jalna Rd) and Jet Airways (☎2441392; Jalna Rd). There are daily flights to Delhi, with a stopover in Mumbai. Fares start from around ₹1500.

Bus

Ordinary buses head to Ellora from the MSRTC bus stand every half hour (₹28, 45 minutes) and hourly to Jalgaon (₹122, four hours) via Fardapur (₹80, two hours). The T-junction near Fardapur is the drop-off point for Ajanta (see p141 for more details)

Train

Aurangabad's train station (Station Rd East) is not on a main line, but two heavily booked trains, the *Tapovan Express* (2nd class/chair ₹102/338, 7½ hours, 2.35pm) and the *Janshatabdi Express* (2nd class/chair ₹127/420, 6½ hours, 6am) run daily to/from Mumbai.

❶ Getting Around

The taxi stand is next to the MSRTC bus stand; share jeeps also depart from here for destinations around Aurangabad, including Ellora. Expect to pay ₹600 for a full-day rickshaw tour, or ₹900 in a taxi.

Ellora

02437

A hammer and chisel can create art that lasts. Come to the World Heritage Site–listed **Ellora cave temples** (Indian/foreigner ₹10/250; ⏰dawn-dusk Wed-Mon), located 30km from Aurangabad, and you'll know exactly what we mean. The epitome of ancient Indian rock-cut architecture, these caves were chipped out laboriously over five centuries by generations of Buddhist, Hindu and Jain monks. Unlike the caves at Ajanta (p139), which are carved into a sheer rock face, the Ellora caves line a 2km-long escarpment, the gentle slope of which allowed architects to build elaborate courtyards in front of the shrines, and render them with sculptures of a surreal quality.

Official guides can be hired at the ticket office in front of the Kailasa Temple for ₹700. Most guides have an extensive knowledge of cave architecture, so try not to skimp. If your tight itinerary forces you to choose between Ellora or Ajanta, Ellora wins hands down.

◉ Sights

KAILASA TEMPLE   Hindu Temple
Halfway between a cave and a religious shrine, this **rock-cut temple**, built by King Krishna I of the Rashtrakuta dynasty in AD 760, was built to represent Mt Kailasa (Kailash), Shiva's Himalayan abode. To say that the assignment was daring would be an understatement. Three huge trenches were bored into the sheer cliff face with hammers and chisels, following which the shape was 'released', a process that entailed removing 200,000 tonnes of rock!

Kailasa Temple

The temple houses several intricately carved panels, depicting scenes from the Ramayana, the Mahabharata and the adventures of Krishna. Also worth admiring are the immense **monolithic pillars** that stand in the courtyard, flanking the entrance on both sides, and the southeastern gallery that has 10 giant and fabulous panels depicting the different avatars of Lord Vishnu.

BUDDHIST CAVES

The southernmost 12 caves are Buddhist *viharas* (monasteries), except Cave 10, which is a *chaitya* (assembly hall).

Cave 1, the simplest *vihara*, may have been a granary. **Cave 2** is notable for its ornate pillars and the imposing seated Buddha, which faces the setting sun. **Cave 3** and **Cave 4** are unfinished and not well-preserved.

Cave 5 is the largest *vihara* in this group, at 18m wide and 36m long; the rows of stone benches hint that it may once have been an assembly hall.

Cave 6 is an ornate *vihara* with wonderful images of Tara, consort of the Bodhisattva Avalokitesvara, and of the Buddhist goddess of learning, Mahamayuri, looking remarkably similar to Saraswati, her Hindu equivalent. **Cave** is an unadorned hall, but from here you can pass through a doorway to **Cave 8**, the first cave in which the sanctum is detached from the rear wall. **Cave 9** is notable for its wonderfully carved fascia.

Cave 10 is the only *chaitya* in the Buddhist group and one of the finest in India. Its ceiling features ribs carved into the stonework; the grooves were once fitted with wooden panels.

Cave 11, the Do Thal (Two Storey) Cave is entered through its third basement level, not discovered until 1876. Like Cave 12, it probably owes its size to competitio with the more impressive Hindu caves of the same period.

Cave 12, the huge Tin Thal (Three Storey) Cave, is entered through a courtyard. The locked shrine on the top floor contains a large Buddha figure flanked by his seven previous incarnations

HINDU CAVES

The Buddhist caves are calm and contemplative, but drama and excitement characterise the Hindu group (Caves 13 to 29).

Buddha statue in Cave 10, Kailasa Temple

All these temples were cut from the top down, so it was never necessary to use scaffolding – the builders began with the roof and moved down to the floor.

Cave 13 is a simple cave, most likely a granary. **Cave 14**, the Ravana-ki-Khai, is a Buddhist *vihara* converted to a temple dedicated to Shiva sometime in the 7th century.

Cave 15, the Das Avatara (Ten Incarnations of Vishnu) Cave, is one of the finest at Ellora. The two-storey temple contains a mesmerising Shiva Nataraja, and Shiva emerging from a lingam (phallic image) while Vishnu and Brahma pay homage.

Caves 17 to **20** and **22** to **28** are simple monasteries.

Cave 21, known as the Ramesvara Cave, features interesting interpretations of familiar Shaivite scenes depicted in the earlier temples.

The large **Cave 29**, the Dumar Lena, is thought to be a transitional model between the simpler hollowed-out caves and the fully developed temples exemplified by the Kailasa.

JAIN CAVES   Caves

The five Jain caves may lack the artistic vigour and ambitious size of the best Hindu temples, but they are exceptionally detailed. The caves are 1km north of the last Hindu temple (Cave 29) at the end of the bitumen road.

Cave 30, the Chhota Kailasa (Little Kailasa), is a poor imitation of the great Kailasa Temple and stands by itself some distance from the other Jain temples.

In contrast, **Cave 32**, the Indra Sabha (Assembly Hall of Indra), is the finest of the Jain temples. Its ground-floor plan is similar to that of the Kailasa, but the upstairs area is as ornate and richly decorated as the downstairs is plain.

Cave 31 is really an extension of Cave 32. **Cave 33**, the Jagannath Sabha, is similar in plan to 32 and has some well-preserved sculptures. The final temple, the small **Cave 34**, also has interesting sculptures. On the hilltop over the Jain temples, a 5m-high image of Parasnath looks down on Ellora.

 Eating

The spotless **MTDC Ellora Restaurant & Beer Bar** (mains ₹60-90; ⊙9am-5pm), located within the complex, is a good place to settle in for lunch, or pack takeaways in case you want to picnic beside the caves.

❶ Getting There & Away

Buses regularly ply the road between Aurangabad and Ellora (₹28); the last bus departs from Ellora at 8pm. Share jeeps leave when they're full with drop-off outside the bus stand in Aurangabad (₹40). A full-day autorickshaw tour to Ellora, with stops en route, costs ₹600; taxis charge around ₹900.

Ajanta
☎02438

Fiercely guarding its horde of priceless artistic treasures from another era, the **Buddhist caves of Ajanta** (Indian/foreigner ₹10/250, video ₹25; ⊙9am-5.30pm Tue-Sun), 105km northeast of Aurangabad, could well be called the Louvre of ancient India. Much older than Ellora, their venerable twin in the World Heritage Sites listings, these secluded caves date from around the 2nd century BC to the 6th century AD and were among the earliest monastic institutions to be constructed in the country.

 **Sights & Activities**

THE CAVES   Caves

The 30 caves of Ajanta line the steep face of a horseshoe-shaped rock gorge bordering the Waghore River flowing below.

Cave 1, a Mahayana *vihara*, was one of the last to be excavated and is the most beautifully decorated. This is where you'll find a rendition of the **Bodhisattva Padmapani**, the most famous and iconic of the Ajanta artworks. A verandah in front leads to a large congregation hall, housing sculptures and narrative murals known for their splendid perspective and elaborate detailing of dress, daily

DISCOVER MUMBAI (BOMBAY) & AROUND   MAHARASHTRA

life and facial expressions. The colours in the paintings were created from local minerals, with the exception of the vibrant blue made from Central Asian lapis lazuli.

Cave 2 is also a late Mahayana *vihara* with deliriously ornamented columns and capitals, and some fine paintings. The ceiling is decorated with geometric and floral patterns.

Cave 4 is the largest *vihara* at Ajanta and is supported by 28 pillars. Although never completed, the cave has some impressive sculptures, including scenes of people fleeing from the 'eight great dangers' to the protection of Avalokitesvara.

Cave 6 is the only two-storey *vihara* at Ajanta, but parts of the lower storey have collapsed. Inside is a seated Buddha figure and an intricately carved door to the shrine.

Cave 7 has an atypical design, with porches before the verandah, leading directly to the four cells and the elaborately sculptured shrine.

Cave 9 is one of the earliest *chaityas* at Ajanta. Although it dates from the early Buddhist period, the two figures flanking the entrance door were probably later Mahayana additions. Columns run down both sides of the cave and around the 3m-high dagoba (stupa) at the far end. The vaulted roof has traces of wooden ribs.

Cave 10 is thought to be the oldest cave, dating from 200 BC. Similar in design to Cave 9, it is the largest *chaitya*. One of the pillars to the right bears the engraved name of John Smith, the British officer who rediscovered the caves in 1819 and left his mark here for posterity.

Cave 16, a *vihara*, contains some of Ajanta's finest paintings and is thought to have been the original entrance to the entire complex.

Cave 17, with carved dwarfs supporting the pillars, has Ajanta's best-preserved and

most varied paintings. Famous images include a princess applying make-up, a seductive prince using the old trick of plying his lover with wine, and the Buddha returning home from his enlightenment to beg from his wife and astonished son.

Cave 19, a magnificent *chaitya*, has a remarkably detailed facade; its dominant feature is an impressive horseshoe-shaped window. Two fine, standing Buddha figures flank the entrance. Inside is a three-tiered dagoba with a figure of the Buddha on the front.

Cave 24, had it been finished, would be the largest *vihara* at Ajanta. You can see how the caves were constructed – long galleries were cut in and then the rock between them was broken through.

Cave 26, a largely ruined *chaitya*, is now dramatically lit, and contains some fine sculptures that shouldn't be missed. On the left wall is a huge figure of the 'reclining Buddha', lying back in preparation for nirvana.

Cave 27 is virtually a *vihara* connected to the Cave 26 *chaitya*.

 Eating

If you pack a picnic, you can enjoy it in the shady park below Caves 22 to 27. There's also a buzzing refreshment centre by the main ticket office (at Ajanta caves), which serves an overpriced vegetarian thali (₹80) and warm beer.

ⓘ Getting There & Away

Buses from Aurangabad will drop you off at the T-junction (where the highway meets the road to the caves), 4km from the site. From here, after paying an 'amenities' fee (₹7), race to the departure point for the green-coloured 'pollution-free' buses (with/without AC ₹12/7), which zoom up to the caves. Buses return on a regular basis (half-hourly, last bus at 6.15pm) to the T-junction.

After the caves close you can board buses to Aurangabad outside the MTDC Holiday Resort in Fardapur, 1km down the main road towards Jalgaon. Taxis are available in Fardapur.

141

Rajasthan

Rajasthan, the Land of Kings, is a fabulous realm of maharajas, majestic forts and lavish palaces. While its people-charged cities throb with the crowds and chaos of emerging India, the treasures of the past hold pride of place in mind and spirit.

The romantic remnants of a rich and glorious past are the elements that draw most visitors to Rajasthan. Yet this iconic region of the subcontinent is not just a historical and architectural feast. It is a land of desert dunes and jungle, camel trains and tigers, glittering jewels and a vibrant culture set against a barren landscape. There are enough festivals here to fill a calendar, vivid colours to complete an artist's palette, and the cityscapes (where else has blue, pink and golden cities?), shopping and cuisine combine to make this one of India's must-visit states.

A painted elephant with his keeper

Rajasthan

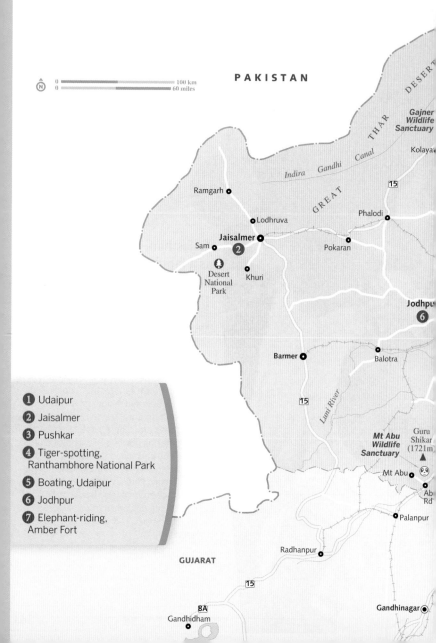

PAKISTAN

0 ——— 100 km
0 ——— 60 miles

DESERT

THAR

Gajner Wildlife Sanctuary

Kolaya

Indira Gandhi Canal

GREAT

15

Ramgarh

Phalodi

Lodhruva

Jaisalmer ②

Pokaran

Sam

Desert National Park

Khuri

Jodhpu

⑥

Barmer

Balotra

15

Luni River

Mt Abu Wildlife Sanctuary

Guru Shikar (1721m) ▲

Mt Abu

29

Ab Rd

Palanpur

① Udaipur
② Jaisalmer
③ Pushkar
④ Tiger-spotting, Ranthambhore National Park
⑤ Boating, Udaipur
⑥ Jodhpur
⑦ Elephant-riding, Amber Fort

GUJARAT

Radhanpur

15

8A

Gandhidham

Gandhinagar

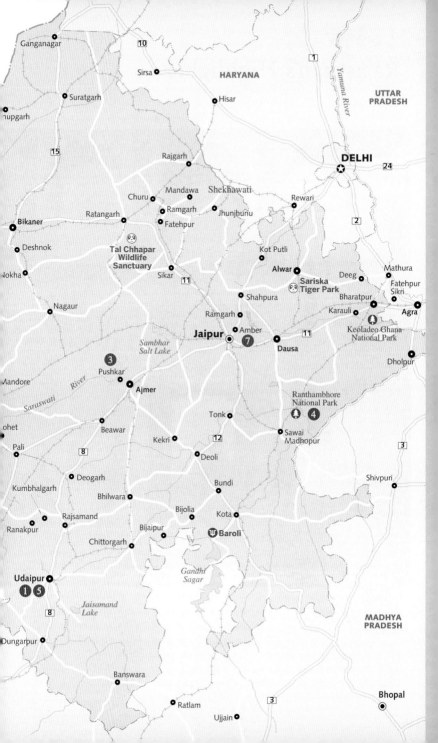

Rajasthan's Highlights

1

Udaipur

Surrounded by the wooded ridges of the Aravalli Hills and centred on two glimmering, mirror-calm lakes, Udaipur (p170) is Rajasthan's most romantic city, home to serene views on sunny rooftops; fantastical, lace-like, cupola-topped palaces, temples and *havelis* (noble houses); and narrow, crooked, colourful streets. Above: Courtyard, City Palace; Top Right: Lake Pichola; Bottom Right: Peacock mosaic, City Palace

Need to Know
TEA The City Palace restaurant has high tea and lake views. **BOAT RIDES** Pay the palace admission fee to reach the City Palace jetty. **For more, see p170 and Map p170.**

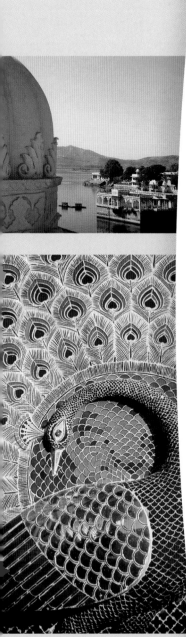

Udaipur Don't Miss List

PIERS HELSON LIVED IN UDAIPUR FOR OVER 12 YEARS. HE HAS WRITTEN BOOKS ON THE CITY AND FOUNDED THE MAGAZINE *OUT & ABOUT IN UDAIPUR*

1 CITY PALACE

The City Palace appears to be a single residence towering above the lake, giving rise to the claim that it is Rajasthan's largest palace complex. However, Udai Singh's original palace continued to be added to on its northern side by as many as 22 later maharanas: it is really four major and several minor palaces with a unique single facade. A blend of Rajput and Mughal styles, its architectural unity has been impeccably maintained.

2 ROYAL CENOTAPHS

When Maharana Amar Singh I (1597–1620) died, he was cremated at Ahar. His son, Maharana Karan Singh raised a magnificent *chatri* or cenotaph in memory of his father. Since then, Ahar has been the Mewar royal family's *mahasati* (cremation site). The memorials are carved with decorations resembling 15th-century temples nearby, and with carved figures representing the maharana and each of his *satis* (his wives who died in his cremation flames).

3 BAGORE-KI-HAVELI

Gangaur Ghat is one of Udaipur's most elegant and noticeable waterfront facades, with its charming triple-arched gateway leading onto a broad lakeside piazza. To the side of this gateway is one of the finest *havelis* (noble houses) in the city, the splendidly restored Bagore-ki-Haveli.

4 TRIBAL MUSEUM

This museum, within the Tribal Research Institute, is Udaipur's best-kept secret. The display is amazingly imaginative, with life-like scenes beautifully created to put the artefacts into context. The institute also boasts an exceptionally well-maintained, well-stocked library.

5 SAHELION-KI-BARI

Enclosed by high walls, separating the park from woodland, 'Garden of the Maidens' feels like a secret garden. The walls served not only to protect the gardens, but to protect those within – this was designed as a haven for the noble and royal ladies of Udaipur. The fountains here function solely by water pressure, with no pumps.

Jaisalmer

Rising from the desert scrub like a beautiful, oversized sandcastle, surrounded by 99 bastions, the city of Jaisalmer (p183) resonates with its history. Despite today's commercialism, it retains a sense of epic romance. Visiting the ancient citadel and exploring the desert on camelback are mirage-like, otherworldly experiences that will stay with you long after you leave.

Need to Know

ADVICE Ask other travellers before choosing a camel-trek operator.
HOTELS The trade-off for cheap rooms may be a hard sell on camel safaris. **For more, see p183 and Map p184.**

2

Jaisalmer Don't Miss List

RADHIKA DHUMAL IS A DELHI-
BASED CONSERVATION ARCHITECT,
OVERSEEING JAISALMER IN JEOPARDY'S
STREETSCAPE PROJECT

1 THE FORT

Jaisalmer Fort (far left and below left) owes its magnificence to its location on the main trade route linking India to Egypt, Arabia, Persia, Africa and the West. Its prosperity was reflected in its *havelis*, intricately carved wood and sandstone mansions, in the magnificent Royal Palace complex, among the oldest recorded buildings in Rajasthan, and in the incomparable Jain Temple complex, dating from the 12th and 13th centuries. Carved in the Dilwara style from the local yellow sandstone, the complex is dedicated to Rakhab and Shambhaydev, the famous Jain Hermits known as Tirhankars.

2 CAMEL TREKKING

No visit to Jaisalmer is complete without a visit to the Thar desert. I recommend a moonlight camel trek over the dunes followed by dinner under the stars.

3 SUNSET VIEWS

The most sublime view of Jaisalmer Fort is from the roof of **Jawahar Niwas Hotel** (www.jawaharniwaspalace .co.in; 1 Bada Bagh Rd), sipping a gin and tonic as the setting sun reflects on the golden sandstone. Originally a royal guesthouse, Jawahar Niwas is sited 800m from the bustle of the fort.

4 HIKING

I would recommend the 5km hike around Jaisalmer Fort's 99 bastions, preferably at dawn, as the city sleeps and your only companions are the slumbering cows.

5 DINING

At Jaisal Italy (p188) in Aklhey Prol, you can dine indoors if the desert nights turn cold, or outside on the terrace while watching a performance of Rajasthani musicians and dancers below.

Pushkar

The pastel-hued pilgrimage destination of Pushkar (p165) is a mystical small town set aro a holy lake. Although it's a popular travellers' stop, the town feels essentially spiritual, and there's always something going on at one of the temples around the lake. The diminutive town also hosts one of India's most famous fairs, the Pushkar Camel Fair (p168).

3

4 Tiger-spotting, Ranthambhore

Ranthambhore (p168) is one of India's most spectacular national parks, an ar of lush, tangled jungle dotted by ruine *chhatris* (cenotaphs) and temples, topped by a magical cliff-top fortress, and inhabited by exotic birds and wild animals, including, of course, tigers. T big cats are used to visitors and you h a good chance of spotting one here.

Boating in Udaipur

Udaipur (p170), prettily pale white and set around several mirror-flat lakes, is India's most romantic place to go boating. Float by boat across Lake Pichola, watching the surface reflect the sunset, the birds flutter overhead, and the distant Aravalli Hills turn from milky blue to shadowy purple.

Jodhpur

The blue city (p177) really is blue, as you'll see when you climb up to its majestic fortress, Mehrangarh, which rears out of its rocky escarpment like a vision from a fairytale. Listen to the blue city's secrets from its soaring ramparts, and get lost in its glittering bazaars, where you can buy polished tubas and trumpets, heaped spices, jewellery and shimmering temple decorations.

Riding by Elephant to Amber Fort

Outside Jaipur, Amber Fort (p167) tops a rocky ridge, coloured peach against the dust of the cliff. Draw closer and the scale of the building becomes clear – this was the Kachhwahas capital before Jai Singh built Jaipur. In the morning, it's possible to ride an elephant up the steep, zigzagging road to the gate. The mighty beasts, driven by mahouts, are usually painted as though for a festival.

Rajasthan's Best…

Palace Hotels

○ **Samode Haveli** (p160) Some beautiful mirrored suites in Jaipur's old city

○ **Rambagh Palace** (p160) Once the Jaipur pad of Maharaja Man Singh II, in 19 hectares of gardens

○ **Jagat Niwas Palace Hotel** (p171) Two adjoining *havelis* overlooking Lake Pichola in Udaipur

○ **Taj Lake Palace** (p173) Romantic white-marble palace

○ **Hotel Nachana Haveli** (p185) A sandstone-carved hotel in a 280-year-old palace in Jaisalmer

Wining & Dining

○ **Indique** (p180) Jodhpur's candle-lit rooftop restaurant, with old-city views

○ **Nirvana** (p181) With panoramic views and delicious food, in Jodhpur

○ **Niro's** (p161) A soothing sanctum serving reliably tasty dishes in Jaipur

○ **LMB** (p162) Pure veg in retro-disco surroundings in Jaipur's old city

○ **Ambrai** (p174) Udaipur's loveliest waterfront restaurant

○ **Sixth Sense** (p167) Chilled rooftop oasis in Pushkar

Forts

○ **Amber Fort** (p167) Magnificent fort outside Jaipur

○ **Mehrangarh** (p177) Muscular edifice overlooking Jodhpur

○ **Ranthambore** (p168) Jungle fort in tiger-inhabited national park

○ **Jaisalmer** (p183) Sandcastle-like desert fortress

Need to Know

Cultural Experiences

Haggling in Jaipur (p163) The Rajasthani capital's glittering bazaars are a delight

Chokhi Dhani (p162) Mock local village, south of Jaipur, with dazzling performing arts, such as dancers with flaming hats

Jaisalmer Desert Villages (p183) The vibrancy of desert life, visited on camel back

Temples in Pushkar (p165) One of Rajasthan's holiest towns, with constant devotional hubbub

ADVANCE PLANNING

○ **Two months before** Book any particularly special palace hotels, especially during the high season (October to March)

○ **One week before** Book train tickets for longer journeys

○ **One day before** Call your hotel to confirm your booking

RESOURCES

○ **Festivals of India** (www.festivalsofindia.in) All about Indian festivals

○ **Incredible India** (www.incredibleindia.org) Official India tourism site

○ **Rajasthan Tourism Development Corporation** (www.rtdc. in) Rajasthan government tourism site

○ **Lonely Planet** (www.lonelyplanet.com/ india/rajasthan) Destination and accommodation information, plus the Thorn Tree travellers' forum

GETTING AROUND

○ **Car & driver** The standard rate hovers around ₹6 per km (petrol prices permitting), with a minimum of 250km per day, plus ₹100–150 per overnight stay

○ **Train** Jaipur, Sawai Madohpur (for Ranthambore), Jaipur, Udaipur, Jodhpur and Jaisalmer are all served by rail. Pushkar's nearest rail hub is Ajmer, 30 minutes' drive away

○ **Bus** All destinations are served by bus; AC Volvo buses tend to be the most comfortable

BE FOREWARNED

○ **Gem scams** Don't get smooth-talked into buying gems with an eye to making a profit

○ **Camel safaris** Ask other travellers for recommendations of the best operators

○ **Pushkar Camel Fair** Prices rocket in Pushkar at the time of its famous camel fair (usually October/November), and you'll need to book well ahead

Left: A painted Indian elephant;
Above: The Amber Fort (p167)
(LEFT) CHRISTER FREDRIKSSON/LONELY PLANET IMAGES ©;
(ABOVE) TIM MAKINS/LONELY PLANET IMAGES ©

Rajasthan Itineraries

The first of these itineraries covers the eastern highlights of Rajasthan, while the second takes in several of the most spectacular desert cities of the western part of the region. For a longer stay you could combine the two journeys.

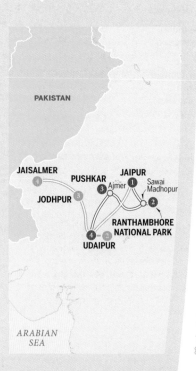

PAKISTAN

JAISALMER
PUSHKAR
JODHPUR
JAIPUR
Ajmer
Sawai Madhopur

RANTHAMBHORE
NATIONAL PARK
UDAIPUR

ARABIAN
SEA

5 DAYS

JAIPUR TO UDAIPUR
Eastern Promise

Start your trip in the pink city of **(1) Jaipur**, visiting its colourful bazaars, City Palace, Amber Fort and Hawa Mahal. Next you can take a train from here to Sawai Madhopur, the nearest station to **(2) Ranthambhore National Park**, to explore the lush jungle landscape of the park, with its myriad wildlife, see its ancient, overgrown fort, and go tiger-spotting.

Returning from Sawai Madhopur, take the train to Ajmer, from where it's a short hop by taxi or bus to the magical small town of **(3) Pushkar**. Spend a day chilling out in this beguilingly pretty pilgrimage and traveller centre, lazing on its rooftop cafes and seeing the sunset from its Monsoon Palace. Next you can either hire a taxi for the next leg of the journey, or return to Ajmer to travel to **(4) Udaipur** by train. The milk-white city of Udaipur, built across several lakes, is the ideal place to end your journey on a high, exploring its impressive City Palace and spending your last day boating on beautiful Lake Pichola before taking an internal flight back to your starting point.

Top Left: Woman dressed for a wedding;
Top Right: Exterior, Patwa-ki-Haveli (p183)
(TOP LEFT) ANDERS BLOMQVIST/LONELY PLANET IMAGES ©;
(TOP RIGHT) KEREN SU/LONELY PLANET IMAGES ©

Western Desert

gain start your trip in the Rajasthani capital, **(1) Jaipur**, visiting the sights of the pink city, cluding the City Palace and Amber Fort, and seeing a blockbusting Bollywood film at its eringue-like, sumptuous Rajmandir Cinema. Next, make your way via train or taxi to the id-back town of **(2) Udaipur** to visit its City Palace, indulge in some lakeside lazing, and ke boats across Lake Pichola against a backdrop of misty blue hills.

The easiest and quickest way to reach **(3) Jodhpur** from Udaipur is to hire a taxi. Thus ou can make your way to the blue city, an amazing impressionistic cityscape overlooked the magnificent fortifications of Mehrangarh. Spend your time here visiting the fort self, for wonderful views over the city, and don't miss the old city's glittering bazaars. lake sure you book ahead for the overnight train to the desert city of **(4) Jaisalmer**, here you can explore the golden sandstone fort, see its beautifully carved *havelis* and ain temples, and take an overnight trip into the desert on camelback, spending the night nder a firmament of stars.

Discover Rajasthan

EASTERN RAJASTHAN

Jaipur

🕿 0141 / 3.21 MILLION

Jaipur, Rajasthan's capital, is an enthralling historical city and the gateway to India's most flamboyant state.

The city's colourful, chaotic streets ebb and flow with a heady brew of old and new. Careering buses dodge dawdling camels, leisurely cycle-rickshaws frustrate swarms of motorbikes, and everywhere buzzing autorickshaws watch for easy prey. In the midst of this mayhem, the splendours of Jaipur's majestic past are islands of relative calm evoking a different pace and another world. At the city's heart, the City Palace continues to house the former royal family; the Jantar Mantar, the royal observatory maintains a heavenly aspect; and the honeycomb Hawa Mahal gazes on the bazaar below.

 Sights

Consider buying a **composite ticket** (Indian/foreigner ₹50/300) which gives you entry to Amber Fort, Central Museum, Jantar Mantar, Hawa Mahal and Narhargarh and is valid for two days from time of purchase.

Old City (Pink City)

The Old City is partially encircled by a crenellated wall punctuated at intervals by grand gateways. The major gates are Chandpol (*pol* means 'gate'), Ajmer Gate and Sanganeri Gate.

CITY PALACE Palace
(Indian/foreigner incl camera & audio guide ₹75/300, video camera ₹200, Chandra Mahal tour ₹2500; ⏱9.30am-5pm) A complex of

Blue-painted laneway, Jodhpur (p177)
JOHNNY HAGLUND/LONELY PLANET IMAGES ©

RICHARD I'ANSON/LONELY PLANET IMAGES ©

Don't Miss **Iswari Minar Swarga Sal**

Piercing the skyline near the City Palace is the unusual **Iswari Minar Swarga Sal** (Heaven-Piercing Minaret), just west of Tripolia Gate. The minaret was erected by Jai Singh's son Iswari, who later ignominiously killed himself by snakebite (in the Chandra Mahal) rather than face the advancing Maratha army; his 21 wives and concubines then did the necessary noble thing and committed *jauhar* (ritual mass suicide by immolation) on his funeral pyre. You can take a spiral staircase to the top of the minaret for excellent views.

View of Jaipur from Iswari Minar Swarga Sal

THINGS YOU NEED TO KNOW
Indian/foreigner ₹5/10, camera ₹10; ⊙9am-4.30pm

courtyards, gardens and buildings, the impressive City Palace is right in the centre of the Old City. The outer wall was built by Jai Singh, but within it the palace has been enlarged and adapted over the centuries. Despite the gradual development, the whole is a striking blend of Rajasthani and Mughal architecture.

JANTAR MANTAR Historic Site
(Indian/foreigner ₹20/100 incl audio guide, optional guide Hindi/English ₹200/250; ⊙9am-4.30pm)
Adjacent to the City Palace is Jantar Mantar, an observatory begun by Jai Singh in 1728 that resembles a collection of

bizarre sculptures. In 2010 it was added to India's list of World Heritage Sites.

HAWA MAHAL Historic Building
(Palace of the Winds; Indian/foreigner incl camera ₹10/50, audio guide Hindi/English ₹80/110, guide ₹200; ⊙9am-5pm) Jaipur's most distinctive landmark, the Hawa Mahal is an extraordinary, fairy-tale, pink-sandstone, delicately honeycombed hive that rises a dizzying five storeys. It was constructed in 1799 by Maharaja Sawai Pratap Singh to enable ladies of the royal household to watch the life and processions of the city.

Jaipur

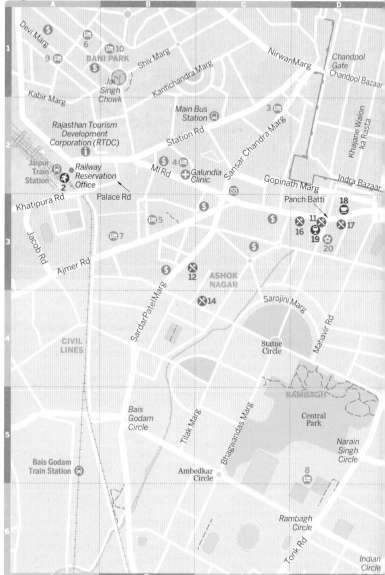

Map of Jaipur showing: Devi Marg, Bani Park (6, 10, 9), Shiv Marg, Jai Singh Chowk, Kabir Marg, Kantichandra Marg, Nirwan Marg, Chandpol Gate, Chandpol Bazaar, Main Bus Station, Station Rd, Rajasthan Tourism Development Corporation (RTDC), Sansar Chandra Marg, Khajane Walon ka Rasta, Jaipur Train Station, Railway Reservation Office, MI Rd (4), Galundia Clinic, Gopinath Marg, Indra Bazaar, Palace Rd, Khatipura Rd, Panch Batti (11, 16, 18, 17, 19, 20), Jacob Rd, Ajmer Rd (5, 7), Sardar Patel Marg (12), Ashok Nagar (14), Sarojini Marg, Civil Lines, Statue Circle, Mahavir Rd, Rambagh, Central Park, Bais Godam Circle, Tilak Marg, Bhagwandas Marg, Narain Singh Circle, Bais Godam Train Station, Ambedkar Circle (8), Rambagh Circle, Tonk Rd, Indian Circle

Tours

RTDC   Sightseeing
(☏22020778; tours@rtdc.in; RTDC Tourist
Information Bureau, Platform 1, Jaipur Railway

Station; ⏲8am-6.30pm Mon-Sat) Offers half-/
full-day tours of Jaipur and its surrounds
for ₹150/200. Its **Pink City by Night
tour** (₹250) departs at 6.30pm, explores
several well-known sights, and includes
dinner at Nahargarh Fort. Tours depart

Sleeping

Around MI Road

HOTEL PEARL PALACE Hotel **$**
(☎ 2373700, 9414236323; www.hotelpearl
palace.com; Hari Kishan Somani Marg, Hathroi
Fort; dm ₹175, r ₹350-1200; ❄ @ 🛜) There's
quite a range of rooms to choose from –
small, large, shared bathroom, private
bathroom, some balconied, some with
AC or fan cooled, and all are spotless.
Congenial hosts Mr and Mrs Singh offer
all manner of services including free pick-
up (8am to 11pm only), money-changing
and travel services. Rightfully popular;
advance booking is highly recommended.

PEARL PALACE HERITAGE Hotel **$$**
(☎ 2375242, 9829404055; www.pearlpalace
heritage.com; 54 Gopal Bari, lane 2; r ₹1500-1800;
❄ @ 🛜) The second hotel for the suc-
cessful Pearl Palace team is a midrange
hotel with several special characteris-
tics and great attention to detail. Stone
carvings adorn the halls and each room
recreates an individual cultural theme
such as a village hut, a sandstone fort or a
mirror-lined palace boudoir.

ATITHI GUEST HOUSE Guesthouse **$**
(☎ 2378679; atithijaipur@hotmail.com; 1 Park
House Scheme Rd; s ₹650-1100, d ₹750-1200;
❄ @ 🛜) This well-presented guesthouse,
set between MI and Station Rds, offers
strikingly clean, simple rooms around a
quiet courtyard. It's central but peaceful,
and the service is friendly and helpful.
There's a spotless kitchen and restaurant
(guests only) and you can also dine on
the very pleasant rooftop terrace.

ALSISAR HAVELI Heritage Hotel **$$**
(☎ 2368290; www.alsisar.com; Sansar Chandra
Marg; s/d from ₹3400/4300; ❄ 🏊) Another
genuine heritage hotel that has emerged
from a gracious 19th-century mansion.
Alsisar Haveli is set in beautiful green
gardens, and boasts a lovely swimming pool and a wonderful dining room.
Its bedrooms don't disappoint either,
with elegant Rajput arches and antique
furnishings.

from Jaipur railway station; the company
also picks up and takes bookings from
the RTDC Hotel Teej, RTDC Hotel Gangaur
and the Tourist Information Bureau at the
main bus station.

Jaipur

Bani Park

The Bani Park area is relatively peaceful (away from the main roads), about 2km west of the old city (northwest of MI Rd).

MADHUBAN   Heritage Hotel **$$**
(☎ 2200033; www.madhuban.net; D237 Behari Marg, Bani Park; s ₹1700-2300, d ₹1900-3600; ❋ @ ☎) Madhuban is an elegant, heritage hotel/guesthouse run by the convivial Dicky and his family. It features a range of bright, spotless, antique-furnished rooms including a suite with a Jacuzzi. Most guests gravitate quickly to the peaceful lawn where they can drink tea, read a newspaper over breakfast, watch a puppet show at night or just pat the dog. Money-changing and travel services are available as is free pick-up from the bus or train station.

UMAID BHAWAN Heritage Hotel **$$**
(☎ 2206426; www.umaidbhawan.com; Kali Das Marg, via Bank Rd, Bani Park; s ₹1400-2400, d ₹1600-2800, ste ₹4000; ❋ @ ☎) This mock-heritage hotel, behind the Collectorate in a quiet cul-de-sac, is extravagantly decorated in traditional style. Rooms are stately, full of marble and carved furniture and the rooftop restaurant is wonderful. Free pick-up is available from the train or bus station and all taxes and breakfast are included in the tariff.

SHAHPURA HOUSE Heritage Hotel **$**
(☎ 2203069; www.shahpurahouse.com; D257 Devi Marg, Bani Park; s/d from ₹3000/3500, ste from ₹4500; ❋ @ ☎ ☎) Elaborately built and decorated in traditional style, this heritage hotel offers immaculate rooms, some with balconies, featuring murals, coloured-glass lamps, flat-screen TVs, and even ceilings covered in small mirror (in the suites).

Old City

SAMODE HAVELI Heritage Hotel **$$$**
(☎ 2632370; www.samode.com; Gangapol; s/d incl breakfast from €190/215/198, ste from €250; ❋ @ ☎) Tucked away in the northeast corner of the old city is this charming 200-year-old building, once th town house of the *rawal* (nobleman) of Samode, Jaipur's prime minister. Rooms have large beds and most have private terraces.

Rambagh Environs

RAMBAGH PALACE Heritage Hotel **$$$**
(☎ 2211919; www.tajhotels.com; Bhawan Singh Marg; r from ₹27,500; ❋ @ ☎) This splendid palace was once the Jaipur pad of Maha-

ja Man Singh II and, until recently, his
amorous wife Gayatri Devi. Veiled in 19
ectares of gardens, there are fantastic
ews across the immaculate lawns. Non-
uests can join in the magnificence by
ining in the lavish restaurants or drinking
ea on the gracious verandah.

Eating

Around MI Road

NIRO'S   Indian $$
(2374493; MI Rd; mains ₹110-350; 10am-
pm) Established in 1949, Niro's is a
ong-standing favourite in MI Rd that
ontinues to shine. Escape the chaos of
he street by ducking into its cool, clean,
mirror-ceiling sanctum to savour veg and
onveg Indian cuisine. Classic Chinese
nd Continental food are available but the
ndian menu is definitely the pick.

FOUR SEASONS   Vegetarian $$
(2373700; D43A Subhas Marg; mains
100-210; noon-3.30pm & 6.30-11pm) Four
Seasons is one of Jaipur's best vegetarian
restaurants and being pure vegetarian
here's no alcohol. It's a vastly popular

place on two levels, with a glass wall to
the kitchens. There's a great range of
dishes on offer, including tasty Rajasthani
specialities, dosas and a selection of
pizzas.

LITTLE ITALY   Italian $$
(4022444; 3rd fl, KK Square, C-11, Prithviraj
Marg; mains ₹165-200; noon-3.30pm & 6.30-
11pm) Easily the best Italian restaurant
in town, Little Italy is part of a small
national chain that offers excellent
vegetarian pasta, risotto and wood-fired
pizzas in cool, contemporary surroundings. The menu is extensive and includes
some Mexican items and first-rate Italian
desserts.

MOTI MAHAL DELUX   North Indian $$
(4017733; MI Rd; mains ₹140-300; 11am-
4pm & 7-11pm) The tantalising menu
features a vast range of veg and nonveg,
including seafood and succulent tandoori
dishes. Snuggle into a comfortable booth
and enjoy the ambience, spicy food and,
last but not least, a delicious *pista kulfi*
(pistachio-flavoured sweet similar to ice
cream). Beer and wine available.

Gateway to Jaipur's City Palace (p156)

ORIEN HARVEY/LONELY PLANET IMAGES ©

Detour:
Chokhi Dhani

Chokhi Dhani means 'special village', and this mock **Rajasthani village** (☎2225001; Tonk Rd; adult/child aged 3-9 incl dinner ₹350/200), 20km south of Jaipur, lives up to its name. As well as the restaurants, where you can enjoy an oily Rajasthani thali meal, there is a bevy of traditional entertainment on offer. Wander around and watch traditional tribal dancers setting fire to their hats, children balancing on poles, and dancers dressed in lion costumes lurking in a wood. You can also take elephant or camel rides.

A return taxi from Jaipur, including waiting time, will cost about ₹600.

PEACOCK ROOFTOP RESTAURANT Multicuisine $$
(☎2373700; Hotel Pearl Palace, Hari Kishan Somani Marg, Hathroi Fort; mains ₹35-120; ⊙7am-11pm) This multi-level rooftop restaurant at the popular Hotel Pearl Palace gets rave reviews for its excellent and inexpensive cuisine (Indian, Chinese and Continental) and relaxed ambience. The mouth-watering food, attentive service, whimsical furnishings and romantic view towards Hathroi Fort make this a first-rate restaurant and the economical prices all the more unbelievable.

DĀSAPRAKASH South Indian $$
(☎2371313; Kamal Mansions, MI Rd; mains ₹90-200; ⊙11am-11pm) Part of a renowned chain, Dāsaprakash specialises in South Indian cuisine including thalis and several versions of *dosa* and *idli* (rice cake). Afterwards you can choose from a wonderful selection of cold drinks and over-the-top ice cream sundaes.

Old City

LMB Vegetarian $$
(☎2560845; Johari Bazaar; mains ₹95-190; ⊙11.30am-3.30pm & 7-11pm) Laxmi Misthan Bhandar, LMB to you and me, is a *sattvik* (pure vegetarian) restaurant in the Old City that's been going strong since 1954. Try the Rajasthan thali followed by the signature *kulfa,* a fusion of *kulfi* and *falooda* (a rose-flavoured drink) with dry fruits and saffron.

GANESH RESTAURANT Vegetarian $
(☎2312380; Nehru Bazaar; mains ₹50-90; ⊙9.30am-11pm) This pocket-sized outdoor restaurant is in a fantastic location on the top of the old city wall near New Gate. The cook is in a pit on one side of the wall, so you can check out your pure vegetarian food being cooked. If you're looking for a local eatery with fresh tasty food, such as *paneer butter masala,* you'll love it.

🍷 Drinking & Entertainment

LASSIWALA Lass
(MI Rd; ⊙7.30am till sold out) This famous, much-imitated institution, opposite Niro's, is a simple place that whips up fabulous, creamy lassis at ₹14/28 for a small/jumbo clay cup. Get there early to avoid disappointment! Will the real Lassiwala please stand up? It's the one that says 'Shop 312' and 'Since 1944', directly next to the alleyway. Imitators spread to the right as you face it.

REDS Bar
(☎4007710; 5th fl, Mall 21, Bhagwandas Marg; ⊙11am-midnight Sun-Fri, 11am-1.30pm Sat) Overlooking the Raj Mandir cinema and MI Rd with views to Tiger Fort, slick Reds is a great place to kick back with a drink or take a meal. Drop into one of the low-slung, red-and-black couches with a beer (bottled or draught), cocktail or mocktail and enjoy the sound system.

OLO BAR Bar

ambagh Palace Hotel, Bhawan Singh Rd;
noon-midnight) A spiffing watering hole
dorned with polo memorabilia and
rched, scalloped windows framing the
eatly clipped lawns. A bottle of beer
osts ₹350 to ₹450 and cocktails
round ₹450.

AJ MANDIR CINEMA Cinema

2379372; Baghwandas Marg; admission
50-110; reservations 10am-6pm, screen-
gs 12.30pm, 3.30pm, 6.30pm & 9.30pm) Just
ff MI Rd, Raj Mandir is *the* place to go
see a Hindi film in India. This opulent
nema looks like a huge pink cream
ake, with a meringue auditorium and a
pyer somewhere between a temple and
isneyland. Bookings can be made one
our to seven days in advance at window
os 7 and 8 – this is your best chance of
ecuring a seat, although forget it in the
arly days of a new release. Alternatively,
harpen your elbows and join the queue
hen the current booking office opens
5 minutes before curtain up.

🔒 Shopping

aipur is a shopper's paradise. You'll have
bargain hard though – shops have
een too many cash-rich, time-
oor tourists.

aipur's Gems

aipur is famous for pre-
ious and semiprecious
tones. There are many
hops offering bargain
rices, but you do need
know your gems.
he main gem-dealing
rea is around the
Muslim area of Pahar
Ganj, in the southeast
f the old city.

Gem Scams – A Warning

If you believe any stories about
buying anything in India to sell at
a profit elsewhere, you'll simply
be proving (once again) that old
adage about separating fools from
their money. Precious stones are
favourites for this game. Don't be
taken in: it's all a scam, and the
gems you buy will be worth only
a fraction of what you pay. Often
the scams involve showing you
real stones and then packing up
worthless glass beads to give you
in their place. Don't let greed cloud
your judgment.

Jantar Mantar observatory (p157)
DIANA MAYFIELD/LONELY PLANET IMAGES ©

Major Trains from Jaipur

DESTINATION	TRAIN NO & NAME	FARE (₹)	DURATION (HR)	DEPARTURE
Agra	12966 *Udaipur-Gwalior Exp*	90/305/385/515/840 (A)	4¼	6.10am
Delhi	12016 *Shatabdi*	535/1015 (B)	5	5.50pm (Thu-Tue)
Delhi	14060 *Jaisalmer-Delhi Exp*	90/155/410/550 (C)	6	5am
Delhi	12413 *Jaipur-Delhi Exp*	100/175/440/590/970 (D)	5	4.30pm
Jaisalmer	14059 *Delhi-Jaisalmer Exp*	145/255/680/930/1555 (D)	13	11.55pm
Jodhpur	12465 *Ranthambhore Exp*	100/180/355/450 (E)	5½	5pm
Jodhpur	14059 *Delhi-Jaisalmer Exp*	90/160/415/565/940 (D)	5½	11.55pm
Sawai Madhoper	12956 *Jaipur-Mumbai Exp*	140/275/355/585 (B)	2	2.10pm
Sawai Madhoper	12466 *Intercity Exp*	65/140/225/275 (E)	2¼	10.55am
Udaipur	12965 *Jaipur-Udaipur Exp*	125/215/435/545/735/1230 (F)	9½	10.25pm

Fares: A – 2nd class/AC chair/3AC/2AC/1AC, B – sleeper, 3AC, 2AC, 1AC, C – 2nd class/ sleeper/3AC/2AC, D – 2nd class/sleeper/3AC/2AC/1AC, E – 2nd class/sleeper/AC chair/3AC, F – 2nd class/sleeper/AC chair/3AC/2AC/1AC.

ℹ Information

Medical Services

Most hotels can arrange a doctor on-site. At Galundia Clinic (☏2361040, 9829061040; dagalundia@doctor.com; MI Rd), Dr Chandra Sen (☏9829061040) is on 24-hour call.

Money

There are plenty of places to change money, including numerous hotels, and masses of ATMs, most of which accept foreign cards.

Tourist Information

RTDC Tourist Reception Centre (☏5155137; www.rajasthantourism.gov.in; Room 21, former RTDC Tourist Hotel; ⊙9.30am-6pm Mon-Fri) Ha maps and brochures on Jaipur and Rajasthan.

ℹ Getting There & Away

Air

There are plenty of domestic flights from Jaipur, mostly run by Indian Airlines, Kingfisher Airlines and Jet Airways, who offer similar prices. Other airlines serving Jaipur include IndiGo and

SpiceJet. Fares and schedules vary widely, so check the airline websites before booking.

Bus

Rajasthan State Road Transport Corporation (RSRTC aka Rajasthan Roadways) buses all leave from the **main bus station** (Station Rd), picking up passengers at Narain Singh Circle (you can also buy tickets here).

Car

You can arrange car and driver hire directly with the driver at the taxi stand at the train station. A much easier way to do this is to utilise the services provided by your hotel. Most hotels will be able to contact drivers (with cars) that are known to the hotel.

Train

The efficient **railway reservation office** (📞135; ⏱8am-2pm & 2.15-8pm Mon-Sat, 8am-2pm Sun) is to your left as you enter Jaipur train station. It's open for advance reservations only (more than five hours before departure).

For same-day travel, buy your ticket at the northern end of the train station on **Platform 1, window 10** (⏱closed 6-6.30am, 2-2.30pm & 10-10.30pm).

ⓘ Getting Around

To/From the Airport

An autorickshaw/taxi costs at least ₹200/350 for the 15km journey into the city centre, or there's a prepaid taxi booth inside the terminal.

Autorickshaw

There are prepaid autorickshaw stands at the bus and train stations. If you want to hire an autorickshaw for local sightseeing, it should cost about ₹200/400 for a half/full day (including a visit to Amber); be prepared to bargain.

Taxi

There are unmetered taxis available which will require negotiating a fare or you can try **Mericar** (📞4188888; www.mericar.in; flagfall incl 3km ₹50, afterwards per km ₹11, 25% night surcharge 10pm-5am). It's a 24-hour service and taxis can be hired for sightseeing for four-/six-/eight-hour blocks costing ₹550/850/1050.

Pushkar

📞0145 / POP 14,789

Pushkar has a magnetism all of its own, and is quite unlike anywhere else in Rajasthan. It's a prominent Hindu pilgrimage town and devout Hindus should visit at least once in their lifetime. The town curls around a holy lake, said to have appeared when Brahma dropped a lotus flower. It also has one of the world's few Brahma temples. With 52 bathing ghats and 400 milky-blue temples, the town literally hums with regular *puja*s (prayers) generating an episodic soundtrack of chanting, drums and gongs, and devotional songs.

The result is a muddle of religious and tourist scenes. The main street

Pedestrian and resting cow, Pushkar
APRIL MACIBORKA/LONELY PLANET IMAGES ©

is one long bazaar, selling anything to tickle a traveller's fancy, from hippy-chic tie-dye to didgeridoos. Despite the commercialism and banana pancakes, the town remains enchantingly small and authentically mystic.

 Sights

TEMPLES
Hindu Temple

Pushkar boasts hundreds of temples, though few are particularly ancient, as they were mostly desecrated by Au-rangzeb and subsequently rebuilt.

BRAHMA TEMPLE
Most famous is the Brahma Temple, said to be one of the few such temples in the world as a result of a curse by Brahma's consort, Saraswati. The temple is marked by a red spire, and over the entrance gateway is the *hans* (goose symbol) of Brahma.

SARASWATI TEMPLE
The one-hour trek up to the hilltop Saraswati Temple overlooking the lake is best made before dawn, though the views are fantastic at any time of day.

PAP MOCHANI (GAYATRI) TEMPLE
The sunrise views over town from the closer Pap Mochani (Gayatri) Temple, reached by a track behind the Marwar bus stand, are also well worth the 30-minute climb.

GHATS
Bathing Gha

Fifty-two bathing ghats surround the lake, where pilgrims bathe in the sacred waters. If you wish to join them, do it with respect. Remember, this is a holy place: remove your shoes and don't smoke, kid around or take photographs.

Sleeping

INN SEVENTH HEAVEN
Boutique Hotel $$

(☎ 5105455; www.inn-seventh-heaven.com; Chotti Basti; r ₹550-2400; ✳ @) You enter this lovingly converted *haveli* (mansion) through heavy wooden doors into an incense-perfumed courtyard, centred

A sadhu (holy man) drinks some tea

ith a marble fountain. There are just 12 idividually decorated rooms on three levls, with traditionally crafted furniture and omfortable beds. On the roof you'll find ne excellent Sixth Sense restaurant as ell as sofas and swing chairs for relaxing ith a book.

OTEL PUSHKAR PALACE   Hotel **$$$**
(2773001; www.hotelpushkarpalace.com; s/d om ₹4225/5150, ste ₹10,850; ✿@✖) Once elonging to the maharaja of Kishangarh, nis top-end hotel boasts a romantic akeside setting. Rooms have carved vooden furniture and beds and the suites ook directly onto the lake. There's also a leasant outdoor dining area overlooking ne lake.

AGAT PALACE HOTEL   Hotel **$$**
(2772953; www.hotelpushkarpalace.com; jmer Rd; s/d ₹3575/4225; ✿@✖) This is lovely heritage-style hotel in new but raditional-style buildings resembling a balace. It's in a quiet spot on the town's utskirts and offers romantic bedrooms vith carved wooden furniture and lovely bathrooms. There are tempting packges including meals and low-season liscounts.

BHARATPUR PALACE   Hotel **$**
(2772320; bharatpurpalace_pushkar@yahoo.o.in; r ₹200-800; ✿) This rambling old building occupies one of the best spots n Pushkar, on the upper levels adjacent o Ghandi Ghat. It features aesthetic blue-washed simplicity: bare-as-bones ooms with unsurpassed views of the holy ake. Room 1 is the most romantic place o wake up: it's surrounded on three sides by the lake.

 Eating

SIXTH SENSE   Multicuisine **$**
(Inn Seventh Heaven, Chotti Basti; mains ₹50-180; ⊘8.30am-4pm & 6-10pm) This chilled rooftop restaurant is a great place to head even if you didn't score a room in its popular hotel. Indian seasonal vegetables

Detour:
Amber Fort

This magnificent **fort** (Indian/foreigner ₹25/200, guide ₹200, audio guide Hindi/English/various European/various Asian ₹100/150/200/250; ⊘8am-6pm, last entry 5.30pm) is more of a palace, built from pale yellow and pink sandstone and white marble, and divided into four main sections, each with its own courtyard.

You can trudge up to the fort from the road in about 10 minutes (cold drinks are available at the top). A seat in a jeep up to the fort costs ₹200 return. Riding up on **elephant back** (₹900 per 2 passengers; ⊘8-11am & 3.30-5.30pm) is a popular alternative.

An autorickshaw/taxi will cost at least ₹150/550 for the return trip. RTDC city tours (see p158) include the Amber Fort.

and rice, vegetable sizzlers, pasta and pizzas are all excellent.

LITTLE ITALY   Italian **$**
(Panchkund Marg; mains ₹80-200; ⊘10am-11pm) This superb garden restaurant has excellent thin-crust, wood-fired pizzas and imported pasta with tasty sauces. As well as homemade pesto and gnocchi, there are some Indian and Israeli dishes and fresh ground Keralan coffee.

SUNSET CAFÉ   Multicuisine **$**
(mains ₹75-200; ⊘7.30am-midnight) Right on the eastern ghats, this cafe has sublime lake views. It offers the usual traveller menu, including curries, pizza and pasta, plus there's a German bakery serving OK cakes. The lakeshore setting is perfect at sunset and gathers a crowd.

Pushkar Camel Fair

Come the month of Kartika, the eighth lunar month of the Hindu calendar and one of the holiest, Thar camel drivers spruce up their ships of the desert and start the long walk to Pushkar in time for Kartik Purnima (Full Moon). Each year around 200,000 people converge here, bringing with them some 50,000 camels, horses and cattle. The place becomes an extraordinary swirl of colour, sound and movement, thronged with musicians, mystics, tourists, traders, animals, devotees and camera crews.

It's hard to believe, but this seething mass is all just a sideshow. Kartik Purnima is when Hindu pilgrims come to bathe in Pushkar's sacred waters. The religious event builds in tandem with the camel fair in a wild, magical crescendo of incense, chanting and processions to dousing day, the last night of the fair, when thousands of devotees wash away their sins and set candles afloat on the holy lake.

HONEY & SPICE Multicuisine **$**
(Laxmi Market off Sadar Bazaar; mains ₹75-120; ⏰**7am-7pm)** Run by a friendly man who is a mine of information, this tiny breakfast and lunch place has delicious South Indian coffee and homemade banana cake. Soups and hearty vegetable stews served with brown rice are thoroughly healthy.

ⓘ Getting There & Away

Frequent buses to/from Ajmer (₹8, 30 minutes), which has the nearest train station with services to Delhi, Agra, Jaipur and Udaipur, stop on the road heading eastwards out of town.

The post office will book train tickets for services out of Ajmer for about ₹15 commission. For around ₹50 private agencies do the same, including transfer to Ajmer.

Ranthambhore National Park
📞07462

This famous national park, open from October to June, is the best place to spot wild tigers in Rajasthan. Comprising 1334 sq km of wild jungle scrub hemmed in by rocky ridges, at its centre is the amazing 10th-century **Ranthambore Fort** (admission free; ⏰6am-6pm).

It's 10km from the town of Sawai Madhopur to the first gate and another 3km to the main gate and Ranthambore Fort. Accommodation is stretched out along the road from the town to the park The train station is in the heart of Sawai Madhopur.

◉ Sights & Activities

The best option is to travel by gypsy, a small, open-topped 4WD that takes five passengers. You still have a good chance of seeing a tiger from the large, open-topped, 20-seater canter, though sometimes other passengers can be rowdy.

Safaris (Indian/foreigner per person in gypsy ₹500/890, in canter ₹425/812, video camera ₹400) take three hours. In October canter and gypsies leave at 6.30am and 2.30pm from November to January they leave at 7am and 2pm; from February to March they leave at 6.30am and 2.30pm; from April to May they leave at 6am and 3pm; and from May to June they leave at 6am and 3.30pm.

Be aware that the rules for booking safaris (and prices) are prone to change. Seats in gypsies and canters can be reserved on the official website (www

ajasthanwildlife.in), though a single
ypsy and five canters are also kept
or direct booking at the **Forest Office**
Ranthambhore Rd; ☺5.30am-7am & noon-2pm).

🛏 Sleeping

HEM VILLAS　　　Boutique Hotel　**$$$**
☎252099; www.khemvillas.com; Ranthamb-
ore Rd; s/d incl all meals & taxes ₹8000/9500,
nts ₹10,600/14,000, cottage ₹14,000/17,000;
🌣) Fateh Singh Rathore is lauded as
he driving force behind the conserva-
on of the tiger at Ranthambhore. His
on Goverdhan, and his daughter-in-law
sha, run this impressive ecolodge set
9 hectares of organic farmland and
eafforested land. The accommodation
anges from rooms in the colonial-style
ungalow to luxury tents to sumptuous
tone cottages.

**HOTEL TIGER SAFARI
ESORT**　　　　　　　Hotel　**$$**
☎221137; www.tigersafariresort.com; d incl
eakfast ₹1280-1600; ❄@☀) This is one
f the best options for those on a budget
vhere the helpful management is adept

at organising safaris, wake-up calls and
early breakfasts before the morning
safari. They can also organise pick-up
and drop-off from the train station and
sightseeing trips to the fort. The spacious
doubles and so-called 'cottages' (larger
rooms with bigger bathrooms) face a
well-kept garden and small pool.

ℹ Getting There & Away

Train

At Sawai Madhopur train station there's a
computerised reservation office (☺8am-8pm
Mon-Sat, to 2pm Sun).

The 12956 *Jaipur-Mumbai Express* departs
Jaipur at 2.10pm, arriving at Sawai Madhopur
(sleeper/3AC/2AC/1AC ₹140/275/355/585)
at 4pm. Going the other way (No 12955) it
departs Sawai Madhopur at 10.45am arriving at
Jaipur at 12.50pm. The 12466 *Intercity Express*
leaves Jaipur at 10.55am, arriving at Sawai
Madhopur (2nd class/sleeper/AC chair/3AC
₹65/140/225/275) at 1.15pm. Going the other
way, the 12465 *Ranthambhore Express* departs
Sawai Madhopur at 2.40pm and reaches Jaipur
at 4.40pm.

busy street in Pushkar

SOUTHERN RAJASTHAN

Udaipur

☎ 0294 / POP 389,317

Beside shimmering Lake Pichola, with the ochre and purple ridges of the wooded Aravalli Hills stretching away in every direction, Udaipur has a romance of setting unmatched in Rajasthan. Fantastical palaces, temples, *havelis* (mansions) and countless narrow, crooked, colourful streets add the human counterpoint to the city's natural charms. Its tag of 'the most romantic spot on the continent of India' was first applied in 1829 by Colonel James Tod, the East India Company's first Political Agent in the region. Today the romance is wearing ever so slightly thin as Udaipur strains to exploit it for tourist rupees.

Take a step back from the hustle, however, and Udaipur still has its magic, not just in its marvellous palaces and monuments but in its matchless setting, the tranquillity of boat rides on the lake, the bustle of its ancient bazaars, the quaint old-world feel of its better hotels, its tempting shops, and lovely countryside to explore on wheels, feet or horseback.

 Sights

LAKE PICHOLA   Lake

Limpid and large, Lake Pichola reflects the cool grey-blue mountains on its rippling mirror-like surface. It was enlarged by Maharana Udai Singh II, following his foundation of the city, by flooding Picholi village, which gave the lake its name.

Udaipur

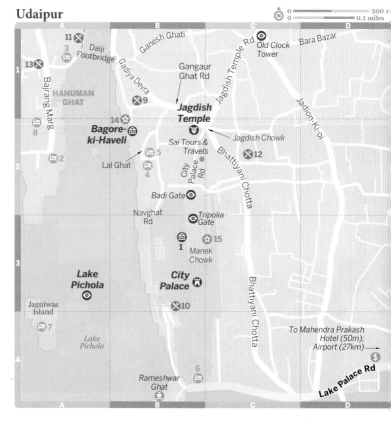

Boat rides (adult/child 30min ₹200/100, ~~r~~ ₹300/150, sunset ₹500/250; ☺10am-5pm) ~~l~~ave roughly hourly from Rameshwar ~~C~~hat in the City Palace gardens. Note that ~~y~~ou also have to pay ₹25 to enter the City ~~P~~alace complex.

~~C~~ITY PALACE   Palace
(~~w~~ww.eternalmewar.in; adult/child ₹25/15, not ~~c~~harged if visiting City Palace Museum; ☺7am-~~8~~pm) Surmounted by balconies, towers ~~a~~nd cupolas towering over the lake, the ~~i~~mposing City Palace is Rajasthan's ~~l~~argest palace, with a facade 244m long ~~a~~nd 30.4m high. Construction was begun ~~b~~y Maharana Udai Singh II, the city's ~~f~~ounder, and it later became a con-~~g~~lomeration of structures (including 11 ~~s~~eparate smaller palaces), though it still ~~m~~anages to retain a surprising uniform-~~i~~ty of design.

~~C~~ITY PALACE MUSEUM
~~a~~dult/child ₹50/30, camera or video ₹200; ☺9.30am-5.30pm, last entry 4.30pm) The ~~m~~ain part of the palace is open as the City ~~P~~alace Museum, with rooms extrava-~~g~~antly decorated with mirrors, tiles and ~~p~~aintings and housing a large, varied col-~~l~~ection of artefacts.

~~J~~AGDISH TEMPLE   Hindu Temple
(☺5.30am-2pm & 4-10pm) Entered by a ~~s~~teep, elephant-flanked flight of steps ~~1~~50m north of the City Palace's Badi Pol entrance, this busy Indo-Aryan temple was built by Maharana Jagat Singh in 1651.

 Tours

City tours (per person excl admission charges ₹140) run by the Rajasthan Tourism Development Corporation (RTDC) leave at 8.30am from the RTDC Hotel Kajri by Shastri Circle (400m northeast of Delhi Gate), and take in the main sights in 4½ hours. Contact the Tourist Reception Centre for more information.

 **Sleeping**

Lal Ghat Area
**JAGAT NIWAS PALACE
HOTEL**   Heritage Hotel **$$**
(☎2420133; www.jagatniwaspalace.com; 23-25 Lal Ghat; r ₹1750-3950, ste ₹6350; ✻ @ ☎) This leading midrange hotel set in two converted lakeside *havelis* takes the location cake. The lake-view rooms are charming, with carved wooden furniture, cushioned window seats and pretty prints. Non-lake-facing rooms are almost as comfortable and attractive, and considerably cheaper.

JAIWANA HAVELI
Hotel $$

(☎2411103; www.jaiwanahaveli.com; 14 Lal Ghat; s/d ₹1890/1990; ❄@🛜) Professionally run by two helpful, efficient brothers, this smart midrange option has spotless, unfussy rooms with good beds, some decorated with attractive block-printed fabrics. Book corner room 11, 21 or 31 for views.

Hanuman Ghat Area

AMET HAVELI
Heritage Hotel $$

(☎2431085; www.amethaveliudaipur.com; s/d/ ste ₹4000/5000/6000; ❄@🛜📶) This 350-year-old heritage building on the lake shore has delightful rooms with cushioned window seats and coloured glass with little shutters.

DREAM HEAVEN
Guesthouse $

(☎2431038; www.dreamheaven.co.in; Hanuman Ghat; r ₹150-600; ❄) A deservedly popular place to come to a halt, with spick-and-span rooms featuring wall hangings and paintings. Bathrooms are smallish, though some rooms have a decent balcony and/or views.

UDAI KOTHI
Hotel $$$

(☎2432810; www.udaikothi.com; Hanuman Ghat; r ₹4000-10,000; ❄@🛜📶) A bit like a five-storey wedding cake, Udai Kothi is a glittery, modern building with lots of traditional touches. The apex is the roof terrace, where you can dine well and swim in Udaipur's *only* rooftop pool (nonguests ₹300).

Lake Palace Road Area

MAHENDRA PRAKASH HOTEL
Hotel $$

(☎2419811; www.hotelmahendraprakash. com; r ₹1400-3000; ❄@🛜📶) Spacious gardens, spick-and-span rooms well furnished in traditional style, a cheery atmosphere and friendly staff are the name of the game at the very well-run Mahendra Prakash. There's a fabulous pool (nonguests ₹100), a decent restaurant and a lawn with tortoises.

Left: Sadhus sitting beneath a carved elephant at Jagdish Temple (p171); **Below:** Women in traditional dress during a spring festival

City Palace

SHIV NIWAS

PALACE HOTEL Heritage Hotel **$$$**
(2528016; www.hrhhotels.com; City Palace
complex; r ₹12,000, ste ₹24,000-80,000;
❄ @ 🛜 ☀) This hotel, in the former
palace guest quarters, has opulent com-
mon areas like its pool courtyard, bar and
lovely lawn garden with a 30m-long royal
procession mural. Some of the suites are
truly palatial, filled with fountains and sil-
ver, but the standard rooms are not great
value. Go for a suite, or just go for a drink,
meal, massage, or swim in the gorgeous
marble **pool** (nonguests ₹300; ⏱ 9am-6pm).
Rates drop dramatically from April to
September.

Other Areas

TAJ LAKE

PALACE Heritage Hotel **$$$**
(2428800; www.tajhotels.com; r ₹37,500-
43,500, ste from ₹150,000; ❄ @ 🛜 ☀) The
icon of Udaipur, this romantic white-
marble palace seemingly floating on

the lake is extraordinary, with open-air
courtyards, lotus ponds and a small,
mango-tree-shaded pool. Rooms are
hung with breezy silks and filled with
carved furniture. Service is superb.
Access is by boat from the hotel's own
jetty in the City Palace gardens. Rates
can vary a lot with season and demand:
check the website.

MOUNTAIN RIDGE Homestay **$$**
(3291478, 9602192902; www.mountainridge.
in; Sisarma; r incl breakfast & dinner ₹1950-
3950; ☀) This country homestay run by a
resident Briton makes a great alternative
to the city noise and hustle, and a good
base for exploring the Udaipur country-
side. It's a lovely stone-built house with
five spacious rooms and great views,
perched on a hilltop near Sisarma village,
6km from the city centre.

If You Like…
Palaces

If you like the City Palace (p173), visit some of Udaipur's other grand houses and palaces.

1 **BAGORE-KI-HAVELI**
(admission ₹30; ☺10am-5pm) This gracious 18th-century *haveli*, set on the water's edge in the Gangaur Ghat area, was built by a Mewar prime minister and has been carefully restored.

2 **SAJJAN GARH (MONSOON PALACE)**
Perched on top of a distant mountain like a fairy-tale castle, this melancholy, neglected late-19th-century palace was constructed by Maharana Sajjan Singh. Visitors stream up here for the marvellous views, particularly at sunset. It's 5km west of the old city as the crow flies, but about 9km by the winding road. At the foot of the hill you enter the 500-hectare **Sajjan Garh Wildlife Sanctuary** (Indian/foreigner ₹10/80, car ₹60, camera/video free/₹200). A good way to visit is with the daily sunset excursion in **taxi No RJ-27-TA 2108** (✆9784400120; per person ₹200), a minivan which leaves Udaipur's Gangaur Ghat at 5pm daily (the charge does not include the sanctuary fees).

 Eating

Lal Ghat Area
JAGAT NIWAS PALACE HOTEL   Indian $$
(✆2420133; 23-25 Lal Ghat; mains ₹120-300; ☺6.30-10.30am, noon-3.30pm & 7-10pm) A wonderful, classy, rooftop restaurant with superb lake views, delicious Indian cuisine and good service. Choose from an extensive selection of rich curries (tempered for Western tastes) – mutton, chicken, fish, veg – as well as the tandoori classics. There's a tempting cocktail menu and the beer is icy. It's wise to book ahead for dinner.

LOTUS CAFE   Multicuisine
(15 Bhattiyani Chotta; dishes ₹50-120; ☺9am-10.30pm) This funky little restaurant plucks out fabulous chicken dishes (predominantly Indian), plus salads, baked potatoes and plenty of vegetarian fare. It's ideal for meeting and greeting other travellers, with a mezzanine to loll about on and cool background sound.

CAFE EDELWEISS   Cafe
(73 Gangaur Ghat Rd; snacks ₹30-80; ☺7a-7pm) The Savage Garden restaurant folks run this itsy piece of Europe that appeals to homesick and discerning travellers with superb baked goods and good coffee. If sticky cinnamon rolls, squidgy blueberry chocolate cake, spinach-and-mushroom quiche or apple strudel don't appeal, give it a miss.

Hanuman Ghat Area
AMBRAI   North Indian $$
(✆2431085; Amet Haveli hotel; mains ₹145-325; ☺12.30-3pm & 7.30-10.30pm) The cuisine at this scenic restaurant – at lake-shore level, looking across to Lake Palace Hotel, Lal Ghat and the City Palace – does justice to its fabulous position. Highly atmospheric at night, Ambrai feels like a French park, with its wrought-iron furniture, dusty ground and large shady trees, and there's a terrific bar to complement the dining.

JASMIN   Multicuisine $
(mains ₹50-80) Very tasty vegetarian dishes are cooked up here in a lovely, quiet, open-air spot looking out on the quaint Daiji footbridge. There are plenty of Indian options, and some original variations on the usual multicuisine theme including Korean and Israeli dishes. The ambience is super-relaxed and service friendly.

QUEEN CAFE   Indian $
(14 Bajrang Marg; mains ₹60-75; ☺8am-10pm) This homey little eatery with just a couple of tables serves up fabulous home-style Indian vegetarian dishes. Try the pumpkin curry with mint and coconut, and the Kashmir pilau with fruit, vegies and coco

...ut. Don't pass on the chocolate desserts either!

City Palace

Note that you have to pay ₹25 to enter the City Palace complex if you're not staying in one of its hotels.

PAANTYA RESTAURANT
Multicuisine $$$

(☎2528016; Shiv Niwas Palace Hotel; mains ₹500-1400) Most captivating in the evening, this semiformal restaurant in the ritzy Shiv Niwas Palace has indoor seating, but if the weather's warm enough it's best out in the open-air courtyard by the pool. Indian classical music is performed nightly, and the food is great. For local flavour try the very tasty *laal maas dhungar,* a Rajasthani spiced and smoked mutton dish.

GALLERY RESTAURANT
Continental $$$

(Durbar Hall; Durbar tea ₹325; ⊙9am-6pm) Alongside the splendiferous Durbar Hall, this elegant little restaurant has beguiling views across Lake Pichola. It does snacks and a continental lunch, but the time to come is between 3pm and 5pm when you can indulge in afternoon tea with cakes and the all-important scones, jam and cream.

 **Entertainment**

DHAROHAR
Dance

(☎2523858; Bagore-ki-Haveli, Gangaur Ghat; admission ₹60, camera ₹50; ⊙7pm) The beautiful Bagore-ki-Haveli hosts the best (and most convenient) opportunity to see Rajasthani folk dancing, with nightly shows of colourful, energetic Mewari, Bhil and western Rajasthani dances, by talented performers.

MEWAR SOUND & LIGHT SHOW
Sound & Light Show

(Manek Chowk, City Palace; lower/upper seating English show ₹150/400, Hindi show ₹100/200; ⊙7pm Sep-Feb, 7.30pm Mar-Apr, 8pm May-Aug) Fifteen centuries of intriguing Mewar history are squeezed into a single atmospheric hour of commentary and light switching – in English from September to April, in Hindi other months.

Elephant murals in a village outside Udaipur

ⓘ Information

Emergency

Police (2414600, 100) There are police posts at Surajpol, Hatipol and Delhi Gate.

Medical Services

GBH American Hospital (3056000; www.gbhamericanhospital.com; 101 Kothi Bagh, Bhatt Ji Ki Bari, Meera Girls College Rd) Modern, reader-recommended private hospital with 24-hour emergency service, about 2km northeast of the old city.

Money

Places to change currency and travellers cheques include the following:

Sai Tours & Travels (168 City Palace Rd; ⊙8am-9pm)

Thomas Cook (Lake Palace Rd; ⊙9.30am-6pm Mon-Sat)

ⓘ Getting There & Away

Air

Air India (2410999; www.airindia.com; 222/16 Mumal Towers, Saheli Rd) Flies to Mumbai daily and to Delhi via Jodhpur also daily

Jet Airways (2561105; www.jetairways.com; Blue Circle Business Centre, Madhuban) Flies direct to Delhi daily, and Mumbai once or twice daily.

Kingfisher Airlines (1800 2093030; www.flykingfisher.com; 4/73 Chetak Circle) Has daily flights to Delhi, Mumbai and Jaipur, with the Jaipur flight continuing to Jodhpur from about October to March.

Train

The computerised main ticket office (⊙8am-8pm Mon-Sat, 8am-2pm Sun) at the station has a window for foreign tourists and other special categories of passenger.

12964 *Mewar Express* Departs Udaipur at 6.15pm and arrives in Delhi's Nizamuddin

Left: Mehrangarh Fort rises above the Blue City of Jodhpur;
Below: A woman preparing some fresh herbs
(LEFT) IZZET KERIBAR/LONELY PLANET IMAGES ©; (BELOW) HUW JONES/LONELY PLANET IMAGES ©

station (sleeper/3AC/2AC/1AC
₹315/816/1102/1846) at 6.30am,
via Sawai Madhopur.

12966 *Udaipur-Gwalior Super Express* Departs
Udaipur at 10.20pm and arrives in Gwalior
(sleeper/3AC/2AC/1AC ₹324/844/1142/1915)
at 12.45pm, via Ajmer and Jaipur
(₹224/559/747/1255, 7½ hours).

🛈 Getting Around

To/From the Airport
The airport is 25km east of town, about 900m
south of Hwy 76 to Chittorgarh. A prepaid taxi to
the Lal Ghat area costs ₹400.

WESTERN RAJASTHAN
Jodhpur
☏0291 / POP 846,400

Mighty Mehrangarh, the muscular fort that
towers over the Blue City of Jodhpur, is a
magnificent spectacle and an architectural masterpiece. Around Mehrangarh's
feet, the old city, a jumble of Brahmin-blue
cubes, stretches out to the 10km-long,
16th-century city wall. The 'Blue City'
really is blue! Inside is a tangle of winding,
glittering, medieval streets, which never
seem to lead where you expect them to,
scented by incense, roses and sewers,
with shops and bazaars selling everything
from trumpets and temple decorations to
snuff and saris.

🎯 Sights & Activities

MEHRANGARH   Fort
(www.mehrangarh.org; museum admission
adult/senior & student incl camera & audio
guide ₹300/250, video ₹200; ⏱9am-5.30pm)
Rising perpendicular and impregnable
from a rocky hill that itself stands 120m
above Jodhpur's skyline, Mehrangarh
is one of the most magnificent forts in

177

Jodhpur

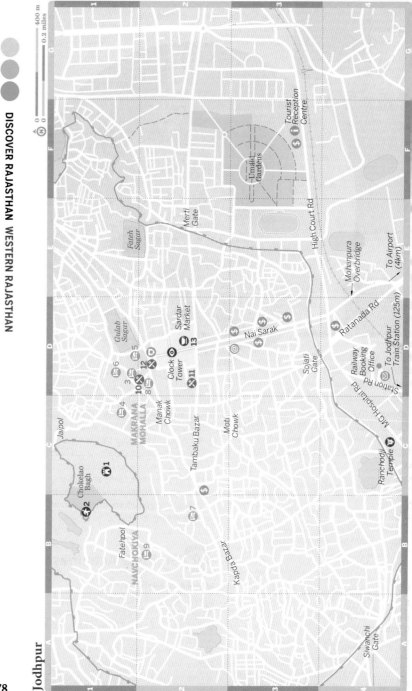

- 400 m
- 0.2 miles

Jodhpur

India. The battlements are 6m to 36m high and as the building materials were chiselled from the rock on which the fort stands, the structure merges with its base. Still run by the Jodhpur royal family, Mehrangarh is chock-full of history and legend.

FLYING FOX
(www.flyingfox.asia; 1/6 zips ₹330/1330; ⊙9am-4pm) This two-hour circuit of six zip lines flies back and forth over walls, bastions and lakes on the north side of Mehrangarh. Safety standards are good, and 'awesome' is the verdict of most who dare.

 Tours

Most guesthouses and hotels can lay on city tours by autorickshaw (half-day/day around ₹350/700) or taxi (around ₹500/1000). If you prefer to organise your own taxi, there's a stand outside the main train station.

 **Sleeping**

Old City

SINGHVI'S HAVELI   Guesthouse **$**
(☎2624293; www.singhvihaveli.com; Ramdevji-ka-Chowk, Navchokiya; r ₹300-1800; ❄@🔊) This red-sandstone, family-run, 500-odd-year-old *haveli* is an understated gem. It's in Navchokiya, one of the most atmospheric yet least touristy parts of the old city,

beneath the western end of Mehrangarh (which you can enter by the Fatehpol gate).

KRISHNA PRAKASH HERITAGE HAVELI   Heritage Hotel **$$**
(☎2633448; www.kpheritage.net; Nayabas, Killikhana; s/d standard ₹850/1050, deluxe incl breakfast ₹1550/1750, ste incl breakfast ₹2450-3500; ❄🌬) This multilevel heritage hotel right under the fort walls is a good-value and peaceful choice, with prettily painted furniture and murals and rooms.

PAL HAVELI   Heritage Hotel **$$**
(☎3293328; www.palhaveli.com; Gulab Sagar; r incl breakfast ₹2500-4000; ❄@) This stunning *haveli,* the best and most attractive in the old city, was built by the Thakur of Pal in 1847. There are 21 charming, spacious rooms, mostly large and elaborately decorated in traditional heritage style, surrounding a cool central courtyard.

RAAS   Boutique Hotel **$$$**
(☎2636455; www.raasjodhpur.com; Tunwarji-ka-Jhalra, Makrana Mohalla; incl breakfast r ₹15,000-18,000, ste ₹26,000; ❄🔊🌬) Developed from a 19th-century city mansion, This is Jodhpur's first contemporary-style boutique hotel. If you fancy a change from the heritage aesthetic, Raas' clean, uncluttered style is just the ticket.

SHAHI GUEST HOUSE   Guesthouse **$$**
(☎2623802; www.shahiguesthouse.net; Gandhi St, City Police; r ₹900-2200; ❄🔊) Shahi is an interesting guesthouse developed from a 350-year-old zenana (women's quarters). There's lots of cool stone, and narrow walkways surrounding a petite courtyard.

The six rooms are individual and cosy and the family is charming. There is a delightful rooftop restaurant with views.

HOTEL HAVELI
Hotel **$$**
(☎ 2614615; www.hotelhaveli.net; Makrana Mohalla; r ₹500-2200; ❄ @ 🛜) This 250-year-old building inside the walled city is a popular, efficient and friendly place. Rooms vary greatly and are individually decorated with colour themes and paintings; many have semibalconies and fort views. The rooftop vegetarian restaurant, Jharokha, has excellent views and nightly entertainment.

Shivam Paying Guest House
Guesthouse **$**
(☎ 2610688; shivamgh@hotmail.com; Makrana Mohalla; r ₹200-700, without bathroom ₹150; ❄) Near the clock tower, this quiet, hassle-free option run by a helpful family has cosy rooms, steep staircases and a lovely little rooftop restaurant.

South of the Old City

DEVI BHAWAN
Heritage Hotel **$$**
(☎ 2511067; www.devibhawan.com; Ratanada; r ₹1800-2300; ❄ @ 🛜 ☂) A charming hotel surrounding a verdant oasis shaded by majestic neem trees. As well as being the most peaceful place in Jodhpur it is also excellent value. There's a superb pool and a good **restaurant** (veg/non-veg thali ₹175/200; ⏱7-10am & 8-10pm).

RATAN VILAS
Heritage Hotel **$$**
(☎ 2613011; www.ratanvilas.com; Loco Shed Rd, Ratanada; r ₹2000-2950; ❄ @ 🛜) Built in 1920, this beauty from a bygone era is quintessential colonial India, with manicured lawns, spacious, spotless and solidly tasteful rooms, and exceptional staff who prepare wonderful meals.

 Eating

It's often convenient to eat in your guesthouse or hotel restaurant (which is usually on the roof, with a fort view), but there are also a number of places well worth going out to.

INDIQUE
Indian **$$**
(☎ 3293328; Pal Haveli, Gulab Sagar; mains ₹200-275) This candle-lit rooftop restaurant at the Pal Haveli hotel is the perfect place for a romantic dinner. Even murky Gulab Sagar lake glistens at night and the views

Gulab Sagar lake, with Mehrangarh Fort (p177) in the distance

to the fort, clock tower and Umaid Bhawan are superb. The food covers traditional tandoori, biryanis and North Indian curries, and you won't be disappointed by the old favourites – butter chicken and rogan josh.

NIRVANA   Indian $$
(1st fl, Tija Mata ka Mandir, Tambaku Bazar; mains ₹90-130, regular/special thali ₹160/250) Sharing premises with a Rama temple, 300m from the clock tower, Nirvana has both an indoor cafe covered in 150-year-old wall paintings of the Ramayana story, and a rooftop eating area with panoramic views. The Indian vegetarian food is among the most delicious you'll find in Rajasthan, and the thalis are wonderful.

JHAROKHA   Multicuisine $
(Hotel Haveli, Makrana Mohalla; mains ₹60-90) The rooftop terraces of the Hotel Haveli host one of the best vegetarian restaurants in Jodhpur. As well as the excellent food and views there's nightly entertainment in the form of traditional music and dance.

JHANKAR CHOTI
HAVELI   Multicuisine $
(Makrana Mohalla; mains ₹70-110; 📶) Stone walls, big cane chairs, prettily painted woodwork and whirring fans set the scene at this semi-open-air travellers' favourite. It serves up good Indian vegetarian dishes plus pizzas, burgers and baked cheese dishes.

ON THE ROCKS   Indian $$
(📞5102701; Circuit House Rd; mains ₹115-325; 🕐12.30-3.30pm & 7.30-11pm) This leafy garden restaurant (candle-lit in the evening) is very popular with locals and tour groups. It has tasty Indian cuisine, including lots of barbecue options and rich and creamy curries, plus a small playground and a cavelike bar (open 11am to 11pm) with a dance floor (for couples only).

OMELETTE SHOP   Cafe $
(Sardar Market; dishes ₹15-25) Located beside the northern gate of Sardar Market, this spot goes through 1000 to 1500 eggs a

day. The egg man has been doing his thing here for over 30 years. Three tasty, spicy boiled eggs cost ₹15, and a two-egg masala and cheese omelette with four pieces of bread is ₹25.

🍷 Drinking

SHRI MISHRILAL HOTEL   Cafe
(Sardar Market; lassi ₹20; 🕐8am-10pm) Just inside the southern gate of Sardar Market, this place is nothing fancy but whips up the most superb creamy *makhania* lassis, a thick and filling saffron-flavoured version of that most refreshing of drinks.

ℹ Information

Om Forex (Sardar Market; internet per hr ₹30; 🕐9am-10pm) Also exchanges currency and travellers cheques.

Police (Sardar Market; 🕐24hr) Small police post inside the market's north gate.

State Bank of India (off High Court Rd; ⏰10am-4pm Mon-Fri, 10am-1pm Sat) Exchanges currency and travellers cheques.

Tourist Reception Centre (☎2545083; High Court Rd; ⏰9am-6pm Mon-Fri) Offers a free map and willingly answers questions.

ℹ Getting There & Away

Air

Jet Airways (☎5102222; www.jetairways.com; Residency Rd) and **Indian Airlines** (☎2510758; www.indian-airlines.nic.in; Circuit House Rd) both fly daily to Delhi and Mumbai, with Indian Airlines' Mumbai flights stopping at Udaipur on the way.

Taxi

You can organise taxis for inter-city trips, or longer, through most accommodation places, or deal direct with drivers. There's a taxi stand outside Jodhpur train station.

Train

The computerised **booking office** (Station Rd; ⏰8am-8pm Mon-Sat, 8am-1.45pm Sun) is 300m northeast of Jodhpur station. There's a tourist quota (Window 786).

Most trains from the east stop at the Raika Bagh station before heading on to the main station, which is handy if you're heading for a hotel on the eastern side of town.

To Jaisalmer, the *Delhi-Jaisalmer Express* (14059) departs at 6.10am, arriving in Jaisalmer (2nd class/sleeper/3AC/2AC/1AC ₹100/165/419/566/944) at 11.45am. The *Jodhpur-Jaisalmer Express* (14810) departs every night at 11pm, arriving at 5am.

To Delhi, the *Mandore Express* (12462) leaves Jodhpur at 7.30pm, reaching Jaipur (sleeper/3AC/2AC/1AC ₹188/458/608/1015) at 12.40am, and Delhi (₹282/723/975/1627) at 6.25am. The *Intercity Express* (12466) departs at 5.55am, reaching Jaipur (2nd class/sleeper/AC chair/3AC ₹110/188/369/458) at 10.45am, and Sawai Madhopur (₹133/227/453/567) at 1.15pm

ℹ Getting Around

To/From the Airport

The airport is 5km south of the city centre, about ₹200/100 by taxi/autorickshaw.

A sadhu on the streets of Jaisalmer

Jaisalmer

☎02992 / POP 58,286

The fort of Jaisalmer is a breathtaking sight: a massive sandcastle rising from the sandy plains like a mirage from a by-gone era. No place better evokes exotic camel-train trade routes and desert mystery. Ninety-nine bastions encircle the fort's still-inhabited twisting lanes. Inside are shops swaddled in bright embroideries, a royal palace and numerous businesses looking for your tourist rupee. Despite the commercialism, it's hard not to be enchanted by this desert citadel.

Sights

JAISALMER FORT   Fort

Founded in 1156 by the Rajput ruler Jaisal and reinforced by subsequent rulers, Jaisalmer Fort was the focus of a number of battles between the Bhatis, the Mughals of Delhi and the Rathores of Jodhpur. You enter the fort from its east side and pass through four massive gates on the zigzagging route to the upper part. The fourth gate opens into a large square, Dashera Chowk, where Jaisalmer Fort's uniqueness becomes apparent: this is a living fort, with about 3000 people residing within its walls.

FORT PALACE
(Indian/foreigner incl audio guide & camera ₹30/250, video ₹50/150; ◷8am-6pm Apr-Oct, 9am-6pm Nov-Mar) Towering over the fort's main square is the former rulers' elegant seven-storey palace. The 1½-hour audio-guide tour, available in six languages, is worthwhile but you must deposit ₹2000 or your passport/driver's licence/credit card.

JAIN TEMPLES
(admission ₹30, camera/video/cellphone ₹70/120/30; ◷7am-1pm) Within the fort walls is a maze-like, interconnecting treasure trove of seven beautiful yellow-sandstone Jain temples, dating from the 15th and 16th centuries.

If You Like...
Mansions

If you like Jaisalmer's Fort Palace, visit these fairy-tale sandstone mansions.

1 PATWA-KI-HAVELI
The biggest fish in the *haveli* pond is Patwa-ki-Haveli, which towers over a narrow lane, with intricate stonework like honey-coloured lace. Divided into five sections, it was built between 1800 and 1860 by five Jain brothers who made their fortunes in brocade and jewellery.

2 SALIM SINGH-KI-HAVELI
(admission incl guide ₹20, camera/video ₹20/50; ◷8am-7pm May-Sep, to 6pm Oct-Apr) This 18th-century *haveli* has an amazing, distinctive shape. The top storey mushrooms out into a mass of carving, with graceful arched balconies surmounted by pale blue cupolas.

3 NATHMAL-KI-HAVELI
(admission ₹20; ◷8am-7pm) This late-19th-century *haveli* used to be a prime minister's house, and is still partly inhabited. It has an extraordinary exterior dripping with carving, and the 1st floor has some beautiful paintings made with 1.5kg of gold.

Tours

The Tourist Reception Centre runs sunset tours to the Sam sand dunes (₹200 per person, minimum four people). Add ₹100 if you'd like a short camel ride too.

Sleeping

Staying in the fort is the most atmospheric and romantic chocie, but you should be aware of the pressure tourism is exerting on the fort's infrastructure. There is a wide choice of good places to stay outside the fort.

Jaisalmer

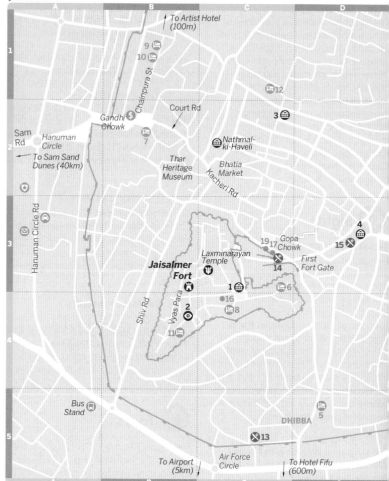

Outside the Fort

DESERT MOON Guesthouse **$**
(☏ 250116, 9414149350; www.desertmoon
guesthouse.com; Achalvansi Colony; s ₹700-800,
d ₹800-1000; ❄) On the northwest edge
of town, 1km from Gandhi Chowk, Desert
Moon is in a peaceful location beneath
the Vyas Chhatri sunset point. The
guesthouse is run by a friendly Indian-
Kiwi couple who offer free pick-up from
the train and bus stations. The 11 rooms
are cool, clean and comfortable and the
rooftop vegetarian restaurant has fort
and *chhatri* (cenotaph) views.

HOTEL PLEASANT HAVELI Hotel **$$**
(☏ 253253; www.pleasanthaveli.com; Chainpura
St; r ₹1200-2000, ste ₹2000-3250; ❄ 🛜)
Recently renovated, this welcoming place
has lots of lovely carved stone, a beautiful
rooftop and just a handful of spacious,
attractive, colour-themed rooms, all with
bathroom and AC.

HOTEL FIFU
Hotel $$

(☎254317; www.fifutravel.com; Bera Rd; r incl breakfast ₹2650; ❄ 📶) Down a dusty lane on the south edge of town, this hotel is a little out of the way, though the beautiful, colour-themed sandstone rooms afford a very peaceful and pleasant stay. The rooftop has tremendous views and a great vegetarian restaurant.

HOTEL NACHANA HAVELI
Heritage Hotel $$

(☎252110; www.nachanahaveli.com; Gandhi Chowk; s/d ₹2500/3000; ❄ @) This 280-year-old royal *haveli,* set around three courtyards – one with a tinkling fountain – is a fascinating hotel. The raw sandstone rooms have arched stone ceilings and the ambience of a medieval castle.

HOTEL GORAKH HAVELI
Hotel $$

(☎9982657525; www.hotelgorakhhaveli.com; Dhibba; s/d ₹1000/1500, AC ₹1500/2500; ❄) A pleasantly low-key spot south of the fort, Gorakh Haveli is a modern place built with traditional sandstone and some attractive carving. Rooms are comfy and spacious, staff are amiable, and there's a reasonable multicuisine rooftop restaurant.

HOTEL RENUKA
Hotel $

(☎252757; hotelrenuka@rediffmail.com; Chainpura St; r ₹200-750; ❄ @) Spread over three floors, Renuka has squeaky clean rooms – the best have balconies, bathrooms and AC. It's been warmly accommodating guests since 1988, so management knows its stuff. The roof terrace has great fort views and a good restaurant.

🌿 ARTIST HOTEL
Hotel $

(☎252082; www.artisthotel.info; Artist Colony; s ₹150-250, d ₹250-500, AC tr ₹1000; ❄) This friendly, Austrian-and-Indian-run establishment helps support – and maintain the artistic traditions of – formerly nomadic musicians and storytellers who are now settled in the same area of

RESIDENCY CENTRE POINT
Guesthouse $

(☎/fax 252883; residency_guesthouse@ yahoo.com; Kumbhara Para; r ₹450) Near the Patwa-ki-Haveli, this friendly, family-run guesthouse has five clean, spacious doubles in a lovely 250-year-old building. Rooms vary in size – budget by price but midrange in quality. The rooftop restaurant has superb fort views and offers home-cooked food.

Jaisalmer

town. There are great fort views from the roof, where frequent musical events take place, and a very good range of European and Indian dishes (mains ₹85 to ₹220) is served.

In the Fort
HOTEL KILLA BHAWAN
Boutique Hotel **$$$**
(☎251204; www.killabhawan.com; 445 Kotri Para; r incl breakfast ₹3850-9400; ❄) A cute mini-labyrinth of a place combining three old houses set right on the fort walls. French-owned and designed, it has vividly coloured rooms, attractive little sitting areas and all sorts of intriguing arts and crafts.

Hotel Paradise Hotel **$**
(☎252674; www.paradiseonfort.com; r ₹300-2000, AC from ₹1050; ❄ @) Right above the fort's southern walls, Paradise has great terraces for lounging, eating and drinking, and nice clean rooms, many with views.

Hotel Siddhartha Hotel
(☎253614; r ₹500-700) Just past the Jain temples, little Siddhartha has well-kept, stone-walled rooms with attached bathrooms; some with street or panoramic views and some have no views.

A sweets maker pounding dough
RICHARD I'ANSON/LONELY PLANET IMAGES ©

Jaisalmer Camel Safaris

Trekking around by camel is the most evocative and fun way to sample Thar Desert life. Don't expect dune seas, however – the Thar is mostly arid scrubland sprinkled with villages and wind turbines, with occasional dune areas popping out here and there.

Most trips now include jeep rides to get you to less frequented areas, often with stops at a few interesting spots en route.

BEFORE YOU GO

Competition between safari organisers is cut-throat and standards vary. Most hotels and guesthouses are very happy to organise a camel safari for you.

You can also organise a safari direct with one of the several reputable specialist agencies in Jaisalmer. Since these agencies depend exclusively on safari business it's particularly in their interest to satisfy their clients. It's a good idea to talk to other travellers and ask two or three operators what they're offering.

A one-night safari, leaving Jaisalmer in the afternoon and returning next morning, with a night on some dunes, is a minimum to get a feel for the experience: you'll probably get 1½ to two hours riding each day.

The best known dunes, at Sam (40km west of Jaisalmer) and Khuri, are always crowded in the evening and are more of a carnival than a back-to-nature experience. 'Non-touristy' and 'off the beaten track' trips take you to other areas, usually southwest from Jaisalmer to the area between Sam and Khuri, or beyond Khuri.

With jeep transfers included, typical rates are between ₹550 and ₹750 per person per day. This should include three meals a day – at least porridge, tea and toast for breakfast, and rice, dhal and chapatis for lunch and dinner – plus as much mineral water and as many blankets as you need, and often thin mattresses. Check that there will be one camel for each rider.

You shouldn't have to pay for a full day if you're returning after breakfast on the last day. One-night safaris starting in the afternoon and ending the following morning are normally charged as about 1½ days.

WHICH SAFARI?

Reputable, established agencies include:

○ **Ganesh Travels** (☏250138; ganeshtravel45@hotmail.com; Fort) Run by camel owners from the villages and has a good basic rate of ₹550 per day.

○ **Sahara Travels** (☏252609; sahara_travels@yahoo.com; Gopa Chowk) Its office is just outside the First Fort Gate. This agency gets good reviews and is run by the proudly bearded and moustachioed LN Bissa, alias Mr Desert. The normal daily rate is ₹700.

○ **Trotters** (☏9414469292; www.trotterscamelsafarijaisalmer.com; Gopa Chowk) Trotters has a daily rate of ₹750 but provides very reliable service.

Whichever agency you go for, insist that all rubbish is carried back to Jaisalmer.

 Eating

As well as the many hotel-rooftop eateries, there's a good number of other places to enjoy a tasty meal, often with a view.

DESERT BOY'S DHANI   Indian $
(Dhibba; mains ₹70-90; ⏰8am-10pm) This is a walled-garden restaurant where tables are spread around a large, stone-paved courtyard with a big tree. Rajasthani music and dance is performed from 8pm to 10pm nightly, and it's a very pleasant place to eat excellent, good-value Rajasthani and other Indian veg dishes.

JAISAL ITALY   Italian $$
(First Fort Gate; mains ₹120-170) Superb all-veg bruschetta, antipasti, pasta, pizza, salad and desserts, plus Spanish omelettes, served in an exotically decorated indoor restaurant (cosy in winter, deliciously air-conditioned in summer) or on a delightful terrace atop the lower fort walls, with cinematic views.

NATRAJ RESTAURANT   Multicuisine $$
(mains ₹110-270) This is an excellent place to eat, and the rooftop has a satisfying view of the upper part of the Salim Singh-ki-Haveli next door. The veg and non-veg food, including tandoori and curries, as well as Chinese and Continental dishes, is consistently excellent, as is the service.

SAFFRON   Multicuisine $$
(Gandhi Chowk; mains ₹70-180) On the spacious roof terrace of Hotel Nachana Haveli, the veg and non-veg food here is excellent and it's a particularly atmospheric place in the evening. The Indian food is hard to beat, though the Italian comes a close second.

ⓘ **Information**

Money

Thomas Cook (Gandhi Chowk; ⏰9.30am-7pm Mon-Sat, 10am-5pm Sun) A reliable moneychanger changing travellers cheques and cash, and providing credit- and debit-card advances.

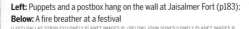
Left: Puppets and a postbox hang on the wall at Jaisalmer Fort (p183);
Below: A fire breather at a festival
(LEFT) DALLAS STRIBLEY/LONELY PLANET IMAGES ©; (BELOW) JOHN SONES/LONELY PLANET IMAGES ©

Tourist Information

Tourist Reception Centre (☏252406;
Gadi Sagar Rd; ⊙9.30am-6pm) Friendly office
with a free (if old) town map and various
brochures. Helpful staff will answer questions.

Getting There & Away

Air

The airport, 5km south of town, opens and
closes intermittently due to border tensions
with Pakistan. In early 2011 it was closed. The
most recent flights were operated by Kingfisher
Airlines (www.flykingfisher.com) to Jodhpur.

Bus

RSRTC buses leave from a stand just off Shiv Rd
on the south side of town. There are buses to
Jodhpur (₹125/155, 5½ hours, 15 daily).

Taxi

One-way taxis should cost about ₹1800 to
Jodhpur or ₹4500 to Udaipur. There is a stand on
Hanuman Circle Rd.

Train

The station (⊙ticket office 8am-8pm Mon-Sat,
8am-1.45pm Sun) is on the eastern edge of town,
just off the Jodhpur road.

Two daily express trains leave for Jodhpur. The
Jaisalmer-Jodhpur Express (14809; sleeper/3AC
₹165/419) departs at 11.15pm, reaching Jodhpur at
5.20am. The 14060 *Jaisalmer-Delhi Express* leaves
at 4.30pm, reaching Jodhpur (sleeper/3AC/2AC
₹165/419/566) at 9.50pm, and continues to Jaipur
(₹262/693/945, 10½ hours from Jaisalmer) and
Delhi (₹331/888/1215, 18½ hours).

Getting Around

Car & Motorcycle

It's possible to hire taxis or jeeps from the stand
on Hanuman Circle Rd. To the Sam sand dunes,
expect to pay ₹500 return, including a wait of
about an hour or so.

Goa & Around

It's green, it's glistening and it's gorgeous: just three of the reasons why Goa has allured travellers for decades. Two million visitors come each year for the silken sand, crystalline shores, coconut culture and *susegad* – a Portuguese-derived term that translates loosely to 'laid-backness'.

But there's more to discover here than the pleasure of warm sand between your toes. Goa is as beautiful and culturally rich as it is tiny and hassle-free, so you can marvel at centuries-old cathedrals, venture out to white-water waterfalls or meander through the capital's charming alleyways, all in between lazy beach days (or weeks). Pour in a dash of Portuguese-influenced food and architecture, infuse with a colourful blend of religious traditions, pepper with parties, and you've got a heady mix that's extremely hard to leave, though it's worth tearing yourself away to make a side trip to the stunning ancient site of Hampi in bordering Karnakata.

Colourful beach shacks, Goa
THOMAS BOEHM/PHOTOLIBRARY

Interior of an Old Goa church

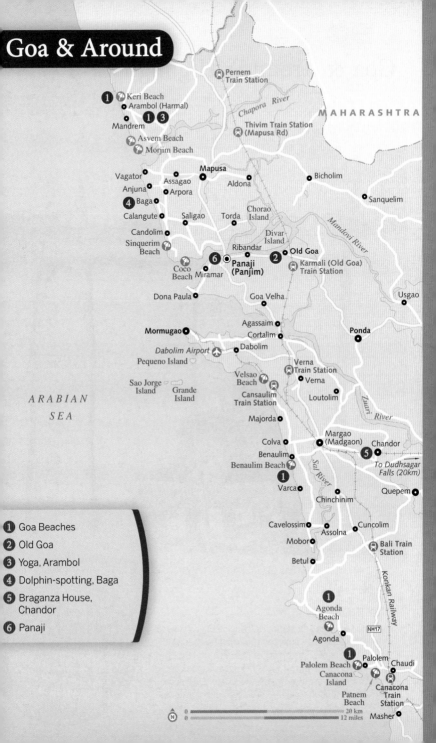

Goa & Around

MAHARASHTRA

Chapora River

❶ Keri Beach
Arambol (Harmal)
Mandrem
❶ ❸

Pernem Train Station

Thivim Train Station (Mapusa Rd)

Asvem Beach
Morjim Beach

Vagator
Assagao
Anjuna
Arpora
❹ Baga
Calangute
Saligao
Candolim
Sinquerim Beach
Coco Beach
Miramar

Mapusa
Aldona

Bicholim

Sanquelim

Chorao Island

Torda

Divar Island
Ribandar

❻ Panaji (Panjim)

Old Goa ❷
Karmali (Old Goa) Train Station

Mandovi River

Usgao

Dona Paula

Goa Velha

Agassaim
Cortalim

Mormugao
Dabolim Airport
Pequeno Island
Dabolim

Ponda

Verna Train Station
Verna
Loutolim

ARABIAN SEA

Sao Jorge Island
Grande Island

Velsao Beach
Cansaulim Train Station

Majorda

Colva
Benaulim
Benaulim Beach
❶
Varca

Margao (Madgaon)
Chandor
❺

Sal River

Zuari River

To Dudhsagar Falls (20km)

Quepem

Chinchinim

Cavelossim
Mobor
Betul

Assolna
Cuncolim

Bali Train Station

Konkan Railway

❶ Goa Beaches
❷ Old Goa
❸ Yoga, Arambol
❹ Dolphin-spotting, Baga
❺ Braganza House, Chandor
❻ Panaji

❶ Agonda Beach
Agonda
NH17

❶ Palolem Beach
Palolem
Chaudi
Canacona Island
Canacona Train Station
Patnem Beach
Masher

0   20 km
0   12 miles

Goa & Around's Highlights

① Goa Beaches

Goa is one of India's best places to kick back on powder-white beaches. In some places the coast has become built up, but there's still plenty of paradise-style, palm-shaded coastline, where it's easy to escape, relax and tuck into fresh-from-the-boat seafood. Here are some local recommendations for Goa's best beach options.

Need to Know

SURVIVAL TIP Don't swim when wasted. **AVOID** Christmas and New Year, when parties rage but so do prices and hoards. **For more, see p202 and Map p193.**

Goa Beaches Don't Miss List

ANTHONY DAS WAS BORN AND BRED IN GOA, AND HAS WORKED IN THE TOURIST INDUSTRY FOR MANY YEARS

1 ARAMBOL BEACH

To the extreme north of Goa, this beach used to be a hippie hang-out in the 1970s, and it's still popular with backpackers rather than mainstream tourists. A short walk away from the beach there's a sweet-water lake. It's scenic, hasn't been over-exploited, and is extremely laid-back.

2 KERI BEACH

Even further north than Arambol, there is Keri Beach, shaded by pine trees, a hassle-free place. Here there are hardly any buildings, just a few shacks. There's a little ferry that runs across the Keri river to arrive at Terekhol Fort, an old Portuguese fortress on the Goa-Maharashtra border.

3 PALOLEM BEACH

Again this is a quiet south Goa beach. The accommodation here is all in tents and cottages, without any big hotels. It's long been on the traveller radar, but it's quite far from the main towns so retains a secluded feel, and there are strict building regulations here. The beach is a little cove, so there are no big waves – it's an ideal place to swim.

4 AGONDA BEACH

Previously a lot of long-stayers in caravans from Europe used to come to Agonda, in south Goa. Visitors also used to stay in local houses as paying guests. But nowadays people tend to stay in cottages; the beach is well-equipped and also very clean, cleaner than many beaches in the north.

5 BENAULIM BEACH

This is beautiful. It's big: a 15km to 20km stretch of white sand. It's very popular with foreign tourists – local tourists tend to prefer the busier beaches close to the main towns. There are lots of five-star hotels close by, and watersports are popular here; they tend to be safer and better organised than other, more remote places.

Old Goa

Gaze at the cathedral-filled remains of Old Goa (p207), which from the 16th to the 18th centuries was the 'Rome of the East'. Only shadows of this history remain, but it's a picturesque place that's full of faded vestiges of Catholic splendour, adapted to the local environment. home to the largest church in Asia, as well as some beautiful 16th- and 17th-century chape

Basilica of Bom Jesus (p209)

Yoga, Arambol

Goa is a great place to practise some alternative therapies and yoga (p212). Fr Ashtanga through to Zen, every kind o spiritually orientated health regime is to be found here. There are plenty of places all over the state to take cours or have treatments such as ayurvedi massage. Try the lovely beach of Arar bol to track down some local practitic ers. Class at a yoga retreat, Goa

Dolphin-spotting, Baga

4

Goa is a nature-lover's paradise, perfect for wildlife-watching, with an abundance of brilliant birdlife and a fine (but well-concealed) collection of fauna, including sambars, barking deer and the odd leopard. Many resorts offer dolphin-spotting rides – try Baga beach (p208) and you'll find someone with a boat eager to show you those adorable grey mammals of the sea. Fishing boat being pushed out to sea, Baga

5

Braganza House, Chandor

You can feel a palpable sense of times gone by in the faded mansions of Goa, such as Braganza House (p216) in Chandor, 15km east of Margao. This glorious 17th-century mansion is full of worn splendour, a Miss Havisham–style spectacle of gorgeous chandeliers, Italian marble floors, rosewood furniture, and antique treasures from Macau, Portugal, China and Europe.

6

Panaji

Is Panaji (p202) India's cutest capital? It's a friendly, manageable and walkable city and its Portuguese-era colonial charms make it a perfect place to lull away a day or two. Stroll the peaceful streets, take a kitschy river cruise, eat delicious vindaloos and end the evening in a cosy local bar.

Goa's Best...

Wining & Dining

○ **Upper House** (p205) Fabulous home-style regional dishes in Panaji

○ **Café Inn** (p221) Great night-time barbecue in Palolem

○ **Shore Bar** (p211) Cliffside, breezy cafe with great vibe and eats in Anjuna

○ **Seasonal beach shacks** (all over) Fresh fish on the menu, toes in the sand

Chill-out Spots

○ **Arambol** (p212) Longtime favourite, north Goa's laid-back beach hang-out

○ **Benaulim** (p215) Broad, open beaches in the south

○ **Palolem** (p218) Stunning crescent of southern beach

○ **Patnem Beach** (p219) Even more secluded than nearby Palolem

Local Culture

○ **Panaji** (p202) Chilled-out Goan capital

○ **Old Goa** (p207) Centre of Indian Catholicism, full of colonial-era churches

○ **Braganza House** (p216) Glorious, faded 17th-century mansion

○ **Goa Chitra** (p215) Ethnographic museum preserving Goa's domestic past.

Character-filled Sleeps

○ **Hotel Bougainvillea** (p210) Ridiculously pretty hotel in a 200-year-old mansion

○ **Palacete Rodrigues** (p210) Cool and quirky mansion with themed rooms

○ **Bhakti Kutir** (p220) A unique jungle retreat

○ **Ciaran's** (p220) Rustic yet sophisticated Palolem beach huts

Need to Know

ADVANCE PLANNING

○ **One month before** Book any particularly special accommodation

○ **Two weeks before** Reserve long train journeys

○ **One day before** Arrange wildlife-spotting boat trips

RESOURCES

○ **Goa Tourism** (www.goa-tourism.com) Good background and tour info

○ **Goa World** (www.goa-world.com) General info on Goan culture

○ **Goa's English dailies** (www.navhindtimes.in & www. oheraldo.in) For the news

BE FOREWARNED

○ **Illegal substances** Being caught, even with small quantities of illegal drugs, can mean a hefty sentence in jail

○ **Strong currents** Check where it's safe to swim before launching into the Arabian Sea

○ **Christmas & New Year** If you're looking for peace and quiet, be aware that this is the most crowded and expensive period

GETTING AROUND

○ **Taxi** Cars and drivers are available to hire in most towns; try your hotel or the local taxi stand

○ **Konkan Railway** This is the main train line running through Goa and connecting with Mumbai

○ **Motorcycle** Very popular all over the region, but take care on the potholed, haphazard Goan roads

○ **Bus** There's an extensive network of buses serving even the smallest towns

Left: Colonial houses, Panaji (p202);
Above: Fish for sale at market, Panaji

(LEFT) GREG ELMS/LONELY PLANET IMAGES ©;
(ABOVE) GREG ELMS/LONELY PLANET IMAGES ©

Goa Itineraries

Central Goa is the state's most cultural part, with its gracious capital Panaji, while the north is the liveliest, harbouring the last remnants of the region's fabled party scene. For utter peace and relaxation, head to the quieter beaches in the south.

5 DAYS

PANAJI TO ARAMBOL
North Goa Explorer

Start your trip in the charming Goan capital, **(1) Panaji**, where you can wander the old town, see its historic buildings, take cruises along the Mandovi River, and dine at delicious, laid-back restaurants. From here you can take a day trip to Old Goa for more sun-bleached colonial-era buildings and a sense of the culture of the region. Next, take a short bus or taxi ride to **(2) Baga** to enjoy some excellent cooking, beach fun and watersports in this lively resort.

From Baga it's an easy day trip to visit the famous flea market at **(3) Anjuna**, which takes place every Wednesday, after which you could head still further north to the appealing beach town of **(4) Arambol**, a corner of Goa that's a well-known traveller magnet, with something of a mainstream festival vibe – the main drag leading to the beach is known as 'Glastonbury St'. For what's left of Goa's party scene, this is where to head. It's hence not the most peaceful or least discovered beach along the coast, but certainly has a great deal of charm, and beach huts aplenty.

Top Left: Market stalls, Anjuna (p209);
Top Right: Checking for holes in fishing nets, Benaulim (p215)
(LEFT) GREG ELMS/LONELY PLANET IMAGES ©; (RIGHT) GREG ELMS/LONELY PLANET IMAGES ©

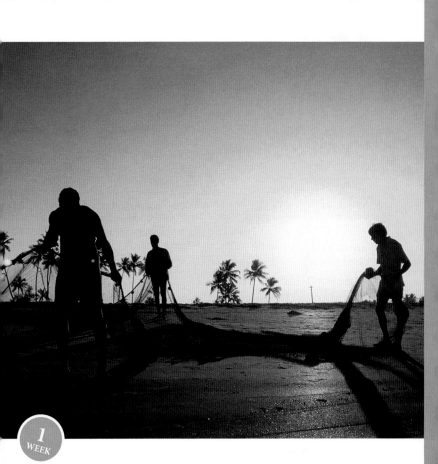

South Goa Relaxer

This itinerary explores the tranquil coastal stretches in the south of Goa, with its white-sand beaches and undiscovered-feeling coves, but you can kick off in the relaxed regional capital of **(1) Panaji**, as with the first itinerary.

Next travel south, either taking the train from Old Goa to the transport hub of Margao and then taking a taxi, or by hiring a taxi all the way to the coastal resort of **(2) Benaulim**, to relax on its long white-sand beach, and explore the surrounding empty and gorgeous coastline, dotted with Portuguese-era mansions and whitewashed churches. From here you can also take a trip to explore inland, heading to the town of **(3) Chandor**, which is home to several fantastical mansions, including the sumptuous, 17th-century Braganza House, of which one wing is fantastically well preserved, while the other is peeling and dilapidated. Next, travel still further south (again, most easily by taxi) to the stunning crescent of beach of **(4) Palolem**, one of Goa's most beautiful spots, with calm seas and plenty of opportunities for yoga and to indulge in alternative therapies while resting up in picturesque beach huts or lusher, low-key resorts set back from the beach.

Discover Goa & Around

CENTRAL GOA
Panaji (Panjim)
POP 98,915

Panaji (more commonly known as Panjim) has yellow houses with purple doors, cats lying in front of bicycles parked beneath oyster-shell windows, paddle-wheel boats moseying along the river that laps the city's northern boundary and a giant church on a hill that looks like a fancy wedding cake. It's a friendly, manageable and walkable city – maybe India's cutest capital – and its Portuguese-era colonial charms make it a perfect place to while away a day or two.

⊙ Sights

CHURCH OF OUR LADY OF THE IMMACULATE CONCEPTION   Church

Panaji's spiritual and geographical centre is its gleamingly picturesque main church, consecrated in 1541. When Panaji was little more than a sleepy fishing village, this place was the first port of call for sailors from Lisbon, who would clamber up here to thank their lucky stars for a safe crossing before continuing to Old Goa, the state's capital until the 19th century, further east up the river.

☞ Tours

The Goa Tourism Development Corporation (GTDC) operates a range of boat trips along the Mandovi River, including daily hour-long **cruises** (₹150; ⊙6pm & 7.15pm) and two-hour **dinner cruises** (₹450;

Person on a giant boulder, Hampi (p222)
ANDERS BLOMQVIST/LONELY PLANET IMAGES ©

8.45pm) aboard the *Santa Monica*. All include a live band and dancers – sometimes lively, sometimes lacklustre – performing Goan folk songs and dances. Cruises depart from the Santa Monica jetty beside the New Patto Bridge, where the **GTDC boat counter** (2437496) also sells tickets.

Three private companies also offer one-hour **night cruises** (adult/child ₹150/free; 6pm, 7pm & 8.30pm) departing from Santa Monica jetty. The GTDC cruises are a little more staid, while others – maybe because of the bars and DJs – can get rowdy with groups of local male tourists.

Sleeping

As in the rest of Goa, prices vary wildly in Panaji depending on supply and demand.

MAYFAIR HOTEL　　　　　　Hotel **$$**
(2223317; Dr Dada Vaidya Rd; s/d from ₹900/1200;) Bright rooms at this friendly family-run hotel have mango-yellow accents, woodblock-print curtains and either balconies on the street side or windows overlooking the backyard garden (think palms, flowers and cats chasing butterflies). Beautiful ground-floor oyster-shell windows and old-fashioned good service make it atmospheric, too.

CASA NOVA　　Guesthouse **$$$**
(9423889181, 7709886212; www.goaholidayaccommodation.com; Gomes Pereira Rd; ste ₹3100) Here's your chance to actually stay in one of Panaji's gorgeous old Portuguese-style homes – if you can get a booking. Casa Nova consists of just one stylish, exceptionally comfy suite, accessed via a little alley and complete with arched windows, wood-beam ceilings and mod cons like a kitchenette. Sister property **Casa Morada** (9822196007,

9881966789; agomes@tbi.in; Gomes Pereira Rd; s/d incl breakfast ₹5000/10,000) is as fancy as Nova is modern. Its two bedrooms and sitting room are full of antique furniture and objets d'art (ergo the no children, no pets policy), with real art on the walls and floors of elegant pale-green marble.

CROWN　　　　　　　　　Hotel **$$$**
(2400060; www.thecrowngoa.com; Jose Falcao Rd; d/ste from ₹5000/10,000; @) Perched high above Panaji, with lovely views from its cool and peaceful pool area, is this great option for a bit of luxury in the midst of the city. Recent renovations have resulted in airy, tastefully done rooms in mustards and whites (some with balconies) with super-modern bathrooms.

AFONSO GUEST HOUSE　　Hotel **$$**
(2222359, 9764300165; St Sebastian Rd; r ₹1500) Run by the friendly Jeanette, this place in a pretty old Portuguese-era town house offers spacious, well-kept rooms with wood-plank ceilings and a pinch of character. The little rooftop terrace, meanwhile, makes for sunny breakfasting (dishes ₹20 to ₹30). It's a simple, serene stay in

Goan specialty Kingfish Xacuti
GREG ELMS/LONELY PLANET IMAGES ©

204

Panaji (Panjim)

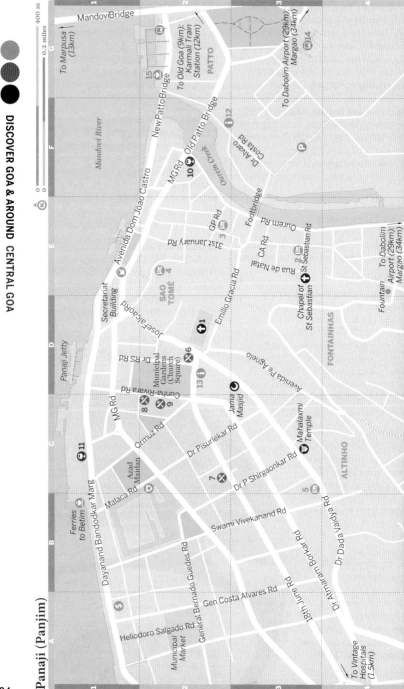

0   0   400 m
0   0.2 miles

MandoviBridge

To Marpusa
(13km)

Mandovi River

Panaji Jetty

Ferries
to Betim

Secretariat
Building

Avenida Dom Joao Castro

MG Rd

New Patto Bridge

Old Patto Bridge

To Old Goa (9km);
Karmali Train
Station (12km)

PATTO

Queula Creek

Dr Alvaro
Costa Rd

Footbridge

Ourem Rd

To Dabolim Airport (29km);
Margao (34km)

SAO
TOMÉ

JosefalcaoRd

31st January Rd

GP Rd

Emilio Gracia Rd

CA Rd

Rua de Natal

St Sebastian Rd

Chapel of
St Sebastian

Fountain

To Dabolim
Airport (29km);
Margao (34km)

FONTAINHAS

Municipal
Gardens
(Church
Square)

Dr RS Rd

Cunha-Rivara Rd

MG Rd

Ormuz Rd

Azad
Maidan

Malaca Rd

Dayanand Bandodkar Marg

Municipal
Market

Heliodoro Salgado Rd

General Bernado Guedes Rd

Gen Costa Alvares Rd

Dr Pisurlekar Rd

Dr P Shirgaonkar Rd

Jama
Masjid

Avenida Pe Agnelo

Mahalaxmi
Temple

ALTINHO

18th June Rd

Swami Vivekanand Rd

Dr Atmaram Borkar Rd

Dr Dada Vaidya Rd

To Vintage
Hospitals
(1.5km)

1
2
3
4
5
6
7
8
9
10
11
12
13
14
15

Panaji (Panjim)

the heart of the most atmospheric part of town with just two small faults: checkout is 9am and it doesn't take bookings.

Eating

You'll never go hungry in Panaji, where food is enjoyed fully and frequently. A stroll down 18th June or 31st January Rds will turn up a number of great, cheap canteen-style options, as will a quick circuit of the Municipal Gardens.

UPPER HOUSE   Goan **$$**
(Cunha-Rivara Rd; mains ₹95-295; ☺11am-10pm) Fans of Goan seafood *and* vegetarians can rejoice in the food at this new spot specialising in home-style regional dishes. Local favourites like crab *xec xec* (crab cooked in a roasted-coconut gravy), pork vindaloo and fish-curry-rice are done the old-fashioned way (the latter even comes with saltwater mango pickle, rarely found outside Goan mothers' kitchens), and even the veg adaptations (eg mixed veg and mushroom *xacuti*) are show-stoppers.

SHER-E-PUNJAB   North Indian **$$**
(18th June Rd; mains ₹70-140; ☺10.30am-11.30pm) A cut above the usual lunch joint, Sher-E-Punjab caters to well-dressed locals with its generous, carefully spiced Punjabi dishes: even a humble *mattar pa-*

neer (unfermented cheese and pea curry) is memorable here. There's a pleasant garden terrace out back, too, open seasonally. The food at the fancier branch of **Sher-E-Punjab** (Hotel Aroma, Cunha-Rivara Rd; mains ₹120-270; ☺11am-3pm & 7-10.30pm) is equally tasty.

GEORGE BAR & RESTAURANT Goan **$$**
(Church Sq; mains ₹75-160; ☺9.30am-10.30pm) Slightly cramped wooden tables and a healthy mix of drunks and families make for a good local, down-to-earth vibe. Seafood's the name of the game here, and it's done especially well in *pilau* (rice cooked in stock; often spelled *pulao* in Goa) and other Goan classics. George is also one of those rare birds in Goa that does good veg; try the biryani or the delish veg *pilau*.

Drinking

Panaji's got pick-me-up pit stops aplenty, especially in Sao Tomé and Fontainhas. Mostly simple little bars with a few plastic tables and chairs, they're a great way to get chatting with locals.

Down the Road   Bar
(MG Rd; ☺11am-2am) This restaurant's balcony overlooking the creek and Old Patto Bridge makes for a good and comfy cocktail spot. The

ground-floor bar is also Panaji's only real late-nighter, with occasional live music.

Quarterdeck　　　　　　　　　Bar
(Dayanand Bandodkar Marg; ⏱11am-10.45pm)
The prices here are on the high side, but the spot right on the water makes up for that. It's the perfect place for an evening drink.

ℹ️ Information

Goa Tourism Development Corporation
(GTDC; ☎2424001/2/3; www.goa-tourism.com; Dr Alvaro Costa Rd; ⏱9.30am-1.15pm & 2-5.45pm Mon-Sat) Pick up maps of Goa and Panaji here and book one of GTDC's host of tours.

Indiatourism (Government of India tourist office; ☎2223412; www.incredibleindia.com; 1st fl, Communidade Bldg, Church Sq; ⏱9.30am-6pm Mon-Fri, to 2pm Sat) Helpful staff can provide a list of qualified guides for tours and trips in Goa. A half-/full-day tour for up to five people costs ₹600/750.

Thomas Cook (☎2221312; Dayanand Bandodkar Marg; ⏱9.30am-6pm Mon-Sat) Changes travellers cheques commission-free and handles currency exchange, wire transfers, cash advances on credit cards, and air bookings.

Vintage Hospitals (☎6644401-05, ambulance 2232533; www.vintage3.com; Cacula Enclave, St Inez) A couple of kilometres southwest of Panaji, Vintage is a reputable hospital with all the fixings.

ℹ️ Getting There & Away

AIR A taxi from Panaji to Dabolim Airport takes about an hour, and costs ₹500.
BUS All government buses depart from the **Kadamba bus stand** (☎local enquiries 2438034), with local services heading out every few minutes. To get to south Goan beaches, take a bus to Margao and change there.

Calangute ₹14, 45 minutes

Margao express; ₹26, 45 minutes

Old Goa ₹8, 15 minutes

State-run long-distance services also depart from the **Kadamba bus stand** (☎interstate enquiries 2438035; ⏱reservations 8am-8pm).
TRAIN Panaji's closest train station is Karmali (Old Goa), 12km to the east, where many long-distance

Detour: Dudhsagar Falls

On the eastern border with Karnataka are Goa's most impressive waterfalls, Dudhsagar Falls (603m). The second highest in India, they're best seen as soon as possible after the rains. Take the 8.13am train to Colem from Margao (check return times in advance; there are only three trains daily in each direction), and from there, catch a jeep for the bumpy 40-minute trip to the falls (₹300 return per person, or ₹1800 for the six-passenger jeep). It's a short but rocky clamber to the edge of the falls themselves.

A simpler but more expensive option is a full-day **GTDC tour** (₹700; ⏱9am-6pm Wed & Sun) from Panaji, Mapusa or Calangute (book at the office in Panaji); you can also arrange excursions with Speedy Travels in Anjuna (see p212) or Day Tripper in Goa (see boxed text, p210).

services stop. Panaji's **Konkan Railway reservation office** (☎2712940; ⏱8am-8pm Mon-Sat) is on the 1st floor of the Kadamba bus stand.

ℹ️ Getting Around

It's easy enough to get around Panaji on foot, and it's unlikely you'll even need a pilot or autorickshaw, which is good because they charge a lot: a rick from Kadamba to your hotel will cost ₹50. Frequent buses run between Kadamba and the municipal market (₹5).

To Old Goa, a taxi costs around ₹300, an autorickshaw ₹150. Lots of taxis hang around the Municipal Gardens, while you'll find autorickshaws and pilots in front of the post office, on 18th June Rd, and just south of the church.

Old Goa

From the 16th to the 18th centuries, when Old Goa's population exceeded that of Lisbon or London, this capital of Goa was considered the 'Rome of the East'. You can still sense that grandeur as you wander the grounds, with its towering churches and cathedral and majestic convents. Its rise under the Portuguese, from 1510, was meteoric, but cholera and malaria outbreaks forced the abandonment of the city in the 1600s. In 1843, the capital was officially shifted to Panaji.

Some of the churches, the cathedral and a convent or two are still in use, but many of the other historical buildings have become museums. It's a fascinating day trip, but it can get crowded: consider visiting on a weekday morning, when you can take in Mass at Sé Cathedral or the Basilica of Bom Jesus (remember to cover your shoulders and legs in the churches and cathedral), and definitely stop by if you're around in the 10 days leading up to the **Feast of St Francis Xavier** on 3 December.

 Sights

SÉ CATHEDRAL   Church

The largest church in Old Goa, the Sé de Santa Catarina, is also the largest in Asia, at over 76m long and 55m wide. Construction began in 1562, under orders from Portugal's King Dom Sebastião, and the finishing touches were made 90 years later. Fairly plain all-round, the cathedral has three especially notable features: the first, up in the belfry, is the **Golden Bell**, the largest bell in Asia; the second is in the screened chapel inside to the right, known as the **Chapel of the Cross of Miracles**, wherein sits a cross said to have miraculously, and vastly, expanded in size after its creation by local shepherds in 1619. The third is the massive gilded *reredos* (ornamental screen behind the altar), which depicts the life of St Catherine, to whom the cathedral is dedicated and who came to a sticky end in Alexandria, Egypt, where she was beheaded.

Old Goa

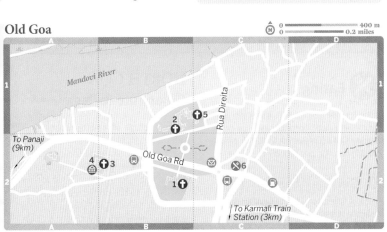

Old Goa

Mandovi River

To Panaji (9km)

Rua Direita

Old Goa Rd

To Karmali Train Station (3km)

TIBOR BOGNAR/ALAN

Don't Miss Museum of Christian Art

This excellent museum, set in a positively stunning space in the restored 1627 **Convent of St Monica**, has a fine collection of 16th- and 17th-century Christian art from Old Goa and around the state. There are some exquisite pieces here – wooden sculptures glittering with gilt and polychrome, processional lamps, tabernacle doors, polychrome paintings and other religious objects from Old Goa's prime – that are almost, but not quite, outdone by the atmospheric interior. The four-storey-high ceilings, exposed wood beams, terracotta work and all-around beauty of the place are worth a visit in their own right.

THINGS YOU NEED TO KNOW

http://christianartmuseum.goa-india.org; adult/child ₹30/free; ☉9.30am-5pm

 Eating

Little tourist restaurants with chai and snacks are peppered around; the basic **Sanjay Cafe** (Old Goa Rd; thalis ₹35, tiffins ₹25-30) has the best food in town.

ℹ **Getting There & Away**

Frequent buses from Old Goa head to Panaji's Kadamba bus stand (₹8, 25 minutes) from Old Goa Rd.

NORTH GOA
Calangute & Baga
POP 15,800

Once a refuge of wealthy Goans, and later a 1960s hot spot for naked, revelling hippies, Calangute today is popular with extended Indian families, groups of Indian bachelors and partying foreigners. Baga, to the north, meanwhile, is the place for drinking and dancing, attracting a younger crowd with clubs open until 4am.

Sleeping & Eating

CAVALA SEASIDE RESORT   Hotel **$$**
(2276090; www.cavala.com; s/d/ste incl breakfast from ₹850/1300/2200; ❄️ 🛜 🏊) Classy, ivy-clad Cavala has been charming Baga-bound travellers for more than 30 years, and continues to deliver clean, simple, nicely furnished rooms among a large complex with two swimming pools (₹150 for non-guests). There's a good vibe about the place and friendly staff, and the bar-restaurant cooks up a storm most evenings, with frequent live music.

LE POISSON ROUGE   French **$$$**
(mains ₹310-390; ⏱7pm-midnight) Baga manages to do fine dining with aplomb, and this French-slanted experience is one of the picks of the place. Simple local ingredients are combined into winning dishes such as beetroot carpaccio (₹185) and red-snapper masala (₹390), and served up beneath the stars.

ℹ Getting There & Around

Frequent buses to Panaji (₹14, 45 minutes) and Mapusa (₹10) depart from the Baga and Calangute bus stands, and a local bus (₹5) runs between the Baga and Calangute stands every few minutes; catch it anywhere along the way. A prepaid taxi from Dabolim Airport to Calangute costs ₹645.

Anjuna

Dear old Anjuna, that stalwart on India's hippy scene, still drags out the sarongs and sandalwood each Wednesday for its famous – and once infamous – flea market. Though it continues to pull in droves of backpackers and long-term hippies, mid-range tourists are also increasingly making their way here. The town itself might be a bit ragged around the edges these days, but that's all part of its cosy charm.

🏃 Activities

Anjuna's charismatic, rocky **beach** runs for almost 2km from the northern village area to the flea market. The northern end shrinks to almost nothing when the tide washes in, but when the tide goes out, it becomes a lovely, and surprisingly quiet, stretch of sand. For more action, **paragliding** (tandem rides ₹1500) sometimes takes place on market days off the headland at the southern end of the beach.

Yoga

There's lots of yoga, reiki and ayurvedic massage offered around Anjuna; look for notices at Café Diogo and the German Bakery. Drop-in classes are organised by **Avalon Sunset** (www.yogainternational organisation.com; classes ₹300-400) and at **Brahmani Yoga** (📞9370568639; www. brahmaniyoga.com; classes ₹500), next to Hotel Bougainvillea. Also consider staying at Yoga Magic or the Ashtanga Purple Valley Yoga Retreat, both lovely resorts with longer-term yoga programs.

🛏 Sleeping

Most accommodation and other useful services are sprinkled along the beach, or down shady inland lanes.

If You Like…
Churches

If you enjoy Old Goa's churches and architecture, seek out these other two gems.

1 CHURCH OF ST FRANCIS OF ASSISI
The gorgeous interior of this 1661 church, built over a 16th-century chapel, is filled with gilded and carved woodwork, murals depicting the life of St Francis, frescoes of decorative flowers and various angels, 16th-century Portuguese tombstones, and another stunning *reredos*.

2 BASILICA OF BOM JESUS
This imposing red-stone church was completed in 1605; its vast, gilded interior contains the last resting place of Goa's patron saint, St Francis Xavier.

If You Like…
Watery Adventures

If you like adventurous excursions, such as to **Dudhsagar Falls** (p210), you'll find numerous other watery activities to enjoy around Goa, based mainly around Baga

1 **BARRACUDA DIVING**
(☎2279409-14, 9822182402; www.barracudadiving.com; Sun Village Resort, Baga; courses from ₹4000) This long-standing diving school offers a range of dives and courses.

2 **LOCAL FISHERMEN**
Congregating around northern Baga beach, fishermen offer dolphin-spotting trips (₹400 per person), visits to Anjuna Market (₹200 per person) and excursions to Arambol and Mandrem (₹1000 per person). Try friendly fisherman Eugenio (☎9226268531).

3 **DAY TRIPPER**
(☎2276726; www.daytrippergoa.com; Gaura Vaddo; ◷9am-5.30pm Mon-Sat Nov-Apr) One of Goa's best tour agencies, Day Tripper runs a variety of trips, including two weekly to Dudhsagar Falls (₹1175) and another sailing through the mangroves of the Cumbarjua River (₹1300).

4 **ARAMBOL HAMMOCKS**
(☎9822389005; www.arambol.com; per 20min ₹1800; ◷9am-6pm) At the north end of Arambol beach you'll find Arambol Hammocks, an established paragliding option.

HOTEL BOUGAINVILLEA　Heritage Hotel　$$
(Granpa's Inn; ☎2273270/71; www.granpasinn.com; d/ste incl breakfast & tax from ₹2200/2950; ❄🛜🏊) This old-fashioned hotel in a 200-year-old yellow mansion is ridiculously pretty. Elegant rooms have that rare combination of charm and luxury, and the pool area is gorgeous, with lots of trees around. The grounds are so lush and shady, in fact, that the place seems a good few degrees cooler than the rest of Anjuna.

VILANOVA　Guesthouse　$
(☎6450389, 9225904244; mendonca90@rediffmail.com; d without/with AC ₹700/900; ❄) Big, clean rooms have fridge, TV, 24-hour hot water and window screens and are set in three Portuguese-style bungalows in a cute little compound. There are good vibes and a comfortable family atmosphere, with friendly staff and a good-value restaurant. We almost hate to tell anyone about it!

🖋 **YOGA MAGIC**　Guesthouse　$$$
(☎6523796; www.yogamagic.net; s/d huts ₹4500/6000, ste ₹6000/8000; 🛜) Solar lighting, vegetable farming and compost toilets are just some of the worthy initiatives practised in this ultraluxurious yoga resort, where hand-printed textiles, reclaimed-wood furniture and organic, gourmet vegetarian food are the order of the day. 'Huts' are of the stunning, dramatic Rajasthani variety. Rates include breakfast; daily yoga classes cost an extra ₹400 per session.

FAIZ'D　Guesthouse　$
(☎9619855350; tents ₹800) The spacious, high-end tents here are lined with embroidered fabric, have tile floors and attached bathrooms, and are set in pretty grounds – like a little tent village – with winding, lamp-lit paths. The location, a stone's throw from the beach, isn't bad, either.

PALACETE RODRIGUES　Heritage Hotel　$$
(☎2273358, 9422056467; www.palacetegoa.com; s/d from ₹850/1000, d/ste with AC ₹1550/1750; ❄) This old-fashioned mansion, filled with antiques, odd corners and bags of fun, tacky charm, is as cool and quirky as they come. Choose your theme: rooms come in Chinese, Vietnamese, Portuguese and, of course, Goan flavours.

PARADISE　Guesthouse　$
(☎9922541714; janet_965@hotmail.com; Anjuna-Mapusa Rd; d ₹600-800, with AC ₹1500; ❄) The friendly, homey Paradise is fronted by an old Portuguese house, and its clean rooms are set in rustic grounds

ull of crowing roosters and sleeping cats. Proprietor Janet and her enterprising family also run a general store, restaurant, internet cafe (₹40 per hour), travel agency, money exchange, Western Union services and beauty parlour (₹250 for head massages). You name it and Janet can probably arrange it for you.

 Eating & Drinking

Inside the flea market on market days (Wednesdays), look for the teensy **Maria's Tea Stall (snacks from ₹10)**, selling tasty chai and snacks made by colourful elderly local Maria herself.

SHORE BAR   Multicuisine   **$$**
(mains ₹120-400) Anjuna has lots of cliffside cafes with the standard traveller-oriented menus, happy hours and stunning coastal views, but the food is overwhelmingly mediocre. Shore Bar is the exception: the grilled baguettes, seafood and especially coffees are supergood (at a price), the walls are adorned with cool art, and loungy day beds and sofas are full of happy, mellow dreadlocked customers. Shore also has a no-commission art gallery and rooms out back. There were rumours at research time about relocating; we hope it's still there by the time you arrive.

GERMAN BAKERY   Multicuisine   **$$**
(pastries ₹30-50, mains ₹70-170;) Leafy and filled with prayer flags, jolly lights and atmospheric curtained nooks, this is a perfect place for a relaxed dinner. Innovative tofu dishes are a speciality: this may be your only chance to try tofu tikka (₹150). There's live music and sometimes Middle Eastern dancers

on Wednesday night and round-the-clock wi-fi (₹100 per hour).

CAFÉ DIOGO   Cafe   **$**
(Market Rd; snacks ₹30-100; 8am-5pm) Probably the best fruit salads in the world are sliced and diced at Café Diogo, a small locally run cafe on the way to the market. Also worth a munch are the generous toasted avocado, cheese and mushroom sandwiches.

WHOLE BEAN TOFU SHOP & VEGETERIA   Cafe   **$$**
(Market Rd; mains ₹60-150; 8am-5pm) One of the only places in Goa where vegans can eat well, this tofu-filled health-food cafe focuses on all things created from that most versatile of beans. Breakfasts include eggs (for the nonvegans) and a surprisingly good tofu scramble with onions and toast (₹130).

6PACK BAR & RESTAURANT   Multicuisine, Bar   **$$**
(Market Rd; mains ₹60-200; 9am-midnight) Everyone loves 6Pack for its excellent 'traditional' – that's code for beef –

Dusk at a beachside cafe, Anjuna
GREG ELMS/LONELY PLANET IMAGES ©

cheeseburgers (₹170), pool table, and festive vibe when sports are shown on the big screen upstairs.

Avalon Sunset Multicuisine **$**
(mains ₹50-140; 🛜) Nice views but so-so food; we only mention it for the wi-fi (₹40 per hour).

ℹ️ Information

Anjuna has three ATMs, clustered together about 100m east of Bank of Baroda (⊙9.30am-2.30pm), which gives cash advances on Visa and MasterCard.

Speedy Travels (📞2273266; ⊙9am-6.30pm Mon-Sat, 10am-1pm Sun) Reliable agency for air and train ticket booking, a range of tours (including one to Dudhsagar Falls), and credit-card advances or currency exchange.

ℹ️ Getting There & Away

Two daily buses to Calangute depart from the main crossroads. Cabs and pilots gather at both stops, and you can hire scooters and motorcycles easily from the crossroads.

Arambol (Harmal)

Arambol first emerged in the 1960s as a mellow paradise for long-haired long-stayers, and ever since, travellers attracted to the hippy atmosphere have been drifting up to this blissed-out corner of Goa, setting up camp and, in some cases, never leaving. As a result, in the high season the beach and the road leading down to it (the town is basically one road) can get pretty crowded – with huts, people and nonstop stalls selling the usual tourist stuff.

 Activities

HIMALAYAN IYENGAR YOGA CENTRE Yoga
(www.hiyogacentre.com) A popular spot for Iyengar yoga, with five-day courses (beginning on Fridays; ₹3000), intensive workshops, children's classes and teacher training all available. The centre is a five-minute walk from the beach, off

Left: Market stalls near Arambol beach;
Below: Boats and beachgoers on Arambol beach
(LEFT) GREG ELMS/LONELY PLANET IMAGES ©; (BELOW) GREG ELMS/LONELY PLANET IMAGES ©

the main road; look for the big banner. HI also has **huts** (**s/d without bathroom ₹250/300**) for students.

 **Sleeping**

Accommodation in Arambol is almost all of the budget variety, and it pays to trawl the cliffside to the north and south of Arambol's main beach stretch for the best hut options. Most are without private bathrooms but with incredible views.

CHILLI'S   Hotel **$**
(☎9921882424; s/d ₹300/400) This clean and simple place, owned by superfriendly and helpful Derick Fernandes, is one of Arambol's best nonbeachside bargains. Chilli's offers 10 nice, no-frills rooms on the beach road, near the beach entrance, all with attached bathroom, fan and hot-water shower; there's an honour system

for buying bottled water, self-service, from the fridge on the landing.

SHREE SAI COTTAGES   Beach Huts **$$**
(☎3262823, 9420767358; shreesai_cottages@ yahoo.com; huts without bathroom ₹1000) A short walk north from the main Arambol beach, Shree Sai has a calm, easygoing vibe and really cute hut-cottages with little balconies and lovely views out over the water. Maybe the best of the beach-hut bunch.

OM GANESH   Beach Huts **$**
(☎9404436447; r & huts ₹800) Popular huts right on the edge of the water, as well as rooms, managed by the friendly Sudir. The seaside Om Ganesh Restaurant is also a great place for lunch or dinner. Note that everyone in the area will tell you that their place is Om Ganesh; it's a family enterprise. Call ahead to avoid confusion.

213

 Eating & Drinking

Sparkly and parachute-silk-draped places to eat are everywhere in Arambol, from the top of the main road down to and along the full length of the beach and cliffs. Many change annually, but 21 Coconuts (for seafood) and Relax Inn (for Italian) are mainstays.

FELLINI Italian **$$**
(mains ₹140-280; ☺11am-11pm) Pizza's the big deal here – the menu has no fewer than 41 different kinds – and the pastas, calzones and paninis, especially with seafood, are also tasty. The tiramisu (₹60) will keep you up at night, thinking back on it fondly.

DOUBLE DUTCH Multicuisine **$$**
(mains ₹110-290) An ever-popular option for its steaks, salads, Thai and Indonesian dishes, and famous apple pies, all in a pretty garden setting. The noticeboard here is also worth a peruse, maybe while munching on a plateful of cookies or a huge sandwich.

ⓘ Information

Internet outfits, travel agents and money changers are as common as monsoon frogs on the road leading down to Arambol's beach, while several agencies towards the top of the road also offer parcel services by post, FedEx and DHL. The closest ATM is in Siolim, about 12km south.
JBL Enterprises (per hr ₹40; ☺8.30am-10.30pm) Internet cafe, travel agency, money and ISD: one-stop shopping.

ⓘ Getting There & Around

A prepaid taxi to Arambol from Dabolim Airport costs ₹975; from Mapusa it's ₹400.

Lots of places in Arambol rent scooters and motorbikes, for ₹200 and ₹300, respectively, per day; we like Derick's, at Chilli's, the best.

SOUTH GOA
Margao (Madgaon)
POP 94,400

The capital of Salcete province, Margao (also known as Madgaon) is the main population centre of south Goa and is a friendly, bustling market town of a man-

Fishing boats on the beach at Arambol

MICHAEL TAYLOR/LONELY PLANET IMAGES ©

geable size for getting things done, or for
etting in and out of the state.

Eating

WAD Indian **$**

New Market; veg thalis ₹40-75, mains ₹60-85)
Margao's best veg food, hands down, is at
he family-friendly, lunch-break favourite
SwaD, across from Lotus Inn. The thalis
re reliably delish, as are the snacks,
South Indian tiffins, mains and all the
other stuff on the 12-page menu of pure-
eg scrumptiousness.

Information

Banks offering currency exchange and 24-hour
ATMs are all around town, especially near the
municipal gardens and along Luis Miranda Rd.

Apollo Victor Hospital (☑2728888; Station Rd,
Malbhat) Reliable medical services.

Margao Residency (☑2715096; www.
goa-tourism.com) Book GTDC trips here.

Thomas Cook (Mabai Hotel Bldg; ◷9.30am-
6pm Mon-Sat)

Getting There & Around

BUS Local buses to Benaulim (₹7), Colva (₹10)
and Palolem (₹27) also swing by the bus stop on
the east side of the Municipal Gardens every 15
minutes or so.

TAXI Taxis are plentiful around the municipal
gardens, train station and Kadamba bus stand,
and they'll go anywhere in Goa, including Palolem
(₹700), Panaji (₹700), Calangute (₹900), Anjuna
(₹1100) and Arambol (₹1600). Except for the train
station, where there's a prepaid booth, you'll have
to negotiate the fare with the driver.

Autorickshaws and pilots are the most popular
way to get around town; most trips cost ₹50 and
₹30, respectively.

TRAIN Margao's well-organised train station,
about 2km south of town, serves the Konkan
Railway and other routes. Its reservation hall
(☑information 2712790, PNR enquiry 2700730;
◷8am-2pm & 2.15-8pm Mon-Sat, 8am-2pm Sun)
is on the 1st floor. Services to Mumbai, Ernakulam
(Kochi) and Thiruvananthapuram (Trivandrum)
are the most frequent.

Colva & Benaulim
POP 10,200

Colva and Benaulim, with their broad,
open beaches, are not the first place
backpackers head – most tourists here
are of the domestic or ageing European
varieties – but are, as a result, slightly less
sceney than Palolem or the beach towns
up north. Perhaps the biggest reason to
stay at either is to explore this part of the
southern coast (which stretches north
as far as Velsao and south as far as the
mouth of the Sal River at Mobor), which
in many parts is empty and gorgeous. The
inland road that runs this length is perfect
for gentle cycling and scootering, with lots
of picturesque Portuguese-era mansions
and whitewashed churches along the way.

Sights & Activities

The beach entrances of Colva and
Benaulim throng with dudes keen to sell
you **parasailing** (per ride ₹600), **jet-skiing**
(per 15min ₹700) and one-hour **dolphin-
watching trips** (per person ₹300).

GOA CHITRA Museum
(☑6570877; www.goachitra.com; St John the
Baptist Rd, Mondo Vaddo, Benaulim; admission ₹200; ◷9am-6pm Tue-Sun) Artist and
restorer Victor Hugo Gomes first noticed
the slow extinction of traditional objects –
everything from farming tools to kitchen
utensils to altarpieces – as a child in
Benaulim. But it wasn't until he was
older that he realised the traditional, and
especially agricultural, local knowledge
was disappearing with them. He created
this ethnographic museum from the
more than 4000 cast-off objects that he
collected from across the state over 20
years (he often had to find elderly people
to explain their uses). In addition to the
organic traditional farm out back, you'll
see plenty of tools and household objects,
Christian artefacts and some fascinating
farming implements, including a massive
grinder for making coconut oil, which,
ingeniously, attaches to a bull who does
all the hard work. Goa Chitra is 3km east
of Maria Hall.

Detour:
Braganza House

Built in the 17th century, this is possibly the best example of what Goa's scores of once grand and glorious mansions have today become. Built on land in Chandor, 15km east of Margao, that was granted by the King of Portugal, the house was divided from the outset into two wings, to house two sides of the same big family.

The **West Wing** (☎2784201; ⏰9am-5pm) belongs to one set of the family's descendents, the Menezes-Bragança, and is filled with gorgeous chandeliers, Italian marble floors, 250-year-old, locally made rosewood furniture, and antique treasures from Macau, Portugal, China and Europe. Mrs Aida Menezes-Bragança lives here today, and will show you around with the help of her assistant. Between them, they struggle valiantly with the upkeep of a beautiful but needy house, whose grand history oozes from every inch of wall, floor and furniture.

Next door, the **East Wing** (☎2784227, 2857630; ⏰10am-6pm) is owned by the Braganza-Pereiras, descendents of the other half of the family. It's nowhere near as grand: paint peels from windows, ceilings sag and antiques are mixed in with cheap knick-knacks and seaside souvenirs. But it's beautiful in its own, lived-in way and has a small but striking family chapel, which contains a carefully hidden fingernail of St Francis Xavier (see p209).

Both homes are open daily. The owners rely on donations for the hefty costs of maintenance: ₹100 per visitor per house is reasonable, though anything extra would, of course, be welcome.

🛏 Sleeping

Colva

SAM'S COTTAGES Hotel $
(☎2788753; r ₹500) Up away from the fray, north of Colva's main drag, you'll find Sam's, a cheerful place with superfriendly owners, spacious, spick-and-span rooms – that were getting a major upgrade when we visited – and pretty and peaceful grounds.

SKYLARK RESORT Hotel $$
(☎2788052; www.skylarkresortgoa.com; r without/with AC from ₹2300/3000; ❄) Clean and fresh rooms here have pretty, locally made teak furniture and block-print bedspreads, which gives them much more ambience than the hotel's generic exterior. The pool outside is also pleasant, and you can always just lounge here if you can't deal with the three-minute walk to the beach.

CASA MESQUITA Guesthouse $
(☎2788173; r ₹300) With just three rooms that go beyond simple and a phone number that may or may not work, this old mansion on the main coast road is the place to go if you like atmosphere. Goodness knows when rooms were last cleaned, but the elderly inhabitants are friendly, the paint's suitably peeling, and the ghosts of better days linger lovingly in the shadows.

SOUL VACATION Hotel $$$
(☎2788144/47; www.soulvacation.in; r incl breakfast ₹6300-7000; ❄🔍🏊) Tasteful rooms are arranged around gardens and a gorgeous pool area at the sleek Soul Vacation, 400m from Colva Beach. New luxury rooms are capacious and sophisticated in cool blues and whites – totally worth the extra money. It's a relaxing (if slightly pretentious) place to unwind.

Benaulim

here are lots of homes around town
dvertising simple rooms to let. This,
ombined with a couple of decent budget
ptions, makes Benaulim a better bet for
ackpackers than Colva.

ALM GROVE COTTAGES Hotel **$$**
(2770059/411; www.palmgrovegoa.com; d
ithout/with AC incl tax from ₹1600/2000; ✴)
ld-fashioned, secluded charm is to be
ad amid the dense foliage at Palm Grove
ottages, hidden among a thicket of trees
n a road winding slowly south out of
enaulim. Guest rooms are atmospheric
some have balconies), and the ever-
opular Palm Garden Restaurant graces
he garden. New rooms (₹2700) – more
rand than cosy – were being construct-
d at the time of research.

**'SOUZA GUEST
IOUSE** Guesthouse **$**
(2770583; d ₹600) This traditional blue
ouse is run by a superfriendly local Goan
amily and comes with bundles of homey
tmosphere, a lovely garden and just
hree spacious, clean rooms – making it
est to book ahead. There's an imposter
'Souza Guest House ((2771307; Vas-
addo Beach Rd; d ₹500) that's not as homey
ut also a good option; rooms are
ompact but airy and clean.

Eating &
Drinking

Colva

Colva's beach has
lenty of shacks offer-
g the standard fare.
t the roundabout
ear the church, you'll
nd chai shops and
hali places, fruit, veg-
table and fish stalls,
nd, at night, *bhelpuri*
fried, savoury rounds of
ough) vendors.

SAGAR KINARA Indian **$**
(Colva Beach Rd; thalis ₹65-85, mains ₹70-120)
A pure-veg restaurant with tastes to
please even committed carnivores, this
great place is super-efficient and serves
up cheap and delicious North and South
Indian cuisine. You might have to wait for
a table among throngs of Indian families
who love it as much as we do.

**LEDA LOUNGE &
RESTAURANT** Continental, Bar **$$**
(mains ₹125-200; ⏱7.30am-midnight) Some-
what pricey Western favourites (pizzas,
salads, sandwiches) meet fancy drinks
(mojitos, Long Island iced teas) at this
comfy, cosmopolitan cafe-lounge. It's a hip
environment for Colva, with contempo-
rary-print sofas lit by artful woven-basket
chandeliers. There's often live music, too.

Benaulim

**MALIBU
RESTAURANT** Indian, Italian **$$**
(mains ₹80-180) With a secluded garden
setting full of flowers, cool breezes and
butterflies, the relatively inland Malibu

Kingfish vindaloo on a bed of rice
GREG ELMS/LONELY PLANET IMAGES ©

is one of Benaulim's tastier and more sophisticated dining experiences, with great renditions of Italian favourites and live jazz and blues on Tuesday evenings.

PEDRO'S BAR & RESTAURANT
Goan, Multicuisine $$
(Vasvaddo Beach Rd; mains ₹70-220; ⏱9am-midnight) In a large, shady garden set back from the beachfront and popular with local and international tourists alike, Pedro's offers standard Indian, Chinese and Italian dishes, as well as a good line in Goan choices and some super 'sizzlers'.

JOHNCY RESTAURANT
Goan, Multicuisine $$
(Vasvaddo Beach Rd; mains ₹75-195; ⏱9.30am-1am) Like Pedro's beside it, Johncy dispenses standard beach-shack favourites from its location just off the sands. Staff are obliging, and food, if not exciting, is fresh and filling.

❶ Information

Colva has plenty of banks and ATM machines strung along the east–west Colva Beach Rd, and a post office on the lane that runs past the eastern end of the church. Benaulim has a single '24-hour' Bank of Baroda ATM, which is sometimes locked.

❶ Getting There & Around

BENAULIM Buses from Benaulim to Margao are frequent (₹7, 15 minutes); they stop at the intersection by Maria Hall. Some from Margao continue south to Varca and Cavelossim. Rickshaws and pilots charge ₹150 to ₹200 for Margao, and ₹50 to ₹60 for the five-minute ride to the beach. Benaulim gets green points for ubiquitous bicycle rentals for ₹50 per day; scooters will cost you ₹200.

COLVA Buses run from Colva to Margao every few minutes (₹10, 20 minutes) until around 7pm.

Benaulim to Palolem

Immediately south of Benaulim are the beach resorts of **Varca** and **Cavelossim**, with wide, pristine sands and a line of roomy five-star hotels set amid landscaped grounds fronting the beach. The most luxe is the (somewhat snooty) **Leela Goa** (☎6621234; www.theleela.com; r from ₹25,000; ❄@🛜🏊) at Mobor, 3km south of Cavelossim. Just beyond it, at the end of the peninsula, you'll find one of the most picturesque spots in Goa, with simple beach shacks serving good food. The **Cafe Beach Hut** (mains ₹70-200) is at another pretty beach-shack spot; the turn-off is halfway between Cavelossim town and Mobor, opposite Old Anchor Dalmia Resort.

Palolem & Around

Palolem's stunning crescent beach was, as recently as 15 years ago, another of Goa's undiscovered gems, with few tourists and even fewer facilities to offer them. Nowadays it's no longer quiet or hidden, but remains

Paragliders at sunset, Colva beach
GREG ELMS/LONELY PLANET IMAGES ©

ne of Goa's most beautiful spots, with a friendly, laid-back pace and lots of budget accommodation along the sands. Nightlife's still sleepy here – there are no real clubs, and the place goes to bed when the music stops at 10pm. But if you're looking for a nice place to lay up, rest a while, swim in calm seas and choose from an infinite range of yoga, massages and therapies on offer, this is your place.

If even Palolem's version of action is too much for you, head south, along the small rocky cove named **Colomb Bay**, which hosts several basic places to stay, to **Patnem Beach**, where a fine selection of beach huts, and a less pretty – but infinitely quieter – stretch of sand awaits.

Note that Palolem, even more so than other beach towns, operates seasonally; many places aren't up and running until November.

 **Activities**

Yoga

Palolem and Patnem are the places to be if you're keen to yoga, belly dance, reiki, t'ai chi or tarot the days away. There are courses and classes on offer all over town, with locations and teachers changing seasonally. Bhakti Kutir (p220) offers daily drop-in yoga classes, as well as longer residential courses, but it's just a single yogic drop in the area's ever-changing alternative-therapy ocean. You'll find info on local yoga, and even cooking, classes at Butterfly Book Shop.

Beach Activities

Kayaks are available for rent on both Patnem and Palolem beaches; an hour's paddling will cost ₹200 to ₹300, including dry bag. Fishermen and other boat operators hanging around the beach offer rides to beautiful **Butterfly Beach**, north of Palolem, for ₹800 to ₹1000 for two people, including one hour's waiting time.

Detour: Cotigao Wildlife Sanctuary

About 9km south of Palolem is this beautiful, remote-feeling **wildlife sanctuary** (☏2965601; admission/camera ₹5/25; ⏱7am-5.30pm). Don't expect to bump into its more exotic residents – including gaurs (Indian bison), sambars (a type of deer), leopards and spotted deer – but blazingly plumed birds, frogs, snakes and monkeys are plentiful. Trails are marked; set off at early morning for the best sighting prospects from one of the sanctuary's two forest watchtowers, set 6km and 9km from the entrance. A rickshaw/taxi from Palolem to the sanctuary will charge ₹500/600 (including a couple of hours' waiting time), and two buses also go here from Chaudi (at 1pm and 6.15pm), making the park's two cottages (₹400 and ₹750) a convenient option.

Trekking

GOA JUNGLE ADVENTURE Outdoor Adventure
(☏9850485641, 9922173517; www.goajungle.com; trekking/canyoning trips from ₹1200/1500) Run by a couple of very professional, very gregarious French guys, this adventure outfit gets rave reviews from travellers for its trekking and canyoning trips. (Canyoning, as owner Emmanuel puts it, is 'part jumping, part abseiling and part sliding' down a cliff.) Trips run from a half-day to several days, and rafting trips are also occasionally offered. Shoes can be rented for ₹150 per day.

Sleeping

Palolem

Most of Palolem's accommodation is of the simple beach-hut variety. Since the huts are dismantled and rebuilt with each passing season, standards can vary greatly from one year to the next. Walk along the beach and check out a few before making your decision; a simple hut without attached bathroom will cost around ₹600.

PALOLEM GUEST HOUSE　　Hotel　**$$**
(☎2644879; www.palolemguesthouse.com; r ₹750-2300; ✳) Towels here have 'Palolem Guest House' embroidered on them: that's the kind of old-school hotel this is. Comfortable rooms are arranged around a leafy garden just a quick walk from the beach, and the food in the courtyard restaurant is excellent.

BHAKTI KUTIR　　Hotel　**$$$**
(☎2643472; www.bhaktikutir.com; cottages ₹2500-4000; @) Ensconced in a thick wooded grove between Palolem and Patnem Beaches, Bhakti's well-equipped rustic cottages are a little on the pricey side, but still make for a unique jungle retreat. There are daily drop-in yoga classes (₹200) and ayurvedic massages, and the outdoor restaurant (mains ₹120 to ₹240) beneath billowing parachute silks, turns out yummy, imaginative, healthful stuff.

ORDO SOUNSAR　　Beach Huts　**$$**
(☎9822488769; www.ordosounsar.com; huts ₹2000-2500, without bathroom ₹1500) Beach huts they might be, but set as far north up Palolem beach as it's possible to go, across a rickety bridge spanning a wide creek, this hidden haven makes a cool, quiet alternative to some of the elbow-to-elbow options further on down the sands. Friendly owner Serafin prides himself on the restaurant's Goan dishes.

CIARAN'S　　Beach Huts　**$$$**
(☎2643477; www.ciarans.com; huts incl breakfast ₹4000; ✳ 🛜) You can barely call the gorgeous lodgings here 'huts'. With actual

Left: Beach shacks, Palolem beach;
Below: Fermenting cashew fruits at a Goan spice farm
(LEFT) GREG ELMS/LONELY PLANET IMAGES ©; (BELOW) GREG ELMS/LONELY PLANET IMAGES ©

windows, stone floors, full-length mirrors, wood detailing and nicer bathrooms than you'll find in most hotels, they're more like small chalets, all arranged around peaceful gardens right at the beach. It's the perfect balance of rustic and sophisticated. Plus, the wi-fi's free.

Dreamcatcher   Beach Huts $$
(2644873; www.dreamcatcher.in; huts from 2000, without bathroom ₹1000) Stylish huts are peppered around a lush garden on the beach, and yoga's offered every day. There's a four-day minimum stay (but you'd probably stay that long anyway).

My Soulmate   Hotel $$
(Shirley's Residency; 9823785250; mysoulmate@gmail.com; r ₹700-800, with AC 1000; ❄) A good spot close to the beach (behind Rainbow Travels), and the best hotel name ever.

Luke's Residence   Guesthouse $$$
(2643003; www.lukesresidence.com; d 2750, without bathroom ₹1750) Praised by its oft-returning guests for its warm hospitality and great food. Most rooms would fit several beach huts inside, and rates include a simple breakfast.

🍴 Eating & Drinking

Both Palolem and Patnem beaches are lined with beach shacks, offering all-day dining and fresh, fresh seafood as the catch comes in and the sun goes down. Many of these change seasonally, but as of press time, Ma-Rita's was winning the readers' choice award.

CAFÉ INN   Cafe $$
(light meals ₹70-240) This huge, fun semi-outdoor place has loud music, sari-clad servers and a cafeteria vibe (in a good way). The shakes, burgers and salads are great, but the evening barbecue (from 6pm to 10pm) will blow you away: pick your base, toppings, sauces and bread to make a mix-and-match masterpiece.

GERMAN BAKERY
Bakery, Multicuisine **$$**

(pastries ₹25-80, mains ₹95-170) Tasty baked treats and excellent coffee are the star at the Nepali-run German Bakery, but the Western breakfasts and Italian and Indian dinners are also super good. It also occasionally has yak cheese from Nepal – how cool is that? Oh, and the whole thing is set in a peaceful garden festooned with flags.

CASA FIESTA
Mexican, Multicuisine **$$**

(mains ₹70-200) Fiesta, like all the restaurants around here, has a little bit of everything on the menu. Its speciality, though, is Mexican, and it makes a valiant attempt at it (and does surprisingly well). The mellow hut ambience is also working, as are the evening barbecues.

SMUGGLERS' INN
Multicuisine **$$**

(mains ₹70-190) If you're craving full English breakfasts or Sunday dinner with all the trimmings, the Smugglers' Inn, with its cosy couches, football on TV and weekly quiz nights, provides that little bit of Britain in the midst of beachside India.

Home
Continental **$$**

(☎2643916; www.homeispatnem.com; mains from ₹100) A hip, relaxed veg restaurant, Home also rents out nicely decorated, light rooms (₹1000 to ₹2500); call to book or ask at the restaurant.

Hira Bar & Restaurant
Indian **$**

(snacks & breakfasts ₹6-23; ☺6am-8.30pm) A good place to start the morning in Palolem with a *pav bhaji* (spiced vegetables and bread) and a chai alongside locals on their way out to work.

Shiv Sai
Multicuisine **$**

(thalis ₹40-50, mains ₹40-100) A local lunch joint knocking out tasty thalis, including Goan fish and veggie versions, and a good line in Western breakfasts like banana pancakes (₹40).

❶ Information

Palolem's main road is lined with travel agencies, internet places and money changers – but no ATMs. For those, head to nearby Chaudi, which also has a supermarket, several pharmacies and all the other amenities you might need. An autorickshaw from Palolem to Chaudi costs ₹50, or you can walk the flat 2km in a leisurely 45 minutes.

Sun-n-Moon Travels (per hr ₹40; ☺8am-midnight) Quick internet.

❶ Getting There & Around

BUS Services to Margao (₹27, one hour, every 30 minutes) and Chaudi (₹5, every 15 minutes), the nearest town, depart from the bus stand down by the beach and stop at the Patnem turn-off.

TAXI & AUTORICKSHAW An autorickshaw from Palolem to Patnem costs ₹50, as does a rick from Palolem to Chaudi. A prepaid taxi from Dabolim Airport to Palolem costs ₹1000, but going the other way, you might get it for ₹800.

TRAIN Many trains that run north or south out of Margao (see p215) stop at the **Canacona Train Station** (☎2643644, 2712790).

KARNATAKA
Hampi
☎08394

Heaps of giant boulders perch precariously over miles of undulated terrain, their rusty hues offset by jade-green palm groves, banana plantations and paddy fields. The azure sky painted with fluffy white cirrus only adds to the magical atmosphere. A Unesco World Heritage Site, Hampi is a place where you can lose yourself among wistful ruins, or simply be mesmerised by the vagaries of nature, wondering how millions of years of volcanic activity and erosion could have resulted in a landscape so captivating.

Sights

VIRUPAKSHA TEMPLE
Hindu Temple

(admission ₹2; ☺dawn-dusk) The focal point of Hampi Bazaar is the Virupaksha Temple, one of the city's oldest structures. The main *gopuram* (gateway tower), almost 50m high, was built in 1442, with a smaller one added in 1510. The main shrine is dedicated to Virupaksha, an incarnation of Shiva.

If Lakshmi (the temple elephant) and her attendant are around, she'll smooch (bless) you for a coin. The adorable

ANDERS BLOMQVIST /LONELY PLANET IMAGES ©

Don't Miss **Vittala Temple**

The undisputed highlight of the Hampi ruins, the 16th-century Vittala Temple stands amid the boulders 2km from Hampi Bazaar. Though a few cement scaffolds have been erected to keep the main structure from collapsing, the site is in relatively good condition.

It's believed work started on the temple during the reign of Krishnadevaraya (1509–29). The temple was never finished or consecrated, yet its incredible sculptural work remains the pinnacle of Vijayanagar art. The outer 'musical' pillars reverberate when tapped, but authorities have placed them out of bounds for fear of further damage (so no more *do-re-mi* for tourists). Don't miss the temple's showcase piece – an ornate **stone chariot** in the temple courtyard, whose wheels were once capable of turning.

THINGS YOU NEED TO KNOW
Indian/foreigner ₹10/250; ⊘8.30am-5.30pm

akshmi gets her morning bath at
.30am, just down the way by the river
hats.

❶ Getting There & Away

umerous travel agents in Hampi Bazaar book
nward tickets or arrange taxis.

Hospet is Hampi's nearest train station. The
rst bus from Hospet (₹12, 30 minutes, half-
ourly) is at 6.30am; the last one back leaves
ampi Bazaar at 8.30pm. An autorickshaw costs
round ₹150.

❶ Getting Around

Once you've seen the main sights in Hampi, explore
the rest of the ruins by bicycle. The key monuments
are haphazardly signposted all over the site. While
they're not adequate, you shouldn't get lost.
Bicycles cost about ₹30 per day in Hampi Bazaar.

Walking the ruins is recommended too, but
expect to cover at least 7km just to see the major
sites. Autorickshaws and taxis are available
for sightseeing, and will drop you as close to
each of the major ruins as they can. A five-hour
autorickshaw tour costs ₹500.

Kerala & South India

Kerala's pace of life is as contagious as the Indian head-wobble – just setting foot on this swathe of green will slow your stride to a blissed-out amble. One of India's most beautiful and successful states, Kerala is a world away from the freneticism of elsewhere, as if India had passed through the Looking Glass and become an altogether more laid-back place.

Besides its famous backwaters, rice paddies, coconut groves, elegant houseboats and delicately spiced, tastebud-tingling cuisine, Kerala also proffers azure seas, white crescents of beach and evocative ex-colonial trading towns. The main problem a visitor might find here is choosing where to linger the longest.

It's a simple step between here and the riches of Tamil Nadu, homeland of one of humanity's living classical civilisations, as well as the serene hill station of Ooty, the French-tinged town of Puducherry and the inspirational temples of Mamallapuram and Madurai.

Punting through the backwaters of Kerala

Shop selling offerings in Sri Meenakshi Temple (p282)

Kerala & South India

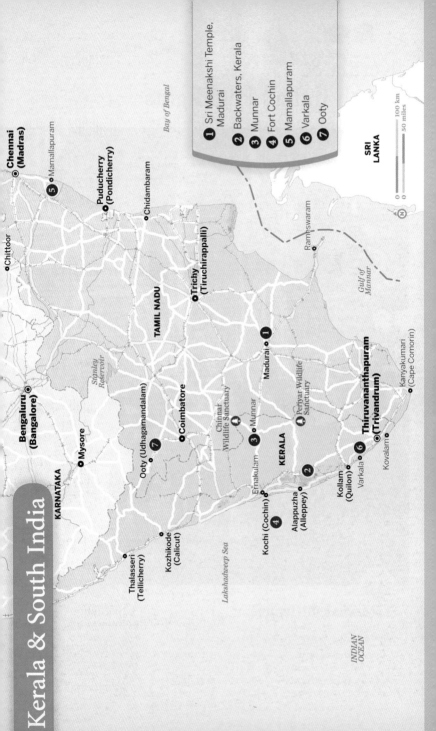

1 Sri Meenakshi Temple, Madurai
2 Backwaters, Kerala
3 Munnar
4 Fort Cochin
5 Mamallapuram
6 Varkala
7 Ooty

SRI LANKA

100 km
50 miles

Bay of Bengal

Chennai (Madras)
Mamallapuram
Chittoor
Puducherry (Pondicherry)
Chidambaram
Rameswaram
Gulf of Mannar

TAMIL NADU

Trichy (Tiruchirappalli)

Stanley Reservoir

KARNATAKA

Bengaluru (Bangalore)

Mysore

Coimbatore

Ooty (Udhagamandalam)

Chinnar Wildlife Sanctuary

Munnar

Madurai

Periyar Wildlife Sanctuary

Thiruvananthapuram (Trivandrum)

Kanyakumari (Cape Comorin)

Ernakulam

KERALA

Kochi (Cochin)

Alappuzha (Alleppey)

Kollam (Quilon)

Varkala

Kovalam

Thalasseri (Tellicherry)

Kozhikode (Calicut)

Lakshadweep Sea

INDIAN OCEAN

Kerala &
South India's Highlights

1

Sri Meenakshi Temple

The labyrinthine Sri Meenakshi Temple is one of India's most breathtaking religious complexes, a 6-hectare complex enclosed by 12 *gopurams*, or entrance towers. It's the pinnacle of South Indian temple architecture, and an amazing place to observe the busy rituals and constant activity that centre on the shrine. Above: Elephant blessing a devotee; Top Right: Rangoli design; Below Right: Statue of elephant god, Ganesh

Need to Know

TIMING Visit the temple from 7am to 9am or 5pm to 7pm. BEST VIEWS The two golden *vimanas* from the east side of the golden lotus tank. For more, see p282 and Map p281.

Sri Meenakshi Temple Don't Miss List

BOBY JOSE IS A TOUR GUIDE
SPECIALISING IN MADURAI AND TAMIL NADU

1 THE SOUTH GOPURAM

This is the only *gopuram* (entrance tower) with parabolic design, and is one of the most beautiful *gopurams* structurally. The *gopuram* was constructed during the late 16th century, and has both Vijayanagar and Nayak architectural characteristics.

2 SCULPTURE ON THE SHIVA SHRINE

There is some marvellous marriage-ceremony sculpture on one of the pillars in front of the *sundareswar* or Shiva shrine. In this scene, Lord Vishnu offers his sister Meenakshi or Parvati to Sundareswarar or Shiva. Vishnu is in a gentle mood, Parvati looks shy, and Shiva courageous – it's a visual feast. This sculpture, along with the Nandi *mandapa* (pillared pavilion), is housed under a high ceiling supported by ornamental pillars typical of the Nayak period.

3 THOUSAND PILLAR HALL

This is a wonder because of the remarkable angularity between all the pillars. The *mandapa* is a huge edifice located in the northeast corner of the temple that actually houses 985 pillars. The group of figures on two rows of pillars at the entrance is a masterpiece in itself.

4 THE GOLDEN VIMANAS

You may view the two golden *vimanas* from the eastern side of the golden lotus tank. The two *vimanas* (towers) and the golden lotus tank are as old as the legends connected with the origin of the shrine.

5 PATH AROUND THE SHIVA SHRINE

I advise visitors to walk around the outside of the Shiva shrine: this circular route is particularly stunning. The monolithic pillars and granite roof are dazzling structures – you can see how the engineering of the era embraced artistry.

Kerala Backwaters

Exploring Kerala's 900km network of waterways that fringe the coast and trickle inland is an experience not to be missed. The main jumping-off point to explore Kerala's southern backwaters is Alappuzha (p245), and from here you can hire an overnight houseboat, or travel around through the narrower canals by canoe.

Need to Know

HOUSEBOATS Try to view before you book. **AVOID** Christmas and New Year; prices soar. **GO GREEN** The greenest boats are punted not motorised. **For more, see p248.**

Kerala Backwaters Don't Miss List

BROUGHT UP ALONGSIDE THE BACKWATERS, DINESH KUMAR RUNS LOCAL TOURS AND HOUSEBOAT TRIPS

1 CANOE & CHAVARA

A motorised canoe ride through Alleppey's inland waters allows a glimpse of the local social life, the nature and its landscape. I recommend seeing a church, the 250-year-old birth house and Chavara Bhavan (Kuttamangalam) of the Reverend Kuriakose Elias. The journey will take you through the zigzagging canals, past rice fields – really you are in the lap of nature.

2 COIR MAKING

In 1902, Londoner William Goodacre started a coir handloom in Muhamma, a village 16km north of Alleppey. When the British left India, Goodacre gave his handloom workers ownership – Kerala's first co-operative society. There are 150 workers here, the oldest aged 82. Take a bus from Alleppey and alight at Muhamma junction (₹7, 40 minutes). Entry is free and it's open Monday to Saturday.

3 RICE PADDIES & A CHURCH

There are three famous rice fields below the water level, called Q, S and T Kayals. Kayal, in Malayalam, refers to the rice fields artificially created from Vembanad Lake. The project was led by local man Paul Murikkan, and it was his dream that he and his wife should be buried near the rice fields, so he built a church and burial grounds here. Sadly, his dream was never fulfilled, and he died alone in Trivandrum, but the church still exists on the deserted lakeshore.

4 HOUSEBOAT ROUTE

There are so many routes, but I suggest leaving from Alleppey at noon, docking overnight in a small lake called Vattakayal, south of C-block rice fields. This location is surrounded by paddy fields and the landscape is lush and green.

5 PUBLIC FERRY

I recommend the public ferries: Alleppey to Nedumudy (via Venattukadu, ₹6) and Alleppey to Kavalam (via Venattukadu, ₹9). Being from the backwaters, I know the beauty of the landscape, and these are some of the loveliest routes.

Trekking Around Munnar

The countryside around Munnar (p252) consists of rolling tea plantations, hued in a thousand shades of green. The lolling hills all around are covered by a sculptural carpet of tea trees, and the mountain scenery is magnificent. Stay in a remote guesthouse and take a trek – you'll often find yourself up above the clouds, watching veils of mist cling below the mountaintops. Tea plantation near Top Station (p255)

Staying in a Heritage Mansion in Fort Cochin

The historic port of Kochi (Cochin; p25 is full of old colonial-era mansions, ma turned into some of South India's love est heritage hotels. It's the ideal place to splash out on some atmospheric, stately accommodation to use as a ba for your explorations of Kochi's island its synagogue, museums and excellen restaurants. Brunton Boatyard Hotel (p257)

Wandering Mamallapuram at Sunset

5

Mamallapuram's World Heritage Site (p270) has incredible temples and carvings. These are best visited at sunset, when the sandstone turns bonfire orange and blood-red. Modern carvers tink-tink with their chisels on the street, enflaming the imagination. They're the inheritors of an ancient tradition – the temple reliefs here may have been especially created to show off the skills of local artists.

Ayurveda in Varkala

6

Kerala's laid-back, low-key resort of Varkala (p243) is strewn along a dramatic string of red-streaked sea cliffs. It's a beautiful setting and the kind of place you find yourself staying longer than you intended. Ayurveda is available all over India, but Kerala is its heartland, and a beach break is one of the ideal opportunities to relax and try out some of the ancient, herb-infused, oil- and massage-based treatments. Volleyball on a Varkala beach

Ooty

7

Travellers often fall in love with this pine-clad retreat (p283), where you can trek into the surrounding dreamy landscape before snuggling in front of roaring fires; it's the ideal hill-station escape in South India, a world away from the frenetic towns elsewhere.

Steam-powered miniature train to Ooty (p285)

Kerala & South India's Best…

Spiritual Sites

○ **Shore Temple, Mamallapuram** (p271) Rock-cut elegance overlooking the sea, symbolising the heights of Pallava architecture

○ **Sri Meenakshi Temple** (p282) A labyrinthine structure that ranks among the greatest temples of India

○ **St Stephen's Church** (p283) A 19th-century edifice with beautiful stained glass and colonial-era cemetery

○ **Pardesi Synagogue** (p260) Exquisite synagogue in the spice port of Mattancherry in Kochi

Heritage Accommodation

○ **Varikatt Heritage** (p239) Trivandrum's most charismatic place to stay

○ **Raheem Residency** (p245) Lovely 1860s beachside home, with exquisite rooms

○ **Malabar House** (p257) Boutique glamour in Fort Cochin

○ **Brunton Boatyard** (p257) Faithful 16th- and 17th-century Dutch and Portuguese architecture

○ **Calve** (p276) Stunning boutique heritage hotel in Puducherry

Wining & Dining

○ **Indian Coffee House** (p239) Trivandrum's extraordinary spiralling cafe tower

○ **Chakara Restaurant** (p247) The gorgeous small restaurant at the Raheem Residency in Alleppey

○ **Dal Roti** (p259) Fort Cochin's finest, with the freshest, tastiest Indian cuisine

○ **Ramathula Hotel** (p261) A legend among locals for its chicken and mutton biryanis

○ **Hotel Saravana Bhavan** (p268) Delish South Indian in Chennai

Chill-out Spots

Varkala (p243) Stunning red-streaked coastal cliffs and long white-sand beaches at Kerala's beachside traveller hot spot

Munnar (p252) Trek, hill and sip chai in the tea plantations around Munnar

Ooty (p283) Lovely, relaxing hill station in Tamil Nadu

Periyar (p249) Wildlife exploration, jungle treks and spice plantations in and around Kerala's most popular national park

Kovalam (p241) Beachside lazing at Kerala's biggest resort

Need to Know

ADVANCE PLANNING

○ **One month before** Book ahead at heritage hotels

○ **Two weeks before** Reserve train tickets or arrange a car and driver through an agency

○ **One day before** Call to reconfirm hotel bookings

RESOURCES

○ **Kerala Tourism** (www.keralatourism.org) Information offices in most major towns

○ **Tamil Nadu.com** (www.tamilnadu.com) News and directory

○ **Tamil Nadu Forest Department** (www.forests.tn.nic.in) National parks, ecotourism and permit information

○ **Tamil Nadu Tourism** (www.tamilnadutourism.org)

○ GETTING AROUND

○ **Train** Kerala's efficient railway system is often the quickest way between towns along the coast

○ **Car & Driver** A taxi – for one or several days – is the most convenient way to travel, but can be slower than the train on some routes, especially after the monsoon

○ **Boat** Ferries serve towns around Kerala's backwaters

○ **Bus** Good for getting to smaller towns, but less convenient than a taxi

BE FOREWARNED

○ **High season** Kerala's backwaters and beach resorts have a high season around November to March; around mid-December to mid-January, prices creep up further

○ **Great deals** To be had during the monsoon (June to September)

○ **National parks closure** Most Kerala parks close for one week for a tiger census during the months of January or February (check with the tourist office for dates)

ft: Woman selling fresh fish in village market;
above: Narrow footbridge, Kerala backwaters

Kerala & South India Itineraries

The first of these itineraries concentrates on the high-lights of the glorious southern region of Kerala, while the second also takes in some of the major sights in fascinating neighbouring Tamil Nadu.

MAMALLAPURAM ❶

❷ PUDUCHERRY (PONDICHERRY)

KOCHI (COCHIN)   MUNNAR
❹   ❺
ALAPPUZHA (ALLEPPEY)   ❸ MADURAI
❺   ❹
PERIYAR WILDLIFE SANCTUARY
VARKALA ❸   THIRUVANANTHAPURAM
❶ (TRIVANDRUM)
❷ KOVALAM   SRI LANKA

5 DAYS

TRIVANDRUM TO MUNNAR
Kerala Triangle

Launch off from Kerala's gentle state capital, **(1) Trivandrum**, popping in to its appealing museums and zoological park before heading straight for the coast, either to Kerala's busiest, but still small-scale resort of **(2) Kovalam**, with its perfect small crescents of beach, or to the more laidback, traveller-oriented resort of **(3) Varkala**, which straggles along the top of stunning coastal cliffs, and is formed of a cluster of small hotels and guesthouses – it's a Hindu place of pilgrimage as well as a holiday destination, and you'll see priests doing *puja* (worship) on the beach. From here you can head to the fascinating historic spice port of **(4) Kochi**. Stay in lovely Fort Cochin with its colonial-era mansions, excellent restaurants and cafes, cantilevered Chinese fishing nets, and spice-port history and synagogue within walking distance in Mattancherry. From Kochi, it's an easy trip into the foothills of the Western Ghats to the scrappy-looking town of **(5) Munnar**, which is sublimely set, surrounded by rolling tea plantations. It's the perfect place to stay in a remote mansion, relax and go trekking into the hills.

1 WEEK

MAMALLAPURAM TO ALAPPUZHA (ALLEPPEY)
Temples & Tranquillity

Begin your trip in Tamil Nadu, picking your way through the dramatic, ruined temples of **(1) Mamallapuram** by sunset, before gorging on fresh seafood. Next, make your way to French-tinged **(2) Puducherry**, with its colonial-era buildings and bobo vibe, to eat steak, browse some boutiques and practise some yoga. From Puducherry, you can go on to **(3) Madurai**, with its extraordinary Sri Meenakshi Temple, a riot of Dravidian sculpture that's regarded as South India's finest temple complex. From here, it's about a half-day trip to Kerala's **(4) Periyar Wildlife Sanctuary**, where you'll spot some animals and birds if you're

lucky by taking a boat trip across the sanctuary lake, and you can also opt for longer jungle trails. You can then make your way to the tree-shaded, bustling town of **(5) Alapphuzha (Alleppey)**, the gateway to Kerala's famous southern backwaters, huge spidery networks of canals that spread like tendrils inland, opening out into vast lakes. You can hire a houseboat and dine and sleep under the stars, or take a canoe out along the narrower canals, passing villages and tableau after tableau of the fascinating social and practical experiences of village life.

Dancers on Kovalam beach (p241)
PAUL BEINSSEN/LONELY PLANET IMAGES ©

Discover Kerala & South India

Palm-fringed beach, Varkala (p243)
CRAIG PERSHOUSE/LONELY PLANET IMAGES ©

KERALA
Thiruvananthapuram (Trivandrum)

☏ 0471 / POP 889,191

For obvious reasons, Kerala's capital Thiruvananthapuram is still often referred to by its colonial name: Trivandrum. Most travellers merely springboard from here to the nearby beachside resorts of Kovalam and Varkala, though laid-back, hill-enclosed Trivandrum, with its bevy of Victorian museums in glorious neo-Keralan buildings, is deserving of more time, if you can spare it.

◎ Sights & Activities

ZOOLOGICAL GARDENS & MUSEUMS
Zoo, Museums

Yann Martel based the animals in his *Life of Pi* on those he observed in Trivandrum's **zoological gardens** (☏ 2115122; admission ₹10, camera ₹25; ◷ 9am-6pm Tue-Sun). Here are shaded paths meandering through woodland and lakes, where animals such as tigers, macaques and birds frolic in massive open enclosures that mimic their natural habitats.

The park contains a gallery and two museums. The **Napier Museum** (admission ₹10; ◷ 9am-5pm Tue & Thu-Sun, 1-5pm Wed) has an eclectic display of bronzes, Buddhist sculptures, temple carts and ivory carvings. The carnivalesque interior is stunning and worth a look in its own right. The dusty **Natural History Museum** (admission ₹10; ◷ 9am-5pm Tue & Thu-Sun, 1-5pm Wed) has hundreds of stuffed animals and birds, and a fine skeleton collection. The **Shri Chitra Art Gallery** (admission ₹5; ☻9am-5pm Tue & Thu-Sun, 1-5pm Wed) has paintings by the Rajput, Mughal and Tanjore schools.

Sleeping

VARIKATT HERITAGE   Homestay **$$$**
(☏2336057; www.varikattheritage.com; Punnen Rd; r ₹4000-5000) Trivandrum's most charismatic place to stay is the 250-year-old house of Colonel Roy Kuncheria. It's a wonderful bungalow flanked by verandahs and a cinnamon tree and orchids in hanging pots. Every antique has a family story attached to it. Lunch and dinner available (₹300).

GRACEFUL HOMESTAY   Homestay **$$**
(☏2444358; www.gracefulhomestay.com; Philip's Hill; downstairs s/d ₹1300/1500, upstairs s/d ₹2000/2500 incl breakfast; @ ☎) In Trivandrum's leafy suburbs, this is owned by Sylvia and run by her brother Giles, and is an attractive house set in a couple of hectares of garden. The pick of the rooms has an amazing covered terrace overlooking palm trees.

Eating

For some unusual refreshments with your meal, look out for *karikku* (coconut water) and *sambharam* (buttermilk with ginger and chilli).

INDIAN COFFEE HOUSE   Indian **$**
Station (Central Station Rd; dishes ₹12-50; ☻7am-11pm); Zoo (Museum Rd; ☻8.30am-6pm)

The Central Station Rd link of the chain serves its yummy coffee and snacks in a crazy red-brick tower that looks like a pigeon coop from outside, and has a spiralling interior lined inside by bench tables. You have to admire the hard-working waiters. It's a must-see.

KALAVARA FAMILY RESTAURANT   Indian **$$**
(Press Rd; dishes ₹60-140; ☻lunch & dinner) A bustling favourite of Trivandrum's middle class, this is decorated by curious half-awnings and serves up scrummy Keralan fish dishes. Our money's on the fish *molee* (fish in coconut sauce; ₹130).

❶ Getting There & Away

Air

There are flights to Mumbai (from ₹5200), Kochi (from ₹2300), Chennai (Madras, from ₹3800) and Delhi (from ₹7500).

All airline bookings can be made at the efficient Airtravel Enterprises (☏3011412; www.ategroup.org; New Corporation Bldg, MG Rd).

Bus

For buses operating from the KSRTC bus stand (☏2323886), opposite the train station, see the table below.

Buses leave for Kovalam beach (₹15, 30 minutes, every 20 minutes) between 5.40am and 10pm from the southern end of the East Fort bus stand on MG Rd.

Train

Trains are often heavily booked, so it's worth visiting the reservation office (☏139; ☻8am-8pm Mon-Sat, to 2pm Sun) at the train station.

Buses from Trivandrum (KSRTC Bus Stand)

DESTINATION	FARE (₹)	DURATION (HR)	FREQUENCY
Alleppey	97	3½	every 15min
Ernakulam (Kochi)	135	5	every 20min
Varkala	36	1¼	hourly

Thiruvananthapuram (Trivandrum)

Within Kerala there are frequent trains to Varkala (2nd class/AC chair ₹36/279, one hour) and Ernakulam (₹74/259, 4½ hours), with trains passing through Alleppey (₹59/347, three hours).

🛈 Getting Around

The **airport** (☏ 2501424) is 8km from the city and 15km from Kovalam; take local bus 14 from the East Fort and City Bus stand (₹6). Prepaid taxi

Thiruvananthapuram (Trivandrum)

ouchers from the airport cost ₹250 to the city and ₹400 to Kovalam.

Autorickshaws are the easiest way to get around, with short hops costing ₹10 to ₹20.

Kovalam
☎ 0471

Once a calm fishing village clustered around its crescents of beach, nowadays Kovalam is Kerala's most developed resort. It's a touristy place and the shore is built up with hotels, but it remains an appealing place to have some fun by the sea, though it has more than its fair share of resident touts and tourist tat.

Check out the endless views along the coast by climbing Kovalam's **lighthouse** (Indian/foreigner ₹10/25, camera/video ₹20/25; ⊗3-5pm). Not recommended for small children, or for those with vertigo.

Dangers & Annoyances

There are strong rips at both ends of Lighthouse beach that carry away several swimmers every year. Swim only between the flags in the area patrolled by lifeguards – green flags show the area is safe, red flags warn of danger zones.

Activities

SANTHIGIRI Massage
(☎ 2482800; www.santhigiriashram.org; near Lighthouse Beach; ⊗8am-8pm) Try this place for excellent massages and Ayurvedic treatments. For ₹750/900 for 60/90 minutes you can have a four-handed massage while listening to the sound of the waves outside. Twenty-one-day

panchakarma costs ₹64,250, including accommodation in big, airy rooms, and food.

Sleeping

Beachfront properties are the most expensive and have great sea views.

TREETOPS Guesthouse $$
(☎ 2481363; treetopsofkovalam@yahoo.in; r ₹900; @) Indeed in the treetops, this friendly expat-owned place is a breath of fresh air, hidden away from the hustle. The three bright, sparkling-clean rooms have hanging chairs on the terraces, the view from the roof is awesome, and there's a yoga centre next door.

BEACH HOTEL II Hotel $$$
(☎ 2481937; www.thebeachhotel-kovalam.com; r ₹3000, with AC ₹4000; ❋) The Beach Hotel's upmarket new cousin, this is a stylish hotel with the best views on the seafront. Rooms have plate-glass windows opening onto terraces, and the decor is simple chic, with printed sheets and curtains and white walls. It's home to the new Oasia terrace restaurant.

PARADESH INN Guesthouse $$
(☎ 9995362952; inn.paradesh@yahoo.com; Paradesh House, Avaduthura; s/d ₹1250/1350; @) Next door to Treetops, tranquil Italian-run Paradesh Inn resembles a Greek island hideaway, a whitewashed building highlighted in blue. Each of the six fan-cooled rooms has a hanging chair outside, there are sweeping views from the rooftop and fab breakfasts.

BEACH HOTEL Guesthouse **$$**
(2481937; www.thebeachhotel-kovalam.com;
s/d ₹1500/2500) Brought to you by the
long-running German Bakery, this uberhip
beachfront property has rooms designed
with minimalist flair, ochre tones and
finished with smart, arty touches. Plus
Waves restaurant is just upstairs.

LEELA Hotel **$$$**
(2480101; www.theleela.com; r from ₹14,000;
❄ @ ☎ ☒) The only top-end option in
town, the Leela is located in extensive
grounds on the headland north of Hawah
beach. There are three swimming pools,
an ayurvedic centre, a gym, two private
beaches, several restaurants and more.
Rooms are sumptuous, with period touches, colourful textiles and Keralan artwork.

 Eating

Each evening, dozens of open-air restaurants line the beach promenade displaying the catch of the day – just pick a fish,

settle on a price (per serve around ₹150,
tiger prawns over ₹400) and decide how
you want it prepared. Unlicensed places
will serve alcohol in mugs, or with the bottles hidden discreetly out of sight.

MALABAR CAFE Indian **$$**
(mains ₹90-300) The busy tables tell their
own story: this place, with its plastic
chairs, candlelight at night, and view
through pot plants to the crashing waves
offers tasty food and good service.

WAVES Multicuisine **$$**
(mains ₹100-480) With its broad, burnt-
orange balcony, ambient soundtrack and
wide-roaming menu proffering everything
from *weisskraut mit chinnken* (roast cab-
bage and bacon) to Thai curries, this is a
foreign-tourist magnet.

Devi Garden Restaurant Indian **$**
(NUP Beach Rd; mains ₹50-150; ⊙ 7.30am-11pm)
Garden is overstating it, but this tiny, family-run
eatery whips up great veg and nonveg Indian
food for refreshingly reasonable prices.

Left: Fishermen haul in their catch, Kovalam;
Below: Hermit crab on a Keralan beach
(LEFT) TIM MAKINS/LONELY PLANET IMAGES ©; (BELOW) HIRA PUNJABI/LONELY PLANET IMAGES ©

ⓘ Information

Almost every shop and hotel will change money. In Kovalam there's a National Bank of India and near the hospital a CBS **ATM** taking Visa cards. Otherwise, there are Federal Bank and ICICI ATMs at Kovalam Junction.

Tourist Facilitation Centre (☎2480085; ⏰9.30am-5pm) Helpful, inside the entrance to the Kovalam Beach Resort.

Upasana Hospital (☎2480632) Has English-speaking doctors who can take care of minor injuries.

ⓘ Getting There & Away

BUS Buses connect Kovalam and Trivandrum every 20 minutes between 5.30am and 10.10pm (₹9, 30 minutes); catch them from the entrance to Leela resort. There are two buses daily to Ernakulam (₹140, 5½ hours), stopping at Kallambalam (for Varkala; ₹50, 1½ hours), Kollam (₹70, 2½ hours) and Alleppey (₹110, four hours). There's another 6.30am bus to Ernakulam.
TAXI A taxi between Trivandrum and Kovalam beach is around ₹400.

Varkala
☎0470 / POP 42,273

Perched almost perilously along the edge of dizzying cliffs, Varkala has a naturally beautiful setting and is a low-key resort that's geared to a backpacker demographic. Even though this kind of tie-dye commercialism can grate on the nerves, Varkala is still a great place to watch the days slowly turn into weeks.

Dangers & Annoyances

The beaches at Varkala have strong currents; even experienced swimmers have been swept away. This is one of the most dangerous beaches in Kerala, so be careful and swim between the flags or ask the lifeguards where's the best place to swim.

Activities

Laksmi's — Massage
(📞 9895948080; Clafouti Beach Resort; manicure/pedicure from ₹400/600, henna ₹300, massage ₹800; ⏰ 9am-7pm) This tiny place offers great beauty treatments such as threading and waxing as well as massages (women only).

Olympia House — Massage
(📞 9349439675; massages ₹600) Mr Omanakuttan at is a qualified massage instructor, in both ayurveda and other schools.

Eden Garden — Massage
(📞 2603910; www.eden-garden.net; massage from ₹1000) Offers a more upmarket ayurvedic experience, and offers single treatments and packages.

Sleeping

Most places to stay are crammed in along the north cliff; some open only for the tourist onslaught in November. Less-developed Odayam beach, about 1km further north of Varkala's black beach, is a tranquil alternative.

VILLA JACARANDA — Guesthouse **$$$**
(📞 2610296; www.villa-jacaranda.biz; d incl breakfast ₹4600-5600) The ultimate in understated luxury, this romantic retreat has just a handful of huge, bright rooms in a large house, each with a balcony and decorated with a chic blend of minimalist modern and period touches. The delicious breakfast is served on your verandah.

EDEN GARDEN — Resort **$$**
(📞 2603910; www.edengarden.in; r from ₹1200, luxury ste ₹5500) Overlooking peaceful paddy fields, this place has rooms with high wooden ceilings and attractive wooden furniture, set around a lush lily pond. Suites are organically shaped like white space-mushrooms, but inside they are romantic and fantastical, with intricate paintwork, round beds and mosaic circular baths. A recommended ayurvedic resort is based here.

Local snacks *idlis* and *wadi*, served with coconut chutney and *sambar*, Chennai

GREG ELMS/LONELY PLANET IMAGES

TAJ GATEWAY HOTEL   Hotel **$$$**
(☎ 6673300; www.tajhotels.com/gateway;
s/d ₹4400/5200; ❄ @ ☲) Rebranded,
revamped, refurbished, the Taj Varkala is
looking hot – especially the new rooms,
with beds covered in gleaming linen and
mocha cushions, and glass shower cubi-
cle complete with electric blind. There's a
fantastic pool (nonguests ₹400).

JICKY'S   Guesthouse **$$**
(☎ 2606994; www.jickys.com; s ₹400, d ₹600-
1750, cottage ₹900-1000) Way back in the
palm groves, family-run Jicky's remains
friendly as they come. The regular rooms
are lovely and fresh, surrounded by lots of
leafiness, and there are now also two double cottages, and some larger rooms for
three to four in two smaller whitewashed,
wooden-shuttered buildings.

 Eating

Most restaurants in Varkala offer the
same mishmash of Indian, Asian and
Western fare to a soundtrack of easy-
listening trance; they open from around
8am to 11pm. Those that are unlicensed
will usually serve alcohol discreetly.

CAFÉ DEL MAR   Multicuisine **$$**
(dishes ₹110-400) This is the kind of place
you return to for its efficient service, good
coffee, whirring fans, great position over-
looking the cliffs, and the specials of the
day chalked up on a board outside.

TRATTORIAS   Multicuisine **$$**
(meals ₹80-200) Smarter-than-most Tratto-
rias has an Italian coffee machine and the
usual wide-ranging menu, but specialises
in pasta and even has some Japanese
dishes.

NOTHIN' DOING   Indian **$$**
(Hindustan Hotel; mains ₹120-280; ⏱7-10.30am,
noon-3pm & 7-10.15pm) The rooftop restau-
rant topping this carbuncle offers tasty
enough nonveg and veg fare, but the real
reason to come here is the view from the
balcony (with just a couple of tables) over
the action of the beach.

ℹ **Information**

A 24-hour ATM at the temple junction takes Visa
cards, and there are more ATMs in Varkala town.
Many of the travel agents lining the cliff do cash
advances on credit cards and change travellers
cheques.

ℹ **Getting There & Away**

There are frequent trains to Trivandrum (2nd
class/AC chair ₹21/140, one hour) and Kollam
(₹17/140, 30 minutes), as well as three daily
services to Alleppey (₹35/153, two hours). From
Temple Junction, three daily buses pass by on
their way to Trivandrum (₹30, 1½ to two hours).

ℹ **Getting Around**

It's about 2.5km from the train station to Varkala
beach, with rickshaws covering the distance for
₹40 to ₹50.

Alappuzha (Alleppey)
☎ 0477 / POP 282,700

Hmm, those Venice comparisons might
work if Venice shrank, acquired a few
breeze-block buildings and imported
some tooting rickshaws. But step out
of the hectic centre, and Alappuzha is
graceful and greenery-fringed, set around
its grid of canals. Explore the vast watery
highways of the region and you'll experi-
ence one of Kerala's most mesmerisingly
beautiful and relaxing experiences.

 Tours

Any of the dozens of travel agencies in
town, guesthouses, hotels or the KTDC
can arrange canoe-boat tours of the
backwaters; also see the boxed text,
p248.

 **Sleeping**

RAHEEM RESIDENCY   Hotel **$$$**
(☎ 2239767; www.raheemresidency.com;
Beach Rd; s/d from €140/170; ❄ 🛜 ☲) This
thoughtfully renovated 1860s heritage

Below: Local children in the Keralan backwaters near Alappuzha;
Right: Men compete in an annual snake boat race, Alappuzha

home is a delight to visit, let alone stay in. The 10 rooms here have been restored to their former glory and have bathtubs, antique furniture and period fixtures.

PALMY RESIDENCY   Guesthouse **$**
(☎ 2235938; www.palmyresort.com; opposite Matha Jetty, Finishing Point Rd; r ₹350) Run by the friendly folk of Palmy Resort, this has to be the best deal in town. It's in a brand-new building in a fab location – just over the new Matha footbridge from the bus station, but set back from the road amid lush greenery.

CHERUKARA NEST   Homestay **$**
(☎ 2251509; www.cherukaranest.com; d incl breakfast ₹750, with AC ₹1200; ❄ @) Set in well-tended gardens, with a pigeon coop at the back, this lovely heritage home has the sort of welcoming family atmosphere that makes you miss your grandma. There are four large character-

ful rooms, each sporting lots of polished wood touches and antediluvian doors with ornate locks. Great value.

PALMY LAKE RESORT   Homestay **$**
(☎ 2235938; www.palmyresort.com; Punnamada Rd East; cottages d ₹750) With six handsome cottages, some in bamboo and some in concrete, there's loads of charm and peace at this stunning value homestay, 3.5km north of Alleppey. It's set among palm groves near the backwaters, with gracious owner Bigi and his wife Macy providing delicious meals on request.

THARAVAD   Homestay **$$**
(☎ 242044; www.tharavadheritageresort.com; west of North Police Station; d ₹1000, with AC ₹2000; ❄) Between the town centre and the beach, in a quiet canalside location, this ancestral home (the owner's grandfather was an ayurvedic doctor) has lots of glossy teak and antiques, five characterful rooms and well-maintained gardens.

 Eating

ROYALE PARK HOTEL   Indian **$$**

YMCA Rd; meals ₹90-200; ⊙7am-10pm; 📶) There is an extensive menu at this swish hotel restaurant, and the food is excellent, including scrumptious veg thalis for ₹100. You can order from the same menu in the upstairs bar and wash down your meal with a cold Kingfisher.

**CHAKARA
RESTAURANT**   Multicuisine **$$$**

(📞2230767; Beach Rd; mini Kerala meal 350, mains ₹420; ⊙1-3pm & 7-9.30pm) The restaurant at Raheem Residency is Alleppey's finest, with seating on a bijou open rooftop with views over to the beach. The menu creatively combines traditional Keralan and European cuisine. Local Indian wine is available.

**HARBOUR
RESTAURANT**   Multicuisine **$$**

(📞2230767; Beach Rd; meals ₹90-120; ⊙10am-10pm) This beachside, casual little brick hut is run by the swish Raheem Residency. It's more casual and budget-conscious than the hotel's restaurant, but promises equally well-prepared cuisine, and is good to drop by for a cold beer (large Kingfisher ₹110).

· ·

🛈 **Information**

DTPC Tourist Reception Centre (📞2253308; www.alappuzhatourism.com; ⊙8.30am-6pm) Remarkably rudimentary tourist info.

Tourist Police (📞2251161; ⊙24hr) Next door to the DTPC.

UAE Exchange (📞2264407; cnr Cullan & Mullackal Rds; ⊙9.30am-6pm, to 4pm Sat, to 1pm Sun) For changing cash and travellers cheques.

The Backwaters

The undisputed main attraction of a trip to Kerala is travelling through the 900km network of waterways that fringe the coast and trickle inland. Long before the advent of roads, these waters were the slippery highways of Kerala, and many villagers still use paddle-power as their main form of transport.

HOUSEBOATS

Renting a houseboat designed like a *kettuvallam* (rice barge) is usually worth every rupee. Drifting through quiet canals, eating delicious Keralan food, meeting local villagers and sleeping on the water; it's a haven from the clamour.

Houseboats cater for couples (one or two double bedrooms) and groups (up to seven bedrooms!). Food (and an onboard chef to cook it) is generally included in the quoted cost. Be warned that this is the biggest business in Kerala, and some operators are unscrupulous. The quality of boats varies widely, from rust buckets to floating palaces – try to check out the boat before agreeing on a price.

In the high season you're likely to get caught in backwater-gridlock – some travellers are disappointed by the number of boats on the water. It's not possible to travel by houseboat between Alleppey and Kollam, or between Alleppey and Kochi. Expect a boat for two people for 24 hours to cost about ₹4500 to ₹6000; for four people, ₹5500 to ₹8000; more for larger boats or for AC. Shop around to negotiate a bargain. Prices triple from around 20 December to 5 January.

VILLAGE TOURS & CANOE BOATS

Village tours usually involve groups of five to six people, a knowledgeable guide and an open canoe or covered *kettuvallam*. The tours (from Kochi, Kollam or Alleppey) last from 2½ to six hours and cost between ₹300 and ₹650 per person. They include visits to villages to watch coir-making, boat building, toddy (palm beer) tapping and fish farming. A traditional Keralan lunch may be provided.

In Alleppey, rented canoe boats offer a nonguided laze through the canals on a small, covered canoe for up to four people (two people for two/four hours ₹150/600) – a great way to spend a relaxing afternoon.

PUBLIC FERRIES

If you want the local backwater transport experience, there are State Water Transport boats between Alleppey and Kottayam (₹10 to ₹11, 2½ hours) departing Alleppey at 7.30am, 9.35am, 11.30am, 2.30pm and 5.15pm; they leave Kottayam at 6.40am, 11.30am, 1pm, 3.30pm and 5.15pm.

ENVIRONMENTAL ISSUES

Environmental problems, such as pollution, land reclamation, and industrial and agriculturel development threaten the backwaters and the communities that live on their banks. It's estimated that water levels have dropped by two-thirds since the mid-19th century, and many migratory birds no longer visit the area.

Pollution from houseboat motors is becoming a major problem as boat numbers swell every season. The Keralan authorities have introduced an ecofriendly accreditation system for houseboat operators. Among the criteria for a 'Green Palm Certificate' are the installation of solar panels and sanitary tanks for the disposal of waste. Consider choosing one of the few remaining punting, rather than motorised, boats if possible.

reshly split coconut as an afternoon snack, Keralan backwaters

ORIEN HARVEY/LONELY PLANET IMAGES ©

Getting There & Away

Boat

Ferries run to Kottayam from the boat jetty on VCSB (Boat Jetty) Rd; see the boxed text on p248.

Bus

From the KSRTC bus stand, frequent buses head to Trivandrum (₹97, 3½ hours, every 20 minutes) and Ernakulam (Kochi, ₹39, 1½ hours). The Varkala bus (₹97, 3½ hours) leaves at 10.40am daily.

Train

There are several trains to Ernakulam (2nd class/ AC chair ₹59/202, 1½ hours) and Trivandrum (₹59/202, three hours) via Kollam (₹45/165, 1½ hours). Four trains a day stop at Varkala (2nd class/AC chair ₹50/178, two hours). The train station is 4km west of town.

Getting Around

An autorickshaw from the train station to the boat jetty and KSRTC bus stand is around ₹50. Several guesthouses around town hire out scooters for ₹200 per day.

Periyar Wildlife Sanctuary

☏ 04869

South India's most popular wildlife sanctuary, **Periyar** (☏ 224571; www.peri yartigerreserve.org; Indian/foreigner ₹25/300; ⏰ 6am-6pm) encompasses 777 sq km and a 26-sq-km artificial lake created by the British in 1895. The vast region is home to bison, sambar, wild boar, langur, 900–1000 elephants and 35–40 tigers. Firmly established on both the Indian and foreigner tourist trails, the place can sometimes feel a bit like Disneyland-in- the-Ghats, but its mountain scenery and jungle walks make for an enjoyable visit. Bring warm and waterproof clothing.

Kumily, 4km from the sanctuary, is a growing strip of hotels, spice shops and Kashmiri emporiums.

 Activities

FOREST DEPARTMENT BOATS Boating (per adult/child ₹40/20; ⏰ departures 7.30am, 10am, 11.30am, 1.30pm & 3.30pm) These small- er, more decrepit boats offer a chance to get a bit closer to the animals than on KTDC trips, and are driven by sanctuary

249

Below: Wild Asian elephants in Periyar Wildlife Sanctuary;
Right: Tourists on bamboo raft, Periyar Wildlife Sanctuary

trained tribal guide. Note that leeches are common after rain.

workers who may offer commentary. Entry to the park doesn't guarantee a place on the boat; get to the **ticket office** (⏰6.30am-4pm) 1½ hours before each trip to buy tickets. The first and last departures offer the best wildlife-spotting prospects, and October to March are generally the best times to see animals.

KTDC BOAT TRIPS Boating
(lower/upper deck ₹75/150; ⏰departures 2hr tours 7.30am & 3.30pm, 1hr tours 10am, 7am, 11.30am & 1.30pm) One- or two-hour trips around the lake are the usual way of touring the sanctuary. They can be enjoyable, though often packed, rowdy and not an ideal way to spot wildlife.

JUNGLE PATROLS Guided Tours
(up to 5 people ₹500; ⏰departures 6.30am & 10pm) These three-hour tours cover 4km or 5km and are the best way to experience the park close up, accompanied by a

SPICE GARDENS & PLANTATIONS Gardens
Interesting spice tours cost around ₹450/750 by autorickshaw/taxi (two to three hours) and can be arranged by most hotels. If you want to see a tea factory in operation, do it from here – tea-factory visits are not permitted in Munnar.

If you'd rather do a spice tour independently, you can visit a few excellent gardens outside Kumily. The 1-hectare **Abraham's Spice Garden** (☎222919; tours ₹100; ⏰7am-6.30pm) has been going for 56 years. **Highrange Spices** (☎222117; tours ₹100; ⏰7am-6pm), 3km from Kumily, has 4 hectares where you can see ayurvedic herbs and vegetables growing. A rickshaw to either spice garden and back will be around ₹250.

SANTHIGIRI AYURVEDA Ayurveda
(☎223979; Vandanmedu Junction) An excellent and authentic place for the ayurvedic

experience, offering top-notch massage (₹650 to ₹1500), sirovasthi (₹1200) and long-term treatments lasting seven to 14 days.

 **Sleeping**

Inside the Sanctuary

LAKE PALACE
Hotel $$$

(☏223888; www.ktdc.com; r incl all meals ₹16,000-25,000) Located on an island in the middle of the Periyar Lake, this is the best value of the government hotels inside the park. It is a stunningly restored old palace that has six charismatic rooms, all decorated with flair using antique furnishings and a selection of modern conveniences (like flat-screen TVs). Transport is by boat across the lake.

Kumily

GREEN VIEW HOMESTAY
Homestay $$

(☏224617; www.sureshgreenview.com; Bypass Rd; r incl breakfast ₹600-1750) Grown from its humble homestay origins to be practically hotel-size today, Greenview is a smashing place that manages to retain its personal and friendly family welcome, and continues to get rave reviews.

CLAUS GARDEN
Homestay $$

(☏222320; www.homestay.in; r ₹800-1000) Set well away from the hustle and bustle, this lovely big building has gently curving balconies, warm, bright colours in spades, and is surrounded by a lush green garden. The excellent rooms are spacious and have neat touches like colourful blankets, rugs and artwork.

Spice Village
Hotel $$$

(☏0484-3011711; crs@cghearth.com; Thekkady Rd; villas ₹12,000-22,000; ☀) This place has captivating, spacious cottages that are smart yet cosily rustic, in pristinely kept grounds.

251

If You Like...
Safaris

If you want to go deeper into the Periyar Sanctuary and its surrounding jungle, try these adventurous options.

1 ECOTOURISM CENTRE
(☎224571; www.periyartigerreserve.org; ⊙9am-5pm) Organises full-day border hikes (₹750), three-hour elevated cloud walks (₹200), 4km to 5km nature walks (₹100), three-hour 'jungle patrols' (₹500) and full-day bamboo rafting trips (₹1000). Excursions usually require a minimum of four to five people. There are also two-day 'tiger trail' treks (per person ₹3000, solo ₹5000), conducted by former poachers, which cover 20km to 30km.

2 JUNGLE SAFARIS
(per person ₹1600-2000; ⊙5am-6.30pm) Most hotels and agencies around town can arrange all-day 4WD jungle safaris, which cover over 40km of jungle trails bordering the park. Tours also include meals and a paddleboat trip.

Its restaurant does lavish lunch/dinner buffets (₹1000 each).

Eating

There are plenty of good cheap veg restaurants in the bazaar area.

PERIYAR CAFE Indian **$**
(meals ₹40-140) Painted in kindergarten-bright colours and papered with zinging ads, this cheery diner serves up loads of North and South Indian dishes at sensible prices. Near the park entrance, it's perfect for an early breakfast or quick lunch between animal-spotting trips.

EBONY'S CAFE Multicuisine **$**
(Bypass Rd; meals ₹70-100) This small, friendly 1st-floor joint serves up a tasty assortment of Indian and Western food with a smile and a background of traveller-friendly music.

❶ Information

DTPC office (☎222620; ⊙10am-5pm Mon-Sat) Behind the bus stand, not as useful as the Ecotourism Centre.

Ecotourism Centre (☎224571; ⊙9am-5pm) For park tours and walks.

State Bank of Travancore (⊙10am-3.30pm Mon-Fri, to 12.30pm Sat) Changes travellers cheques and currency; has an ATM accepting foreign cards.

Wildlife Information Centre (☎222028; ⊙6am-6pm) Above the boat jetty in Thekkady.

❶ Getting There & Away

Buses originating or terminating at Periyar start and finish at Aranya Nivas, but they also stop at the Kumily bus stand, at the eastern edge of town.

Eight buses daily operate between Ernakulam (Kochi) and Kumily (₹110, five hours).

Tamil Nadu buses leave every 30 minutes to Madurai (₹42 to ₹56, four hours) from the Tamil Nadu bus stand just over the border.

Munnar
☎04865 / POP 68,000 / ELEV 1524M

Wander just a few kilometres outside the scruffy little hill station of Munnar and you'll be engulfed in a sea of a thousand shades of green. The lolling hills all around are covered by a sculptural carpet of tea-trees, and the mountain scenery is magnificent – you're often up above the clouds, watching veils of mist cling below the mountaintops. Once known as the High Range of Travancore, today Munnar is the commercial centre of some of the world's highest tea-growing estates.

◎ Sights & Activities

The main reason to be in Munnar is to explore the lush, tea-filled hillocks that surround it. Hotels, homestays, travel agencies, autorickshaw drivers and practically every passer-by will want to organise a day of sightseeing for you:

shop around.

Tours

[Th]e DTPC runs a couple of fairly rushed [al]l-day tours to points around Mun[n]ar. The **Sandal Valley Tour (per person** [₹]50; 9am-6pm) visits Chinnar Wildlife [Sa]nctuary, several viewpoints, waterfalls, [pl]antations, a sandalwood forest and vil[la]ges. The **Tea Valley tour (per person ₹300;** [1]0am-6pm) visits Echo Point, Top Station [an]d Rajamalai (for Eravikulam National [P]ark), among other places. You can hire [a] day's taxi to visit the main local sights [fo]r around ₹1100 – there's a taxi office in [M]unnar.

Sleeping

[Th]e best options are mostly outside Mun[na]r town centre.

[A]round Town

[I]NA COTTAGES Homestay **$**
(230349; r incl tax ₹800-1000) On the [ou]tskirts of town but immersed in lush tea [pl]antations, the 10 rooms in this hospi[ta]ble homestay are an outstanding deal.

[fa]lling green coconuts, Tamil Nadu

Frilly touches in the rooms and stunning vistas come as standard, as do the local information and hospitable cups of tea provided by the legendary Mr Iype, who has been namechecked in travel books by Devla Murphy and Bill Aitken. However, wild boars mean going out for a wander after 7pm is a no-no.

JJ COTTAGE Homestay **$**
(230104; jjcottagemunnar@sancharnet. in; d ₹350-800) The mothering family at this superb place will go out of its way to make sure your stay is comfortable. The varied and uncomplicated rooms are ruthlessly clean, bright and have TV and geysers. The one deluxe room has frilly pink curtains and sweeping views.

Munnar Hills

ROSE GARDENS Homestay **$$$**
(04864-278243; www.rosegardens.com; NH49 Rd, Karadipara; r ₹3500) Around 10km south of Munnar. Despite its handy location on the main road, with good bus connections, this is a peaceful spot overlooking Tomy's idyllic plant nursery, with over 240 types of plants. Rooms are large and comfortable, and the family are charming, with two young sons. Rajee's home cooking

is delicious, the coffee home-grown, the honey from their hives. Cooking lessons are free.

DEW DROPS
Guesthouse $$

(☎ 0484-2216455; www.dewdropsmunnar.com; Kallar; r incl breakfast ₹1200) Set in the thick forest around 20km south of Munnar, this fantastic, remote place lies on 97 hectares of spice plantation and farmland. The resplendent building is expertly constructed, with seven bright, simple rooms. Each room has a verandah on which you can sit and enjoy the hush and the small restaurant has 280-degree views. The peace here is Zen. It's 20km from Munnar; call for a pick-up (₹50 per person).

BRITISH COUNTY
Guesthouse $$

(☎ 2371761; touristdesk@satyam.net.in; ET City Rd, Anachal; person full board ₹2000) Around 11km southeast of Munnar, with its verandah facing a stunning panorama, this appealing little guesthouse has two nice fresh rooms with views. There's a

simple little treehouse for rent too, and steps lead down into the valley. Taxi from Munnar will cost ₹400. This is the overnight base for the Tourist Desk's Munnar Hillstation Tour from Kochi.

 Eating

Early morning food stalls in the bazaar serve breakfast snacks and cheap meals.

SN ANNEXE
Indian $$

(AM Rd; meals ₹55-130; ⊙ 7am-10pm) SN's little sis has a nice deep-orange look with slatted blinds at the windows. It's madly popular with families for its great range of thalis: take your pick from special, Rajasthani, Gujarati, Punjabi and more, plus a dazzling array of veg dishes.

EASTEND
Indian $$

(Temple Rd; dishes ₹120-170; ⊙ noon-3.30pm & 6.30-10.30pm) In the same-named hotel this frilly-curtained, smartish place is the

Left: Houseboat, Kerala backwaters (p248);
Below: Detail of Kathakali dancer's costume, Fort Cochin (p261)
(LEFT) CHRISTER FREDRIKSSON/LONELY PLANET IMAGES ©; (BELOW) KIMBERLEY COOLE/LONELY PLANET IMAGES ©

est spot in town to head
or nonveg Indian dishes,
with Chinese, North and South
ndian and Kerala specialities on the
menu.

ℹ Information

here are ATMs near the bridge, south of the
azaar.

TPC Tourist Information Office (✆231516;
Iway-Munnar Rd; ⊙8.30am-7pm) Marginally
elpful.

orest Information Centre (✆231587;
ipmunnar@sify.com; ⊙8am-5pm)

tate Bank of Travancore (✆230274;
⊙10am-3.30pm Mon-Sat, to noon Sun) Has an
TM.

ourist Information Service (✆230349,
447190954) Joseph Iype is a walking Swiss-
rmy knife of Munnar information – he no
nger has an office in town, but will supply
formation on trekking, taxis and so on, if
ou call.

ℹ Getting There & Away

Roads around Munnar are in poor condition and
can be affected by monsoon rains, so bus times
may vary. The main **KSRTC bus station** (AM Rd)
is south of town, but it's best to catch buses from
stands in Munnar town (where more frequent
private buses also depart).

There are around 10 buses a day to Ernakulam
(Kochi; ₹80, 5½ hours).

Around Munnar

Top Station, on Kerala's border with
Tamil Nadu, has spectacular views
over the Western Ghats. From Munnar,
four daily buses (₹35, 1½ hours, from
7.30am) make the steep, 32km climb
in around an hour; you can also book a
return taxi (₹750).

Kochi (Cochin)

☎ 0484 / POP 1.36 MILLION

Serene Kochi has been drawing traders and explorers to its shores for over 600 years. Nowhere in India could you find such a mix: giant fishing nets from China, a 400-year-old synagogue, ancient mosques, Portuguese houses and crumbling remains of the British Raj. The result is an unlikely blend of medieval Portugal, Holland and an English village grafted onto the tropical Malabar Coast.

Mainland **Ernakulam** is the hectic transport and cosmopolitan hub of Kochi, while the historical towns of **Fort Cochin** and **Mattancherry** remain wonderfully serene.

Sights

FORT COCHIN   Area

At the tip of Fort Cochin sit the unofficial emblems of Kerala's backwaters: cantilevered **Chinese fishing nets**. They are a legacy of traders from the 1400 AD court of Kubla Khan and the enormous, spiderlike contraptions require at least

four, strong people to operate their counterweights at high tide. Unfortunately, modern fishing techniques are making these labour-intensive methods less and less profitable.

MATTANCHERRY PALACE   Palace

(Dutch Palace; ☎ 2226085; Bazaar Rd; admission ₹5; ☉ 8am-5pm) Admission is a bargain to this interesting building. Presented by the Portuguese in 1555, Mattancherry Palace was a generous gift to the Raja of Kochi, Veera Kerala Varma (1537–61) as a gesture of goodwill. More probably, it was used as a sweetener to securing trading privileges. The Dutch renovated the palace in 1663, hence its alternative name, the Dutch Palace.

The star attractions here are the astonishingly preserved Hindu **murals**. The ladies' bedchamber downstairs features a cheerful, impressively multitasking Krishna, using his eight hands and two feet to engage in foreplay with eight happy milkmaids, while also managing to play the flute. Put those cameras away, though. Photography is prohibited.

Fisherman mending nets, with Chinese cantilevered nets behind, Fort Cochin

ANTHONY PLUMMER/LONELY PLANET IMAGES

Tours

**OURIST DESK INFORMATION
OUNTER** Boating, Wildlife Watching
his private organisation (p261) runs
ne popular full-day **Water Valley Tour
ay tour ₹650)** through local canals and
goons. A canoe trip through smaller
anals and villages is included, as is lunch
nd hotel pick-ups.

TDC Boating
ne KTDC Tourist Reception Centre
261) has **backwater tours (½-day tour
50)** at 8.30am and 2pm, and tourist
otor-boat tours (2½hr tour ₹150) around
ort Cochin at 9am and 2pm. It has full-
ay **houseboat backwater trips (day tour
300; ☺8am-6.30pm)**, where you stop to
ee local weaving factories, spice gardens
nd, most importantly, toddy tapping!

**LEPHANT TRAINING
AMP** Wildlife Tours
dmission free; ☺7am-6pm) Most hotels and
ourist offices can arrange a day trip out
this camp at Kudanadu, 50km from
ochi. Here you can go for a ride (₹200)
nd even help out with washing the gentle
easts if you arrive at 8am. Entry is free,
hough the elephant trainers will expect
small tip. A return trip out here in a taxi
hould cost around ₹700 to ₹1200.

Sleeping

ort Cochin is an ideal place to escape
ne noise and chaos of the mainland – it's
anquil and romantic, with some excel-
nt accommodation choices.

ort Cochin

MALABAR HOUSE Hotel **$$$**
2216666; www.malabarhouse.com; Parade
round Rd; r €220, ste incl breakfast €300-360;
⚙@☎) What may just be one of the fan-
iest boutique hotels in Kerala, Malabar
aunts its uberhip blend of modern col-
urs and period fittings like it's not even
rying. It has a restaurant and wine bar.

Detour:
Chinnar Wildlife Sanctuary

About 10km past Marayoor and
60km northeast of Munnar, this
wildlife sanctuary (www.chinnar.
org; Indian/foreigner ₹10/100, camera/
video ₹25/150; ☺7am-6pm) hosts
deer, leopards, elephants and the
endangered grizzled giant squirrel.
Trekking (3hr trek ₹150) and **tree
house** (s/d ₹1000/1250) or **hut** (s/d
₹1500/1800) accommodation within
the sanctuary are available, as
well as ecotour programs such as
river-trekking, cultural visits and
waterfall hikes (around ₹150).
For details contact the Forest
Information Centre in Munnar
(p255). Buses from Munnar can
drop you off at Chinnar (₹35, 1½
hours); taxi hire for the day will cost
around ₹1100.

BRUNTON BOATYARD Hotel **$$$**
(☎2215461; brunton boatyard@cghearth.com;
River Rd; r ₹18,700-25,000; ⚙@☎) This
imposing hotel faithfully reproduces 16th-
and 17th-century Dutch and Portuguese
architecture in its grand complex. All of
the rooms look out over the harbour, and
have bathtub and balconies with a refreshing sea breeze that beats AC any day.

NOAH'S ARK Homestay **$$**
(☎2215481; www.noahsarkcochin.com; 1/508
Fort Kochi Hospital Rd; r ₹2750-2900; ⚙@)
An upmarket, huge modern house, with
a sweeping spiral staircase from the
reception room and a variety of gleam-
ingly clean, appealing rooms (one with a
balcony), plus a friendly welcome.

WALTON'S HOMESTAY Guesthouse **$$**
(☎ 2215309; www.waltonshomestay.com;
Princess St; r incl breakfast ₹1200-2400, with AC
₹1600-2600; ❄) The fastidious Mr Walton
offers big wood-furnished rooms in his
lovely old house that's painted a nautical
white with blue trim. There's a lush gar-
den out the back and a large secondhand
bookshop downstairs.

TEA BUNGALOW Hotel **$$$**
(☎ 3019200; www.teabungalow.in; 1/1901 Ku-
numpuram; r ₹7500; ❄ @ ☎) This mustard-
coloured colonial building was built
in 1912 as headquarters of a UK spice
trading company before being taken over
by Brooke Bond tea. Graceful rooms are
decorated with flashes of strong colour

Kochi (Cochin)

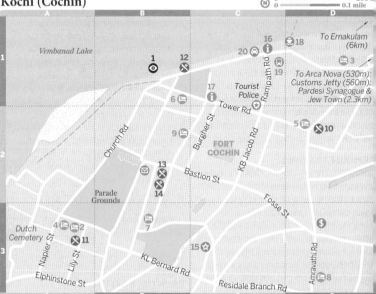

Kochi (Cochin)

nd carved wooden furniture, and have
Bassetta-tiled bathrooms.

RAINTREE LODGE   Guesthouse **$$**
3251489; www.fortcochin.com; Peter Celli St;
₹2300; ✲) The intimate and comfortable
rooms at the Raintree flirt with boutique-
hotel status. Each room has a great blend
of contemporary style and carved wood
furniture. Try to get an upstairs room with
a (tiny) balcony.

BERNARD BUNGALOW   Guesthouse **$$**
2216162; www.bernardbungalow.com; Parade
Ground Rd; r ₹2500-3500; ✲) This gracious
place has the look of a 1940s summer
cottage, housed in a fine 350-year-old
house that boasts a large collection of interesting rooms. The house has polished
floorboards, wooden window shutters,
balconies and verandahs, and is filled with
lovely period furniture.

SUI HOUSE   Homestay **$$$**
2227078; http://suihousecochin.com; Maulana
Azad Rd; r incl breakfast & tax ₹4000; ✲) This
is the home of the antique-dealer owner
of gorgeous Caza Maria in Jew Town Rd.
There are four mammoth turquoise rooms
in this grand family villa. The sumptuous
communal drawing room is filled with
more antiques, and a hearty breakfast is
served in the outdoor courtyard.

OLD HARBOUR HOTEL   Hotel **$$$**
2218006; www.oldharbourhotel.com;
Tower Rd; r incl tax ₹8250-14,200; ✲ @ ☎)
Set around an idyllic garden, with lily
ponds and a small pool, the dignified
Old Harbour is housed in a 300-year-old
Dutch/Portuguese heritage building. The
elegant mix of period and modern styles
and bright colour accents are luxurious
without being over the top.

 **Eating & Drinking**

Covert beer consumption is de rigueur
at most of the Fort Cochin restaurants,
and more expensive in the licensed ones
(₹100 to ₹165).

Detour:
Kerala Folklore Museum

This incredible private **museum**
(0484-2665452; Folklore Junction,
Thevara; admission ₹200; 9.30am-
7pm) on the southeast outskirts of
Ernakulam is well worth the journey.
It includes over 5000 artefacts from
ancient temples and beautiful old
houses, collected by its antique-
dealer owner over three years.

Fort Cochin
Behind the Chinese fishing nets are several **fishmongers** (seafood per kg ₹200-400),
from whom you can buy fish (or prawns,
scampi, lobster), then take your selection to the nearby row of shacks where
they will cook it and serve it to you (fish
about ₹200 to ₹400 per kg, cooking
₹100 per kg).

DAL ROTI   Indian **$$**
(Lily St; meals ₹70-170; lunch & dinner)
Friendly and knowledgeable owner
Ramesh will hold your hand through his
expansive North Indian menu, which
even sports its own glossary, and help
you dive in to his delicious range of
vegetarian, eggetarian and nonvegetar-
ian options.

TEAPOT   Cafe **$**
(Peter Celli St; snacks ₹40-60, meals ₹140-180)
This atmospheric place is the perfect
venue for 'high tea', with teas, sandwiches
and full meals served in chic, airy rooms.
Witty tea-themed accents include loads
of antique teapots, tea chests for tables
and a gnarled, tea-tree based glass table.
The cheesecake is divine.

MEDIUM FORMAT COLLECTION/BALAN MADHAVAN/ALA

Don't Miss **Pardesi Synagogue & Jew Town**

Originally built in 1568, this synagogue was partially destroyed by the Portuguese in 1662, and rebuilt two years later when the Dutch took Kochi. It features an ornate gold pulpit and elaborate, hand-painted willow-pattern floor tiles from Canton, China, which were added in 1762.

THINGS YOU NEED TO KNOW

(admission ₹5; ⏱10am-1pm & 3-5pm Sun-Thu, closed Jewish holidays)

SHALA Keralan **$$**
(Peter Celli St; meals ₹180-220; ⏱noon-3.30pm & 6.30-11pm) With high ceilings, whirring fans, and white walls adorned with striking paintings, Shala is owned by the same management as Kailah Art Cafe, and serves well-presented meals that include vegetable side dish and rice, such as coconut fish curry or vegetable of the day, all made by local women.

ARCA NOVA South Indian **$$**
(2/6A Calvathy Rd; mains ₹225-290; ⏱12.30-2.30pm & 7.30-10.30pm) The waterside restaurant at the Fort House Hotel is a prime choice for a leisurely lunch (mosquitoes may join you for dinner), particularly specialising in fish, with dishes such as fish wrapped in banana leaf.

CASA LINDA Multicuisine **$$**
(Dispensary Rd; mains ₹85-300) This modern dining room above the hotel of the same name might not be much to look at, but it's all about the food here. Chef Dipu once trained with a Frenchman and whips up delicious local Keralan dishes alongside French imports like Poisson de la Provencale (fish fried in oil and herbs, Provence-style). The Keralan dry-fried coconut prawns, made to a loving mother's recipe, are scrumptious.

MALABAR JUNCTION
International **$$$**

(2216666; Parade Ground Rd; mains ₹380-
00) Set in an open-sided pavilion, the
restaurant at Malabar House is movie-
star cool, with white-tableclothed tables
in a courtyard close to the small pool.
There's a seafood-based, European-style
menu and Grover's Estate wine (quaf-
ble, Indian) is served. The signature
dish is the impressive seafood platter
with grilled vegetables (₹1500). Upstairs,
the bar serves upmarket snacks such
as tapioca-and-cumin fritters in funkily
dashing surroundings.

Mattanchery & Jew Town

Ramathula Hotel
Indian **$**

(Gayees Junction, Mattancherry; biryani ₹40-45;
lunch & dinner) This place is legendary among
locals for its chicken and mutton biryanis – get
there early or you'll miss out. It's better known by
the chef's name, Kayikka's.

Kaza Maria
Multicuisine **$$**

(Bazaar Rd; mains around ₹120-200) With cooks
trained by a travelling Frenchman, this is an
enchanting, bright blue, antique-filled space
with funky music and a changing daily menu of
North Indian, South Indian and French dishes.

Ernakulam

GRAND PAVILION
Indian **$$**

(MG Rd; meals ₹90-350; ❄) This is the
restaurant at the Grand Hotel and is as
retro-stylish as the hotel itself. It serves a
some of a menu that covers dishes from
the West, North India, South India and
most of the rest of the Asian continent.
The *meen pollichathu* (fish cooked in
banana leaves) gets the thumbs up.

Entertainment

There are several places in Kochi where
you can view Kathakali, a dramatic pres-
entation of plays, usually based on Hindu
epics the Ramayana, the Mahabharata
and the Puranas. The performances are
certainly made for tourists, but they're

also a good introduction to this intriguing
art form.

SEE INDIA FOUNDATION
Cultural Program

(2376471; devankathakali@yahoo.com; Ka-
lathiparambil Lane, Ernakulam; admission ₹150;
make-up 6pm, show 6.45-8pm) One of the
oldest Kathakali theatres in Kerala, it has
small-scale shows with an emphasis on
the religious and philosophical roots of
Kathakali.

KERALA KATHAKALI CENTRE
Cultural Program

(2217552; www.kathakalicentre.com; KB Jacob
Rd, Fort Cochin; admission ₹250; make-up
from 5pm, show 6-7.30pm) In an intimate,
wood-lined theatre, this place provides
a useful introduction to Kathakali. The
centre also hosts performances of the
martial art of *kalarippayat* at 4pm to 5pm
daily, traditional music at 8pm to 9pm
Sunday to Friday and classical dance at
8pm to 9pm on Saturday.

ⓘ Information

Medical Services

Lakeshore Hospital (2701032; NH
Bypass, Marudu) It's 8km southeast of central
Ernakulam.

Medical Trust (2358001; www.
medicaltrusthospital.com; MG Rd)

Money

UAE Exchange (9.30am-6pm Mon-Fri, to 4pm
Sat); Ernakulam (2383317; Perumpillil Bldg,
MG Rd); Ernakulam (3067008; Chettupuzha
Towers, PT Usha Rd Junction); Fort Cochin
(2216231; Amravathi Rd) Foreign exchange
and travellers cheques.

Tourist information

There's a tourist information counter at the
airport. Many places distribute a free brochure
that includes a neat map and walking tour entitled
Historical Places in Fort Cochin.

KTDC Tourist Reception Centre (2353234;
Shanmugham Rd, Ernakulam; 8am-7pm) Also
organises tours.

Tourist Desk Information Counter Ernakulam (☎ 2371761; touristdesk@satyam.net.in; ⏱8am-6pm); Fort Cochin (☎ 2216129) A private tour agency that's extremely knowledgeable and helpful about Kochi and beyond.

Tourist Police Ernakulam (☎ 2353234; Shanmugham Rd, Ernakulam; ⏱8am-6pm); Fort Cochin (☎ 2215055; ⏱24hr)

ⓘ Getting There & Away

Air

For flights from Ernakulam, Kochi's mainland transport hub, see the boxed table (p263).

Bus

The **KSRTC bus stand** (☎ 2372033; ⏱reservations 6am-10pm) is in Ernakulam next to the railway halfway between the two train stations.

Train

Ernakulam has two train stations, Ernakulam Town and Ernakulam Junction. Reservations for both are made at the Ernakulam Junction **reservations office** (☎ 132; ⏱8am-8pm Mon-Sat, 8am-2pm Sun).

There are trains to Trivandrum (2nd class/AC chair ₹70/255, 4½ hours), via Alleppey (₹39/16 1½ hours).

ⓘ Getting Around

To/From the Airport

Kochi International Airport (☎ 610125; http://cochinairport.com) is at Nedumbassery, 30km northeast of Ernakulam. Taxis to/from Ernakulam cost around ₹500, and to/from Fort Cochin around ₹650. Ernakulam's mad traffic means that the trip can take over 1½ hours in the daytime, though usually less than one hour at night.

Boat

Ferries are the fastest form of transport between Fort Cochin and the mainland. One-way fares are ₹2.50 (₹3.50 between Ernakulam and Mattancherry).

ERNAKULAM There are services to both Fort Cochin jetties (Customs and Mattancherry) every 25 to 50 minutes (5.55am to 9.30pm) from Ernakulam's main jetty.

Carved wooden elephant inlaid with fish bone, Kochi

KIMBERLEY COOLE/LONELY PLANET IMAGE

Ernakulam Flights & Bus Services

DOMESTIC FLIGHTS FROM ERNAKULAM

DESTINATION	AIRLINE	FARE (₹)	DURATION (HR)	FREQUENCY
Chennai	IC	2300	1	1 daily
	9W	2900	1½	3 daily
	IT	2800	1½	1 daily
Delhi	IC	5900	3	2 daily
	9W	6300	3	3 daily
Goa	IT	6200	5	1 daily
	SG	9350	5	1 daily
Mumbai	IC	5500	2	1 daily
	9W	5300	2	1 daily
	IT	4700	2	1 daily
	SG	4900	2	2 daily
Trivandrum	IC	2300	¾	1 daily
	6E	2200	¾	1 daily

Note: Fares are one way. Airline codes: IC – Air India; 9W – Jet Airways; IT – Kingfisher; 6E – IndiGo; SG – SpiceJet.

MAJOR BUSES FROM ERNAKULAM

The following bus services operate from the KSRTC bus stand.

DESTINATION	FARE (₹)	DURATION (HR)	FREQUENCY
Alleppey	34	1½	every 20min
Kumily (for Periyar)	90	5	8 daily
Munnar	86	4½	every 30min
Trivandrum	140	5	every 30min

Ferries also run every 20 minutes or so to llingdon and Vypeen Islands (6am to 10pm).

RT COCHIN Ferries run from Customs Jetty to nakulam between 6.20am and 9.50pm. Ferries o hop between Customs Jetty and Willingdon and 18 times a day from 6.40am to 9.30pm onday to Saturday).

Car and passenger ferries cross to Vypeen and from Fort Cochin virtually nonstop from m until 10pm.

Local Transport

There are no real bus services between Fort Cochin and Mattancherry Palace, but it's an enjoyable 30-minute walk through the busy warehouse area along Bazaar Rd.

Taxis charge round-trip fares between the islands, even if you only go one way – Ernakulam Town train station to Fort Cochin should cost around ₹200.

TAMIL NADU
Chennai (Madras)

🕿044 / POP 6.6 MILLION

Chennai doesn't always make an over-whelmingly positive first impression. The streets are clogged with traffic, the weather is oppressively hot, the air is suf-focatingly heavy with smog (although it is generally regarded as one of the cleanest cities in India), and sights of any particu-lar interest are rather thin on the ground.

The charm of the city of Chennai lies in its inhabitants; the enthusiasm of Chennaites for their hometown starts to infect you after a while, and they're friendlier and more down to earth than most jaded big-city dwellers. Chennai is so chilled out you wouldn't even know it's an economic powerhouse, much less a queen of the showbiz world with a pulsating theatre scene: India's fourth-largest city is its most humble. Look beyond the initial impression and let its layers envelop you.

 Sights

Egmore & Central Chennai

GOVERNMENT MUSEUM   Museum
(www.chennaimuseum.org; 486 Pantheon Rd, Egmore; Indian/foreigner ₹15/250, camera/video ₹200/500; ⏰9.30am-5pm Sat-Thu)
Housed across several British-built buildings known as the Pantheon Com-plex, this excellent museum is Chennai's best.

The main building has a respectable **archaeological section** representing all the major South Indian periods, including Chola, Vijayanagar, Hoysala and Chalukya. Don't miss the intricate marble reliefs on display from Amaravathi temple in Andhra Pradesh, or the poignant *sati* stones commemorating women who burned on their husbands' funeral pyres.

In Gallery 3, the **bronze gallery** has a superb and beautifully presented

ollection of Chola art.
mong the impressive pieces
the bronze of Ardhanarishvara, the
ndrogynous incarnation of Shiva and
arvati.

Tours

TDC (☏ 25367850; www.tamilnadutourism.
rg; 2 Wallajah Rd, Triplicane; ☉ 10am-5.30pm
on-Fri) conducts half-day city tours
hon-AC/AC ₹140/200) and day trips to
Mamallapuram (₹385/550), Puducherry
₹500/750) and Tirupathi (₹915/1135).
very full moon there's an overnight
ilgrimage trip to Tiruvannamalai
₹385/630).

Storytrails (☏ 9600080215,
2124214; www.storytrails.in) runs highly
ecommended neighbourhood walking
ours based around themes such as
ance, jewellery and bazaars, as well as
ours specially aimed at children.

Sleeping

Hotels in Chennai are pricier than in the
rest of Tamil Nadu and don't as a rule
offer much bang for your buck.

Egmore

HOTEL CHANDRA PARK Hotel **$**
(☏ 28191177; info@hotelchandrapark.com; 9
Gandhi Irwin Rd; s/d with AC incl breakfast from
₹899/999; ✴) How do they do it? Prices
keep rising around Chennai but Chandra
Park's prices remain mysteriously low.
Standard rooms are small but have clean
towels and tight, white sheets. Throw in a
decent bar, a hearty buffet breakfast and
classy front lobby, and this place offers
superb value by Chennai standards.

FORTEL Hotel **$$$**
(☏ 30242424; info@cischennai.in; 3 Gandhi
Irwin Rd; s/d incl breakfast from ₹3500/4000;
✴) Right opposite Egmore station and

Chennai (Madras)

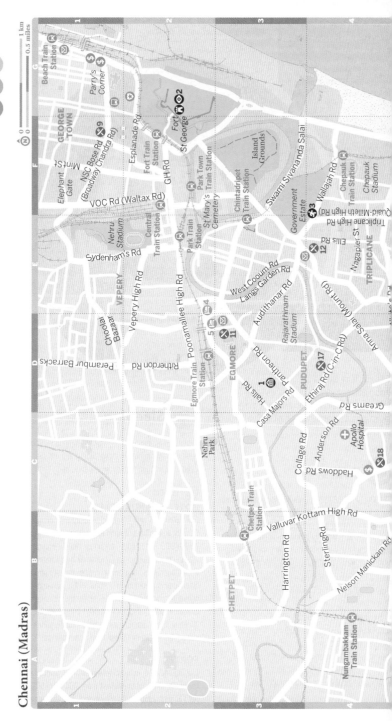

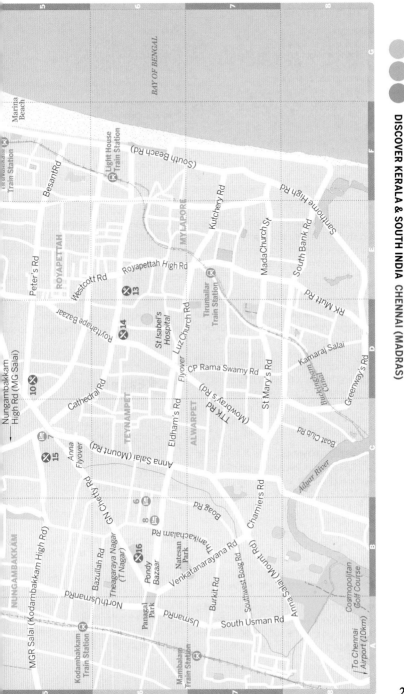

BAY OF BENGAL

Marina Beach

Light House Train Station

Besant Rd

ROYAPETTAH

Peter's Rd

Westcott Rd

Royiahape Bazaar

(South Beach Rd)

MYLAPORE

Royapettah High Rd

Kutchery Rd

MadaChurch St

South Bank Rd

Santhome High Rd

Tirumailar Train Station

Luz Church Rd

St Isabel's Hospital

CP Rama Swamy Rd

PK Mutt Rd

Kamaraj Salai

Greenway's Rd

Boat Club Rd

St Mary's Rd

ALWARPET

TTK Rd (Mowbray's Rd)

Eldham's Rd

Flyover

Cathedral Rd

TEYNAMPET

Anna Salai (Mount Rd)

Anna Flyover

Nungambakkam High Rd (MG Salai)

Chamiers Rd

Buckingham Canal

Adyar River

Cosmopolitan Golf Course

NUNGAMBAKKAM

MGR Salai (Kodambakkam High Rd)

Nungambakkam High Rd

Bazullah Rd

Theagaraya Nagar (T.Nagar)

GN Chetty Rd

NorthUsmanRd

Pondy Bazaar

Panagal Park

UsmanRd

Natesan Park

Thanikachalam Rd

Boag Rd

Venkatanarayana Rd

Burkit Rd

South Usman Rd

Southwest Boag Rd

Anna Salai (Mount Rd)

To Chennai Airport (10km)

Kodambakkam Train Station

Mambalam Train Station

267

Chennai (Madras)

remarkably quiet for it, the Fortel is cool and stylish in a dark wood-and-white-walls way, with comfy cushion-laden beds and two good restaurants.

South Chennai

LOTUS   Hotel **$$**
(☎ 28157272; www.thelotus.inn; 15 Venkatraman St, T Nagar; s/d incl breakfast from ₹2000/2700; ❄ 🛜) An absolute gem, the Lotus offers a quiet setting away from the main roads, a great veg restaurant, and fresh, stylish, sparkling rooms with wood floors and cheerful decor. There are good deals if you stay for a while, and if you want a kitchen nook with gadgets ahoy, the ₹3800 suite is excellent value.

RESIDENCY TOWERS   Hotel **$$**
(☎ 28156363; www.theresidency.com; Sir Theagaraya Nagar Rd, T Nagar; s/d incl breakfast from ₹5200/5700; ❄ @ 🛜 ⊗) At this price, it's like Residency Towers doesn't know what a good thing it has going: five-star elegance with personality. Every floor is decorated differently, but rooms all have sliding doors in front of windows to block out light and noise, dark-wood furniture and thoughtful touches. Wi-fi is free.

PARK HOTEL   Boutique Hotel **$$$**
(☎ 42676000; www.theparkhotels.com; 601 Anna Salai; s/d from ₹10,500/11,500; ❄ @ 🛜) We love this uberchic boutique hotel,

which flaunts stylish elements like framed old Bollywood posters, towering indoor bamboo gardens and oversized doors. The rooms are petite but have lovely lush bedding, and all the mod cons including funky bathrooms separated from the boudoir by an opaque glass wall. It's all pretty swish, and as a bonus the pricier rooms include airport pick-up and drop-off.

 # Eating

Chennai is packed with classic 'meals' joints, which serve thalis for lunch and dinner, and tiffin (snacks) such as *idlis* (fermented rice cakes) and dosas other times.

Egmore
HOTEL SARAVANA BHAVAN   South Indian **$**
Egmore (21 Kennet Lane; ◷6am-10.30pm); George Town (209 NSC Bose Rd); Mylapore (101 Dr Radhakrishnan Salai; ◷7am-11pm); Thousand Lights (293 Peter's Rd; ◷lunch & dinner); Triplicane (Shanthi Theatre Complex, 48 Anna Salai; ◷7am-11pm) Dependably delish, 'meals' at the Saravana Bhavans run around ₹50, though the Mylapore locale has some 'special meals' for ₹100 and up. The Thousand Lights branch is more upscale, with silver cutlery.

PONNUSAMY HOTEL   Indian **$**

(Wellington Estate, 24 Ethiraj Rd; mains ₹80-110; ☺lunch & dinner) This well-known nonveg place serves curry, biryani and Chettinad specialities. Look out for interesting options like brain fry and rabbit masala. You may be ordered to wash your hands before you can sit down.

Nungambakkam & Around

TUSCANA PIZZERIA   Italian **$$$**

(www.tuscanarestaurants.com; 19, 3rd St, Wallace Garden, Nungambakkam; large pizzas ₹295-525; ☺lunch & dinner) This, my pizza-loving friends, is the real deal, and Chennai is embracing it fast. Tuscana serves authentic thin-crust pizzas with toppings like prosciutto, as well as interesting takes like hoi sin chicken pizza. Pasta and desserts are also top-notch. The expat owner, who is serious about food, also runs a Greek restaurant, **Kryptos**, just round the corner in Kader Nawaz Khan Rd.

KUMARAKOM   Indian **$$**

(Kodambakkam High Rd, Nungambakkam; mains ₹60-160; ☺lunch & dinner) You may have to queue for a table at this classy, popular Keralan restaurant with dark-wood furniture, cool AC and busy waiters. The seafood is the standout – try the prawns masala – but everything's fresh and tasty.

ⓘ Information

Medical Services

Apollo Hospital

(☎28293333, emergency 28290792; www.apollohospitals.com; 21 Greams Lane) Cutting-edge hospital popular with international 'medical tourists'.

Money

ATMs are everywhere; there's a cluster at the front of Central station.

State Bank of India George Town (22 Rajaji Salai, George Town; ☺10am-4pm Mon-Fri, 10am-1pm Sat); Anna Salai (Anna Salai; ☺10am-4pm Mon-Fri, 10am-1pm Sat)

Thomas Cook Anna Salai (Spencer Plaza, Phase I; ☺9.30am-6.30pm); Egmore (45 Montieth Rd; ☺9.30am-6pm Mon-Sat, 10am-4pm Sun); George Town (20 Rajaji Salai; ☺9.30am-6pm Mon-Sat); Nungambakkam (Eldorado Bldg, 112 Nungambakkam High Rd; ☺9.30am-6.30pm Mon-Fri, 9.30am-noon Sat) Changes currency and travellers cheques with no commission.

Tourist Information

India Tourism Development Corporation (ITDC; ☎28281250; www.attindiatourism.com; 29 Cherian Cres, Egmore; ☺10am-5.30pm Mon-Sat) Hotel and tour bookings only; they're not very helpful.

Tamil Nadu Tourism Complex (TTDC; ☎25367850; www.tamilnadutourism.org;

Rickshaw driver, Chennai
TOM COCKREM/LONELY PLANET IMAGES ©

Major Trains from Chennai (Madras)

DESTINATION	TRAIN NO & NAME	FARE (₹)	DURATION (HR)	DEPARTURE
Kochi	6041 *Alleppey Exp*	269/728/998	11¾	9.15pm CC
Madurai	6127 *Guruvayur Exp*	212/564/772	8¾	7.50am CE
	2635 *Vaigai Exp*	132/471	8	12.40pm CE

Departure codes: CC – Chennai Central, CE – Chennai Egmore. Shatabdi fares are chair/ executive; Express and Mail fares are 2nd/chair car for day trains, sleeper/3AC/2AC for overnight trains.

2 Wallajah Rd, Triplicane; ⏱10am-5.30pm Mon-Fri) State tourist offices from all over India. The tour-booking desk at the Tamil Nadu office (☏25383333) is supposedly open 24 hours.

❶ Getting There & Away

Air

The international Anna terminal (☏22560551) of Chennai Airport in Tirusulam, 16km southwest of the centre, is efficient and not too busy, making Chennai a good entry or exit point. The domestic Kamaraj terminal (☏22560551) is next door.

Bus

Most Tamil Nadu (SETC) and other government buses operate from the chaotic Chennai Mofussil Bus Terminus (CMBT; Jawaharlal Nehru Salai, Koyambedu), better known as Koyambedu CMBT, 7km west of town.

An autorickshaw charges around ₹150.

Train

Interstate trains and those heading west generally depart from Central train station, while trains heading south depart from Egmore. The Train Reservation Complex (☏general 139; ⏱8am-8pm Mon-Sat, 8am-2pm Sun) is in a separate 10-storey building just west of Central station; the Foreign Tourist Assistance Cell (one of the best we've ever dealt with) is on the 1st floor. Egmore's booking office (☏28194579) keeps the same hours.

❶ Getting Around

To/From the Airport

The cheapest way to reach the airport is by MRTS train to Tirusulam station, 300m across the road from the terminals. An autorickshaw will cost you at least ₹250/350 for a day/night trip.

Both terminals have prepaid taxi kiosks. If you want to bypass Chennai altogether, the kiosks can organise taxis straight from here to destinations including Puducherry (₹4000).

Autorickshaw

Rickshaw drivers in Chennai routinely quote astronomical fares for both locals and tourists alike. Since you have no chance of getting a driver to use the meter, expect to pay at least ₹40 for a short trip down the road.

Mamallapuram (Mahabalipuram)

☏044 / POP 12,345

This World Heritage Site was once a major seaport and second capital of the Pallava kings, and a saunter through the town's great carvings and temples at sunset, when the sandstone turns bonfire orange and blood red and modern carvers tink-tink with their chisels on the street, enflames the imagination.

In addition to ancient archaeological wonders, there's the traveller ghetto of Othavadai Cross St. Stores sell things

rom Tibet, 'Indian' clothes that few
ndians would probably ever wear, toilet
paper, hand sanitiser and used books, and
you know you have landed, once again, in
the Kingdom of Backpackistan.

⊙ Sights

You can easily spend a full day exploring
the temples, *mandapams* and rock carv-
ngs around Mamallapuram. Apart from
the Shore Temple and Five Rathas, admission is free. Official guides from the
Archaeological Survey of India can be
found at archaeological sites and hired
or around ₹50 (give more if the tour is
good); they're well worth the money.

SHORE TEMPLE   Hindu Temple
(combined ticket with Five Rathas Indian/for-
eigner ₹10/250, video ₹25; ⊙6.30am-6pm)
Standing like a magnificent fist of rock-
cut elegance overlooking the sea, the
Shore Temple symbolises the heights of
Pallava architecture and the maritime
ambitions of the Pallava kings. Its small
size belies its excellent proportion and
the supreme quality of the carvings, many

of which have been eroded into vaguely
Impressionist embellishments. Originally
constructed in the 7th century, it was
later rebuilt by Narasimhavarman II and
houses two central shrines to Shiva. The
temple is believed to be the last in a series
of buildings that extended along a since
submerged coastline; this theory gained
credence during the 2004 tsunami, when
receding waters revealed the outlines of
what may have been sister temples.

FIVE RATHAS   Hindu Temples
(Five Rathas Rd; combined ticket with Shore
Temple Indian/foreigner ₹10/250, video ₹25;
⊙6.30am-6pm) Carved from single pieces
of rock, the Five Rathas are low-lying
monoliths that huddle in more ancient
subtlety than grandeur. Each temple is
dedicated to a Hindu god and named for
one of the Pandavas, the five hero-broth-
ers of the epic Mahabharata, plus their
common wife, Draupadi.

The shrines are meant to resemble
chariots (*ratha* is Sanskrit for chariot),
and were hidden in the sand until
excavated by the British 200 years ago.
Outside each *ratha* is a carving of an
animal mount of the gods.

Stone sculptor, Mamallapuram

GANESH RATHA & AROUND
Hindu Temple

This *ratha* is northwest of Arjuna's Penance. Once a Shiva temple, it became a shrine to Ganesh (Shiva's elephant-headed son) after the original lingam (phallic symbol) was removed. Just north of the *ratha* is a huge boulder known as **Krishna's Butter Ball**. Immovable, but balancing precariously, it's a favourite photo opportunity.

Tours

Hi! Tours (☎27443360; www.hi-tours.com; 123 East Raja St; ⊙9.30am-6pm) runs bicycle tours to sights like the Tiger Cave. Tours run from 8am to 2pm and include guide and lunch; depending on the tour, prices are around ₹350 per person.

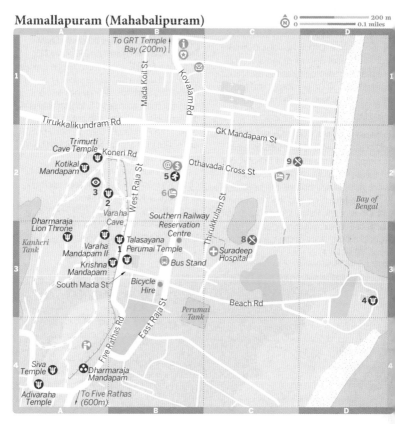

Mamallapuram (Mahabalipuram)

⊚ Sights
1 Arjuna's Penance	B3
2 Ganesh Ratha	A2
3 Krishna's Butter Ball	A2
4 Shore Temple	D3

⊕ Activities, Courses & Tours
5 Hi! Tours	B2

🛏 Sleeping
6 Hotel Mamalla Heritage	B2
7 Tina Blue View Lodge & Restaurant	C2

⊗ Eating
8 Gecko Café	C3
9 Le Yogi	C2

South Indian thali of curries, rice, pappadam and yoghurt

GREG ELMS/LONELY PLANET IMAGES ©

Sleeping

HOTEL MAMALLA HERITAGE Hotel **$$**
(27442060; www.hotelmamallaheritage.
com; 104 East Raja St; s/d from ₹1600/1800;
❄ 🛜 ⛱) In town, this corporate-y place
has large, comfortable rooms, all with
fridge, spotlessly sparkling bathrooms
and charmingly friendly service. The
pool's a decent size, and there's a quality
veg and rooftop restaurant.

**TINA BLUE VIEW LODGE
& RESTAURANT** Hotel **$**
(27442319; 34 Othavadai St; r ₹250-500)
Tina is one of Mamallapuram's originals
and kind of looks it, with some frayed
and faded edges, but remains deserv-
edly popular for its whitewashed walls,
blue accents and tropically pleasant
garden, as well as tireless original
owner Xavier ('I am same age as Tony
Wheeler!').

GRT TEMPLE BAY Resort **$$$**
(27443636; www.radisson.com/mamal
lapuramin; s/d incl breakfast from ₹8000/9000;
❄ @ 🛜 ⛱) This is the best of the luxury
resorts that lie to the north of town. It's

got everything you need to feel like waterfront royalty, including 24-hour service,
a spa, sauna, health club and prices that
are probably a little much, all things
considered. Prices jump in December/
January.

Eating & Drinking

Restaurateurs near Othavadai Cross
St provide open-air ambience, decent
Western mains and bland Indian curries. If
you want real Indian food, there are good
cheap veg places and biryani joints near
the bus stand. Most places – licensed or
not – serve beer, but be sensitive to the
11pm local curfew.

GECKO CAFÉ Multicuisine **$$**
(www.gecko-web.com; off Othavadai Cross St;
mains ₹100-200) Two friendly brothers run
this cute little spot on a thatch-covered
rooftop above the family home. The menu
choices and prices aren't that different to
other tourist-oriented spots, but there's
more love put into the cooking here, and
the decor is fun.

273

PAUL HARDING/LONELY PLANET IMAGES

Don't Miss **Arjuna's Penance**

As if we couldn't wax more poetic on Mamallapuram's stonework, along comes this relief carving, one of the greatest of its age and certainly one of the most convincing and unpretentious works of ancient art in India. Inscribed into a huge boulder, the penance bursts with scenes of Hindu myth (notice the *nagas*, or snake-beings, that descend a cleft once filled with water, meant to represent the Ganges) and everyday vignettes of South Indian life.

THINGS YOU NEED TO KNOW

West Raja St

LE YOGI Multicuisine **$$**
(Othavadai St; mains ₹90-160) This is some of the best Western food in town; the steaks, pastas and pizzas are genuine and tasty (if small), service is good, and the airy dining area, with wooden accents and flickering candlelight, is romantic as all get out.

ℹ Information

Ruby Forex (East Raja St; ⊙9.30am-7pm Mon-Sat)

Suradeep Hospital (☎27442390; 15 Thirukkulam St; ⊙24hr) Recommended by travellers.

ℹ Getting There & Away

There are at least 30 buses a day running to/from Chennai (₹30, two hours, 30 daily). To Chennai airport take bus 108B (₹25, two hours, 9am and 8pm daily). There are also at least nine daily buses to Puducherry (₹35, two hours), and Kanchipuram (₹24, two hours) via Tirukkalikundram; there's a faster direct private bus to Kanchipuram daily at 6am. Two daily buses run to Tiruvannamalai (₹36, three hours, 9.30am and 8pm).

Taxis are available from the bus station. Long-distance trips require plenty of bargaining. It's about ₹1400 to Chennai or the airport.

You can make train reservations at the Southern Railway Reservation Centre (East Raja St).

Puducherry (Pondicherry)

☎0413 / POP 220,749

Let's get something clear: if you came to Puducherry (which used to be called Pondicherry and is almost always referred to as 'Pondy') expecting a Provençal village in South India, you're in for some sore disappointment, *mon ami*. Most of Pondy is Tamil Nadu: honk-scream-screech-honk-chaos Tamil Nadu. Running through this is a thin trickle of colonial Pondy: some cobblestones, mustard-yellow townhouses, and here and there a shady boulevard that could put you in mind of gendarmes marching past sari-clad belles – HONK!

On top of everything are hotels, restaurants and 'lifestyle' shops that sell a vision of *vieux Asie* created by savvy entrepreneurs and embellished by Gallic creative types who arrived here on the French hippie trail.

Sights & Activities

FRENCH QUARTER   Old Neighbourhood

Pocketed away in the eastern alleys are a series of cobbled roads, white and mustard buildings in various states of romantic *déshabillé*, and a slight sense of Gallic glory gone by, otherwise known as the French Quarter. The best way to explore these streets is via Puducherry's **heritage walk**. Start at the north end of Goubert Ave, the seafront promenade, and wander south past the **French consulate** and the **Gandhi Statue**. Turn right at the **Hôtel de Ville** (town hall) on Rue Mahe Labourdonnais, past the shady **Bharathi Park**. From there it's a matter of pottering south through Dumas, Romain Rolland and Suffren Sts.

SRI AUROBINDO ASHRAM   Ashram

(cnr Marine St & Manakula Vinayagar Koil St) Founded in 1926 by Sri Aurobindo and a Frenchwoman known as 'the Mother' (whose visage is *everywhere* here), this ashram seeks to synthesise yoga and modern science. After Aurobindo's death, spiritual authority (and minor religious celebrity) passed to the Mother, who died in 1973 aged 97. A constant flow of visitors files through the **main ashram building** (⊘8am-noon & 2-5pm).

SRI MANAKULA VINAYAGAR TEMPLE   Hindu Temple

(Manakula Vinayagar Koil St; ⊘5.45am-12.30pm & 4-9.30pm) Pondy may have more churches than most towns, but this is still India, and the Hindu faith still reigns supreme. Don't miss the chance to watch tourists, pilgrims and the curious get a head pat from the temple elephant who stands outside Sri Manakula Vinayagar Temple, dedicated to Ganesh and tucked down a backstreet just south of the Sri Aurobindo Ashram. The temple also contains over 40 skilfully painted friezes.

Tours

The local tourist office runs half-day sightseeing tours (₹100 to ₹150, 1.30pm to 5pm) to the Sacred Heart Church, Auroville and Sri Aurobindo Ashram. Full-day tours (₹200 to ₹250, 9.45am to 5pm) cover the same area plus the botanical gardens, Puducherry Museum, Sri Manakula Vinayagar Temple and the Chunnambar water sports complex.

Shanti Tours (Romain Rolland St; ⊘8am-9pm Mon-Sat, 9am-6pm Sun) offers recommended two-hour **walking tours** (per person ₹200) of Puducherry with informed, multilingual guides.

Sleeping

If you've been saving for a special occasion, splurge here, because Puducherry's lodgings are as good as South India gets.

Sri Aurobindo Ashram runs a lot of local budget accommodation. The lodgings are clean and you'll be around like-minded souls (ie the budget – and karma – conscious). But they come with rules: 10.30pm curfew and no smoking or alcohol. For information and reservations, contact the **Sri Aurobindo information centre** (☎2233604; bureaucentral@ sriaurobindoashram.org; Cottage Complex, cnr Rangapillai St & Ambour Salai; ⊘6am-8pm).

Puducherry (Pondicherry)

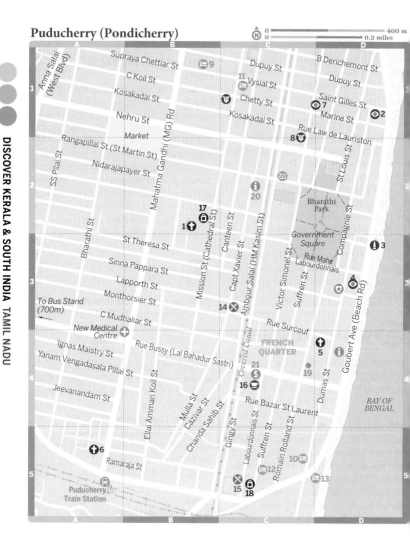

0 — 400 m
0 — 0.2 miles

CALVE Boutique Hotel **$$$**
(☏ 2224261; www.calve.in; 36 Vysial St; r incl breakfast ₹3555-5355; ❄) This excellent heritage option, located on a quiet, tree-shaded boulevard, combines a soaring sense of high-ceilinged space with egg-white walls, wooden shutters, flat-screen TVs, huge niche-embedded mattresses and a warm backdrop of Burmese teak ceilings and banisters. Add gorgeous tiled floors, beautiful furniture and big baths, and you've got a winner.

DUMAS GUEST HOUSE Boutique Hotel **$$**
(☏ 2225726; www.dumasguesthouse.com; 36 Dumas St; d from ₹2000; ❄) All whitewash and dark wood, this antique-filled heritage option has real personality. Enjoy the carved doors, quiet gardens, slight quirkiness in the decor, and very friendly multilingual staff.

LES HIBISCUS Boutique Hotel **$$**
(☏ 2227480; www.leshibiscus.com; 49 Suffren St; d incl breakfast ₹2500; ❄ @) Not dissimi-

Puducherry (Pondicherry)

lar to the Dumas in its white-and-wood heritage style, Hibiscus has just four high-ceilinged rooms with gorgeous antique beds and flat-screen TVs. Travellers have raved about the friendly, helpful owner, and the tasty complimentary breakfast that will set you up for the whole day.

KAILASH GUEST HOUSE   Hotel **$**
(☎2224485; www.kailashguesthouse.in; cnr Vysial & Mission Sts; s/d from ₹500/750; 🌣) The best value for money in this price range; Kailash has simple, superclean rooms and friendly management. It's geared to traveller needs, with communal areas, shared fridge and clothes-drying facilities, and bike rental.

PARK GUEST HOUSE   Ashram Hotel **$**
(☎2224644; 1 Goubert Ave; s/d from ₹450/600) This is the most sought-after ashram address in town thanks to its wonderful seafront position. All front rooms face the sea and have their own porch or balcony, and there's a large garden area for morning yoga or meditation. These are the best-value AC rooms in town.

 Eating

Puducherry is a culinary highlight of Tamil Nadu; you get the best of South Indian cooking plus several restaurants specialising in well-prepped French and Italian cuisine.

SATSANGA   Multicuisine **$$**
(☎2225867; 30-32 Labourdonnais St; mains ₹170-350; ⏱lunch & dinner) This deservedly popular garden spot serves excellent continental cuisine and, like most places in this genre, a full Indian menu as well. The large variety of sausages, pâté and lovely homemade bread and butter goes down a particular treat, as do the steaks. Satsanga Epicerie, next door, sells French and Italian food supplies; pasta, cheese, even vacuum-packed *jamon* (ham).

SALLE A MANGER   Indo-French **$$**
(www.calve.in; Calve hotel, 36 Vysial St; mains ₹150-300; 🌣) The speciality here is 'Creole' food, using recipes sourced from Pondy's French-Indian families and using lots of seafood and spices: try the Fish Vindali, full of fresh flavours. Like the decor – all teak and teal-coloured walls – the food has an Indo-Chinese vibe.

If You Like…
Colonial-era Architecture

Puducherry has one of the best collections of over-the-top cathedrals in India. *(Merci, French missionaries.)* If you've enjoyed your wander around the French Quarter, go in search of these beauties.

1 CHURCH OF OUR LADY OF THE IMMACULATE CONCEPTION
(Mission St) This church, a robin's-egg-blue-and-cloud-white, typically Jesuit edifice, was completed in 1791.

2 SACRED HEART CHURCH
(Subbayah Salai) The brown-and-white grandiosity of Sacred Heart Church is set off by stained glass and a Gothic sense of proportion.

3 NOTRE DAME DE ANGES
(Dumas St) The mellow pink-and-cream 'Our Lady of Angels', built in 1858, looks sublime in the late-afternoon light. The smooth limestone interior was made using eggshells in the plaster.

KASHA KI AASHA   Cafe $$
(www.kasha-ki-aasha.com; 23 Rue Surcouf; mains ₹125-225; ⊙8am-7pm Mon-Sat) You'll get a great pancake breakfast, good lunches (try the 'European-style thali') and delicious cakes served on the pretty rooftop of this colonial-house-cum-craftshop-cum-cafe. Indo-European fusion food includes chips with chutney, and pizza dosa. The heat in some dishes has been dialled back a bit for Western tastes, but it's all delicious.

Drinking & Entertainment

Although this is one of the better spots in Tamil Nadu to sink a beer, closing time is a decidedly un-Gallic 11pm. If you're here on a Friday or Saturday, get ready for some late-night fun, when Pondy stays open until (drum roll)...11.30pm! With low taxes on alcohol, Puducherry has a reputation for cheap booze. The reality is you'll really only find cheap beer in 'liquor shops' or the darkened bars attached to them. Many of the garden and rooftop restaurants in the French Quarter have pleasant bar areas, especially Satsanga and Le Club.

L'E-SPACE COFFEE & ARTS   Cafe
(2 Labourdonnais St; ⊙8am-11pm) A battered, quirky little semi-open-air cafe for breakfasts, juice, coffee, a bite and some fine cocktails (₹160 to ₹180). Staff are friendly, locals and tourists congregate here, and all in all it's the most social traveller spot in Pondy.

ⓘ Information

Puducherry keeps European hours and takes a long lunch break; you can expect most businesses to be closed from about 1pm to 3.30pm.

Medical Services
Lal Bahadur Shastri St between Bharathi St and MG Rd is packed with clinics, pharmacies and two 24-hour hospitals.
New Medical Centre (☏2225289; 470 MG Rd; ⊙24hr)

Money
Nilgiris Supermarket (cnr Mission & Rangapillai Sts) has a forex counter (⊙9am-5.30pm Mon-Sat) upstairs.
Thomas Cook (Labourdonnais St; ⊙9.30am-6.30pm Mon-Sat) Foreign exchange next to L'e-Space Coffee & Arts.

Tourist information
Puducherry tourist office (☏2339497; 40 Goubert Ave; ⊙9am-5pm)

Travel Agencies
Shanti Travels (Romain Rolland St; ⊙8am-9pm Mon-Sat, 9am-6pm Sun) Helpful French-run agency offering bus, train and air ticketing, as

well as walking tours, day trips, longer tours and airport pick-ups from Chennai.

Getting There & Away

Bus

The bus stand is 500m west of town. Services include Chennai (₹56, 3½ hours, 50 daily) and Mamallapuram (₹35, two hours, five daily). There's a booking office (⏱7am-2pm & 4-9pm) at the station.

Taxi

Air-conditioned taxis between Puducherry and Chennai cost around ₹3500; it should be cheaper to/from Chennai airport.

Train

There are two direct services a day to Chennai Egmore (₹52, five hours, 5.35am and 2.35pm), and one to Tirupathy (₹79, nine hours, 1.40pm). There's a computerised booking service for southern trains at the station.

Madurai

📞 0452 / POP 1.2 MILLION

Chennai may be the heart of Tamil Nadu, but Madurai claims her soul. No European-built port town this: Madurai is Tamil-born and Tamil-rooted, one of the oldest cities in India, a metropolis that traded with ancient Rome and outlasted her destruction.

Tourists, Indian and foreign, usually come here to see the temple of Sri Meenakshi Amman, a labyrinthine structure that ranks among the greatest temples of India. Otherwise, Madurai, perhaps appropriately given her age, captures many of India's most glaring dichotomies: a city centre dominated by a medieval temple, an economy increasingly driven by IT, all overlaid with the energy and

excitement of a typically Indian city slotted into a much more manageable package than Chennai's sprawl.

Sights

GANDHI MEMORIAL MUSEUM
Museum

(admission free, camera ₹50; ⏱10am-1pm & 2-5.30pm) Housed in an old *tamukkam* (old exhibition pavilion) of the Rani Mangammal is this excellent museum set in spacious and relaxing grounds. The maze of rooms contains an impressively moving and detailed account of India's struggle for independence from 1757 to 1947, and the English-language signs pull no punches about British rule. Included in the exhibition is the blood-stained dhoti (long loincloth) that Gandhi was wearing at the time he was assassinated in Delhi in 1948; it's here because he first took up wearing the dhoti as a sign of native pride in Madurai in 1921. The **Gandhian Literary Society Bookstore** (⏱Mon-Sat) is behind the museum. The **Madurai Government Museum** (Indian/

DISCOVER KERALA & SOUTH INDIA MADURAI

Pilgrim at Sri Meenakshi Temple (p282)
PAUL BEINSSEN/LONELY PLANET IMAGES ©

foreigner ₹5/100, camera ₹20; ⏲9.30am-5pm Sun-Thu) is next door in the same grounds. Inside is a small collection of archaeological finds, sculpture, bronzes, costumes and paintings.

TIRUMALAI NAYAK PALACE
Historical Building

(Indian/foreigner ₹10/50, camera/video ₹30/100; ⏲9am-1pm & 2-5pm) What Sri Meenakshi Temple is to Nayak religious architecture, the Tirumalai palace is to the secular, although it's just a shell that's in a state of rot today. The main event is the entrance gate, main hall and Natakasala (Dance Hall), with their faded yellow plasterwork, lion and *makara* (crocodile-elephant creature) sculptures and a series of murals that hints at the opulence the Nayak rulers once enjoyed. The rectangular courtyard is known as Swargavilasa (Celestial Pavilion).

🛏 Sleeping

Most of Madurai's accommodation is concentrated in the area between the train station and Sri Meenakshi Temple.

Town Hall Rd, running eastwards from the train station, has a knot of budget hotels, but Madurai's best-value accommodation is the string of almost identical midrange hotels along West Perumal Maistry St, near the train station. Rooms without AC are generally good value and it's worth taking the step up from budget joints. Most have rooftop restaurants with temple and sunset views.

MADURAI RESIDENCY
Hotel $$

(✆2343140; www.madurairesidency.com; 15 West Marret St; s/d incl breakfast from ₹800/1000; ❄ @) The service is stellar and the rooms are comfy and fresh at this winner, which has the highest rooftop restaurant in town. There's 24-hour internet in the lobby, and breakfast is included in the room rates.

HOTEL KEERTHI
Hotel $$

(✆4377788; www.hellomadurai.in/hotelkeerthi; 40 West Perumal Maistry St; r from ₹990; ❄) Don't be fooled by the nondescript lobby; this spotless, shiny hotel has rooms that are small but surprisingly stylish and modern, with groovy bedspreads, funky wall mirrors, picture walls and flat-screen TVs.

Man lying on a bed of hot coals during a trance ritual, Kerala

Madurai

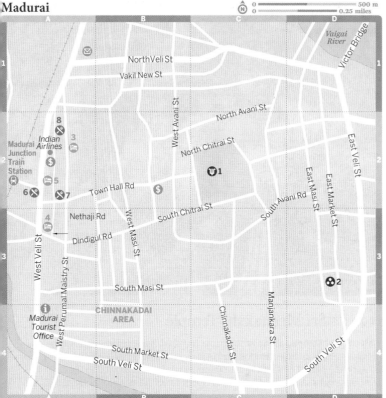

ROYAL COURT MADURAI Hotel **$$$**
(4356666; www.royalcourtindia.com; 4 West
Veli St; s/d from ₹2800/3100;) The
Royal Court manages to blend a bit of
white-sheeted, hardwood-floored colonial
elegance with modern amenities, such as
wi-fi in all rooms, that makes it an excel-
lent, centrally located top-end choice for
someone who needs a bit of spoiling.

 Eating

Along West Perumal Maistry St the
rooftop restaurants of a string of hotels
offer breezy night-time dining and
temple views (don't forget the mosquito
repellent); most also have AC restau-
rants open for breakfast and lunch.
Street stalls selling sweets, dosas, *idli*

Madurai

◎ Sights
1 Sri Meenakshi Temple	C2
2 Tirumalai Nayak Palace	D3

🛏 Sleeping
3 Hotel Keerthi	A2
4 Madurai Residency	A3
5 Royal Court Madurai	A2

✕ Eating
6 British Bakery	A2
7 Shoppers Shop	A2
8 Surya Restaurant	A2

and the like are ubiquitous, especially
near the train station. **Shoppers Shop**
(Town Hall Rd; 8am-11pm) is a well-stocked
grocery store that has a good selection
of Western foods.

281

CRAIG PERSHOUSE/LONELY PLANET IMAGES

Don't Miss **Sri Meenakshi Temple**

The Sri Meenakshi Temple, abode of the triple-breasted, fish-eyed goddess Meenakshi Amman ('fish-eyed' is an adjective for perfect eyes in classical Tamil poetry), is considered by many to be the height of South Indian temple architecture, as vital to the aesthetic heritage of this region as the Taj Mahal is to North India. It's not so much a temple as a 6-hectare complex enclosed by 12 *gopurams* (gateway towers), the highest of which looms 52m over Madurai, and all of which are carved with a staggering array of gods, goddesses, demons and heroes.

According to legend, the beautiful Meenakshi was born with three breasts and a prophecy: her superfluous breast would melt away when she met her husband. The event came to pass when she met Shiva and became his consort. The temple of the cosmic couple was designed in 1560 by Vishwanatha Nayak and built during the reign of Tirumalai Nayak, but its history goes back 2000 years.

Much of the temple is off-limits to non-Hindus, but lay people can enter at the eastern *gopuram*. From here you can see the outer rings of the concentric corridors that enclose the sanctums of Meenakshi and Shiva, worshipped here as Sundareswarar, the 'beautiful lord'. Be on the lookout for statues of deities encrusted in small balls of butter, thrown at the gods as offerings from their devout worshippers.

Note that dress codes have been tightened: no legs should be exposed for either gender, nor women's shoulders; if you're deemed to be immodestly dressed, you can buy a dhoti (long loincloth) from nearby shops. Early mornings or late evenings are the best times for avoiding crowds. 'Temple guides' charge negotiable fees (rarely below ₹200), so prepare to haggle – and be aware that they are often touts for emporiums and tailor shops.

THINGS YOU NEED TO KNOW

camera ₹30; ⏱4am-12.30pm & 4-9.30pm

BRITISH BAKERY
Cafe $

(West Veli St; mains ₹30-75; ⏰lunch & dinner) A clean, popular snack joint with shakes, ice cream, iced tea and other refreshing drinks, along with fries, sandwiches, fried rice and Indian snacks.

SURYA RESTAURANT
Multicuisine $

(110 West Perumal Maistry St; mains ₹45-115; ⏰dinner) The rooftop restaurant of Hotel Supreme offers a superb view over the city, stand-out service and a nice pure veg menu, but the winner here has got to be the cold coffee, which might as well have been brewed by God when you sip it on a dusty, hot (ie every) day.

ℹ️ Information

Money

ATMs are plentiful.

State Bank of India (West Veli St) Has foreign-exchange desks and an ATM; almost next door to Royal Court.

VKC Forex (Zulaiha Towers, Town Hall Rd; ⏰9am-6pm) An efficient place to change travellers cheques and cash.

Tourist Information

Madurai tourist office (☎2334757; 180 West Veli St; ⏰10am-5.45pm Mon-Fri) Not a lot of help, but they'll give you a brochure and map if you ask.

ℹ️ Getting There & Away

Air

Indian Airlines (☎2341234, airport 2690771; West Veli St; ⏰10am-5pm Mon-Sat) flies daily to Mumbai and Chennai, as does **SpiceJet** (☎1800 180 3333; www.spicejet.com), which also flies to Delhi. **Jet Airways** (☎2690771; www.jetairways.com) flies daily to Chennai, and **Kingfisher Airlines** (☎1800 209 3030; www.flykingfisher.com) flies daily to Chennai and Bengaluru. None of these last three airlines has an office in town, but airport counters are open at flight times.

Train

Madurai Junction train station is on the main Chennai–Kanyakumari line. There are at least nine daily trains to Chennai. Some other services include Trivandrum and Mumbai.

ℹ️ Getting Around

The airport is 12km south of town and taxis cost ₹250 to the town centre. Autorickshaws ask around ₹130.

Central Madurai is small enough to get around on foot.

Ooty (Udhagamandalam)

☎0423 / POP 93,921 / ELEV 2240M

Ooty may be a bit bustling for some tastes, but most travellers quickly fall in love with this pine-clad retreat, where trekkers congregate in front of roaring fires before setting out into the surrounding green dream. Even the typical chaos of India becomes somehow subdued in the shadow of the hills.

Sights

ST STEPHEN'S CHURCH
Church

(Church Hill Rd; ⏰10am-1pm & 3-5pm Mon-Sat, services 8am & 11am Sun) Perched above the town centre, the immaculate St Stephen's Church, built in 1829, is the oldest church in the Nilgiris. Throughout its history, St Stephen's has racially shifted from hosting an exclusively British congregation to an Anglo-Indian orphanage to falling under the auspices of the Church of South India. Look out for lovely stained glass, huge wooden beams hauled by elephant from the palace of Tipu Sultan some 120km away, and the sometimes kitschy, sometimes touching, slabs and plaques donated by colonial-era churchgoers.

BOTANICAL GARDENS
Garden

(adult/child ₹20/10, camera/video ₹30/75; ⏰7am-6.30pm) Established in 1848, these lovely gardens are a living gallery of the natural fauna of the Nilgiris. Look out for a fossilised tree trunk believed to be around 20 million years old, and on busy days, roughly 20 million Indian tourists.

Ooty (Udhagamandalam)

Activities

Trekking

Trekking is pretty much de rigueur in Ooty. On day trips you can wander through evergreen forest, tea plantations, over lookouts, into local villages and, generally, catch a bus back to town. Most guesthouses will set you up with guides, or you can hire your own. Expect to pay, depending on the size of your group, ₹300 to ₹900 for a full-day trek.

Horse Riding

Alone or with a guide, you can hire horses outside the boathouse on the north side of the lake; the rides mostly consist of a short amble along bitumen, although you

Ooty (Udhagamandalam)

◎ Sights

🛏 Sleeping

🍴 Eating

can explore the woods and hills for more money. Prices run from ₹50 for a short ride to ₹100 to ₹200 for an hour (more with a guide), which takes you partway around the lake.

Sleeping

HOTEL SWEEKAR Hotel **$**
(2442348; Race View Rd; d ₹350-400)
Definitely the best value for money in
town, the Sweekar hosts guests in simple
but very clean rooms in a traditional Ooty
cottage that sits at the end of a lavender-
hed path. It's run by an incredibly
friendly Bahai manager.

WILLOW HILL Hotel **$$**
(2223123; www.willowhill.in; 58/1 Havelock
Rd; d ₹900-2000) Sitting high above town,
Willow Hill's large windows provide great
views of Ooty. Rooms have wooden floors
and a distinct alpine-chalet-chic; the most
expensive ones offer a private garden.

FERNHILLS PALACE Hotel **$$$**
(2443911; www.fernhillspalace.co.in; Fernhill
Post; 2-night packages ₹13,250-33,950) The
Maharaja of Mysore's summer palace has
been lovingly restored in colourfully gorgeous, ridiculously over-the-top princely
colonial style; if you can afford to stay
here, you really should. Play billiards, walk
in the garden and check out old photos of
he Ooty Hunt while sipping Scotch in the
atmospheric Fox Hunt Bar.

Eating & Drinking

**KABAB
CORNER** North Indian **$$**
(Commercial Rd; mains ₹60-
00; ☺lunch & dinner) This
is the place for meat-
eaters who are tiring
of the nonstop veg of
South India. It might
not look like much
from the outside, but
here you can tear
apart perfectly grilled
and spiced chunks of
lamb, chicken and, if
you like, paneer, sopping

up the juices with pillowy triangles of
naan.

**GARDEN
RESTAURANT** South Indian **$**
(Nahar Hotel, Commercial Rd; mains ₹50-90;
☺lunch & dinner) Slightly upmarket South
Indian food in a clean hotel-restaurant set-
ting, along with juices, ice creams, snacks
and even pizza; the pizza's made in the
hotel's **Sidewalk Café**, which has good veg-
etarian Western food at fairly high prices.

ⓘ Getting There & Away

Train

The miniature train – one of the Mountain Railways
of India given World Heritage status by Unesco in
2005 – is the best way to get here. Departures and
arrivals at Mettupalayam connect with the *Nilgiri
Express,* which runs between Mettupalayam and
Chennai. The miniature train departs Mettupalayam
for Ooty at 7.10am daily (1st/2nd class ₹142/21,
five hours). If you want a seat in either direction,
be at least 45 minutes early or make a reservation
at least 24 hours in advance. From Ooty the train
leaves at 3pm and takes about 3½ hours.

Family on a motorcycle, Tamil Nadu
JOHNNY HAGLUND/LONELY PLANET IMAGES ©

Darjeeling, Varanasi & the Northeast

Up in the cool northern hills the 'toy train' of the Darjeeling Himalayan Railway chugs its way up to the British-era hill station of Darjeeling. It's a quintessential remnant of the Raj, where views of massive Khangchendzonga towering over the surrounding tea estates rank as one of the region's most inspiring sights.

The West Bengal capital Kolkata (Calcutta) is a cultural and gastronomic, somewhat mind-blowing feast, peppered with remnants of grandiose colonial-era architecture. This fascinating metropolis, full of head-spinning contrasts, forms a perfect springboard to exploring the life and death rituals beside the Ganges in the extraordinary holy city of Varanasi, as well as the Buddhist holy city of Sarnath, where the Buddha received enlightenment. It's also an easy trip to the breathtaking, virtuoso erotic carvings of the Unesco World Heritage temple complex at Khajuraho.

Tea estate, Darjeeling
RICHARD I'ANSON / LONELY PLANET IMAGES ©

Drying off on a ghat, Varanasi

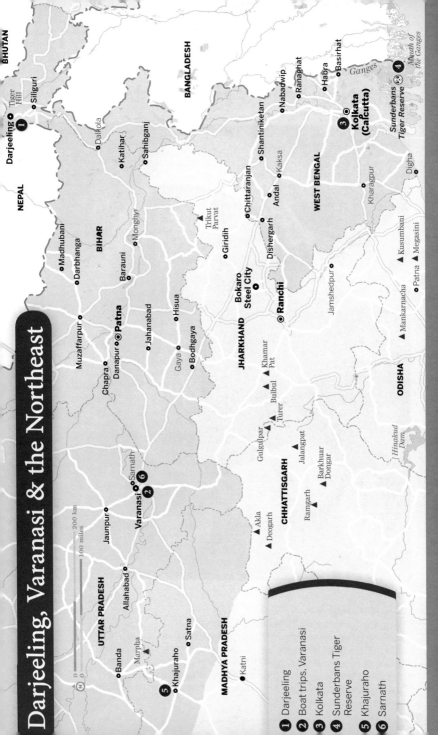

Darjeeling, Varanasi & the Northeast

① Darjeeling
② Boat trips, Varanasi
③ Kolkata
④ Sunderbans Tiger
   Reserve
⑤ Khajuraho
⑥ Sarnath

Darjeeling, Varanasi & the Northeast's Highlights

① Darjeeling

A quintessential Indian hill station, Darjeeling is a place to escape the heat of the plains, relax and drink tea. It resonates with Raj-era history, its views of massive Khangchendzonga towering over the surrounding tea estates rank as one of the region's most inspiring sights, and the approach via 'toy train' through the mountains is one of India's iconic journeys.

Need to Know

VIEWS The weather is best from October to December and March to May. **TEA** Drink it without milk, with a slice of lemon. For more, see p310 and Map p312.

Darjeeling Don't Miss List

TEA EXPERT RAJAH BANERJEE IS THE FOURTH GENERATION OF THE BANERJEE FAMILY TO OWN AND RUN THE MAKAIBARI TEA ESTATE, NEAR KURSEONG

1 THE TOY TRAIN

The heritage Darjeeling toy train, a unique steam-powered narrow gauge chugging up from Kurseong ('land of the white orchid') to Darjeeling ('land of the thunderbolt'), is a must for visitors. Passengers can almost touch the flora from the windows, and hop off, make a swift purchase from a shop and hop on, such is the romantic speed of the train. It meanders through the three main valleys of the region, Kurseong, Sonada and Darjeeling, with views of spectacular flora interspersed with well-groomed tea gardens.

2 HISTORICAL REMNANTS

The remnants of the British Raj resonate at the Hotel Windamere and in the memorabilia at the Tea Planters Club, and the Himalayan Mountaineering Institute offers a rare insight into the famous mountaineers who have conquered Everest, while also grooming future conquerors.

3 SUNRISE FROM TIGER HILL

The early morning sunrise from Tiger Hill is an event to be treasured forever. It's the only spot in the world – regally poised at nearly 3000m – to offer the broad sweep of the eternal Himalyan range from Everest and Khangchendzonga to Makalu. The miracle is not only to witness this majestic display, but also to experience the rapid emergence of the sun over the horizon.

4 TEA PLANTATION VISIT

To discover more about what makes Darjeeling tick, visit a tea plantation for a day trip to understand the process. It's also possible to participate as a long-term volunteer, working on a tea estate – some of the plantations offer programs where you can work as a volunteer while staying with a local village family.

5 ORCHID GROWERS

Take a day trip to the orchid growers of Kalimpong town, situated an hour's drive away from Darjeeling. It's a beautiful journey through virgin alpine and tropical forests.

Boat Trips in Varanasi

The best way to see the tumultuousness and birth and death rituals in the holy city of Varanasi (p321) is to take a dawn boat trip along the Ganges. It's inspiring to see the colour and clamour of pilgrims bathing and performing *puja* (worship) in the mellow morning light. Eaevening is another great time to be by the ghats, lighting a lotus candle and letting it float away on the water.

Experiencing Kolkata Culture

India's intellectual and cultural capital, Kolkata (Calcutta; p298) is full of faded colonial-era buildings such as the grandiose Victoria Memorial and S Paul's Cathedral, with its pre-Raphaeli stained glass. On first glance, this mig seem a frenetic, bamboozling city, but it's a fantastic place to wander, dine an experience local culture. Mosaic detail, St Pa Cathedral (p299)

Sunderbans Tiger Reserve

Home to one of the world's largest concentrations of tigers, Sunderbans (p311) is a 2585-sq-km reserve encompassing a network of broad channels and semi-submerged mangroves, with almost 300 Royal Bengal tigers, as well as other wildlife such as spotted deer, 2m-long water monitors and darting kingfishers.

4

5

Khajuraho

The temples at Khajuraho (p330) are exquisite examples of Indo-Aryan architecture, but it's their liberally embellished carvings that have made them famous. Around the outsides of the temples are bands of virtuoso stonework showing a storyboard of life a millennium ago – gods, goddesses, warriors, musicians, real and mythological animals, and lots and lots of sex.

6

Buddhist Sarnath

The Buddha gave his first sermon in Sarnath (p329), preaching his message of the middle way to nirvana after he achieved enlightenment at Bodhgaya, and the Emperor Ashoka erected magnificent monasteries and stupas here in the 3rd century BC, which still stand. This is one of the most important Buddhist sites in the world, and attracts many followers who come to pay tribute.

Darjeeling, Varanasi & the Northeast's Best...

Wining & Dining

○ **Kewpies** (p305) Feels like a dinner party of Bengali specialities in the chef's eclectic, old-fashioned home

○ **Brown Bread Bakery** (p325) Food is organic, international and terrific, and all for a good cause

○ **Blue Lassi** (p327) Varanasi's best lassis for over 70 years

○ **Pizzeria Vaatika Cafe** (p326) Delicious pizza overlooking Varanasi's Assi Ghat

○ **Raja's Café** (p336) Khajuraho's finest; great location, setting and Indian menu

Viewpoints

○ **Victoria Memorial** (p298) The magnificently photogenic view across reflecting ponds from the northeast

○ **Bhanu Bhakta Sarani** (p315) An early morning stroll from Chowrasta around the north side of Observatory Hill offers stunning views

○ **Bhutia Busty Gompa** (p314) Darjeeling gompa with Khangchendzonga providing a spectacular backdrop

○ **Dasaswamedh Ghat** (p319) The view over Varanasi's most colourful and lively ghat

Sacred Sites

○ **Observatory Hill** (p311) Sacred to both Buddhists and Hindus, the site of the original Dorje Ling monaster that gave Darjeeling its name

○ **Sangam** (p317) The auspicious point where two of India's holiest rivers, the Ganges and the Yamuna, meet one of Hinduism's mythical rivers, the Saraswat

○ **Varanasi** (p319) Where pilgrims wash away a lifetime of sins in the sacred waters or cremate their loved ones

○ **Sarnath** (p329) Where the Buddha came to preach his message of the middle way to nirvana after he achieved enlightenment at Bodhgaya

Left: Wall painting in Bhutia Busty Gompa (p314);
Above: A pilgrim in the Ganges at sunrise
(LEFT) ANTONY GIBLIN / LONELY PLANET IMAGES ©; (ABOVE) CHRIS BEALL / LONELY PLANET IMAGES ©

Need to Know

Natural Splendour

- **Padmaja Naidu Himalayan Zoological Park** (p311) One of India's best, specialising in Himalayan fauna

- **Sunderbans Tiger Reserve** (p311) Home to the world's largest concentrations of tigers

- **Khangchendzonga** (p315) India's highest peak and the world's third-highest mountain

- **Tiger Hill** (p310) Incredible views over a 250km stretch of Himalayan horizon, including Everest

ADVANCE PLANNING

- **One month before** Book accommodation, especially in high season (usually November to March)

- **One week before** Book any long-distance rail journeys

- **One day before** Book your seat on the Darjeeling Himayalan Railway (toy train)

GETTING AROUND

- **Air** The most convenient airport is Kolkata

- **Train** Trains serve Kolkata, Varanasi and Khajuraho; Darjeeling can be reached via picturesque 'toy train'

- **Car & driver** Possible to arrange at taxi stands or through hotels in most towns; the most convenient way to reach smaller towns

RESOURCES

- **West Bengal Tourist Department** (www.wbtourism.com) Information and online booking for WBTDC lodges

- **Bengali Recipes** (http://sutapa.com) To evoke and create Bengali flavours

- **Uttar Pradesh Tourism** (www.up-tourism.com)

- **News and Listings** (www.calcuttaweb.com) What's happening in Kolkata

- **Varanasi District Information** (www.varanasi.nic.in)

BE FOREWARNED

- **Avoid the crowds** During the month-long 'puja season', around the Durga Puja, Dasain/Dushera and Diwali festivals, Darjeeling's resorts get booked out; visit in November to avoid the crowds

- **Pack** Some warm clothes if you're heading to the mountains in the winter

- **Arrival** There are touts aplenty in Varanasi; when you arrive, try to look as if you know what you're doing

- **Donations** In Khajuraho you may receive requests for pens, coins, sweets etc; if you want to give, it's preferable to donate to a local charity or school

Darjeeling, Varanasi & the Northeast Itineraries

The first itinerary travels from Kolkata to beautiful Darjeeling: you're remarkably close to Bhutan, Nepal and Bangladesh. The second itinerary heads west, to the ghats of Varanasi and the temples of Khajuraho.

KOLKATA TO DARJEELING
Northeastern Hop

5 DAYS

Start your trip in **(1) Kolkata**, India's second-biggest city, and explore its feast of colonial-era architecture, full of faded glory; it has some splendid restaurants where you can dine fantastically well and sample Bengali cooking, one of the country's most favoured and delectable cuisines. On the next day, take a tour southwards to **(2) Sunderbans Tiger Reserve**, which is about three hours from Kolkata. This network of channels and mangrove swamps is part of the world's largest river delta and is home to one of the largest concentrations of tigers on the planet.

Returning to Kolkata, next head further north, making sure you take the 'toy train' for the last section of the trip to **(3) Darjeeling**, in the lush northeastern corner of India. This graceful hill station is spread over a steep mountain ridge, surrounded by tea plantations, with a backdrop of jagged Himalayan peaks. Climb Tiger Hill to see the sun rise with a view of Khangchendzonga, visit a tea estate and sip the world's finest tea, and explore the local gompas and pagodas set in breathtaking scenery amid the hills.

KOLKATA TO KHAJURAHO

Ghats & Temples

Start your trip in the frenetic yet fascinating city of **(1) Kolkata**, eating delicious Bengali food and wandering around the city's colonial-era architecture. From here you can take a train westwards to the thrilling holy city of **(2) Varanasi**, a place that encompasses life and death in an extraordinary swirl of colour, ritual and mayhem. The Hindu rites of death are played out across its bathing ghats – take an early morning boat ride along the Ganges to experience a sense of otherworldly spirituality.

Next make your way further west, with a brief stop in **(3) Allahabad** to see Sangam, a particularly auspicious point where two of India's holiest rivers, the Ganges and the Yamuna, meet the mythical Saraswati, before heading on to the incredible carved temples of **(4) Khajuraho** with their beautifully preserved artworks that depict a dizzying array of erotic images. This World Heritage Site is a dazzling symphony of temple art, famous for its fecund images of rampant sexuality, but also a remarkable feat of virtuoso carving. Nowadays it's possible to take an overnight train from here to Delhi, which is a neat way of ending the trip.

Devotees bathe in the river at Sangam, Allahabad (p317)

Discover Darjeeling, Varanasi & the Northeast

Cooking chapatis in a Sikh temple, Kolkata
RICHARD I'ANSON / LONELY PLANET IMAGES ©

WEST BENGAL
Kolkata (Calcutta)

India's second-biggest city is a daily festival of human existence, simultaneously noble and squalid, cultured and desperate. By its old spelling, Calcutta conjures up images of human suffering to most Westerners. But locally, Kolkata is regarded as India's intellectual and cultural capital. While poverty is certainly in your face, the dapper Bengali gentry continues to frequent grand old gentlemen's clubs, back horses at the Calcutta Racetrack and tee off at some of India's finest golf courses.

As the former capital of British India, Kolkata retains a feast of colonial-era architecture, albeit much in a photogenic state of semi-collapse.

 Sights

Chowringhee Area

VICTORIA MEMORIAL Historic Building
(VM; Map p302; Indian/foreigner ₹10/150; ⊙10am-5pm Tue-Sun, last tickets 4.30pm)
The incredible Victoria Memorial is a vast, beautifully proportioned festival of white marble: think US Capitol meets Taj Mahal. Even if you don't want to go in, the building is still worth admiring from afar: there's a magnificently photogenic view across reflecting ponds from the northeast. Or you can get closer by paying your way into the large, well-tended **park** (admission ₹4; ⊙5.45am-5.45pm). By day, entrance is from the north or south gates (with ticket booths at both), though you can exit to the east.

Kolkata (Calcutta)

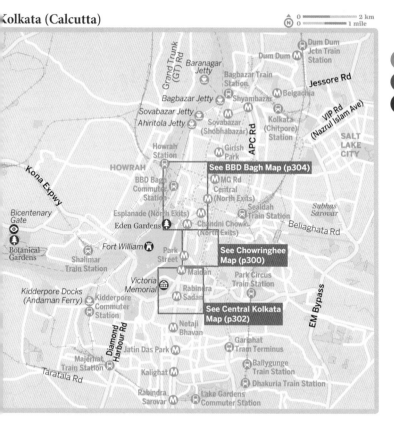

In the evenings the VM makes a spectacular canvas for a 45-minute English-language **sound-and-light show** (Indian/foreigner ₹10/20; ⏲7.15pm Tue-Sun Nov-Feb, 7.45pm Tue-Sun Mar-Jun) that's better than you might initially fear from the very dated opening slide sequence.

ST PAUL'S CATHEDRAL Cathedral
(Map p302; Cathedral Rd; ⏲9am-noon & 3-6pm) With its central crenellated tower, this 1847 cathedral would look quite at home in Cambridgeshire. It has a remarkably wide nave and features a stained-glass west window by pre-Raphaelite maestro Sir Edward Burne-Jones.

AUROBINDO BHAWAN Sacred Site
(Map p302; 8 Shakespeare Sarani; ⏲8am-8pm) Revolutionary-turned-guru Sri Aurobindo was born in Calcutta in 1872 and his grand childhood mansion-home has been preserved as an Aurobindo centre. Its garden forms an oasis of peace in the city centre and there's an open-air meditation space where you can sit as you wish or join half-hour **group meditations** at 7pm on Thursdays or Saturdays.

MAIDAN Park
(Map p302, p300) After the 'Black Hole of Calcutta' fiasco, a moated 'second' Fort William was constructed in 1758 in octagonal, Vaubanesque form. The whole village of Gobindapur was flattened to give the new fort's cannons a clear line of fire. Though sad for then-residents, this created the **Maidan** (pronounced moi-dan), a 3km-long park that is today as fundamental to Kolkata as Central Park is to New York City.

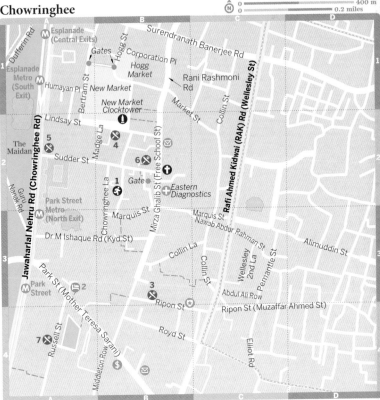

Chowringhee

BBD Bagh Area

BBD BAGH
Area

(Map p304) Originally called Tank Sq,
BBD Bagh is a large square centred on a
palm-lined central reservoir-lake ('tank')
that once supplied the young city's water.
Some locals still call it by its later-colonial
name **Dalhousie Square**, commemorating British Lieutenant-Governor Lord Dalhousie. With delicious irony, the square
is now re-renamed after the nationalists
who tried to assassinate him.

North-Central Kolkata

MARBLE PALACE
Museum

(off Map p304; 46 Muktaram Babu St; ☺10am-
3pm, closed Mon & Thu) Resplendent yet
slightly run-down, this grand 1835 raja's
mansion is astonishingly overstuffed with
statues, Victoriana, Belgian glassware

Chowringhee

◑ Activities, Courses & Tours
1 Backpackers B2

◺ Sleeping
2 Park Hotel A3

◉ Eating
3 Arsalan B3
4 Blue & Beyond B2
   Gangaur .... (see 7)
5 Jong's/Zaranj A2
6 Raj's Spanish Cafe B2
7 Teej A4

and fine if bedraggled paintings including
supposedly original works by Murillo,
Joshua Reynolds and three by Rubens.
Before arriving you need to get a permission note from one of the tourist offices

see p307). With this note, admission is technically free. However, the (obligatory) guide solicits tips of ₹50 to ₹100 per group.

 Tours

Personal, accompanied city-walks that last around four hours are available through expat-run **Kali Travel Home** (☑ 25550581, 9007778504; www.traveleast india.com; ₹350-600) and youthful **CalWalks** (☑ 9830184030; www.calcuttawalks.com; from 1200). Both are enthusiastic and flexible as to the area covered and both offer a range of alternative Kolkata experiences.

Best known for their mangrove boat trips, **Backpackers** (Map p300; ☑ 9836177140; www.tourdesundarbans.com; ottee Lane) also offer innovative two-part city tours on the back of a motorbike (₹1500). Tours drive past several well-known sites and add curiosities like Kolkata's giant trash-mountain, Tangra Chinatown, a burning ghat, a Shiva temple (join the prayers) and a brief drive through the red-light district.

 Sleeping

Decent hotel accommodation in Kolkata often costs about the same as in Europe. AC hotels add 10% luxury tax (5% on cheaper rooms) and some tack on further service charges. For fairness we quote total prices. Most places charging under ₹1000 won't take bookings. Top-end places are often very significantly discounted on websites like www.yatra.com and www.agoda.com.

City Centre

Most hotels here cater for business clientele.

CHROME Boutique Hotel **$$**
(Map p302; ☑ 30963096; www.chromehotel.in; 226 AJC Bose Rd; s/d from ₹8800/9350; ❄ ☎) Sleep in a brilliantly executed artistic statement that looks like a seven-storey Swiss cheese by day, a colour-pulsing alien communicator by night. Rooms have optical illusion decor, the 5th-floor landing hides a mini-library and a rooftop pool is under construction. Bleeping music masks traffic noise.

Man carrying bushels of flowers to market, Kolkata

Central Kolkata

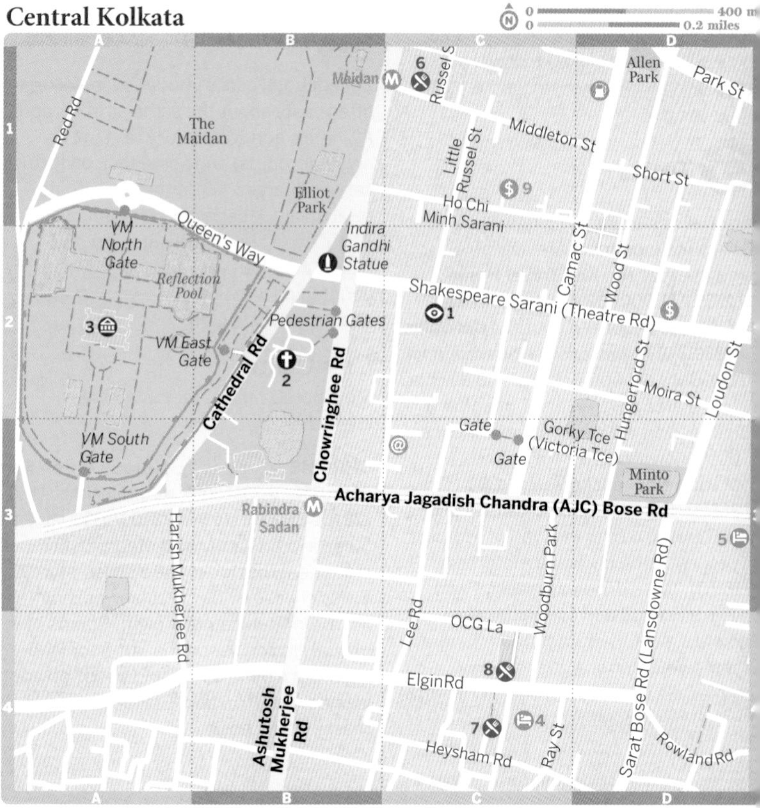

PARK HOTEL Hotel **$$$**
(Map p300; ☎22499000; www.theparkhotels.com; 17 Park St; s/d from ₹13,200/15,400; ❄@📶🏊) Perfectly central and hosting much of the city's nightlife, two of the Park's pricier floors use very stylish black-on-black decor while 'Residency' floors go for a more classical feel. Annoyances include reverberating music that can disturb light sleepers and a front desk where staff seem constantly overstretched.

ALLENBY INN Guesthouse **$$**
(Map p302; ☎24869984; allenbyinn@vsnl.net; 1/2 Allenby Rd; r ₹3300; ❄@) With fashionable trimmings and lashings of abstract art, some of the 20 rooms are very large, though towels could be softer and mattresses thicker. Two 5th-floor rooms share a dining area and small kitchen. They also offer guests wired internet access (per hour ₹20).

Central Kolkata

Sights
1 Aurobindo Bhawan C2
2 St Paul's Cathedral B2
3 Victoria Memorial A2

Sleeping
4 Allenby Inn C4
5 Chrome D3

Eating
6 Fire & Ice C1
7 Kewpies C4
8 Oh! Calcutta C4

Information
9 Globe Forex C1

Outer Kolkata

Due to distant locations and lack of convenient transport links, we don't review several of the city's top business hotels, which include the impressive **Hyatt Regency** (http://kolkata.regency.hyatt.com), eco-friendly **Sonar** (www.itcwelcomgroup.in/hotels/itcsonar.aspx) and the antique-softened 1990s **Taj Bengal** (www.tajhotels.com).

TOLLYGUNGE CLUB Guesthouse $$
(☏24732316; www.tollygungeclub.org; d/ste ₹4743/5014; 🛜❄🏊) The Tolly's idyllic setting with mature tropical trees, roosting birds and velvet-smooth golf greens creates a mind-boggling contrast to the deafening chaos of surrounding Kolkata. All guest rooms are sparkling clean but while some have functional motel-style decor, others have been very stylishly revamped to the standards of a boutique hotel.

 Eating

Most restaurants add 12.5% tax to bills. A few posher places add further 'service charges'. Don't miss sampling Bengali cuisine. At its best it's a wonderful discovery with a whole new vocabulary of names and flavours. In cheaper Bengali places, portions are often tapas-sized so order two or three dishes along with rice/*luchi* (deep-fried flatbread) and sweet *khejur* (chutney).

Upper Chowringhee Area
AROUND SUDDER ST

RAJ'S SPANISH CAFE Cafe $
(Map p300; Taberna Vasca, off Sudder St; mains ₹25-150; ⏰7.30am-10pm; 🛜) Excellent coffee, juices, pancakes and ₹25 wi-fi (plenty of power-points too) makes this a great any-time traveller cafe. The menu includes a small but very well-made selection of Spanish dishes (tortilla, pisto manchego) and delicious pesto-pasta (₹90). Decor is simple but welcoming with a cushioned sitting space and a small outdoor area.

If You Like...
Colonial-era Architecture

If you like the faded grandeur of the Victoria Memorial and St Paul's Cathedral, seek out these impressive buildings around BBD Bagh.

1 GENERAL POST OFFICE (GPO)
(Map p304; BBD Bagh; ⏰7am-8pm Mon-Sat, 10am-4pm Sun, parcel service 10am-4pm Mon-Sat) In 1866 the GPO was built on the ruins of the original Fort William, site of the infamous 'Black Hole of Calcutta'.

2 RAJ BHAVAN
(Map p304; http://rajbhavankolkata.nic.in; ⏰closed to public) This grand governor's mansion was designed in 1799 and modelled on Kedleston Hall, the Derbyshire home of the Curzon family.

3 HIGH COURT BUILDING
(Map p304; http://calcuttahighcourt.nic.in) Another of Kolkata's greatest architectural triumphs is this 1872 building, loosely inspired by the medieval Cloth Hall in Ypres (Belgium).

4 ST JOHN'S CHURCH
(Map p304; KS Roy Rd; ⏰8am-5pm) This stone-spired 1787 church, surrounded by columns, contains a small, portrait-draped room once used as an office by Warren Hastings, the first Governor-General of British India. (You'll find it on the right as you enter.)

JONG'S/ ZARANJ East Asian, Indian $$$
(Map p300; ☏22490369; Sudder St; mains ₹400-840; ⏰12.30-3pm & 7.30-11pm Wed-Mon) Two suave if pricey restaurants in one. Jong's serves Chinese, under-spiced Thai and other Asian cuisines in a magnificently wood-panelled room that feels like a Raj-oriental gentleman's club. Smart-casual Zaranj has a more modern vibe and takes the taste-buds on a gourmet tour of India. Some meals include rice but with most it's ₹100 extra.

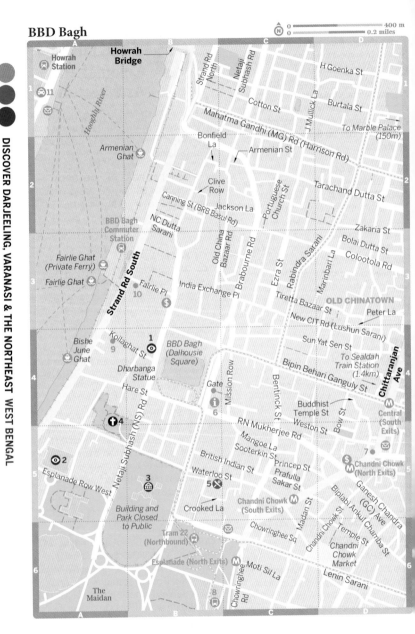

BLUE & BEYOND   Multicuisine **$$**
(Map p300; 9th fl, Lindsay Hotel, Lindsay St;
mains ₹120-190; ⏱11am-11pm) The open-air
rooftop terrace offers views over New
Market and there's a well air-conditioned
dining room in case rain or excessive heat
make sitting there impractical. A wide-
ranging menu encompasses Bengali fish
dishes, Irish stew and ratatouille at prices
that are very reasonable for a restaurant
that's licensed to serve alcohol.

BBD Bagh

PARK ST AREA

FIRE & ICE　　　　　Italian **$$$**

(Map p302; ☎ 22884073; www.fireandice
pizzeria.com; Kanak Bldg, Middleton St; mains
₹290-550, ☺noon-11.15pm) Self-consciously
handsome wait-staff sporting black shirts
and bandannas bring forth real Italian
pastas and pizzas whose fresh-baked thin
crusts are Kolkata's best.

ARSALAN　　　　　Mughlai **$$**

(Map p300; 119A Ripon St; mains ₹95-205;
☺noon-11.30pm) The decor is striking and contemporary without
being upmarket. The high ceilings with gilt insets contrast
with plain tables at which
the main attractions are
melt-in-mouth chicken
tikka and celebrated
biryanis that come with
a free palette of extras
(lemon, chilli, onion,
mint chutney).

TEEJ　　　　　Rajasthani **$$$**

(Map p300; ☎ 22170730; www.teej.in; 1st fl, 2
Russell St; mains ₹145-255, thalis ₹338-450;
☺noon-3.30pm & 7-10.30pm) Superbly
painted with Mughal-style murals, the
interior feels like an ornate Rajasthani
haveli (traditional residence) and the
excellent, 100% vegetarian food is pre-
dominantly Rajasthani, too. Downstairs,
much cheaper if stylistically neutral
Gangaur serves dosas and ₹124 thalis in
AC comfort.

City Centre

KEWPIES　　　　　Bengali **$$**

(Map p302; ☎ 24861600; 2 Elgin Lane; most
dishes ₹73-175, thalis ₹250-540; ☺12.30-3pm &
7.30-11pm Tue-Sun) Dining at Kewpies feels
like being invited to a dinner party in the
chef's eclectic, gently old-fashioned home
(avoid the charmless annex-room, north
door). First-rate Bengali food comes in
small but fairly priced portions. Minimum
spend is ₹250 per person.

The proprietor of a curd shop
RICHARD I'ANSON / LONELY PLANET IMAGES ©

Right: Victoria Memorial (p298) at dusk;
Below: Women hanging saris up to dry, Kolkata

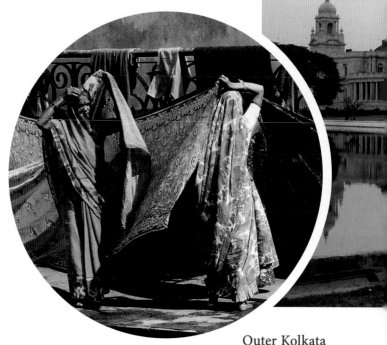

OH! CALCUTTA   Bengali $$$

(Map p302; ☎22837161; 4th fl, Forum Mall, Elgin Rd; mains ₹280-460; ⏰12.30-3pm & 7.30-11pm) Shutter-edged mirror 'windows', bookshelves and B&W photos create a casually upmarket atmosphere in this suave if pricey Bengali-fusion restaurant. *Luchi* (₹102 for six) are feather-light and fresh lime brings out the subtleties of *koraishatir dhokar dalna* (pea-cakes in ginger; ₹312).

BBD Bagh Area

Song Hay   Chinese $

(Map p304; ☎22480974; 3 Waterloo St; lunches ₹25-75, dinner mains ₹50-110; ⏰11am-10.30pm) This modest but prize-winning restaurant cooks authentic Chinese food at prices that are especially reasonable before 5pm when half-priced, half-size portions are available.

Outer Kolkata

BHOJOHARI MANNA   Bengali $

Branch 6 (☎24663941; 18/1 Hindustan Rd; dishes ₹45-210; ⏰noon-10pm); Ekdalia (9/18 Ekdalia Rd; dishes ₹20-190; ⏰noon-10pm) One of Kolkata's best respected chains for genuine if pre-prepared Bengali food, this is a fine place to try coconut-tempered *chingri malaikari* (₹145), a dish where the prawns are so big they speak lobster. The tiny original Ekdalia branch is jam-packed and basic, the only decor being sketches by the father of celebrated film director Satyajit Ray.

6 BALLYGUNGE PLACE   Bengali $$

(☎24603922; 6 Ballygunge Pl; mains ₹85-205; ⏰12.30-3.30pm & 7-10.30pm) In a sturdy but not overly formal century-old mansion, the lunchtime buffets (₹366) allow a good introduction to Bengali food with five main courses plus chutneys, rice and desserts.

🍷 Drinking

A Kolkata delight is making street-side tea stops for ₹2 mini-cuppas served in disposable *bhaar* (environmentally friendly earthenware thimbles).

ℹ Information

Medical Services

For listings see www.kolkatainformation .com/diagnostic.html and www.calcuttaweb .com/doctor.php.

Eastern Diagnostics (Map p300; 135 Mirza Ghalib St; ⊙7.30am-8.30pm) Doctors' consultations cost ₹200. Handy for Sudder St.

Money

Globe Forex (Map p302; 11 Ho Chi Minh Sarani; ⊙9.30am-6.30pm Mon-Fri, 9.30am-2.30pm Sat) City-centre exchange with unusually good rates for cash and travellers cheques.

Tourist Information

Cal Calling (₹45) Useful monthly info-booklet sold at Oxford Bookstore.

West Bengal Tourism (Map p304; ☏22437260; westbengaltourism.gov.in; 3/2 BBD Bagh; ⊙10.30am-1.30pm & 2-5.30pm Mon-Fri, 10.30am-1pm Sat) Comfortable, recently redecorated office mostly set up to sell tours (last sales 4.30pm). They also have booths at the airport, both domestic terminal (⊙8am-9pm) and international terminal (⊙11am to 6.30pm Monday to Saturday).

ℹ Getting There & Away

Air

Long-haul destinations from **Netaji Subhash Bose International Airport** (NSBIA; www. nscbiairport.org) include Frankfurt on Lufthansa and London on **Air India** (Map p304; ☏22114433; 39 Chittaranjan Ave; ⊙10am-6.30pm Mon-Sat). Alternatively, connect via Dubai (Emirates),

Kolkata Trains & Planes

DOMESTIC FLIGHTS FROM KOLKATA

DESTINATION	AIRLINES (& NO OF FLIGHTS PER WEEK IF LESS THAN DAILY)	DURATION	FARES FROM
Chennai	9W, 6E, SG, AI, I7	2hr	₹3030
Delhi	6E, 9W, AI, SG, IT, S2	2hr	₹3030
Goa	IT via Mumbai, SG via Delhi	4½hr	₹3710
Jaipur	6E, SG	2½hr	₹3030
Mumbai	9W, 6E, IT, AI, SG, S2	2½hr	₹3735
Varanasi (via Delhi)	SG	8hr	₹2315

6E=IndiGo, 9W=Jet Airways, AI=Air India, I7=Paramount, IT=Kingfisher, S2=JetLite, SG=SpiceJet

MAJOR TRAINS FROM KOLKATA

Departures daily unless otherwise stated.

USEFUL FOR	TRAIN	DURATION (HR)	DEPARTURES	FARES (FOR SLEEPER/3AC/2AC UNLESS OTHERWISE STATED)
Chennai	12841 Coromandal	26½	2.50pm (HWH)	₹461/1242/1700
	12839 Chennai Mail	28	11.45pm (HWH)	₹461/1242/1700
Delhi	12303/12381 Poorva	23	8.05am/8.20am (HWH)	₹426/1143/1561
	12313 SDAH Rajdhani	17	4.50pm (SDAH)	2AC/1AC ₹2030/3395
Mumbai CST	12810 Mumbai Mail	33¼	8.15pm (HWH)	₹508/1374/1883
Varanasi	13005 Amritsar Mail	15	7.10pm (HWH)	₹269/776/1065

HWH=Howrah, SDAH=Sealdah, KOAA=Chitpur

Singapore (Spice Jet), Bangkok (Thai Airways) or Dhaka (United Airways Bangladesh).

Car

Car rental companies, including Wenz (📞9330018001; www.wenzcars.com) and Ruia (www.ruiacarrentals.com), can organise long-distance chauffeured rides.

Train

Check whether your long-distance train departs from Howrah (Haora; HWH, Map p304), Sealdah (SDAH, Map p299) or 'Kolkata' (Chitpore; KOAA, Map p299) Station.

Before buying your tickets, check 'train between stations' on indianrail.gov.in to see if there's a Foreign Tourist quota left (using the 'Enter Quota' line). If so, head for the Eastern Railways' Foreign

Tourist Bureau (Map p304; ☎ 22224206; 6 Fairlie Pl; ☺10am-5pm Mon-Sat, 10am-2pm Sun) with a book to read – waits can be long but there are sofa-seats. Computerised booking offices (Map p304; Koilaghat St; ☺8am-8pm Mon-Sat, 8am-2pm Sun) offer tickets on the wider train network but have no tourist quota. Sudder St travel agencies can save you the trek and can sometimes manage to find tickets on 'full' trains but check what their commission will be before booking.

Getting Around

To/From the Airport

NSBIA Airport is 5km east of Dum Dum, itself 20 minutes by metro (₹6) from central Kolkata. With massive construction works underway to expand and modernise the airport, you can expect changes to come. Vehicle access is currently from Gate 1, 900m southwest of the terminals where a shopping and hotel complex is under construction, or from Gate 2 on Jessore Rd, around 400m northwest of the terminals. Note that the airport's left-luggage service has closed.

AC BUS New air-con airport buses (₹40, around one hour) run every half-hour from the terminal area to Esplanade Bus Station (Bhutan bus yard; Map p304). There are also less-frequent services to Tollygunge (via the bypass) and to Howrah.

TAXI Prepaid, fixed-price taxis from the airport to Dum Dum metro/Sudder St/Howrah cost ₹140/240/240. Pay before leaving the terminal (beware that there's sometimes quite a queue) then cross over to the rank of yellow cabs, ignoring touts in between. After 10pm very few fixed-rate taxis are available and others will charge far more.

Ferry

The fastest and most agreeable way from central Kolkata to Howrah train station is generally by river ferry (Map p304; ₹4; ☺8am-8pm) departing every 15 minutes from various jetties including Bagbazar, Armenian (not Sundays), Fairlie, Bishe June and Babu Ghat. Reduced service on Sundays.

Metro

Kolkata's busy one-line metro (www.mtp. indianrailways.gov.in; ₹4-8; ☺7am-9.45pm Mon-Sat, 2-9.45pm Sun) has trains every six to 15 minutes. Extensions are being built to Dakshineswar and to the airport, while a second line (Howrah–Sealdah–Salt Lake) is planned eventually. For Sudder St use Esplanade or Park St. There's a cursory baggage check on entering. Theoretically you may not carry bags over 10kg (nor may you carry ghee, leaves or dead bodies for that matter).

Taxi rank outside Howrah Station

PETER STUCKINGS / LONELY PLANET IMAGES ©

Rickshaw

Kolkata is the last bastion of human-powered 'tana rickshaws', especially around New Market. During monsoon, high-wheeled rickshaws are the transport most able to cope in the worst-flooded streets. Although rickshaw pullers sometimes charge foreigners disproportionate fares, many are virtually destitute, sleeping on the pavements beneath their rented chariots at night so tips are heartily appreciated.

Autorickshaws squeeze aboard five passengers to operate as share-taxis along fixed routes.

Taxi

Kolkata's ubiquitous yellow Ambassador cabs charge a minimum fare of ₹22 for up to 1.9km. Ensure that the meter's on (usually easier when flagging down a passing cab than if approaching a parked one) but be aware that what it shows is NOT what you'll pay. To calculate short-trip fares, double the meter reading and add two rupees. For longer trips, that system will be a couple of rupees under, so consult the driver's conversion chart or ask for a fare print-out. Fares rise after 10pm.

Beware that around 1pm, much of the city's one-way road system reverses direction! Not surprisingly many taxis are reluctant to make journeys around this time.

There are prepaid taxi booths at Howrah Station (Map p304), Sealdah Station and at both airport terminals, but such taxis are infamously hard to find at night.

Darjeeling

🕿 0354 / POP 109,160 / ELEV 2135M

Spread in ribbons over a steep mountain ridge, surrounded by emerald-green tea plantations and with a backdrop of jagged white Himalayan peaks floating over distant clouds, the archetypal hill station of Darjeeling is rightly West Bengal's premier attraction. When you aren't gazing at Khangchendzonga (8586m), you can explore colonial-era buildings, visit Buddhist monasteries and spot snow leopards and red pandas at the nearby zoo.

 Sights

TIGER HILL   Viewpoint
To watch the dawn light break over a spectacular 250km stretch of Himalayan horizon, including **Everest** (8848m), **Lhotse** (8501m), and **Makalu** (8475m) to the far west, rise early and get over

Bhutia Busty Gompa (p314)

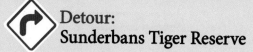

Detour:
Sunderbans Tiger Reserve

Home to one of the largest concentrations of tigers on the planet, this 2585-sq-km **wildlife reserve** (Indian/foreigner ₹15/150) is a network of channels and semisubmerged mangroves forming the world's largest river delta. Royal Bengal tigers (officially estimated to number close to 300) lurk in the impenetrable depths of the mangrove forests and swim the delta's innumerable channels. Although they do sometimes kill villagers working in the Sunderbans, tigers are typically shy and sightings are rare. Nevertheless, cruising the broad waterways through the world's biggest mangrove sanctuary (now a Unesco World Heritage Site) to see wildlife, whether it be spotted deer, a 2m-long water monitor or a luminescent kingfisher, is a world away from Kolkata's chaos.

West Bengal Tourism (see p307) organises weekly boat cruises from September to April, costing from ₹2300 per person for one night and two half-days, including food and onboard accommodation. Trips that include a worthwhile extra day start from ₹3100.

Backpackers (☎ 9836177140; www.tourdesundarbans.com; 11 Tottee Lane, Kolkata) is an extremely professional and knowledgeable outfit that conducts highly recommended tours of the jungles, including birdwatching and local music sessions. All-inclusive prices are ₹4000/4500 per person for one-/two-night trips, give or take a few hundred depending on the number of people in your group.

to **Tiger Hill** (2590m), 11km south of Darjeeling, above Ghum.

The sunrise over the Himalaya from here has become a major tourist attraction, with convoys of jeeps leaving Darjeeling for Tiger Hill every morning around 4.30am. At the summit, you can either pay ₹10 to stand in the pavilion grounds, or buy a ticket for one of the heated lounges in the pavilion (₹20 to ₹40).

Organised sunrise trips (usually with a detour to Batastia Loop on the way back) can be booked through a travel agency or directly with jeep drivers at the Clubside taxi stand. It's also possible to jump on a jeep going to Tiger Hill from along Gandhi or Laden La Rds between 4am and 4.30am, allowing you to check whether skies are clear before you go. Return trips cost around ₹80 per person or ₹600 to ₹800 for a vehicle.

OBSERVATORY HILL   Sacred Site
Sacred to both Buddhists and Hindus, this hill was the site of the original Dorje Ling monastery that gave the town its name. Today, devotees come to a temple in a small cave, below the crest of the hill, to honour Mahakala, a Buddhist deity and an angry form of the Hindu god Shiva. A path leading up to the hill through giant Japanese cedars starts about 300m along Bhanu Bhakta Sarani from Chowrasta.

PADMAJA NAIDU HIMALAYAN ZOOLOGICAL PARK   Zoo
(admission incl Himalayan Mountaineering Institute Indian/foreigner ₹40/100; ⊙ 8.30am-5.30pm Fri-Wed, ticket counter closes 4pm) This zoo, one of India's best, was established in 1958 to study, conserve and preserve Himalayan fauna. Housed within the rocky and forested environment are Himalayan megafauna such as musk deer, snow leopards, red pandas, Siberian tigers and Tibetan wolves.

The zoo is a pleasant 20-minute downhill walk from Chowrasta along Jawahar Rd West; alternatively, take a private taxi (₹70) from the Chowk Bazaar bus/jeep station.

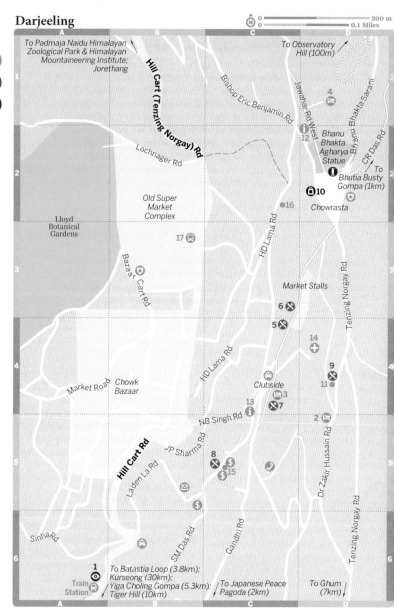

Darjeeling

To Padmaja Naidu Himalayan Zoological Park & Himalayan Mountaineering Institute; Jorethang

To Observatory Hill (100m)

Hill Cart (Tenzing Norgay) Rd

Bishop Eric Benjamin Rd

Jawahar Rd West

Bhanu Bhakta Sarani

CR Das Rd

Lochnager Rd

Bhanu Bhakta Agharya Statue

To Bhutia Busty Gompa (1km)

Old Super Market Complex

Lloyd Botanical Gardens

Bazaar Cart Rd

HD Lama Rd

Chowrasta

Market Stalls

Tenzing Norgay Rd

Market Road

Chowk Bazaar

HD Lama Rd

Clubside

NB Singh Rd

Dr Zakir Hussain Rd

Hill Cart Rd

JP Sharma Rd

Laden La Rd

SM Das Rd

Gandhi Rd

Tenzing Norgay Rd

Sinha Rd

To Batastia Loop (3.8km); Kurseong (30km); Yiga Choling Gompa (5.3km); Tiger Hill (10km)

Train Station

To Japanese Peace Pagoda (2km)

To Ghum (7km)

HIMALAYAN MOUNTAINEERING INSTITUTE   Museum

(HMI; ☎2254087; www.hmi-darjeeling.com; admission incl zoo Indian/foreigner ₹40/100; ☺8.30am-4.30pm Fri-Wed) Tucked away within the grounds of the zoo, this prestigious mountaineering institute was founded in 1954 and has provided training for some of India's leading mountaineers. Within the complex is the fascinating **Everest Museum**.

Darjeeling

Tours

During the high season the Darjeeling Gorkha Hill Council (DGHC) and other travel agencies offer a variety of tours around Darjeeling, usually including the Zoo, Himalayan Mountaineering Institute, Tibetan Refugee Self-Help Centre and several viewpoints. See p310 for Tiger Hill sunrise tour information.

Taxis can be hired for custom tours for around ₹750 per half-day.

Sleeping

Only a small selection of Darjeeling's many hotels is mentioned here. Prices given are for the high season (October to early December and mid-March to June), when it's wise to book ahead. In the low season prices can drop by 50%.

Top-end hotels offer rooms on the 'American Plan', with breakfast, lunch and dinner included; taxes and service charges usually add 15% to 20% to the bill.

**ANDY'S
GUESTHOUSE** Guesthouse **$**
(2253125; 102 Dr Zakir Hussain Rd; s/d from 300/400) This simple, spotless, stone-walled budget place has airy, carpeted rooms, a comfy common area and a rooftop terrace with a great view. Mrs Gurung provides a friendly boarding-house atmosphere (no restaurant) that makes it quieter than most other budget places. There's a good laundry service.

DEKELING HOTEL Guesthouse **$$**
(2254159; www.dekeling.com; 51 Gandhi Rd; d without bathroom ₹700, d ₹1300-2200; @) Spotless Dekeling is full of charming touches like coloured diamond-pane windows, a traditional *bukhari* (wood-burning heater) in the cosy lounge/library, wood panelling and sloping-attic ceilings, plus some of the best views in town. Tibetan owners Sangay and Norbu are the perfect hosts.

WINDAMERE HOTEL Heritage Hotel **$$$**
(2254041; www.windamerehotel.com; Jawahar Rd West; s/d full board from ₹7300/9400; @) This quaint, rambling relic of the Raj on Observatory Hill offers Darjeeling's most atmospheric digs. The charming superior room block was once a boarding house for British tea planters, and the well-tended grounds are spacious with lots of pleasant seating areas. The comfortable rooms, fireplaces and hot water bottles offer just the right measures of comfort and fustiness; a bit like staying at a rich aunt's house.

313

If You Like…
Monasteries & Views

If you like views such as those from Tiger Hill (p310) or Observatory Hill (p311), then try these other fascinating, beautiful places.

1 BHUTIA BUSTY GOMPA

This is the most scenic of them all, with Khangchendzonga providing a spectacular backdrop. Originally on Observatory Hill, it was rebuilt in its present lower location by the chogyals (kings) of Sikkim in the 19th century, and houses fine murals depicting the life of Buddha. To get here, follow CR Das Rd steeply downhill for five minutes from Chowrasta Sq, past a trinity of colourful Buddhist rock carvings. Climbing back up is a 20-minute slog.

2 YIGA CHOLING GOMPA

(Ghum; camera per photo ₹10) The region's most famous monastery has wonderful old murals and is home to 30 monks of the Gelugpa ('Yellow Hat') school. Built in 1850, it enshrines a 5m-high statue of Jampa (Maitreya, or Future Buddha) and 300 beautifully bound Tibetan texts. It's just west of Ghum, about a 10-minute walk off Hill Cart Rd.

3 JAPANESE PEACE PAGODA

(⏱ pujas 4.30–6am & 4.30–6.30pm) Perched on a hillside at the end of AJC Bose Rd, this gleaming white pagoda is one of more than 70 built around the world by the Japanese Buddhist Nipponzan Myohoji organisation. Drumming resonates through the forested grounds during their daily puja (prayers). It's a pleasant, 30-minute (gently) uphill walk from Clubside along Gandhi and AJC Bose Rds.

Eating

Most restaurants close their doors by 8pm or 9pm.

SONAM'S KITCHEN Continental $
(142 Dr Zakir Hussain Rd; mains ₹80-120; ⏱8am-2pm & 5-8pm) Providing an island of real brewed coffee in an ocean of tea, Sonam serves up lovely breakfasts, French toast, pancakes, fresh soups (nettle in season) and pasta; the deliciously chunky wholemeal sandwiches can be packed to go for picnics. Home-style dinner mains need to be pre-ordered at least an hour in advance so someone can dash up the street to stock up at the nearby veg stalls. It's a tiny place so try not to linger during mealtimes.

FRANK ROSS CAFÉ Multicuisine $
(14 Nehru Rd; mains ₹60-120, set breakfast ₹90-120) There's a diner-feel at this strictly vegetarian self-service place, with a wide-ranging menu, including pizzas, South Indian dosa and even enchiladas and nachos. The attached Frank Ross Pharmacy has groceries for self-caterers.

PARK RESTAURANT Indian/Thai $$
(☎2255270; 41 Laden La Rd; mains ₹70-140) The intimate Park is deservedly very popular for its tasty North Indian curries and surprisingly authentic Thai dishes, including small but tasty tom kha gai (coconut chicken soup) and spicy green papaya salad. Grab a seat early or make a reservation.

GLENARY'S Indian/Continental $$
(Nehru Rd; mains ₹120-210; ⏱noon-9pm, later in high season) This elegant restaurant atop the famous bakery and cafe receives mainly rave reviews: of note are the continental sizzlers, Chinese dishes, tandoori specials and veg gratin (good if you're off spicy food). We've heard a few grumbles that it's coasting on its reputation, but most people love it.

KUNGA'S Tibetan $
(51 Gandhi Rd; mains ₹60-90) Kunga's is a cosy wood-panelled place run by a friendly Tibetan family, strong on noodles and momos (dumplings), with excellent juice and fruit museli curd.

DEKEVAS Tibetan $
(51 Gandhi Rd; mains ₹60-90) Next door to Kunga's, this is a similarly good place, offering Tibetan butter tea, tsampa and a range of noodles for connoisseurs who can tell their thenthug (Tibetan noodles) from their sogthug (different Tibetan noodles).

TIM MAKINS / LONELY PLANET IMAGES ©

Don't Miss Khangchendzonga Views

The Himalayan skyline is a major attraction in Darjeeling. The skyline is dominated by **Khangchendzonga** (8586m), India's highest peak and the world's third-highest mountain (until 1852 it was thought to be the world's highest). The name 'Khangchendzonga' is derived from the Tibetan words for 'great five-peaked snow fortress'. On either side of the main massif are **Kabru** (7338m), **Jannu** (7710m) and **Pandim** (6691m), all serious peaks in their own right.

Apart from popular dawn views from **Tiger Hill**, an early morning stroll around **Bhanu Bhakta Sarani**, which runs from Chowrasta around the north side of Observatory Hill, offers several stunning viewpoints.

ℹ Information

Emergency

Police assistance booth (Chowrasta)

Sadar Police Station (☎2254422; Market Rd)

Medical Services

Planter's Hospital (D&DMA Nursing Home; ☎2254327; Nehru Rd) The best private hospital.

Money

A number of shops and hotels around Darjeeling can change cash and travellers cheques at fairly good rates; shop around.

Axis Bank (Rink Mall; ⊗10.30am-3pm Mon-Fri) Changes cash and Amex travellers cheques, with an ATM.

Poddar's (Laden La Rd; ⊗9am-8.30pm) Better rates than the State Bank next door and changes most currencies and travellers cheques at no commission. It accepts credit cards and is a Western Union agent. It's inside a clothing store.

State Bank of India (Laden La Rd; ⊗10am-2pm & 3-4pm Mon-Fri) Changes cash US dollars, euros and pounds sterling, plus US-dollar Amex travellers cheques, with a commission of ₹100 per transaction. It has an adjacent ATM, another in Chowrasta; both accept Visa cards.

TIM MAKINS / LONELY PLANET IMAGES

Don't Miss **Darjeeling Himalayan Railway**

The Darjeeling Himalayan Railway, known affectionately as the **Toy Train**, made its first journey along its precipice-topping, 60cm-wide tracks in September 1881 and is one of the few hill railways still operating in India. The train has been a Unesco World Heritage Site since 1999.

There is a daily steam service to Kurseong and a diesel train to NJP train station. It's an exhausting seven- to eight-hour haul to/from NJP, so if you simply want to experience the train, consider the steam train to/from Kurseong.

During the high season there are also joy rides (₹240) that leave Darjeeling at 10.40am (14D), 1.20pm (16D) and 4pm (18D) for a two-hour steam-powered return trip. The service stops for half an hour in **Ghum**, India's highest railway station, to visit the small **railway museum**, and pauses on the way back at the scenic **Batastia Loop**.

Book at least a day ahead at the **train station**, or online.

THINGS YOU NEED TO KNOW

Darjeeling Himalyan Railway (www.dhrs.org); railway museum (admission ₹20; ⊙10am-1pm & 2-4pm); train station (Hill Cart Rd); online bookings (www.irctc.co.in)

Tourist Information

Darjeeling Gorkha Hill Council Tourist Reception Centre (DGHC; ☎2255351; Silver Fir Bldg, Jawahar Rd West; ⊙10am-5pm Mon-Sat, except 10am-1pm every 2nd Sat, 10am-1pm Sun high season) The staff are friendly, well organised and the best source of information in Darjeeling.

Travel Agencies

Most travel agencies in town can arrange local tours, including the DGHC. Other reliable agencie and their specialities include the following:

Adventures Unlimited (☎9933070013; www. adventuresunlimited.in; Dr Zakir Hussain Rd) Offers Goecha La treks, kayaking, paragliding, motorbike trips and mountain bike rental

₹450 per day); ask about the cycle itinerary to Kurseong and back via Senchul Reservoir.

Samsara Tours, Travels & Treks (☑2252874; samsara1@sancharnet.in; 7 Laden La Rd) Helpful and knowledgeable agency offering rafting and trekking trips.

Somewhere Over the Rainbow Treks & Tours (☑9832025739; kanadhi@yahoo.com; HD Lama Rd; ⏱8am-6pm, later in high season) Organises off-the-beaten track walks around Darjeeling, starting from US$40 per day.

ℹ Getting There & Away

Air

The nearest airport is 90km away at Bagdogra, about 12km from Siliguri, which has flights to Kolkata and Delhi (some via Guwahati) on Air India, Jet Airways, Kingfisher, Go Air and Spice Jet.

Jeep & Taxi

Numerous share jeeps leave the crowded Chowk Bazaar bus/jeep stand for Siliguri (₹90 to ₹110, three hours).

Train

The nearest major train station is at New Jalpaiguri (NJP), near Siliguri. Tickets can be bought for major services out of NJP at the Darjeeling train station (⏱8am-2pm).

ℹ Getting Around

There are several taxi stands around town, but rates are absurdly high for short hops. Darjeeling's streets can be steep and hard to navigate. You can hire a porter to carry your bags up to Chowrasta from Chowk Bazaar for around ₹60.

UTTAR PRADESH
Allahabad
☎0532 / POP 1,049,579

For all its importance in Hindu mythology, Indian history and modern politics, Allahabad is a surprisingly relaxed city that offers plenty in terms of sights, but little in the way of in-yer-face hassle.

Brahma, the Hindu god of creation, is believed to have landed on earth in Allahabad, or Prayag as it was originally

known, and to have called it the king of all pilgrimage centres.

◉ Sights & Activities

SANGAM   Sacred Site
This is the particularly auspicious point where two of India's holiest rivers, the **Ganges** and the **Yamuna**, meet one of Hinduism's mythical rivers, the **Saraswati**. All year round, pilgrims row boats out to this holy spot, but their numbers increase dramatically during the annual **Magh Mela**, a six-week festival held between January and March, which culminates in six communal 'holy dips'. Every 12 years the massive **Kumbh Mela** pilgrimage takes place here, attracting millions of people, while the **Ardh Mela** (Half Mela) is held here every six years.

Old boat hands will row you out to the sacred confluence for around ₹50 per person, or ₹250 to ₹500 per boat.

ANAND BHAVAN   Museum
(admission Indian/foreigner ₹10/50; ⏱9.30am-5pm Tue-Sun) This picturesque two-storey building is a shrine to the Nehru family, which has produced five generations of leading politicians from Motilal Nehru to the latest political figure, Rahul Gandhi.

🛏 Sleeping

ROYAL HOTEL   Hotel **$**
(☑2427201; Nawab Yusuf Rd; r ₹150-350) This wonderful old building, also near the train station, used to be royal stables but was converted into a hotel by the King of Kalakankar, a former princely state, after he was refused entry into a British-run hotel nearby. It's also basic, and very rundown, but has bags of character and the rooms (with 6m-high ceilings), and their bathrooms, are absolutely enormous.

GRAND CONTINENTAL   Hotel **$$$**
(☑2260631; www.birhotel.com; Sardar Patel Marg; s ₹3000-4500, d ₹4000-5500, ste ₹6000-8000; ❄ @ 🛜 🏊) Rooms are a bit old-fashioned, with carpeted floors and

Detour:
Tea Tourism

The best places to learn about tea production are **Makaibari Estate** in Kurseong and **Happy Valley** outside Darjeeling. March to May is the busiest time, but occasional plucking also occurs from June to November.

Stay overnight with a tea-pickers family at a **homestay** (📞9832447774; www.volmakaibari.org; per person incl food ₹600) at Makaibari Estate and join your hosts for a morning's work. Pick your own leaves, watch them being processed and return home with a batch of your very own hand-picked Darjeeling tea.

Want to splurge? Accommodation doesn't get any more exclusive than top-end **Glenburn** (www.glenburnteaestate.com; s/d ₹11,000/14,000), between Darjeeling and Kurseong, a working tea estate/resort that boasts five staff for every guest (it was rumoured to have inspired film director Wes Anderson to make *The Darjeeling Limited*).

nonmatching furniture, but they're larger than other top-end choices in town, and staying here means you can use the delightful swimming pool, housed in a beautiful open-air marble courtyard. There's also a good-quality restaurant and a bar where evening *ghazal* performances are held. Wi-fi is free.

Eating

INDIAN COFFEE HOUSE Cafe $
(MG Marg; coffee from ₹13, mains ₹20-32; 🕗8am-9pm) This large, airy, 50-year-old coffee hall is a top choice for breakfast, with waiters in fan-tailed headgear serving up delicious South Indian fare – dosa, *idli* (fermented rice cakes), *uttapam* (savoury rice pancakes) – as well as eggs omelettes and toast.

SHAHENSHAH Indian $
(MG Marg; mains ₹20-80; 🕚11am-10.30pm) Watch young chefs frying up their creations from a couple of stalls set around a half open-air seating area with plastic tables and chairs and a high corrugated iron roof. This is no-nonsense, cheap eating, but popular with the locals, with a nice atmosphere. The menu includes *uttapam, paratha* (flaky bread cooked on a hotplate), a few Chinese dishes, pizza and some absolutely cracking dosa.

ℹ️ Information

ATMs dot the Civil Lines area.

Apollo Clinic (📞3290507; MG Marg; 🕗8am-8pm) A modern private medical facility with 24-hour pharmacy.

UP Tourism (📞2408873; rtoalld_upt@yahoo.co.in; 35 MG Marg; 🕙10am-5pm Mon-Sat) At the Rahi Ilawart Tourist Bungalow. Very helpful.

ℹ️ Getting There & Away

Air

Bamrauli airport is 15km west of Allahabad. **Air India** (📞2581370; 🕗incoming flights), at the airport, has daily flights to Delhi from ₹4500, except on Sunday. An autorickshaw to the airport costs ₹150 to ₹200, a taxi about ₹350.

Bus

From the Civil Lines Bus Stand regular buses run to Varanasi (₹85, three hours). More comfortable AC buses are much less frequent and about twice the price. To get to Delhi or Agra, change in Lucknow, or take a train.

Train

Allahabad Junction is the main station. Daily trains run to Varanasi (15017 *Gorakhpur Express*, sleeper/3AC/2C ₹120/243/326, four hours, 8.35am), Delhi, Agra (12403 *ALD MTJ Express*, sleeper/3AC/2AC ₹220/561/755, 7½ hours, 11.30pm) and Kolkata. Trains also run to Satna from where you can catch buses to Khajuraho.

Varanasi

0542 / POP 1.2 MILLION

Brace yourself. You're about to enter one of the most blindingly colourful, unrelentingly chaotic and unapologetically indiscreet places on earth. Pilgrims come to the ghats lining the River Ganges here to wash away a lifetime of sins in the sacred waters or to cremate their loved ones. Most visitors agree it's a magical place, but it's not for the faint-hearted. Here the most intimate rituals of life and death take place in public and the sights, sounds and smells in and around the ghats – not to mention the almost constant attention from touts – can be overwhelming. Persevere. Varanasi is unique, and a walk along the ghats or a boat ride on the river will live long in the memory.

 Sights

GHATS   Ghats

Spiritually enlightening and fantastically photogenic, Varanasi is at its brilliant best by the ghats, the long stretch of steps leading down to the water on the western bank of the Ganges. Most are used for bathing but there are also several 'burning ghats' where bodies are cremated in public. The main one is Manikarnika: you'll often see funeral processions threading their way through the backstreets to this ghat. The best time to visit the ghats is at dawn when the river is bathed in a yellow light as pilgrims come to perform *puja* (literally 'respect'; offering or prayers) to the rising sun, and at sunset when the main *ganga aarti* (river worship ceremony) takes place at Dasaswamedh Ghat.

About 80 ghats border the river, but the main group extends from Assi Ghat, near the university, northwards to Raj Ghat, near the road and rail bridge.

A boat trip along the river provides the perfect introduction, although for most of the year the water level is low enough for you to walk freely along the whole length of the ghats.

Old City Stretch

Varanasi's liveliest and most colourful ghat is **Dasaswamedh Ghat**, easily reached at the end of the main road from Godaulia Crossing. The name indicates that Brahma sacrificed (*medh*) 10 (*das*) horses (*aswa*) here. Every evening at 7pm an elaborate *ganga aarti* ceremony with *puja,* fire and dance is staged for all to admire.

Manikarnika Ghat, the main burning ghat, is the most auspicious place for a Hindu to be cremated. Dead bodies are handled by outcasts known as *doms,* and are carried through the alleyways of the old city to the holy Ganges on a bamboo

Steps leading up from the Ganges
GAVIN QUIRKE / LONELY PLANET IMAGES ©

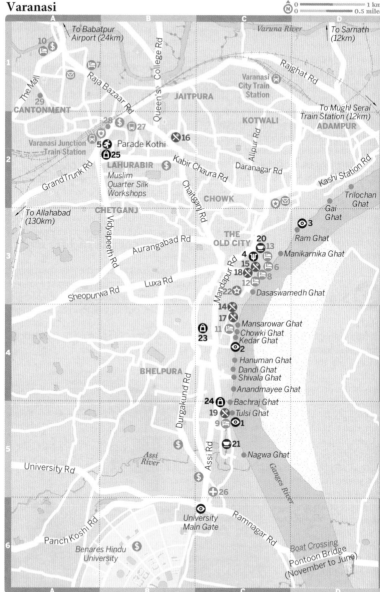

stretcher swathed in cloth. The corpse is doused in the Ganges prior to cremation. Huge piles of firewood are stacked along the top of the ghat; every log is carefully weighed on giant scales so that the price of cremation can be calculated. Each type of wood has its own price, sandalwood being the most expensive. There is an art to using just enough wood to completely incinerate a corpse.

You can watch cremations but always show reverence by behaving respectfully

Varanasi

Photography is strictly prohibited. You're almost guaranteed to be led by a priest, or more likely a guide, to the upper floor of a nearby building from where you can watch cremations taking place, and then asked for a donation (in dollars) towards the cost of wood. If you don't want to make a donation, don't follow them.

Northern Stretch

VISHWANATH TEMPLE   Hindu Temple
There are temples at almost every turn in Varanasi, but this one, also called the Golden Temple, is the most famous of the lot. It is dedicated to Vishveswara – Shiva as lord of the universe. The current temple was built in 1776 by Ahalya Bai of Indore; the 800kg of gold plating on the tower and dome was supplied by Maharaja Ranjit Singh of Lahore 50 years later.

The area is full of soldiers because of security issues and communal tensions. Bags, cameras and mobile phones must be deposited in lockers (₹25 to ₹50) before you enter the alleyway it's in. Non-Hindus are not allowed inside the temple itself, although this is not always strictly enforced.

 **Activities**

RIVER TRIPS   Boating
A dawn rowing boat ride along the Ganges is a quintessential Varanasi experience. The atmospheric, early morning light is particularly inspiring, and all the colour and clamour of pilgrims bathing and performing *puja* unfolds before you. An hour-long trip south from Dasaswamedh Ghat to Harishchandra Ghat and back is also popular, but be prepared to see a burning corpse at Harishchan-

The Varanasi Shakedown

If you thought the touts and rickshaw-wallahs were annoying in Agra, wait till you get to Varanasi. The attention here – particularly around the ghats and the Old City – is incredible, but with a bit of mental preparation it needn't spoil your enjoyment of this unique city.

The first issue is getting to your accommodation when you arrive – and not the one your rickshaw or taxi driver wants to take you to. Arrange a hotel pick-up if you can, or tell your driver that you have arranged to meet friends at a landmark near the hotel, then walk from there. Don't tell drivers the name of your hotel, even if they guess – they'll just spin yarns about it being closed, full, burnt down or full of gangsters.

While wandering the ghats and *galis* (alleyways) you'll be fielding persistent offers from touts and drivers of 'cheapest and best' boat trips, guides, tour operators, travel agents, silk shops and money changers (to name a few). Take them with good humour but, even if they seem appealing to your budget, resist all offers. Authorised guides can be organised through the UP Tourism office. It's safer – and cheaper – to arrange boat trips in groups (and cheaper to arrange them directly with the boat hand). Also resist offers to 'follow me for a better view'.

While most of the above is little more than a mild irritation, Varanasi, like all cities, does have a darker side. A criminal element operates mainly around the train and bus stations, so take extra care with your valuables in these places, and be cautious when walking alone at night.

Of course, not everyone is out to fleece you, and meeting the locals is a valuable part of every travel experience. Visitors who display confidence, patience and humour – and take sensible precautions – usually avoid any major problems.

---

dra. Early evening is an equally enchanting time to be on the river, when you can light a lotus flower candle (₹10) and set it adrift on the water before watching the nightly *ganga aarti* ceremony (7pm) at Dasaswamedh Ghat directly from the boat.

Boats, available at most ghats, cost about ₹100 per person per hour, but you'll need to be prepared for some hard bargaining.

Another trip worth considering is the lazy one-hour motorboat trip to Ramnagar Fort, which should cost around ₹100 per person from Dasaswamedh Ghat.

Many guesthouses offer boat trips, although they're more expensive than dealing with the boatmen directly.

 ## Tours

UP TOURISM OFFICE City Tour
(☎ 2506670; Varanasi Junction train station; half-/full day tour per person ₹900/1400; ⏰ 7am-7pm) If time is short, UP Tourism can arrange guided tours by taxi of the major sites, including a 5.30am boat ride and an afternoon trip to Sarnath.

 ## Sleeping

The majority of Varanasi's budget hotels – and some midrange gems – are concentrated in the most interesting part of the city – the tangle of narrow streets back from the ghats along the

River Ganges. There's a concentration round Assi Ghat, while others are in the crazy, bustling northern stretch of alleys between Scindhia and Meer Ghat, part of an area we refer to as the Old City.

Old City Area

GANPATI GUESTHOUSE
Guesthouse $

(☏2390059; www.ganpatiguesthouse.com; Meer Ghat; r without bathroom ₹350-550, r 700-1000; @ 🛜) Loads more character than next-door Hotel Alka, which is also a great choice, this old red-brick building has a pleasant, shaded, wi-fi–enabled courtyard as well as plenty of balcony space dotted around offering fine river views. Nicely painted rooms are colourful and clean and the ones facing out onto the Ganges (₹550) are lovely and spacious.

HOTEL ALKA
Guesthouse $

(☏2401681; www.hotelalkavns.com; Meer Ghat; ₹450-750, with AC ₹800-1700; ❄ @) An excellent ghat-side option, Alka has pretty much spotless rooms that open onto, or overlook, a large, plant-filled courtyard. In the far corner, a terrace juts out over Meer Ghat for one of the best views in all of Varanasi, a view shared from the balconies of the pricier rooms.

UMA GUESTHOUSE
Guesthouse $

(☏2403566, 9628698015; brownbreadbakery@yahoo.com; s/d without bathroom ₹150/250, d ₹300) Part of the Learn for Life Society run by the excellent Brown Bread Bakery, this homely place has basic but clean rooms that are looked after by some of the women involved with the charity. A percentage of your bill goes to the charity that runs the school behind the guesthouse. Bookings should be made through the bakery, where you can also ask about volunteering or donating.

KEDARESWAR
Hotel $$

(☏2455568; www.kedareswarguesthouse.com; Chowki Ghat; d ₹600, with AC ₹1000-1600; ❄) Housed in a brightly painted, aquamarine green building, this friendly place has small but immaculate rooms with sparkling bathrooms. There's only one cheaper non-AC room, so it might be worth phoning ahead. Chowki Ghat is right beside Kedar Ghat.

Morning yoga by the Ganges, Varanasi

GAVIN GOUGH / LONELY PLANET IMAGES ©

Varanasi's Top 5 Ghats

- **Dasaswamedh Ghat** Especially for the evening *ganga aarti* ceremony.

- **Manikarnika Ghat** Varanasi's primary cremation ghat.

- **Assi Ghat** Large and lively, especially early evenings.

- **Harishchandra Ghat** Another prominent cremation ghat.

- **Panchganga Ghat** Dominated by Alamgir Mosque.

SHIVA GANGES VIEW PAYING GUEST HOUSE Guesthouse $$

(2450063; www.varanasiguesthouse.com; Mansarowar Ghat; r ₹2000-2500, with AC ₹3000, ste ₹5000; ❄) Next to Lotus Lounge Restaurant, this delightful, bright-red brick building is part of the city's paying-guesthouse scheme. Rooms here ooze character, with central double beds, high ceilings, chunky door and window shutters, and some attractive ornaments on shelves. All have river views and spotlessly clean bathrooms. Home-cooked food is also available. The one downside is that the manager can be a bit pushy.

RASHMI GUESTHOUSE Hotel $$$

(2402778; www.rashmiguesthouse.com; Man Mandir Ghat; d ₹2500-6500; ❄ @) Sparkling white-tiled corridors and marble staircases lead to clean and modern rooms, which are small but smart. Many have views of Man Mandir Ghat, although the excellent rooftop **Dolphin Restaurant** offers the best views of all. Ayurvedic massage (₹1250) is also available.

Assi Ghat Area

HOTEL GANGES VIEW Hotel $$

(2313218; www.hotelgangesview.com; Assi Ghat; r ₹1000, with AC ₹3000; ❄) Simply gorgeous, this beautifully restored and maintained colonial-style house overlooking Assi Ghat is crammed with books, artwork and antiques. Rooms are spacious and immaculate and there are some charming communal areas in which to sit and relax, including a lovely 1st-floor garden terrace. Book ahead.

PALACE ON GANGES Hotel $$$

(2315050; palaceonganges@indiatimes.com; Assi Ghat; d ₹2500-3500; ❄ @) Each room in this immaculate heritage accommodation is individually themed on a regional Indian style, using antique furnishings and colourful design themes. The colonial, Rajasthan and Jodhpur rooms are among the best. The spa and massage centre (Ayur Arogyam) is also very good.

CHAITANYA GUEST HOUSE Guesthouse $

(2313686; Assi Ghat; s/d ₹350/400, d with AC ₹800; ❄) In complete contrast to next-door Sahi River View Guesthouse, Chaitanya has just four rooms: a single, two doubles and a double with AC. All are comfortable, with high ceilings and clean bathrooms, and are well looked after by friendly staff.

SAHI RIVER VIEW GUESTHOUSE Guesthouse $

(2366730; sahi_rvgh@sify.com; Assi Ghat; r from ₹250, with AC from ₹625; ❄) There's a huge variety of rooms at this friendly place. Most are good quality and clean, and some have interesting private balconies. Each floor has a pleasant communal seating area with river view, creating a great feeling of space throughout.

Cantonment Area

HOTEL SURYA Hotel $$

(2508465; www.hotelsuryavns.com; 20/51 The Mall; s/d ₹600/800, with AC from ₹1200/1500; ❄ @ 🛜 ❄) Varanasi's cheapest hotel with a swimming pool, Surya has OK modern rooms, built around a huge lawn area that includes a laid-back Middle Eastern-style cafe (**Mango Tree**).

GATEWAY HOTEL GANGES Hotel $$$
(☎2503001; www.thegatewayhotels.com; Raja
Bazaar Rd; r ₹9000-10,500, ste ₹11,500-13,500;
🅿@🛜🏊) Varanasi's best hotel is set in
3 hectares of beautiful gardens with fruit
trees, a tennis court, a pool, an outdoor
yoga centre and the old maharaja's guest-
house. You can walk, cycle or take a ride in
a maharaja's buggy around the grounds.

 Eating

Look out for locally grown *langda aam*
(mangoes) in summer or *sitafal* (custard
apples) in autumn. *Singhara* is a blackish
root that tastes like water chestnut.

Old City Area

**BROWN BREAD
BAKERY** Mulitcuisine $$
(17 Tripura Bhairavi; mains ₹75-230; ☺7am-
10pm; @) Not only does this place lead
the way socially and environmentally – it
supports a local school, runs a women's
empowerment group and uses organic
produce wherever possible – but the
food is also terrific. The fabulous menu
includes more than 20 varieties of cheese
and more than 30 types of bread, cookies
and cakes as well as main courses from
around the world.

**MADHUR MILAN
CAFE** Indian $
(Dasaswamedh Ghat Rd; mains
₹24-60; ☺8am-10pm) Popular
with locals, this no-non-
sense restaurant serves
up a range of good-val-
ue, mostly South Indian
dishes, including dosa,
idli and *uttapam,* and
paratha. Thalis start
from ₹45, and they
have lassis.

LOTUS LOUNGE Multicuisine $$
(Mansarowar Ghat; mains ₹90-200; ☺8am-
10pm) A great place to chill, this laid-back,
half-open-air restaurant, with broken-tile
mosaic flooring and wicker chairs, has
a terrace that juts out over Mansarowar
Ghat. The menu's a mixed bag, with fresh
coffee, set breakfasts, salads, pasta and
curries.

APSARA RESTAURANT Multicuisine $
(24/42 Ganga Mahal; mains ₹35-80) This cosy
AC restaurant has cushioned seats, good
music and friendly staff. The multicuisine
menu includes Indian, Chinese, Continen-
tal, Japanese, Israeli and Korean food, and
there's a small rooftop area.

DOLPHIN RESTAURANT Indian $$$
(Rashmi Guest House, Man Mandir Ghat; mains
₹110-300) Quality food, quality location;
Dolphin – the rooftop restaurant at Rashmi
Guest House – is perched high above
Man Mandir Ghat and is a fine place for an
evening meal. Watch food being prepared
through the glass-walled kitchen by the AC
restaurant, or sit out on the breezy balcony.

Narrow street in Old City, Varanasi.
STEVEN GREAVES / LONELY PLANET IMAGES ©

Rowboat for hire on the Ganges

ANDERS BLOMQVIST / LONELY PLANET IMAGES ©

Assi Ghat Area

PIZZERIA VAATIKA CAFE
Multicuisine **$$**

(Assi Ghat; pizza ₹65-100; ⏱7am-10pm) Sit in the shady garden terrace overlooking Assi Ghat while you munch your way through top-notch pizza baked in a wood-fired oven. None of that thick-crust nonsense here – it's all thin and crispy, as every pizza should be. Don't forget to leave some room for the delicious apple pie.

Cantonment Area

CANTON RESTAURANT
Indian **$$$**

(Hotel Surya, The Mall; mains ₹100-300; ⏱7am-11pm) Housed in a 150-year-old heritage building, Hotel Surya's excellent main restaurant has a colonial elegance, and on warm evenings you can eat out on the large lawn. The menu includes high-quality Indian dishes as well as some Chinese and Continental.

VARUNA RESTAURANT
North Indian **$$$**

(Gateway Hotel Ganges, Raja Bazaar Rd; mains ₹200-1450; ⏱lunch & dinner) As you'd expect from Varanasi's best hotel, this is one of the city's top restaurants. Elegant without being stuffy, Varuna's specialities include classic North Indian and Afghan dishes, the sumptuous maharaja thali and tandoor kebabs. There's live sitar and tabla music every evening.

EDEN RESTAURANT
Indian **$$$**

(Hotel Pradeep, Kabir Chaura Rd; mains ₹110-250) Hotel Pradeep's rooftop restaurant, complete with garden, manicured lawns and wrought-iron furniture, is a lovely place for a candle-lit evening meal. Note that staircase-weary waiters will be very appreciative if you order at the ground-floor AC restaurant behind the lobby before heading up to the roof. The good-quality Indian menu is the same in both restaurants.

Drinking & Entertainment

Wine and beer shops are dotted discreetly around the city, usually away from the river. Note that it is frowned upon to drink alcohol on or near the holy Ganges. For bars, head to midrange and top-end hotels away from the ghats.

here's nightly live **classical music** at Brown Bread Bakery, Puja Hotel and Varuna Restaurant at Gateway Hotel Ganges, to name but a few.

The **International Music Centre Ashram** (☎2452303; keshavaraonayak@hotmail.com), hidden in the tangle of backstreets off Bengali Tola, has small **performances** (₹100) on Wednesday and Saturday evenings.

AUM CAFE Cafe

(www.touchoflight.us; ⊙7am-5.30pm Tue-Sun; 🛜) Run by a friendly American woman who has been coming to India for more than 20 years, this cute and colourful cafe has fabulously fresh juices, coffee and lassis as well as some delicious snacks and sandwiches. The back of the menu lists the ayurvedic qualities of all the ingredients used. There are also massage therapies and body piercing available. Up the steps from Assi Ghat.

OPEN HAND Cafe

(www.openhandonline.com; ⊙8am-8pm Mon-Sat; 🛜) A cafe-cum-gift shop with fresh coffee and juices and a range of cakes and snacks plus a few main courses. There's free wi-fi plus a large selection of gorgeous handicrafts (jewellery, toys, clothing) made in the local community.

PRINSEP BAR Bar

(Gateway Hotel Ganges, Raja Bazaar Rd; ⊙noon-11pm) For a quiet drink with a dash of history try this tiny bar, named after James Prinsep, who drew wonderful illustrations of Varanasi's ghats and temples. Beers start at ₹225, cocktails ₹200.

🔒 Shopping

Varanasi is justifiably famous for silk brocades and beautiful Benares saris, but being led by touts and rickshaw drivers to a silk shop is all part of the Varanasi shuffle and virtually everyone involved will try to rip you off.

Varanasi is also a good place to shop for sitars (starting from ₹3000) and tablas (from ₹2500). The cost depends primarily on the type of wood used.

Mango is cheapest, while teak and vijaysar (a wild Indian herb, the bark of which is used in ayurvedic medicine) are of the highest quality.

BABA BLACKSHEEP Silk

(☎2454342; Bhelpura; 9am-8pm) Trustworthy, non-pushy and frequently recommended by our readers, this is a great place to come for silks (scarves/saris from ₹250/3000) and pashminas (shawls from ₹1300).

BENARES ART & CULTURE Handicrafts

(Shivala Rd; ⊙10am-8pm Mon-Sat) This centuries-old *haveli* (traditional, ornately decorated residence) stocks quality carvings, sculptures, paintings and wooden toys all made by local artists. Prices are fixed.

MEHROTRA SILK FACTORY Silk

(☎2200189; www.mehrotrasilk.com; ⊙10am-8pm) Tucked away down a tiny alleyway near the main train station, this pocket-sized, fixed-priced shop is a fun place to buy silk scarves (from ₹250), saris (from ₹1600) and bedspread sets (from ₹5000).

ℹ️ Information

Heritage Hospital (☎2368888; www.heritagehospitals.com; Lanka) English-speaking staff and doctors; 24-hour pharmacy in reception. Casualty to the right.

No 1 Lassi in all Varanasi

Your long, thirsty search for the best lassi in town is over. Look no further than **Blue Lassi** (lassis ₹10-30; ⊙9am-11.30pm), a tiny, hole-in-the-wall yoghurt shop that has been churning out the freshest, creamiest, fruit-filled lassis for more than 70 years.

State Bank of India (📞2343742; The Mall; 🕐10am-2pm & 2.30-4pm Mon-Fri, 10am-1pm Sat) Changes travellers cheques and cash.

Tourist Police (📞2506670; UP Tourism office, Varanasi Junction train station; 🕐6am-7pm) Tourist police wear sky-blue uniforms.

UP Tourism (📞2506670; Varanasi Junction train station; 🕐9am-5pm) The patient Mr Umashankar at the office inside the train station has been dishing out reasonably impartial information to arriving travellers for years; he's a mine of knowledge, so take advantage of it if you arrive here by train. Can give details of Varanasi's paying guesthouse scheme and guided tours.

❶ Getting There & Away

Air

Indian Airlines (📞Cantonment office/airport 2502529/2622494; 🕐10am-5pm Mon-Sat) has direct flights to Delhi (around ₹3000, daily), Mumbai (₹5000, daily), Kathmandu (₹7800, Tuesday, Thursday, Saturday and Sunday) and Khajuraho (₹3000, Monday, Wednesday and Friday). Other airlines are based at the airport.

Bus

The main bus stand is opposite Varanasi Junction train station. Allahabad (₹82, three hours, every 30 minutes) is also served by one or two AC buses that are more comfortable but at least twice the price.

Train

Luggage theft has been reported on trains to and from Varanasi so you should take extra care. A few years ago there were reports of drugged food and drink, so it's probably still best to politely decline any offers from strangers.

Varanasi Junction train station, also known as Varanasi Cantonment (Cantt) train station, is the main station. Foreign tourist quota tickets (p446) must be purchased at the helpful **Foreign Tourist Centre** (🕐8am-8pm Mon-Sat, 8am-2pm Sun), a ticket office just past the UP Tourism office, on your right as you exit the station.

There are several daily trains to Allahabad, Gorakhpur and Lucknow. A few daily trains leave for New Delhi and Kolkata, but only two daily trains goes to Agra. The direct train to Khajuraho only runs on Monday, Wednesday and Saturday. On other days, go via Satna from where you can catch buses to Khajuraho. See the table on p329.

❶ Getting Around

To/From the Airport

An autorickshaw to Babatpur Airport, 22km northwest of the city, costs ₹200. A taxi is about ₹400.

Taxi & Autorickshaw

Prepaid booths for autorickshaws and taxis are directly outside Varanasi Junction train station and give you a good benchmark for prices around town. First pay a ₹5 administration charge at the booth then take a ticket which you give to your driver, along with the fare, once you've reached your destination. Fares include:

Airport auto/taxi ₹200/400

Man praying by the Ganges, Varanasi
APRIL MACIBORKA / LONELY PLANET IMAGES ©

Handy Trains from Varanasi

DESTINATION	TRAIN NO & NAME	FARE (₹)	DURATION (HR)	DEPARTURES
Allahabad	11094 *Mahangari Exp*	120/277/373	3	11.30am
Khajuraho	21108 *BSB-Kurj Link E*	200/531/725	12	5.10pm*
Kolkata (Howrah)	12334 *Vibhuti Exp*	306/806**	14	6.10pm
New Delhi	12559 *Shiv Ganga Exp*	306/806/1095	12½	7.15pm

All fares are sleeper/3AC/2AC; *Mon, Wed, Sat only; **sleeper/3AC.

Assi Ghat auto/taxi ₹70/200

Dasaswamedh Ghat auto/taxi ₹60/150

Sarnath auto/taxi ₹80/250

Half-day tour (four hours) auto ₹300

Full-day tour (eight hours) auto ₹600

Sarnath
📞 0542

Buddha came to Sarnath to preach his message of the middle way to nirvana after he achieved enlightenment at Bodhgaya and gave his famous first sermon here. In the 3rd century BC emperor Ashoka had magnificent stupas and monasteries erected here as well as an engraved pillar. When Chinese traveller Xuan Zang dropped by in AD 640, Sarnath boasted a 100m-high stupa and 1500 monks living in large monasteries. However, soon after, Buddhism went into decline and, when Muslim invaders sacked the city in the late 12th century, Sarnath disappeared altogether. It was 'rediscovered' by British archaeologists in 1835.

Today it's one of the four important sites on the Buddhist circuit (along with Bodhgaya, Kushinagar and Lumbini in Nepal) and attracts followers from around the world.

 Sights

DHAMEKH STUPA & MONASTERY RUINS
Historic Site

(park Indian/foreigner ₹5/100, video ₹25; 🕑 dawn-dusk) The impressive 34m **Dhamekh Stupa** is set in a peaceful park of monastery ruins. It is historically significant as it marks the spot where the Buddha preached his first sermon. The floral and geometric carvings are 5th century AD, but some of the brickwork dates back as far as 200 BC.

Nearby is a 3rd-century BC **Ashoka Pillar** with an edict engraved on it. It once stood 15m tall and had the famous four-lion capital (now in the museum) perched on top of it, but all that remains are five fragments of its base.

CHAUKHANDI STUPA
Sacred Site

(🕑 dawn-dusk) This large ruined stupa dates back to the 5th century AD, and marks the spot where Buddha met his first disciples while travelling from Bodhgaya to Sarnath. The incongruous, octagonal tower on top of the stupa is Mughal and was constructed here in the 16th century to commemorate the visit of Emperor Humayun.

Eating

Vaishali Restaurant   Indian $
(mains ₹20-100; ⏰7am-9pm) Large 1st-floor
restaurant serving mostly Indian dishes, but
some Chinese too.

Green Hut   Multicuisine $
(meals ₹40-90; ⏰8.30am-8.30pm) A breezy
open-sided cafe-restaurant offering dosa,
snacks and chicken dishes.

ℹ Getting There & Away

An autorickshaw costs about ₹100 from
Varanasi's Old City.

MADHYA PRADESH
Khajuraho
☎07686 / POP 19,286

The erotic carvings that swathe Khajuraho's three groups of World Heritage–listed temples are among the finest temple
art in the world. The Western Group of
temples, in particular, contains some
stunning artwork.

Dangers & Annoyances

Most of the hassle tourists experience
comes in the form of seemingly endless
demands for money, pens and photo
fees, often from children. Also be wary
of commission-driven operations such
as guides offering to take you to a local
school or charity.

Sights

TEMPLES   Hindu/Jain

The temples are superb examples of
Indo-Aryan architecture, but it's their
liberally embellished carvings that have
made Khajuraho famous. Around the
outsides of the temples are bands of
exceedingly artistic stonework showing
a storyboard of life a millennium ago –
gods, goddesses, warriors, musicians and
real and mythological animals.

Two elements appear repeatedly –
women and sex. While the *mithuna* (pairs
of men and women, usually depicted in
erotic poses) are certainly eye-catching,
the erotic content should not distract
from the great skill underlying the
sculptures.

*WESTERN GROUP – INSIDE THE FENCED
ENCLOSURE*
Khajuraho's most striking and best-
preserved temples are those within the
fenced-off section of the **Western Group**
(Indian/foreigner ₹10/250, video ₹25; ⏰dawn-
dusk), and are the only temples here you
have to pay to see. An Archaeological Survey of India (ASI) guidebook to Khajuraho
(₹99) and a 90-minute audio guide (₹50)
are available at the ticket office.

Varaha, dedicated to Vishnu's boar
incarnation, and the locked **Lakshmi**
are two small shrines facing the large
Lakshmana Temple. Inside Varaha is a
wonderful, 1.5m-high sandstone boar,
dating from AD 900 and meticulously
carved with a pantheon of gods.

The large **Lakshmana Temple** took
20 years to build and was completed in
about AD 954 during the reign of Dhanga
according to an inscribed slab in the
mandapa (pillared pavilion in front of a
temple). It's arguably the best-preserved
of all Khajuraho temples. You'll see
carvings of battalions of soldiers here –
the Chandelas were generally at war
when they weren't inventing new sexual
positions.

The 30.5m-long **Kandariya-Mahadev**,
built between 1025 and 1050, is the
largest temple in town and represents
the highpoint of Chandelan architecture.
It also has the most representations of
female beauty and sexual aerobics, all
crammed into three central bands.

Mahadeva, a small ruined temple on
the same platform as Kandariya-Mahadev
and Devi Jagadamba, is dedicated to
Shiva, who is carved on the lintel of its
doorway. It houses one of Khajuraho's
finest sculptures – a *sardula* (mythical
beast – part lion, part some other animal –
possibly human) caressing a 1m-high lion.

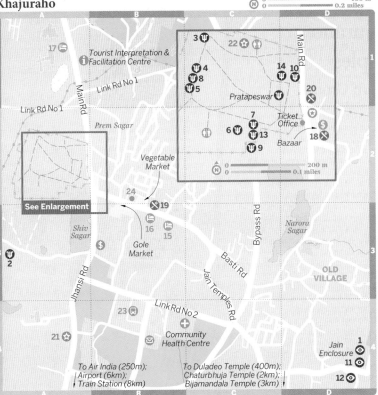

Khajuraho

Khajuraho

⊙ Sights

1	Adinath	D4
2	Chausath Yogini	A3
3	Chitragupta	C1
4	Devi Jagadamba	C1
5	Kandariya Mahadev	C1
6	Lakshmana Temple	C2
7	Lakshmi	C2
8	Mahadeva	C1
9	Matangesvara	C2
10	Nandi Shrine	D1
11	Parsvanath Temple	D4
12	Shanti Nath	D4
13	Varaha	C2
14	Vishvanath Temple	D1

⊜ Sleeping

15	Hotel Harmony	B3
16	Hotel Surya	B3
17	Lalit Temple View	A1

⊗ Eating

18	Madras Coffee House	D2
19	Mediterraneo	B3
20	Raja's Café	D1

⊙ Entertainment

21	Kandariya Art & Culture	A4
22	Sound-and-Light Show	C1

⊕ Transport

23	Bus Stand	B4
	Train Reservation Office	(see 23)
24	Yashowaran Taxi Driver Union	B2

Khajuraho Temples

Western Group

The sheer volume of artwork at Khajuraho's best-preserved temples can be overwhelming. Initiate yourself with this introductory tour, which highlights some of those easy-to-miss details.

First, admire the sandstone boar ❶ in the Varaha shrine before heading towards Lakshmana Temple ❷ to study the south side of the temple's base, which has some of the raunchiest artwork in Khajuraho: first up, a nine-person orgy; further along, a guy getting very friendly with a horse. Up on the temple platform see a superb dancing Ganesh carved into a niche (south side), before walking to the west side for graceful *surasundaris* (nymphs): one removing a thorn from her foot; another draped in a wet sari; a third admiring herself in a mirror.

Next is Khajuraho's largest temple, Kandariya-Mahadev ❸. Carvings to look for here include the famous handstand position (south side), but the most impressive thing about this temple is the scale of it, particularly its soaring rooftops.

Mahadeva ❹ and Devi Jagadamba ❺ share the same stone plinth as Kandariya-Mahadev, as do four beautifully carved *sardula* (part-lion, part-human mythical beasts), each caressing a stone lion – one is at the entrance to Mahadeva; the other three stand alone on the plinth.

Walk north from here to Chitragupta ❻, with beautiful carvings hidden on the west side, as well as elephant friezes around the temple's base (north side). The interior here is particularly impressive.

Continue east to Vishvanath Temple ❼ for more fabulous carvings before admiring the impressive statue of Vishnu's bull in the Nandi shrine ❽ opposite.

Handstand Position
Perhaps Khajuraho's most famous carving, this flexible flirtation is above you as you stand on the south side of the awesome Kandariya-Mahadev.

Sikharas
Despite its many fine statues, perhaps the most impressive thing about Kandariya-Mahadev is its soaring *sikharas* (temple rooftops), said to represent the Himalayan abode of the gods.

Devi Jagadamba Temple ❺

Kandariya-Mahadev Temple ❸

Mahadeva Temple ❹

NORTH →

Toilets

Sardula Statue
There are four lion-stroking *sardula* (part-lion, part-human mythical beasts) on this huge stone plinth, but this one, guarding the entrance to Mahadeva, is our favourite.

Kama Sutra Carvings
Although commonly referred to as Kama Sutra carvings, Khajuraho's erotic artwork does not properly illustrate Vatsyayana's famous sutra. Debate continues as to its significance: to appease evil spirits or imply rulers here were virile, thus powerful? Interestingly, the erotic carvings are never located close to the temple deity.

DANIEL MCCROHAN

DANIEL MCCROHAN

Listen Up

The audio guide only covers two temples but it is very detailed, so is a really useful introduction.

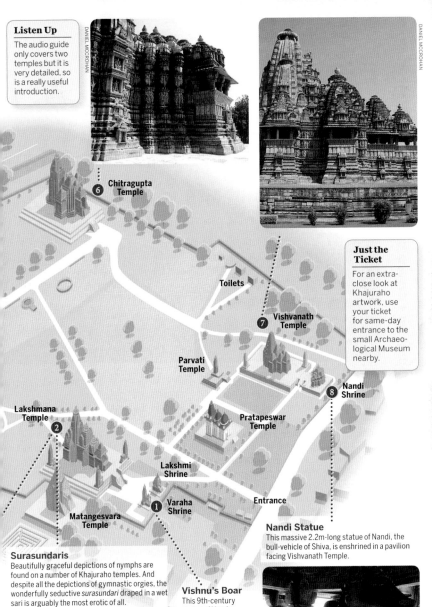

6 Chitragupta Temple

Just the Ticket

For an extra-close look at Khajuraho artwork, use your ticket for same-day entrance to the small Archaeological Museum nearby.

Toilets

7 Vishvanath Temple

Parvati Temple

Lakshmana Temple 2

Pratapeswar Temple

8 Nandi Shrine

Lakshmi Shrine

Matangesvara Temple

1 Varaha Shrine

Entrance

Nandi Statue

This massive 2.2m-long statue of Nandi, the bull-vehicle of Shiva, is enshrined in a pavilion facing Vishvanath Temple.

Surasundaris

Beautifully graceful depictions of nymphs are found on a number of Khajuraho temples. And despite all the depictions of gymnastic orgies, the wonderfully seductive *surasundari* draped in a wet sari is arguably the most erotic of all.

Vishnu's Boar

This 9th-century statue of Varaha, the boar incarnation of Vishnu, is carved all over with figures of Bramanical gods and goddesses. Under Varaha's foot notice the serpent Seshanaga in a devotional posture, and the feet of a goddess, now missing.

Devi Jagadamba was originally dedicated to Vishnu, but later to Parvati and then Kali. The carvings include *sardulas* accompanied by Vishnu, *surasundaris*, and *mithunas* frolicking in the third uppermost band.

North of Devi Jagadamba, **Chitragupta** (1000–25) is unique in Khajuraho – and rare among North Indian temples – in being dedicated to the sun god Surya. While its condition is not as good as the other temples, it has some fine carvings of *apsaras* and *surasundaris* (celestial nymphs), elephant fights and hunting scenes, *mithuna* and a procession of stone-carriers.

Believed to have been built in 1002, the **Vishvanath Temple** and **Nandi Shrine** are reached by steps on the northern and southern side. Elephants flank the southern steps. Vishvanath anticipates Kandariya-Mahadev, with which it shares *saptamattrikas* (seven mothers) flanked by Ganesh and Virabhandra, and is another superlative example of Chandelan architecture.

WESTERN GROUP – OUTSIDE THE FENCED ENCLOSURE
Skirting the southern boundary of the fenced enclosure, **Matangesvara** is the only temple in the Western Group still in everyday use. It may be the plainest temple here (suggesting an early construction), but inside it sports a polished 2.5m-high lingam (phallic image of Shiva).

The ruins of **Chausath Yogini**, beyond Shiv Sagar, date to the late 9th century and are probably the oldest at Khajuraho. Constructed entirely of granite, it's the only temple not aligned east to west. The temple's name means 64 – it once had 64 cells for the *yoginis* (female attendants) of Kali, while the 65th sheltered the goddess herself. It is reputedly India's oldest *yogini* temple.

EASTERN GROUP – JAIN ENCLOSURE
While not competing in size and erotica with the western-enclosure temples, **Parsvanath Temple**, the largest of the Jain temples in the walled enclosure, is

notable for the exceptional skill and precision of its construction, and for its sculptural beauty. Some of the best-preserved of Khajuraho's most famous images can be seen here, including the woman removing a thorn from her foot and another applying eye make-up, both on the south side. Although the temple was originally dedicated to Adinath, a jet-black image of Parsvanath was substituted about a century ago. Both an inscription on the *mahamandapa* doorway and its similarities with the slightly simpler Lakshmana Temple date it to 950–70.

The adjacent, smaller **Adinath** has been partially restored over the centuries. With fine carvings on its three bands of sculptures it's similar to Khajuraho's Hindu temples, particularly Vamana.

Shanti Nath, built about a century ago, houses components from older temples, including a 4.5m-high Adinath statue with a plastered-over inscription on the pedestal dating to about 1027.

SOUTHERN GROUP

A dirt track runs to the isolated **Duladeo Temple**, about 1km south of the Jain enclosure. This is the youngest temple, dating to 1100–1150. Its relatively wooden, repetitious sculptures, such as those of Shiva, suggest that Khajuraho's temple builders had passed their artistic peak by this point, although they had certainly lost none of their zeal for eroticism.

Anticipating Duladeo and its flaws, the ruined **Chaturbhuja Temple** (c 1100) has a fine 2.7m-high, four-armed statue of Vishnu in the sanctum. It is Khajuraho's only developed temple without erotic sculptures.

Just before Chaturbhuja there's a signed track leading to **Bijamandala Temple**. This is the excavated mound of an 11th-century temple, dedicated to Shiva (judging by the white marble lingam at the apex of the mound). Although there are some exquisitely carved figures, unfinished carvings were also excavated, suggesting that what would have been Khajuraho's largest temple was abandoned as resources flagged.

Sleeping

HOTEL SURYA
Hotel $

(☏274144; www.hotelsuryakhajuraho.com; Jain Temples Rd; r from ₹300, with AC from ₹700; ❄@) There's a huge range of decent-value rooms in this sprawling, well-run hotel with whitewashed corridors, marble staircases and a lovely courtyard garden out back. Some rooms have TV. Some have balconies. There's yoga and massage, and the atmosphere is generally laid-back.

HOTEL HARMONY
Hotel $$

(☏274135; Jain Temples Rd; r ₹500, with AC ₹1000; ❄@🛜) Cosy, well-equipped rooms off marble corridors are tastefully decorated with green and brown furnishings and come with cable TV. Yoga and massage available. Wi-fi costs ₹40.

LALIT TEMPLE VIEW
Hotel $$$

(☏272111; www.thelalit.com; Main Rd; s/d from ₹14,000/15,000; ❄@🛜🏊) Sweeps aside all other five-star pretenders with supreme luxury, impeccable service and astonishingly high prices. Rooms are immaculate with large plasma-screen TV, wood-carved furniture and tasteful artwork. Guests who don't have temple-view rooms can see the Western Group from the delightful lotus-shaped pool.

Eating

RAJA'S CAFÉ
Multicuisine $$

(Main Rd; mains ₹60-200; ⏰8am-10pm) Raja's has been on top of its game for more than 30 years, and recently added a **coffee stall** (coffee from ₹50) so that punters can now enjoy quality fresh coffee as well as superb food. The central location is great, as is the restaurant design, with a delightful wrought-iron spiral staircase linking a shaded courtyard with a temple-view terrace. But it's the food that steals the show. The Indian dishes are wonderful – the paneer *kofta* (unfermented cheese and vegetable balls) and chicken *kababi* (barbecued chicken pieces marinated in yoghurt), in particular – and there's good-quality Italian and Chinese too.

MEDITERRANEO
Italian $$$

(Jain Temples Rd; mains ₹100-300, pizza ₹240-345; ⏰7.30am-10pm) High-quality food, served on a lovely terrace overlooking the street, includes chicken, salads and organic wholewheat pasta, but it's all about the pizza here, baked in the wood-fired oven and easily the best in town. Beer and wine is also available.

Taking offerings to temple, Khajuraho
PAUL BEINSSEN / LONELY PLANET IMAGES ©

MADRAS COFFEE
HOUSE South Indian $

(cnr Main & Jain Temples Rds; mains ₹30-60; ⊙8am-9.30pm) Good, honest South Indian fare – dosa, idli, uttapam and thali – as well as coffee and chai, served in a simple, slimline cafe-restaurant. Ideal for breakfast.

Entertainment

Admittedly, the temples do look magical illuminated with technicolour floodlights, but the one-hour **sound-and-light show** (Indian/foreigner ₹50/300; ⊙Hindi 8.20pm Nov-Feb, 7.40pm Mar-Oct, English 7.10pm Nov-Feb, 6.30pm Mar-Oct) chronicling the history of Khajuraho is still about 45 minutes too long.

Folk dancing can be seen at the comfortable indoor theatre at **Kandariya Art & Culture** (✆274031; Jhansi Rd; admission ₹350; ⊙7-8pm & 8.45-9.45pm).

ℹ Information

Community health centre (✆272498; Link Rd No 2; ⊙9am-1pm & 2-4pm) Limited English, but helpful staff.

State Bank of India (✆272373; Main Rd; ⊙10.30am-4.30pm Mon-Fri, 10.30am-1.30pm Sat) Changes cash and travellers cheques. There are ATMs beside Raja's Cafe and Paradise Restaurant.

Tourist Interpretation & Facilitation Centre (✆274051; khajuraho@mptourism.com; Main Rd; ⊙10am-9pm) Leaflets on state-wide tourist destinations. Also has a stand at the airport and train station.

Tourist police booth (✆272690; Main Rd; ⊙6am-10pm)

ℹ Getting There & Away

Air

Jet Airways (✆274406; ⊙10am-3.30pm), at the airport, has a daily 1.45pm flight to Delhi (from ₹4200, 3½ hours) via Varanasi (from ₹3800, 40 minutes). **Air India** (✆274035; Jhansi Rd;

⊙10am-4.50pm Mon-Sat), closer to town, has 2pm flights to the same two cities, but only on Monday, Wednesday and Friday.

Taxi

Yashowaran Taxi Driver Union is opposite Gole Market. Fares include: airport (₹150), train station (₹250), Varanasi (₹6800) and Agra (₹7000).

Train

Three useful trains leave from Khajuraho train station:

On Mondays, Wednesdays and Saturdays the 22447 *Khajuraho–Nizamuddin Express* leaves for Delhi (sleeper/3AC/2AC ₹273/713/960, 6pm, 11½ hours) via Agra (sleeper/3AC/2AC ₹210/527/699, 8½ hours).

On Tuesdays, Fridays and Sundays the 21107 *Bundelkhand Link Express* leaves for Varanasi (sleeper/3AC/2AC ₹198/522/694, 11pm, 12 hours) via Chitrakut (five hours) and Allahabad (eight hours).

Train tickets can be bought from the train reservation office (✆274416; ⊙8am-noon & 1-4pm Mon-Sat, 8am-2pm Sun) at the bus stand. You must book tickets at least four hours before departure.

Coming to Khajuraho the 21108 leaves Varanasi on Mondays, Wednesdays and Saturdays at 5.10pm and passes Allahabad (10.25pm) and Chitrakut (1.03am) before arriving in Khajuraho (5.15am). The 22448 leaves Delhi's Hazrat Nizamuddin station on Tuesdays, Fridays and Sundays at 10.15pm and passes Agra (11.20pm) before arriving in Khajuraho (6.05am).

ℹ Getting Around

Bicycle is a great way to get around. Several places along Jain Temples Rd rent them (per day ₹20 to ₹50).

Cycle-rickshaws should cost ₹10 to ₹20 wherever you go in Khajuraho, and around ₹100/200 for a half-/whole-day tour. Autorickshaws are about double the price.

Taxis to and from the airport/train station charge ₹150/250, autorickshaws ₹50/80, but if you don't have too much luggage it's easy enough to wave down a bus or a shared jeep (₹10) as it heads along Jhansi Rd either into or out of town.

Northern Mountains & Amritsar

Soaring Himalayan peaks and steamy lowland jungles, revered temples and renowned ashrams, peaceful hill stations and busy cities: the Northern Mountains are truly an active traveller's delight, with some of India's best trekking, climbing, rafting, yoga schools, holiday towns and wildlife watching.

In many places to the northwest, you might think you've accidentally stumbled into Tibet. But those ancient Buddhist monasteries clinging to sheer cliffsides, those troves of Buddhist arts and the home-away-from-home of the Dalai Lama are just another part of the essence of Himachal. The unforgettable Himalayan lands of Ladakh are patchworked with timeless monasteries, arid canyons and stark, snow-topped mountainscapes that can soar to 7000m. And a hop, skip and jump south, and you're in the realm of the Punjab, with the glorious Golden Temple, Sikhism's holiest shrine, the gleaming jewel at its heart.

A monk looks out from a monastery rooftop, Ladakh

Floating market on Dal Lake (p375)
RICHARD I'ANSON/LONELY PLANET IMAGES ©

Northern Mountains & Amritsar

Under Administration of Pakistan

Under Administration of China

External boundaries shown reflect the requirements of the government of India. Some boundaries may not be those recognised by neighbouring countries. Lonely Planet always tries to show on maps where travellers may need to cross a boundary (and present documentation) irrespective of any dispute.

Kargil

2 Leh

Kolahoi Glacier

6 Srinagar

Parkachik Glacier

JAMMU & KASHMIR

Darung Drung Glacier

Padum

Banggong Co

0   100 km
0   50 miles

Kishtwar

Jammu

Dalhousie

3 Manali

Bara Shigri Glacier

PAKISTAN

Pathankot

McLeod Ganj **5**

HIMACHAL PRADESH

CHINA TIBET

Lahore

1 Amritsar

Bhakra Dam

Beas

Sutlej

Shimla

Khatling Glacier

Firozpur

Sutlej

Ludhiana

PUNJAB

Chandigarh

UTTARAKHAND

Mussoorie

Gangotri Glacier

Dehra Dun

Rishikesh

Abuhar

Bathinda

Yamuna

4 Corbett Tiger Reserve

RAJASTHAN

Nainital

1 Golden Temple, Amritsar

2 Leh

3 Manali

4 Corbett Tiger Reserve

5 McLeod Ganj

6 Srinagar

Panipat

HARYANA

UTTAR PRADESH

✪ Delhi

Ganges

Bareilly

Northern Mountains & Amritsar's Highlights

1 Golden Temple

Sikhism's holiest shrine, this gold-plated gurdwara (Sikh temple) glitters in the middle of its sacred pool of placid water and draws millions of pilgrims from all over the world. Whatever your faith, Amritsar's gilded temple will undoubtedly be a glowing highlight of your visit to India.

Need to Know

DRESS CODE Keep your head covered; wear modest attire. **EATING** Anyone can enjoy the langar (meal) free of charge, though donations are welcomed. **For more, see p386.**

Golden Temple Don't Miss List

SHIREEN KUMAR IS A TEACHER, LOCAL CULTURE ENTHUSIAST, AND UNOFFICIAL GUIDE TO THE TEMPLE

1 THE MAIN SHRINE

A confection of white marble. gilded frescoes and ornate domes, the main shrine has three storeys. Under a canopy studded with jewels on the ground floor is the Guru Granth Sahib, the holy book of the Sikhs. Beginning early in the morning and lasting until long past sunset, hymns are chanted to the exquisite accompaniment of flutes, drums and stringed instruments.

2 PALKI SAHIB

The Palki Sahib ceremony takes place twice a day where the Guru Granth Sahib is reverently brought to the temple in a decorative palanquin at around 4am, and is taken back to the Akal Takht at 9.30pm amid rousing devotion and thronging devotees. Check ahead regarding the timings, as these vary according to the season.

3 PILGRIMS' LUNCH

Langar (meal) preparation takes place in the community kitchen, where all persons, irrespective of race, religion or gender, perform a voluntary selfless service (*sewa*), serving food to the 35,000 pilgrims who visit the temple each day. The kitchen contains elaborate machines that make up to 6000 chapatis per hour. This is the busiest section of the temple and remains open 24/7. It symbolises the Sikh principle of inclusiveness and oneness of humankind.

4 AKAL TAKHT

Akal Takht is the highest Sikh religious authority, located in the Harmandir Sahib. It is decorated with inlaid marble, gold-leafed domes and wall paintings. The Guru Granth Sahib is kept in the Akal Takht at night. From around 6.30pm to 7.30pm every day, historic weapons are also on display here.

5 THE CENTRAL SIKH MUSEUM

The Central Sikh Museum is on the 2nd floor of the temple's main entrance, and has fascinating galleries display artefacts, coins, weapons, images and remembrances of Sikh gurus, warriors and saints. Details are also given in English.

Gompas in Leh

Studding the dramatic scenery around Leh (p379), stately stupas rise from the hilltops, oft
surrounded by ancient carvings or covered in brightly coloured reliefs. The spirituality of th
places seems to resonate through a combination of the surrounding natural splendour and
the locations and beauty of the monuments themselves. Mural from Phyang Gompa, near Leh

3 Adrenalin-seeking in Manali

Manali (p363) might be one of the mou
tains' most hippie and laid-back travell
magnets, but there's plenty to get the
pulse racing here, amid breathtaking
mountain scenery. This is one of the
best places in India for adventure tourism, with activities such as trekking,
paragliding, rafting and skiing all at you
fingertips. Paragliding above Solang Nullah (p366

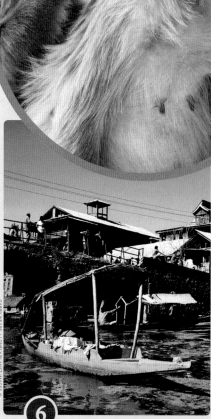
GRANT DIXON / LONELY PLANET IMAGES ©

Corbett Tiger Reserve

④

There are 175 tigers at the Corbett Tiger Reserve (p357) in Uttarakhand, and that's the reason most visitors come here, but even if you don't spot one, the reserve is an end in itself. It's 1318 sq km of grassland, sal forest and river habitats, populated with wild elephants, sloth bears, languor monkeys, peacocks, deer, crocodiles, wild boars, monitor lizards and over 600 species of birds. Rhesus macaques grooming each other at Corbett Tiger Reserve

GARRY WEARE / LONELY PLANET IMAGES ©

⑤

Tibetan Buddhism in McLeod Ganj

McLeod Ganj (p368), nicknamed 'Little Lhasa', is situated high in the fresh air of the Himalayas. You may feel as if you've stumbled into Tibet – it is the ideal place to clear your head, see Tibet in exile and understand something about Tibetan Buddhism. Prayer wheels at the Tsuglagkhang Complex p369

⑥

Boating in Srinagar

A caricatured Raj experience is to be had on the colonial-style, deluxe houseboats on Dal Lake (p375), with tea in the afternoon and boat trips out to Moghul Gardens. The scenery is breathtaking, the lake lying in a valley that is ringed by snowcapped mountains, and you can glide across the waters in a traditional *shikara* boat, visiting local markets and seeing life lived on the water.

Northern Mountains & Amritsar's Best..

Wining & Dining

○ **Imperial Square** (p351) Mussoorie's finest, with huge windows overlooking Gandhi Chowk

○ **Little Buddha Cafe** (p355) An ultra-loungey treehouse restaurant in Rishikesh

○ **Lazy Dog Lounge** (p367) A class act in Manali: eat indoors, relaxing on floor cushions, or out in the garden

○ **Moonpeak Thali** (p371) In McLeod Ganj; try a Himachali Thali for a smattering of delicious local dishes

○ **Mughal Darbar** (p376) Indulge in Kashmiri specialities at Srinagar's finest

Temples

○ **Jakhu Temple** (p360) Shimla's most famous temple, dedicated to the Hindu monkey god, Hanuman

○ **Hadimba Temple** (p364) An ancient stone and wood mandir in Manali

○ **Tsuglagkhang** (p369) One of Tibetan Buddhism's holiest places, in McLeod Ganj

○ **Golden Temple** (p386) Sikhism's holiest shrine

Views

○ **Gun Hill** (p350) Take a cable car from Mussoorie for breathtaking panoramas

○ **Shankaracharya Hill** (p375) A thickly forested hill in Kashmir, offering views over Dal Lake and beyond

○ **Shanti Stupa** (p381) A hilltop stupa with stunning views of Leh

○ **Hotel Indus** (p387) This modern Amritsar hotel has a fantastic view of the Golden Temple from its rooftop

Left: Woman with angora rabbit, Hadimba Temple (p364); **Above:** Shanti Stupa (p3.

(LEFT) RICHARD I'ANSON / LONELY PLANET IMAGES ©; (ABOVE) GUYLAIN DOYLE / LONELY PLANET IMAGES ©

Heritage Accommodation

o **Kasmanda Palace Hotel** (p351) Mussoorie's romantic hotel, a white Romanesque castle (c 1836)

o **Hotel Padmini Nivas** (p351) Built in 1840 by a British colonel, a green-roofed hotel with charm

o **Ananda Spa** (p357) Pure luxury in the palace of the Maharaja of Tehri-Garhwal

o **Chapslee** (p361) All-out Raj treatment in Shimla: the ostentatious former home of Raja Charanjit Singh of Kapurthala

o **Houseboats** (p377) The 1930s-style houseboats on the lakes of Srinagar; a serene experience

Need to Know

ADVANCE PLANNING

o **One month before** Book heritage or other special hotels, especially in the high season

o **One week before** Book long-distance train journeys or arrange a long-term driver and car through a local agency

o **One day before** Call to reconfirm your accommodation; ring ahead if you want to take part in adventure activities

RESOURCES

o **Himachal Tourism** (www.hptdc.gov.in) Regional tourist-board site, including accommodation and transport information

o **Punjab Government Website** (www.punjabgovt .nic.in) All about the Punjab

o **Haryana Online** (www .haryana-online.com) Includes history and cultural information on the Punjab

GETTING AROUND

o **Air** There are airports at Leh, Srinagar and Amritsar; Khullu is the nearest airport to Manali, 50km away

o **Train** The railway will take you as far as Rishikesh and Shimla

o **Car & driver** Hiring a taxi for a day or several days is the easiest way to access more remote places

o **Bus** Serves smaller towns that the train doesn't reach

BE FOREWARNED

o **Best weather** Himachal's best-weather seasons are May to mid-July and mid-September to early November

o **Amritsar accommodation** Hotels in Amritsar quickly fill during weekends and festivals, so book ahead

o **Litter** Dispose of litter carefully and avoid using plastic bottles where possible; both McLeod Ganj and Leh have places to refill water bottles

Northern Mountains & Amritsar Itineraries

These itineraries cover India's heart of Tibetan Buddhism, the tranquil lakes of Srinagar, the spectacular Golden Temple and adventure tourism in Manali.

5 DAYS

MCLEOD GANJ TO LEH
Houseboats & Mountaintops

Start your trip at the home of the Dalai Lama in exile, **(1) McLeod Ganj**, which will give you a taste of Tibetan culture and the chance to learn more about Tibetan Buddhism in beautiful mountainous surroundings.

Continue with your car and driver, if the security situation permits, to the incredible region of Kashmir. It's a journey through beautiful landscapes into the Kashmir valley where the capital **(2) Srinagar** lies like a jewel ringed by snow-dusted mountains, the town itself set around mirror-flat lakes. Rest up for a few days and take *shikara* (small boat) rides around the lakes, seeing the local markets, visiting the Moghul Gardens, and enjoying your stay on the wonderful, if Raj-theme-park-style, 1930s houseboats, complete with afternoon tea in the drawing room. You'll almost feel like dressing for dinner. Next fly from Srinagar into **(3) Leh**, into the otherworldly region of Ladakh, where you'll feel on top of the world, exploring its fascinating architecture and trekking into the moonscape-like mountains to finish your trip on a high note.

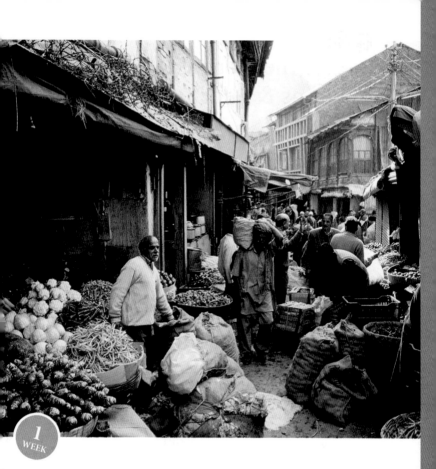

1 WEEK

Northwestern Triangle

tart your trip in the Punjab, visiting the Golden Temple in **(1) Amritsar**. This is not only a reathtakingly spiritual and holy place, but also spectacular architecturally, a glimmering old and silver edifice above its tranquil water tanks, and a peaceful haven in the heart of ne city. From here, the easiest way to continue would be to hire a car and driver (or take train for part of the journey), to make your way eastwards to the lovely hill station of **) Shimla**. For the last section of the journey make sure you take the little narrow-gauge y train up from Kalka, just north of Chandigarh. Shimla itself, with its colonial-era archi- cture and grand heritage hotels, is a beautiful place to relax after the hectic city, with alks into the thickly forested green on all sides and sweeping views.

From Shimla, retaining your car and driver, head still further north to **(3) Manali**, for beautiful Himalayan setting, laid-back traveller vibe and some adrenalin-pumping dventure activities such as mountain biking, rafting, walking and trekking.

Top Left: Celebration at the Tsuglagkhang Complex (p369); **Top Right:** Vegetable market, Shimla (p359)

(TOP LEFT) JOHN SONES / LONELY PLANET IMAGES ©; (TOP RIGHT) RICHARD I'ANSON / LONELY PLANET IMAGES ©

Discover the Northern Mountains & Amritsar

UTTARAKHAND
Mussoorie
📞 0135 / POP 29,319 / ELEV 2000M

Perched on a ridge 2km high, the 'Queen of Hill Stations' vies with Nainital as Uttarakhand's favourite holiday destination. When the mist clears, views of the green Doon Valley and the distant white-capped Himalayan peaks are superb, and in the hot months the cooler temperatures and fresh mountain air make a welcome break from the plains below. Although Mussoorie's main bazaars can at first seem like a tacky holiday camp for families and honeymooners, there are plenty of walks in the area, interesting Raj-era buildings and an upbeat atmosphere.

👁 Sights & Activities

GUN HILL   Viewpoint
From midway along the Mall, a **cable car** (return ₹55; ⊙8am-9pm May-Jul & Oct, 10am-6pm Aug-Sep & late Nov-Apr) runs up to Gun Hill (2530m), which, on a clear day, has views of several peaks, including Bandarpunch.

WALKS   Walking
When the clouds don't get in the way, the walks around Mussoorie offer great views. **Camel's Back Road** is a popular 3km promenade from Kulri Bazaar to Gandhi Chowk, and passes a rock formation that looks like a camel. **Trek Himalaya** (📞2630491; Upper Mall; ⊙9.30am-8pm) can organise guides for around ₹650 a day.

Namgyal Tsemo Monastery, Leh
KIMBERLEY COOLE / LONELY PLANET IMAGES ©

Tours

MVN BOOTH Sightseeing

(2631281; Library bus stand; 10am-5pm Mon-Sat) GMVN organises a number of local bus tours, including to Kempty Falls (three-hour tour ₹70), and Dhanoltri, Surkhanda Devi Temple and Mussoorie Lake (full-day tour ₹160). Tours can also be booked at the Uttarakhand tourism office on the Lower Mall.

Sleeping

Peak season is summer (May to July) when hotel prices shoot to ridiculous heights. There's a midseason during the honeymoon period around October and November, and over Christmas and New Year. At other times you should be able to get a bargain. The following prices are for midseason, unless otherwise specified.

HOTEL BROADWAY Hotel $

(2632243; Camel's Back Rd, Kulri Bazaar; d 600-1200, low-season discount 50%) The best of the budget places by a country mile, this historic 1880s wooden hotel with colourful flowerboxes in the windows oozes character without sacrificing comfort.

**KASMANDA PALACE
HOTEL** Heritage Hotel $$$

(2632424; www.kasmandapalace.com; ₹4000-6500, low-season discount 20%) Located off the Mall, this is Mussoorie's most romantic hotel. The white Romansque castle was built in 1836 for a British officer and was bought by the Maharaja of Kasmanda in 1915.

**HOTEL PADMINI
NIVAS** Heritage Hotel $$$

(2631093; www.hotelpadmininivas.com; the Mall; d ₹1875-2400, ste ₹2850-3300; @) Built in 1840 by a British colonel and then bought by the Maharaja of Rajpipla, this green-roofed heritage hotel has real old-fashioned charm. Large rooms with quaint sun rooms, suites and even a private cottage are well appointed and beautifully furnished.

Eating

IMPERIAL SQUARE Continental $$

(2632632; Gandhi Chowk; mains ₹120-320; 7.30am-11pm;) The tastefully understated Imperial, with huge windows overlooking Gandhi Chowk, scores high – on decor, service and, importantly, food. For breakfast there's even waffles. The attached **hotel** (d ₹4000, off-season discount 30%) has excellent rooms with valley views.

**LOVELY OMELETTE
CENTRE** Fast Food $

(The Mall, Kulri Bazaar; mains ₹35-60; 8am-9pm) Mussoorie's most famous eatery is also its smallest – a cubbyhole along the Mall that serves what many say are the best omelettes in India (a Facebook page for the restaurant started by an omelette lover has over 2000 friends).

**KASMANDA PALACE
RESTAURANT** Multicuisine $$

(2632424; mains ₹110-350) The regal restaurant at this Raj-era hotel (found north of the Mall) is the perfect escape from Mussoorie's holiday bustle. The woodpanelled dining room is intimate but not stuffy, and the garden restaurant is fine for a lazy lunch or summer evening.

Information

Money

Trek Himalaya (2630491; Upper Mall; 9.30am-8pm) Exchanges major currencies and travellers cheques at a fair rate.

Tourist Information

Uttarakhand Tourism office (2632863; Lower Mall; 10am-5pm Mon-Sat) Near the cable-car station.

Getting There & Away

Bus

Frequent buses leave from Dehra Dun's Mussoorie bus stand (next to the train station) for Mussoorie (₹35, 1½ hours). Some go to the Picture Palace bus stand (2632259) while others go to the

Library bus stand (☎2632258) at the other end of town – if you know where you're staying it helps to be on the right bus. The return trip takes an hour. There are no direct buses to Rishikesh – change at Dehra Dun.

Taxi

From taxi stands at both bus stands you can hire taxis to Rishikesh (₹1300).

Train

The **Northern Railway booking agency** (☎2632846; Lower Mall, Kulri Bazaar; ◷8-11am & noon-3pm Mon-Sat, 8am-2pm Sun) books tickets for trains from Dehra Dun, which is Mussoorie's nearest railway hub, and has regular connections with Delhi, as well as services to/from Varanasi and Kolkata (Calcutta).

Rishikesh

☎0135 / POP 79,591 / ELEV 356M

Ever since the Beatles rocked up at the ashram of the Maharishi Mahesh Yogi in the late '60s, Rishikesh has been a magnet for spiritual seekers. Today it styles itself as the 'Yoga Capital of the World', with masses of ashrams and all kinds of yoga and meditation classes. Most of this action is north of the main town, where the exquisite setting on the fast-flowing Ganges, surrounded by forested hills, is conducive to meditation and mind expansion. But it's not all spirituality and contorted limbs. Rishikesh is now a popular white-water rafting centre, backpacker hang-out, and gateway to treks in the Himalaya.

◉ Sights

LAKSHMAN JHULA & AROUND   Area
The defining image of Rishikesh is the view across the Lakshman Jhula hanging bridge to the huge, 13-storey wedding-cake temples of **Swarg Niwas** and **Shri Trayanbakshwar**. Built by the organisation of the guru Kailashanand, they resemble fairyland castles and have dozens of shrines to Hindu deities on each level, interspersed with jewellery and textile shops.

🏃 Activities

Yoga & Ashrams

SRI SANT SEVA ASHRAM   Mixed Yoga
(☎2430465; www.santsewaashram.com; Lakshman Jhula; d ₹150-600, with AC ₹1000; @) Overlooking the Ganges in Lakshman Jhula, the large rooms here are popular, s book ahead. The more expensive rooms have balconies with river views. The yoga classes are mixed styles and open to all. Beginner (₹100) and intermediate and advanced (₹200) sessions run daily.

**PARMARTH NIKETAN
ASHRAM**   Hatha Yoga
(☎244008; www.parmarth.com; Swarg Ashram; r ₹600) Dominating the centre of Swarg Ashram and drawing visitors to its evening *ganga aarti* (river worship ceremony) on

Rishikesh

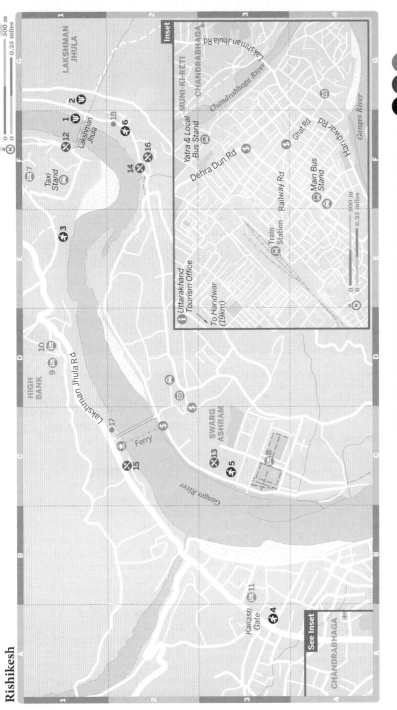

Inset

MUNI-KI-RETI

CHANDRABHAGA

Chandrabhaga River

Yatra & Local Bus Stand

Dehra Dun Rd

Lakshman Jhula Rd

Railway Rd

Ghat Rd

Haridwar Rd

Main Bus Stand

Ganges River

Train Station

Uttarakhand Tourism Office

To Haridwar (19km)

500 m
0.25 miles

LAKSHMAN JHULA

Lakshman Jhula

Taxi Stand

HIGH BANK

Lakshman Jhula Rd

Ferry

Ganges River

SWARG ASHRAM

Kailash Gate

See Inset

CHANDRABHAGA

500 m
0.25 miles

353

the riverbank, Parmarth has a wonderfully ornate and serene garden courtyard. The price includes a room with a private bathroom, all meals and hatha yoga lessons.

Rafting, Kayaking & Trekking

A number of companies offer full- and half-day rafting trips, putting in upstream and paddling back to Rishikesh. The official rafting season runs from 15 September to 30 June. A half-day trip starts at about ₹800 per person, while a full day costs from ₹1500. Most companies also offer all-inclusive Himalayan treks to places such as Kuari Pass, Har ki Dun and Gangotri from around ₹2300 per day.

De-N-Ascent Expeditions Kayaking, Trekking
(☎2442354; www.kayakhimalaya.com; Tapovan Sarai, Lakshman Jhula) Specialist in kayaking lessons and expeditions. Also organises trekking trips.

Garhwal Himalayan Explorations Trekking, Rafting
(☎2442267; www.thegarhwalhimalayas.com; Lakshman Jhula Rd, Muni-ki-Reti; 8am-8pm) Himalayan trekking and rafting trips.

Sleeping

High Bank

NEW BHANDARI SWISS COTTAGE Hotel $
(☎2435322; d ₹300-800, AC cottages ₹1200-1800; ❄@) One of the last places on the High Bank lane, this is a large, popular place with rooms ranging from clean and simple to simply impressive.

HIGH BANK PEASANTS COTTAGE Hotel $$
(☎2431167; d ₹600-800, with AC ₹1500-2000; ❄@) A High Bank original, this is the most upmarket accommodation here (it's closer to midrange than budget). Lovely gardens feature flowering trees and giant

Left: The ashrams, temples and hotels of Rishikesh;
Below: An Ashtanga yoga practitioner, Rishikesh
(LEFT) & (BELOW) CHRISTER FREDRIKSSON / LONELY PLANET IMAGES ©

cacti, there are wicker chairs on the balconies, and the spacious rooms are neatly furnished.

Lakshman Jhula

DIVINE GANGA COTTAGE   Hotel $
(☏2442175; www.divinegangacottage.com; r ₹300-600; ❄@) Tucked away from the hubbub and surrounded by small rice paddies and local homes with gardens, the huge upstairs terrace has supreme river views. Sweet rooms for the price have nice beds, and some have writing tables.

Swarg Ashram & Muni-ki-Reti

GREEN HOTEL   Hotel $$
(☏2434948; www.hotelgreen.com; Swarg Ashram; d with/without AC ₹750/1300; ❄@) In a small enclave of hotels down an alleyway, the newly renovated Green has bright rooms with tasteful furnishings, hot showers and flat-screen TVs. There are peaceful views of the hills – but not the river – from the rooftop terrace. Hallways on some floors are connected by wooden bridges over the atrium.

VASUNDHARA PALACE   Hotel $$$
(☏2442345; www.hotelvasundharapalace. com; Muni-ki-Reti; s/d ₹2950/3550, ste ₹5500; ❄≋) Rishikesh's top riverside hotel, this modern high-rise has luxurious, tastefully designed rooms, an elegant restaurant, and a rooftop pool and health spa with river views – unfortunately, views from the rooms are blocked by apartments.

 Eating

Lakshman Jhula

LITTLE BUDDHA CAFE   Multicuisine $$
(mains ₹70-140; ⊙8am-11pm) This funky treehouse-style restaurant has an ultra-loungey top floor, tables overlooking the Ganga, and really good international food.

355

Pizzas are big and the mixed vegetable platter is a serious feast.

DEVRAJ COFFEE CORNER Cafe **$**
(snacks & mains ₹30-100; ⏰8am-9pm) Perched above the bridge and looking across the river to Shri Trayanbakshwar temple, this German bakery is a sublime spot for a break at any time of the day. The coffee is the best in town and the menu ranges from specialties like brown bread with yak cheese to soups and sizzlers, along with the usual croissants and apple strudel.

PYRAMID CAFE Multicuisine **$**
(mains ₹35-95; ⏰8am-10.30pm; 📶) Sit on cushions inside pyramid-shaped tents, choosing from a menu of home-cooked Indian food, plus a few Tibetan and Western dishes including pancakes.

Swarg Ashram & Ram Jhula

MADRAS CAFE Indian **$**
(Ram Jhula; mains ₹50-120) This local institution dishes up tasty South and North Indian vegetarian food, thalis, a mean

mushroom curry, whole-wheat pancakes and the intriguing Himalayan health pilau as well as super-thick lassis.

GREEN ITALIAN RESTAURANT Italian **$$**
(Swarg Ashram; mains ₹60-150) Wood-fired vegetarian pizzas and imported pastas including gnocchi and cannelloni keep the customers coming back to this spotless, glass-fronted restaurant in the heart of Swarg.

High Bank

Backpackers gather at the popular restaurants on High Bank. This is the only area in town where you'll find meat on the menu.

OASIS RESTAURANT Multicuisine **$$**
(mains ₹45-190) At New Bhandari Swiss Cottage, this restaurant has some character, with candle-lit tables in the garden and hanging lanterns inside. The menu covers oodles of world cuisines, from Mexican and Thai to Israeli and Tibetan, and features a number of chicken dishes, including a delicious chilli chicken.

ℹ️ Information

Dangers & Annoyances

Travellers should be cautious of being befriended by sadhus (holy people) – while many sadhus are on genuine spiritual journeys, the orange robes have been used as a disguise by fugitives from the law since medieval times. In modern times, females walking alone may be at risk.

The current in some parts of the Ganges is very strong, and as inviting as a dip from one of the beaches may seem, people drown here every year. Don't swim out of your depth.

Travellers relax by the Ganges, Rishikesh
CHRISTER FREDRIKSSON / LONELY PLANET IMAGES ©

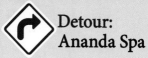

Detour:
Ananda Spa

Part palace, part exclusive luxury resort, this prize-winning **spa** (☎01378-227500; www.anandaspa.com; Badrinath Rd; s/d from US$495/540, ste US$865-1350, villa US$1520-2045; ❄ @ ☎) is the last word in indulgent pampering, and plays host to the rich and famous from India and abroad. Perched high in the hills 18km north of Rishikesh, Ananda Spa occupies part of the palace of the Maharaja of Tehri-Garhwal, spreading out over a manicured estate that includes deluxe accommodation, a six-hole golf course, jogging track, garden restaurants, an amphitheatre and a swimming pool.

Medical Services

Himalayan Institute Hospital (☎2471133; ⊙24hr) The nearest large hospital, 17km along the road to Dehra Dun and 1km beyond Jolly Grant airport.

Shivananda Ashram (☎2430040; www.sivanandaonline.org; Lakshman Jhula Rd) Provides free medical services and a pharmacy.

ⓘ Getting There & Away

Bus

There are regular buses to Dehra Dun (₹33, 1½ hours), where you can change for destinations such as Mussoorie or take trains to Delhi, Varanasi or Kolkata (Calcutta). Private deluxe buses to Delhi (₹350, seven hours) leave from Kailash Gate, just south of Ram Jhula, at 1.30pm and 9.30pm.

Taxi

From the taxi stand near the main bus stand, official taxi rates include Dehra Dun (₹650, 1½ hours), from where you can continue your journey to Mussoorie, or catch a train to Delhi, Varanasi or Kolkata (Calcutta). There are also taxi stands at Ram Jhula and Lakshman Jhula (west bank), charging ₹800 to Dehra Dun.

Train

Bookings can be made at the reservation office (⊙8am-6pm Mon-Sat, to 2pm Sun) at the train station, or at travel agents around Lakshman Jhula and Swarg Ashram (for a fee).

ⓘ Getting Around

Shared *vikrams* run from the downtown Ghat Rd junction up past Ram Jhula (₹10 per person) and the High Bank turn-off to Lakshman Jhula. To hire the entire *vikram* from downtown to Ram Jhula should cost ₹80, and from Ram Jhula to High Bank or Lakshman Jhula is ₹40.

To get to the eastern bank of the Ganges you either need to walk across one of the suspension bridges or take the ferry (one way/return ₹10/15; ⊙7.30am-6.45pm) from Ram Jhula.

Corbett Tiger Reserve

☎05947 / ELEV 400-1210M

This famous **reserve** (⊙15 Nov-15 Jun) was established in 1936 as India's first national park. It's named for legendary tiger hunter Jim Corbett (1875–1955), who put Kumaon on the map with his book *The Man-Eaters of Kumaon*.

Tiger sightings take some luck as the 175 or so tigers in the reserve are neither baited nor tracked. Your best chance of spotting one is late in the season (April to mid-June), when the forest cover is low and animals come out in search of water.

The **reception centre** (☎251489; www.corbettnationalpark.in; Ranikhet Rd; ⊙6am-4pm), where you must get your park entry permit and can sign up for a day trip or overnight safari, is located on the main road in the town of **Ramnagar**, almost opposite the bus stand. From 15 November to 15 June the entry fee (₹200/900 per Indian/foreigner) covers three days and grants access to the entire

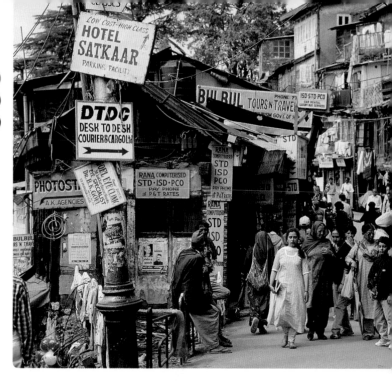

park. Single-day permits (valid for four hours) are available for every zone except Dikhala (₹100/450 per Indian/foreigner). On top of that, there's the jeep vehicle fee (₹500/1500 per Indian/foreigner overnight, ₹250/500 for a single day).

Of Corbett's five zones – Bijrani, Dhikala, Domunda, Jhirna and Sonanadi – Dhikala is the highlight of the park. It's only open from 15 November to 15 June, to overnight guests or as part of a one-day tour booked through the reception centre.

 Tours

The reception centre in Ramnagar runs daily **bus tours** (Indian/foreigner ₹1000/2000) to Dhikala at 5.30am and noon.

Four-wheel drives or the smaller Maruti Gypsies can be hired at the reception centre in Ramnagar, or through your accommodation or a tour agency. The jeep owners have formed a union, so in theory the rates are fixed (on a per jeep basis, carrying up to six people). Half-day safaris (leaving in the morning and afternoon) should cost ₹1000 to Bijrani, ₹1000 to Jhirna, or ₹1500 to Domunda, excluding the entry fees for you and your guide. Trips to Dhikala cost ₹2500. Check prices at the reception centre and at your hotel before hiring a jeep.

 **Sleeping & Eating**

Dhikala

Tourist Hutments (Indian/foreigner ₹1250/2500) offer the best value accommodation in Dhikala and sleep up to six people. Dhikala has a couple of restaurants serving vegetarian food. No alcohol is allowed in the park.

Ramnagar

CORBETT MOTEL   Hotel **$**
(☎ 9837468933; karansafaris@yahoo.co.in; tent ₹400, d/tr ₹500/600) Set in a beautiful mango orchard only a few hundred

Left: A bustling street scene in Shimla;
Below: An elephant in Corbett Tiger Reserve (p357)
(LEFT) PATRICK HORTON / LONELY PLANET IMAGES ©; (BELOW) HIRA PUNJABI / LONELY PLANET IMAGES ©

metres from the train station, Ramnagar's best budget accommodation is a world away from the traffic-clogged centre and offers exceptional service and hospitality. You can stay in sturdy tents or basic but spotless rooms, and the restaurant serves fine food. The owner, Karan, is a well-known local naturalist and can organise jeep safaris into the park. Call ahead for a pick-up.

❶ Getting There & Away

Buses run almost hourly from Ramnagar to Delhi (₹150, seven hours) and Dehra Dun (₹150, seven hours), from where you can take a bus to Mussoorie.

Ramnagar train station is 1.5km south of the main reception centre. The nightly *Corbett Park Link Express* (sleeper/2AC ₹107/417) leaves Delhi at 10.40pm, arriving in Ramnagar at 4.55am. The return trip leaves Ramnagar at 9.40pm, arriving in Old Delhi at 4.15am. For other destinations, change at Moradabad.

HIMACHAL PRADESH
Shimla

☎ 0177 / POP 144,900 / ELEV 2205M

Until the British arrived, there was nothing at Shimla but a sleepy forest glade known as Shyamala (a local name for Kali – the Hindu goddess who is the destroyer of evil). Then a Scottish civil servant named Charles Kennedy built a summer home in Shimla in 1822 and nothing was ever the same again. By 1864 Shimla had developed into the official summer capital of the Raj.

Strung out along a 12km ridge, Shimla is an engaging blend of holiday town and Indian city. Along the Mall and the Ridge, vacationers stroll around licking ice-cream cones, gazing at the views or into store windows. Cascading down the hillsides, bazaars flowing with local life are packed with shops selling hardware, stationery, fabric and spices.

Shimla

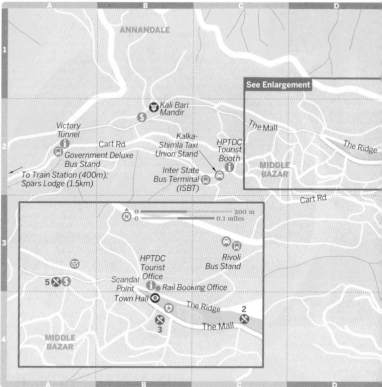

Sights

JAKHU TEMPLE Hindu Temple

Shimla's most famous temple is dedicated to the Hindu monkey god Hanuman; it's therefore appropriate that hundreds of rhesus macaques loiter around harassing devotees for *prasad* (temple-blessed food offerings). Getting here involves a steep 30-minute hike to the top of a hill, starting at the east end of the Ridge. Primate alert: the monkeys on this route can be a menace! Consider renting a walking stick at the start of the walk (from ₹10) to discourage them. Taxis from either stand charge around ₹300 return.

Tours

The HPTDC tourist office organises daily sightseeing bus tours of villages around Shimla. The tours leave from the Rivoli bus stand at around 10.30am. Seats cost ₹160 to ₹250.

The taxi unions also offer one-day sightseeing tours to Kufri, Naldehra, Fagu and Mashobra (₹1000), and to Mashobra, Naldehra and Tattapani (₹1250).

 Sleeping

Hotels in Shimla charge steep rates during the peak tourist season (April to June, October, November and Christmas). At all other times, ask about discounts. In

Shimla

Sleeping

1 Hotel Doegar F3

Eating

2 Ashiana C4
3 Baljee's B4
4 Cafe Sol E3
5 Indian Coffee House A3

Information

6 Great Escape Routes F2

vinter, heating can usually be provided or an extra charge.

:HAPSLEE Heritage Hotel **$$$**
2802542; www.chapslee.com; d with full oard ₹12,500-20,000;) For the full Raj reatment, the outrageously ostentaious former home of Raja Charanjit Singh of Kapurthala is perched atop Elysium Hill, about 4km north of Shimla. The exclusive mountain retreat s crammed with chandeliers, tapestries, Afghan carpets, big-game trophies, Mughal ceramics, baroque furniture and pieces of Victoriana.

SPARS LODGE Guesthouse **$**
2657908; Museum Rd; s/d ₹660/990; @) On the little road up to the museum, Spars is a real travellers' hotel with an nviting, homey feel. It's bright, clean and airy with a lovely sunny dining room upstairs. The owners are welcoming and the cafe serves great food, including local trout.

HOTEL DOEGAR Hotel **$$**
(2811927; www.hoteldoegar.com; The Ridge; d ₹1000-2500) Many of Shimla's hotels turn on the chintzy honeymoon charm, but Doegar does it with aplomb. The disco decor features mirrored ceilings, timber panelling and harem-style curtains, though all rooms look (and smell) different, so check out a few. The roof terrace has unbeatable views of Shimla, and prices halve in the off season.

OBEROI CECIL Hotel **$$$**
(2804848; www.oberoicecil.com; The Mall; s/d from ₹12,750/14,250, ste from ₹25,750; @) Along the Mall about 2km west of Scandal Point, this grand highrise is Shimla's glitziest five-star hotel. Colonial grandeur outside gives way to luxurious comforts within, and the cavernous colonial-style central atrium has a gorgeous bar and restaurant, open to nonguests.

Eating

Unless otherwise stated, the following eateries are open from 10am to 10pm.

CAFE SOL Multicuisine **$$**
(The Mall; dishes ₹140-400; 11am-10pm) In the atrium on the roof of Hotel Combermere but entered straight off the Mall, Sol serves tasty plates of Mexican, Italian

JOCHEN TACK / IMAGEBROKER

Don't Miss Shimla Toy Train

One of the little joys of Shimla is getting to or from it by the narrow-gauge toy train from Kalka, just north of Chandigarh. Although the steam trains are long gone, it's a scenic four- to six-hour trip, passing through 103 tunnels as it creeps up through the hills. Tiny Shimla train station is 1.5km west of Scandal Point on Cart Rd, about a 15-minute uphill walk.

Ordinary trains (1st/2nd class ₹189/16) run downhill to Kalka at 8.30am, 2.25pm and 6.15pm, returning at 4am, 6am and 12.15pm. To travel in style, catch the posh *Shivalik Express* at 5.40pm (returns at 5.30am; ₹280, 1st class only) or the *Himalayan Queen* at 10.30am (returns at 4pm; ₹167, chair car only). All 1st-class prices include food. The *Himalayan Queen* service connects with the *Himalayan Queen* trains to and from Delhi (chair car/2nd class ₹284/75). The train from Delhi's Hazrat Nizamuddin station leaves at 5.25am, departing from New Delhi station at 5.50am.

There's a rail booking office next to the tourist office on the Ridge; you can also book at the train station.

THINGS YOU NEED TO KNOW

Rail booking office (⏰9am-4pm)

and Mediterranean food, and has the best cake selection in Shimla.

BALJEE'S   Indian **$$**
(The Mall; mains ₹70-240) Opposite the Town Hall, Baljee's gets packed with Indian families, many of whom come for the snacks and South Indian specialties. Breakfasts of omelettes, toast and dosas (lentil-flour

pancakes) are good, and there's a popular counter selling Indian sweets.

INDIAN COFFEE HOUSE   Cafe **$**
(The Mall; dishes ₹20-35; ⏰8.30am-9.30pm) A Shimla institution, the Indian Coffee House is like an old boys' club with its ageing booths, uniformed waiters and blackboard menu. It's the most atmos-

heric place in town for breakfast, cheap
osas and coffee (don't even ask for
ea!).

SHIANA Indian **$$**
The Ridge; dishes ₹65-230; ☺9am-10pm) In
a fanciful circular building on the Ridge,
his is an almost elegant restaurant and
good people-watching spot. As well as
asty Indian dishes there are sizzlers,
Chinese and a few Thai favourites.

CECIL RESTAURANT Multicuisine **$$$**
(☎2804848; Oberoi Cecil, The Mall; mains from
₹400, breakfast/dinner buffet ₹650/950) For a
ormal night out, look no further than the
colonial elegance of the Cecil Restaurant.
An à la carte menu is available but there
are sumptuous buffets for breakfast and
dinner. Book ahead.

❶ Information

Emergency

Indira Gandhi Medical College (☎2803073;
The Ridge, Circular Rd; ☺24hr)

Tourist police (☎2812344; Scandal Point)

Money

Punjab National Bank (The Mall; ☺10am-4pm
Mon-Fri, to 1pm Sat) Changes major currencies
in cash and travellers cheques.

State Bank of India (The Mall; ☺10am-4pm
Mon-Fri, to 1pm Sat) West of Scandal Point; has
an ATM opposite.

Tourist Information

HPTDC tourist office (Himachal Pradesh
Tourist Development Corporation; ☎2652561;
www.hptdc.gov.in; Scandal Point; ☺9am-8pm,
to 6pm Aug, Sep & Dec-Mar) Helpful for advice,
brochures and booking HPTDC buses, hotels
and tours, along with a railway booking window.
There are satellite booths by the Inter State Bus
Terminal and the Victory Tunnel.

Travel Agencies

Great Escape Routes (☎5533037; www.
greatescaperoutes.com; 6 Andi Bhavan, Jakhu)

Specialises in trekking and adventure tours
around Shimla and throughout North India.

YMCA Tours & Treks (☎9857102657; www.
himalayansites.com; Shimla YMCA, The Ridge)
The affable and knowledgeable Anil Kumar
runs day trips around Shimla as well as treks
throughout Himachal and Uttarakhand.

❶ Getting There & Away

Air

Jubbarhatti airport, 23km south of Shimla, is
served by Kingfisher Airlines (☎1800 2093030;
www.flykingfisher.com). Weather permitting, there
are daily flights from Shimla to Delhi.

Taxi

The Kalka-Shimla Taxi Union (☎2658225) has
its stand near the ISBT, while Vishal Himachal
Taxi Operators Union (☎2805164) operates
from the bottom of the passenger lift. Taxis from
the train station or the ISBT to the passenger lift
cost around ₹70; to the airport, around ₹750; to
Dharamsala/McLeod Ganj, around ₹3600/3800;
and to Manali, around ₹3700. There's another taxi
stand next to the Rivoli bus stand.

❶ Getting Around

The only way to get around central Shimla is
on foot. Fortunately, there's a two-part lift (per
person ₹7; ☺8am-10pm, till 9pm Jul-Sep)
connecting the east end of the Mall with Cart Rd, a
15-minute walk east of the ISBT.

Manali

☎01902 / POP 4400 / ELEV 2050M

With magnificent views of the Dhaulad-
har and Pir Panjal Ranges, and with the
fast-flowing Beas River running through
the town, Manali is a year-round magnet
for tourists of all descriptions. Backpackers flock here to hang out in the hippie
villages around the main town; adventure
tourists are lured by the trekking, paragliding, rafting and skiing opportunities; Indian honeymoon couples are seduced by
the picture-perfect scenery and the cool
mountain air; and families are captivated
by their first taste of snow on a day trip to
Rohtang La.

Central Manali

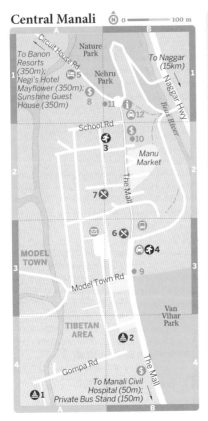

0 ——————— 100 m

contains a two-storey statue of Sakyamuni, the historical Buddha.

Further along the same lane is the more traditional **Gelukpa Cultural Society Gompa** (⊙6am-6pm), with an atmospheric prayer room crammed with statues of bodhisattvas, revered lamas and Buddhist deities. There's also a small workshop producing Tibetan carpets.

Sights & Activities

HADIMBA TEMPLE   Hindu Temple
Also known as the Dhungri Temple, this ancient wood and stone mandir was erected in 1553. Pilgrims come here from across India to honour Hadimba, the wife of Bhima from the Mahabharata. The walls of the temple are covered in woodcarvings of dancers, and horns of bulls and ibex adorn the walls. Hadimba is a 20-minute walk northwest of Manali, or you can take an autorickshaw (₹50).

BUDDHIST MONASTERIES   Buddhist Temples
There's a small Tibetan colony just south of the town centre. The **Himalayan Nyinmapa Buddhist Temple** (⊙6am-6pm)

Tours

In season, the HPTDC offers day tours by bus to Rohtang La (₹290) and Manikaran and the Parvati Valley (₹330), if there are enough takers. Private travel agencies offer similar bus tours.

The **Him-Anchal Taxi Operators Union** (☑252120; The Mall) has fixed-price tours, including Rohtang La (₹1900), Solang Nullah (₹600) and Naggar (₹650).

Adventure Tour Operators

The following places are reliable and well established and can arrange treks, tours and adventure activities – see the boxed text, p366, for more popular options.

Arohi Travels   Outdoor Adventure
(📞254421; www.arohieco adventures) Located off the Mall, and also has an office at Hotel Arohi in Vashisht.

Himalayan Extreme Center   Outdoor Adventure
(📞9816174164; www.himalayan-extreme-center.com) With one office in Old Manali and one in Vashisht, your one-stop shop for any adventure activity.

 Sleeping

Manali has some of the best-value accommodation in the state, though prices are highest during the peak seasons of April to June, September, October and Christmas.

Manali

SUNSHINE GUEST HOUSE   Guesthouse   **$**
(📞252320; Circuit House Rd; r ₹400) This rambling, wooden Raj-era mansion will appeal to lovers of unfussy colonial character rather than modern comforts. Enormous rooms with fireplaces (firewood is extra) and giant bathrooms may be a bit draughty, but the balconies, sunrooms and overgrown garden are straight out of a storybook.

JOHNSON HOTEL   Hotel   **$$$**
(📞253764; www.johnson hotel.in; Circuit House Rd; d ₹2750-3200; ❄ @ 🛜) One of several places named in honour of the Raj-era landowner Jimmy Johnson. This is a classy wood-and-stone hotel that has snug heritage rooms, a century-old lodge and lovely gardens, as well as an excellent restaurant.

NEGI'S HOTEL MAYFLOWER   Hotel   **$$$**
(📞252104; www.negismayflower.com; Club House Rd; r ₹3000; ❄ @) Mayflower is a stately wooden lodge with cascading balconies and cosy but luxurious wood-panelled rooms, some with open fireplaces (firewood costs extra).

BANON RESORTS   Hotel   **$$$**
(📞253026; www.banonresortsmanali.com; d ₹4500-6000, cottages from ₹12,000; ❄ 🛜) This luxury hotel is the most comfortable in Old Manali. Centrally heated rooms in the main hotel are spacious but surprisingly plain, while the two-bedroom cottages are the last word in luxurious peace and privacy.

New buildings by the river, Manali
PATRICK HORTON / LONELY PLANET IMAGES ©

If You Like...
Adventure Activities

Manali is the adventure sports capital of Himachal Pradesh, so if you like activities like those on offer by the listed Adventure Tour Operators (p365), there are plenty more adrenalin-pumping things to do.

1 PARAGLIDING
Paragliding is popular at Solang Nullah from April to October. Short flights start at ₹700 for two minutes, but adventure tour operators can organise longer flights from surrounding take-off points for ₹1500 to ₹3000.

2 RAFTING
White-water rafting trips on the Beas River can be arranged in Manali, starting from Pirdi, 3km downriver from Kullu. There's 14km of Grade II and III white water between Pirdi and the take-out point at Jhiri; trips cost around ₹600 per person. Book through travel agents or directly at Pirdi.

3 OTHER ACTIVITIES
Also available in the area are horse riding (₹900 per day) and canyoning (₹2400 per day). Quad-bike rides around Solang Nullah cost ₹500 for a quick 4km trip, or ₹1500 per hour. Short hot-air balloon rides are sometimes available in Solang Nullah during summer.

Old Manali

Most places close down in late October when many locals head to Goa for the winter.

VEER GUEST HOUSE Hotel $
(✆252710; veerguesthouse@hotmail.com; r ₹400-700; @) Set in a pretty garden, long-running Veer is one of Old Manali's best-value hotels. Rooms in the quaint lime-green original section with wood-plank flooring have plenty of character, while new rooms at the front are bright and slick, with TVs and private balconies.

HIMALAYAN COUNTRY HOUSE Guesthouse $
(✆252294; www.himalayancountryhouse.com; Old Manali; r ₹600-1000) Ensconced at the end of the road in Old Manali, this four-storey stone and timber hotel overlooks the slate roofs of village homes and across to the mountains. It's beautifully designed, with traditional carved doors and compact wood-panelled rooms opening on to shared balconies with the best valley views of any hotel on this side of the Beas.

Eating

Manali

MAYUR Indian/Multicuisine $$
(Mission Rd; dishes ₹70-250; ⊙9am-11pm) Locals rate Mayur highly for its well-prepared North and South Indian specialities. Downstairs is traditional Indian, in decor as well as cuisine, while the contemporary upstairs bistro serves dishes such as croquettes, chicken stroganoff and, oddly, Marmite toast.

IL FORNO Italian $$
(Hadimba Rd; mains ₹140-270; ⊙12.30-10.30pm) Perched on a hillside near Hadimba Temple, Il Forno is a genuine Italian restaurant in a superb Himachal stone and timber building. The wood-fired pizzas, calzone, lasagne and pasta dishes are prepared by a Veronese chef and you can enjoy an espresso or beer with wonderful valley views from the garden terrace.

JOHNSON'S CAFE Continental $$
(Circuit House Rd; dishes ₹120-350; ⊙8am-10.30pm) The restaurant at Johnson Hotel is one of the best in town for European food, with dishes like lamb and mint gravy, smoked chicken, and fig and apple crumble. The restaurant-bar is cosy, but on warm evenings or sunny afternoons, the garden terrace is the place to be.

CHOPSTICKS
Asian **$$**

(The Mall; dishes ₹60-270; ⊘7.30am-10.30pm)
The most popular traveller choice along the Mall in Manali town, this intimate Tibetan-Chinese-Japanese place is always busy. Naturally there are Indian dishes here, too, along with local trout. Cold beers and fruit wines are also served.

Old Manali

All these places close by the start of November.

LAZY DOG LOUNGE
Fusion **$$**

(mains ₹70-300; 🛜) This restaurant/bar overlooking the river features big plates of fresh and flavourful international food that's steps above typical backpacker fare. Sit on chairs, benches or floor cushions in a space that's classy yet earthy, or relax in the outdoor garden. The beer (₹120 to ₹230) and wine (₹180 to ₹1250) lists are plenty long and the desserts will sate your sweet tooth.

DYLAN'S TOASTED & ROASTED
Cafe **$**

(www.dylanscoffee.com; drinks & snacks ₹20-100; ⊘10am-8pm Mon-Sat) Manali's mellowest hang-out, this hole-in-the-wall cabin-style coffee shop in Old Manali serves the best espresso coffee in town, cinnamon tea, hearty breakfasts, garlic cheese toast and wicked desserts like chocolate-chip cookies and 'Hello to the Queen'.

ℹ Information

Medical Services

Manali Civil Hospital (☏253385) Just south of town.

Money

Banks in Manali don't offer foreign exchange but there are private moneychangers, and the State Bank of India has two international ATMs – the one at the bank branch south of the pedestrian mall has shorter queues.

Trans Corp Forex (The Mall; ⊘9.30am-7.30pm) Changes cash and cheques.

Tourist Information

HPTDC booking office (☏252116; The Mall; ⊘7am-8pm, 9am-5pm in winter) Can book seats on HPTDC buses, and rooms in HPTDC hotels.

Tourist office (☏253531; The Mall; ⊘8am-9pm, 10am-5pm Mon-Sat in winter) Helpful for brochures and local information.

The road from Leh to Manali

Right: Trekkers and porters traverse the Pin Parbati Pass, Himalaya;
Below: Tibetan nun and woman knitting at roadside stall, McLeod Ganj

(RIGHT) GARRY WEARE / LONELY PLANET IMAGES © ; (BELOW) RICHARD I'ANSON / LONELY PLANET IMAGES ©

ⓘ Getting There & Away

Air

Manali's closest airport is 50km south at Bhuntar. You can book seats at travel agencies in Manali or at Jagson Airlines (☎ 252843; www. jagsonairlines.com; The Mall).

Taxi

The Him-Anchal Taxi Operators Union (☎ 252120; The Mall) has share minibuses to Leh (₹1600, 14 hours) at 2am from July to mid-October; book a day in advance.

Other one-way fares:

DESTINATION	FARE (₹)
Bhuntar airport	1000
Dharamsala	3500
Leh	15,000

ⓘ Getting Around

Autorickshaw

Autos run to Old Manali and Vashisht for ₹50. If you can't find an auto in the street, head to the Hadimba Auto Rickshaw Booking Office (☎ 253366; The Mall).

McLeod Ganj

☎ 01892 / ELEV 1770M

When travellers talk of heading up to Dharamsala (to see the Dalai Lama...), this is where they mean. Around 4km above Dharamsala town – or 10km via the main bus route – McLeod Ganj is the headquarters of the Tibetan government in exile and the residence of His Holiness the 14th Dalai Lama. Along with Manali, it's the big traveller hang-out in Himachal Pradesh, with many budget hotels, trekking companies, internet

DISCOVER THE NORTHERN MOUNTAINS & AMRITSAR MCLEOD GANJ

cafes, restaurants and shops selling Tibetan souvenirs. Naturally, there's a large Tibetan population here, many of whom are refugees, so you'll see plenty of maroon robes about, especially when the Dalai Lama is in residence.

 Sights

**TSUGLAGKHANG
COMPLEX** Buddhist Temple
(Central Chapel; Temple Rd; ◷nonresidents 5am-8pm) The main focus of visiting pilgrims, monks and many tourists is the Tsuglagkhang, comprising the *photang* (official residence) of the Dalai Lama, the Namgyal Gompa, Tibet Museum and the Tsuglagkhang itself. The revered Tsuglagkhang is the exiles' equivalent of the Jokhang Temple in Lhasa. Sacred to Avalokitesvara (Chenrezi in Tibet), the Tibetan deity of compassion, it enshrines a 3m-high gilded statue of the Sakyamuni

Buddha, flanked by Avalokitesvara and Padmasambhava, the Indian scholar who introduced Buddhism to Tibet.

Next to the Tsuglagkhang is the **Kalachakra Temple**, built in 1992, which contains mesmerising murals of the Kalachakra (Wheel of Time) mandala, specifically linked to Avalokitesvara, currently represented on earth by the Dalai Lama. The remaining buildings form the **Namgyal Gompa**, where you can watch monks debate most afternoons, sealing points of argument with great flourish, a foot stamp and a theatrical clap of the hands.

Just inside the main entry gate is the **Tibet Museum** (admission ₹5; ◷9am-5pm), telling the story of the Chinese occupation and the subsequent Tibetan exodus through photographs, interviews and video clips. A visit here is a must for anyone staying in McLeod Ganj.

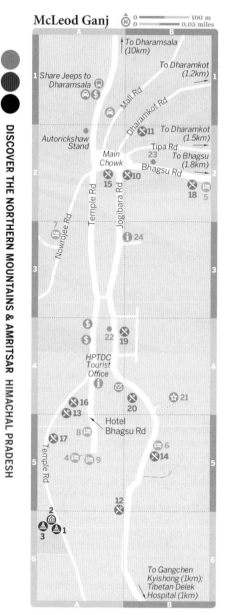

McLeod Ganj

To Dharamsala (10km)
To Dharamkot (1.2km)
Share Jeeps to Dharamsala
Mall Rd
Dharamkot Rd
To Dharamkot (1.5km)
Autorickshaw Stand
Main Chowk
Tipa Rd
To Bhagsu (1.8km)
Bhagsu Rd
Temple Rd
Jogibara Rd
Nowrojee Rd
HPTDC Tourist Office
Hotel Bhagsu Rd
Temple Rd
To Gangchen Kyishong (1km); Tibetan Delek Hospital (1km)

CHONOR HOUSE HOTEL Hotel $$$

(📞221006; www.norbulingka.org; s/d from ₹2300/2900, ste ₹2800/3500; @) Hidden down a track off Hotel Bhagsu Rd, Chonor House is a real gem. It's run by the Nor-bulingka Institute (p373), and rooms are adorned with its wonderful handicrafts and fabrics, from the bedspreads to the murals on the walls.

GREEN HOTEL Hotel $$

(📞221200; www.greenhotel.biz; Bhagsu Rd; r from ₹800; @ 🛜) A long-time traveller favourite, Green has a diverse range of sunny, stylish rooms in two buildings, some with valley and mountain views. The busy restaurant and internet cafe here feel like the hip place to be.

PEMA THANG GUEST HOUSE Hotel $$

(📞221871; www.pemathang.net; Hotel Bhagsu Rd; d ₹825-1155; ❄ 🛜) A tasteful Tibetan-style guesthouse, with a great restaurant and spacious, well-lit rooms with comforting, homey furnishings. The one single room (₹650) is an ideal writer's haven.

OM HOTEL Hotel $

(📞221313; omhotel@hotmail.com; Nowrojee Rd; d with/without bathroom ₹375/200) Conveniently located down a lane below the main square, the friendly family-run Om has pleasing rooms with good views and a great little terrace restaurant that catches the sunset over the valley. A bargain.

ZAMBALA HOUSE Hotel $$$

(📞221121; www.zambalahouse.com; Hotel Bhagsu Rd; d ₹2000-2900; 🛜) Still feeling fresh-out-of-the-box, this place down the same lane as Chonor House has spacious modern rooms with the best bathrooms in town. The views from the upper-floor balconies are so good you might never turn on the flat-screen TV.

HOTEL LADIES VENTURE Hotel $

(📞9816235648; shantiazad@yahoo.co.in; Jogibara Rd; s ₹200, d ₹250-500) Named by the previous lady owners, this peaceful green-and-yellow hotel welcomes all with wraparound balconies, flower pots, a range of tidy rooms and lovely mountain views from the rooftop terrace.

Sleeping

Popular places fill up fast; bookings are advised year-round, especially from April to June, October and November.

McLeod Ganj

Eating

Restaurants

MOONPEAK THALI   Indian **$$**
(Temple Rd; mains ₹70-200; ⊘9am-10.30pm;
⊚) With a stylishly understated dining
room and a tasteful blend of Tibetan and
Indian artwork, this new place might just
have the best food in town. Among
the culinary highlights is the
Himachali Thali, a sampler of
regional dishes. To reach the
tables on the rooftop ter-
race, you walk through the
kitchen – and it's clean!

**OOGO'S CAFE
ITALIANO**   Italian **$$**
(Jogibara Rd; mains
₹60-150) This cute
hole-in-the-wall place
serves up mainly Ital-
ian fare, but with a few
surprises – waffles,
baked potatoes, intrigu-
ing pasta dishes like
'chicken vodka' and even
lamb chops.

GREEN HOTEL   Multicuisine **$**
(Bhagsu Rd; mains ₹50-100; ⊘6.30am-9.30pm;
⊚ ⊚) This traveller-oriented hotel restaurant with comfy chairs and couches
serves good vegetarian food and the

Tibetan *thangka* painting
ANDREW PEACOCK / LONELY PLANET IMAGES ©

earliest breakfasts in town. The internet cafe and wi-fi are a bonus.

COMMON GROUND CAFE
Asian Fusion $$

(www.commongroundsproject.com; Dharamkot Rd; mains ₹60-100; ⏰11am-9pm) The mission of the NGO that runs this restaurant is to promote understanding between Tibetan and Chinese people, and food is used symbolically here. The menu is a sizzling variety of cross-cultural dishes, served in a pleasingly laid-back atmosphere.

MCLLO RESTAURANT
Multicuisine $

(Bus Stand; mains ₹125-225; ⏰10am-10pm) Crowded nightly and justifiably popular, this big place above the noisy main square serves a mind-boggling menu of Indian, Chinese and international fare, including pizzas and pasta. It's also one of the best places to enjoy an icy cold beer (₹115), and it has cider and wines.

PEACE CAFE
Tibetan $

(Jogibara Rd; dishes ₹30-55; ⏰7.30am-9.30pm) This cosy little cafe is always full of monks

chatting and dining, and tasty Tibetan *momos* (dumplings), chow chow (stir-fried noodles with vegetables or meat) and *thukpa* (noodle soup).

LUNG TA
Japanese $

(Jogibara Rd; mains ₹40-60; ⏰noon-8.30pm Mon-Sat) The set menu changes daily at this popular, nonprofit, vegetarian Japanese restaurant. Food and ambience are authentic and many Japanese travellers come here for a taste of home.

NICK'S ITALIAN KITCHEN
Italian $

(Bhagsu Rd; meals ₹50-100; ⏰7am-9pm) At Kunga Guesthouse, Nick's has been serving up tasty vegetarian pizzas, pasta and gnocchi for years. Follow up with heavenly desserts like chocolate brownies with hot chocolate sauce. Eat inside by candlelight or out on the terrace.

Cafes

McLeod has some of the best cafes in North India, with several places serving good espresso coffee, cappuccino and English-style tea.

Beans Cafe
Cafe $$

(Main Chowk; coffees ₹30, mains ₹70-150; ⏰8.30am-9.30pm; @ 🛜) This two-level coffee house serves up satisyingly strong java and has a mixed menu of full meals and yummy desserts. You can get on one of their computers or bring your laptop.

Moonpeak Espresso
Cafe $

(Temple Rd; coffees & meals ₹30-100; ⏰7am-8pm; 🛜) A little bit of Seattle, transported to India. Come for excellent coffee, cakes, imaginative sandwiches and dishes like poached chicken with mango, lime and coriander sauce.

Khana Nirvana
Cafe $

(www.khananirvana.org; Temple Rd; meals ₹35-85) Up a steep stairway, this

Buddhist monk at Norbulingka Institute
GAVIN GOUGH / LONELY PLANET IMAGES ©

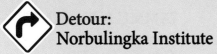

Detour: Norbulingka Institute

The wonderful **Norbulingka Institute** (📞 246405; www.norbulingka.org; 🕐 8am-6pm), about 6km from Dharamsala, was established in 1988 to teach and preserve traditional Tibetan art forms, including woodcarving, statue-making, *thangka* painting and embroidery. The centre produces expensive but exquisite craftworks, including embroidered clothes, cushions and wall-hangings; sales benefit refugee artists. Also here are delightful Japanese-influenced **gardens** and a central **Buddhist temple** with a 4m-high gilded statue of Sakyamuni. On Sundays and the second Saturday of each month the workshops are closed but the rest of the grounds are open.

Set in the gorgeous gardens, **Norling Guest House** (📞 246406; normail@ norbulingka.org; s/d from ₹1400/1800) offers fairy-tale rooms decked out with Buddhist murals and handicrafts from the institute, arranged around a sunny atrium. Meals are available at the institute's Norling Cafe.

A taxi from Dharamsala costs ₹300 return.

community cafe is a relaxed hang-out serving healthy vegetarian breakfasts, soups and salad, pita sandwiches, burritos and organic tea. There's local entertainment most nights.

Drinking & Entertainment

McLeod's bars are mostly clustered around the main *chowk* (town square) and charge around ₹115 for a big bottle of beer.

KHANA NIRVANA Cultural Program
(www.khananirvana.org; Temple Rd) Cool community cafe with a program of arts and entertainment most nights. There's an open-mic night on Monday, documentary films about Tibet on Tuesday, and Tibetan speakers on Sunday.

TIBETAN MUSIC TRUST   Live Music
(📞 9805661031; www.tibetanmusictrust.org; admission by donation) Performances of Tibetan folk music are held with varying regularity at Yonglings School, off Jogibara Rd. The live shows feature dem-

onstrations of traditional regional Tibetan instruments and song.

ℹ️ Information

Medical Services

Tibetan Delek Hospital (📞 222053; Gangchen Kyishong; consultations ₹10; 🕐 outpatient clinic 9am-1pm & 2-5pm)

Money

Several places around town offer Western Union money transfers.

Thomas Cook (Temple Rd; 🕐 9.30am-6.30pm)

Tourist Information

HPTDC tourist office (📞 221205; Hotel Bhagsu Rd; 🕐 10am-5pm, closed Sun Jul-Aug & Dec-Mar) Offers maps and guides, and can also make bookings for HPTDC hotels and buses around Himachal.

Information Office of Central Tibetan Administration (📞 222457; www.tibet.net; Jogibara Rd; 🕐 9am-5.30pm Tue-Sun) For information on Tibetan issues.

Travel Agencies

Numerous travel agencies can book train and bus tickets, and can also arrange tours and treks.

Himachal Travels (☎221428; himachaltravels@sancharnet.in; Jogibara Rd)

Himalaya Tours & Travels (☎220714; www.akupema.net/himalaya; Bhagsu Rd)

ⓘ Getting There & Around

Air

McLeod Ganj's nearest airport is at Gaggal, 15km southwest of Dharamsala. **Kingfisher** (www.flykingfisher.com) flies to Delhi daily at 1pm. Book at a travel agency.

Taxi

McLeod's **taxi stand** (☎221034) is on Mall Rd, north of the Main Chowk. To hire a taxi for the day, for a journey of less than 80km, expect to pay ₹1400. Fares for short hops include Dharamsala's Kotwali Bazaar (₹150), Dharamsala bus station (₹170), Norbulingka Institute (₹350) and the airport (₹600).

JAMMU & KASHMIR

Srinagar

☎0194 / POP 988,000 / ELEV 1730M

Indulgent houseboats on placid Dal Lake, famous Mughal gardens, distinctive Kashmiri wooden mosques and a mild summer climate combine to make Srinagar one of India's top domestic tourist attractions. Except, that is, when intercommunal tensions erupt. Sadly, such eruptions have proved depressingly frequent and throughout summer 2010 paralysing strikes and curfews effectively shut down the city altogether. Visiting Srinagar without thoroughly checking the latest security situation would be foolhardy (see p437).

◉ Sights

Sitting and watching waterborne life go by from a houseboat's carved wooden verandah is one of Srinagar's great pleasures (see the boxed text, p377).

Old City

KHANQAH SHAH-I-HAMADAN   Mosque

(Khanqah-e-Muala; Khawaja Bazaar area) This distinctively spired 1730s Muslim meeting hall is one of Srinagar's most beautiful with both frontage and interiors covered in papier-mâché reliefs and elaborately coloured *khatamband* (faceted wood panelling). Non-Muslim visitors can peek through the door but may not enter.

JAMA MASJID   Mosque

(Nowhatta) This mighty 1672 mosque has room for thousands of devotees between 378 roof-support columns,

Khanqah Shah-i-Hamadan Mosque
RICHARD I'ANSON / LONELY PLANET IMAGES ©

KAREN TRIST / LONELY PLANET IMAGES ©

Don't Miss Dal Lake

Whether you sleep on one of its wonderful time-warp houseboats or just stroll along the Boulevard savouring the sunset, beautifully serene Dal Lake is likely to be your main memory of Srinagar. Mirror-flat waters reflect the misty peaks of the Pir Panjal mountains while gaily painted *shikaras* glide by. These are gondolalike boats, hand-powered with heart-shaped paddles and used to transport goods to market, children to school, and visitors on explorative tours of the lake's floating communities; canal-like passages link all the way to Nagin Lake. Nehru Park is a good starting point for visiting the early morning floating vegetable market.

each fashioned from the trunk of a single deodar tree. Monumental brick gatehouses mark the four cardinal directions.

Central Srinagar

SRI PRATAP SINGH MUSEUM   Museum
(☎2312859; http://spsmuseum.org; Indian/foreigner ₹10/50; ☻10am-4pm Tue-Sun)
Accessed by a footbridge across the Jhelum River then by shimmying through frightening coils of razor wire, this richly endowed historical museum features Mughal papier-mâché work, weaponry and traditional Kashmiri costumes. An impressive new exhibition hall is nearing completion. Bring ID.

KASHMIR GOVERNMENT ARTS
EMPORIUM   Historic Building
(☎2452783; Bund; ☻10am-5.30pm Mon-Sat)
The century-old half-timbered former British Residency Building (restored 2004) is now used as an elegant fixed-price craft showroom where, without sales pressure, you can peruse Kashmiri copperwork, rugs, crewel (embroidered bedcovers) and intricately carved furniture.

Around Dal Lake
SHANKARACHARYA
HILL   Viewpoint, Sacred Site
(☻7.30am-5pm) Thickly forested Shanka-racharya Hill is topped by a small Shiva temple built from hefty blocks of visibly

ancient grey stone. It's now named for a sage who reached enlightenment here in 750 AD, but signs date the octagonal structure as 5th-century and the site is even older. Access is by a winding 5.5km road from Nehru Park (₹150 return by autorickshaw). Walking isn't advisable, given the population of wild bears.

PARKS & GARDENS   Gardens
Srinagar's famous gardens date back to the Mughal era. Most have a similar design with terraced lawns, fountain pools and manicured flowerbeds interspersed with mighty *chinar* (plane trees), pavilions and mock fortress facades.

Built for Nur Jahan by her husband Jehangir, **Shalimar Bagh** (adult/child ₹10/5; ⏱9am-dusk Apr-Oct, 10am-dusk Nov-Mar) is the most famous garden. However, **Nishat Bagh** (adult/child ₹10/5; ⏱9am-dusk Sat-Thu) is more immediately impressive with steeper terracing and a lake-facing panorama.

🛏 Sleeping & Eating

Staying on a houseboat (p377) is one of the city's main attractions, but you might prefer to sleep at least the first night in a hotel while carefully selecting a suitable boat.

HOTEL SWISS   Guesthouse $
(☎2472766; www.swisshotelkashmir.com; Old Gagribal Rd; foreigners d ₹450-850, Indians ₹1200-1800; @) The Swiss has reliably good-value budget accommodation at prices that are discounted for foreigners. There's a peaceful lawn, free fast internet and bicycle hire available. But most of all it's the tirelessly helpful Sufi-spiritual manager which makes the place so congenial.

LALIT GRAND
PALACE   Heritage Hotel $$$
(☎2501001; www.thelalit.com/Srinagar; ste from ₹20,000) Vast period suites in the Maharaja's 1910 palace and a wing of (slightly) cheaper new rooms are all beautifully set above hectares of manicured lawns. The Durbar Hall features royal portraits and one of the world's largest handmade carpets.

MUGHAL DARBAR   Kashmiri $$
(☎2476998; Residency Rd; mains ₹150-300; ⏱10am-10pm) Widely considered the

An elaborate houseboat on Nagin Lake, Srinagar

Houseboats

Srinagar's signature houseboats first appeared in colonial times, because the British were prohibited from owning land. Most houseboats you'll see are less than 30 years old, but some are still palatial, with chandeliers, carved walnut panels, *khatamband* (wooden patchwork) ceilings and sitting rooms redolent of the 1930s Raj era. **Category A** boats are comfy but less grand. Lower categories often lack interior sitting areas. **Category D** boats hopefully stay afloat.

Choosing from 1400 boats is challenging. Some owners are super-friendly families, others are crooks – ask fellow travellers for recent firsthand recommendations.

THINGS TO WATCH OUT FOR

- Don't pre-purchase houseboat packages; *never* book in Delhi.
- Thoroughly check out houseboats in person before agreeing to or paying anything.
- Get a clear, possibly written, agreement stating what the fees cover.
- Don't be pressured into giving 'charity' donations.
- Don't sign up for overpriced treks or excursions (prices are usually far lower in Ladakh).
- Beware isolated or less friendly houseboats. Trust your instincts.
- Don't leave valuables unattended.
- Don't leave your passport with the boat owner.
- Tell a friend, hotelier or the **Houseboat Owners Association** (☎ 2450326; www.houseboatowners.org; TRC Rd; ⊙10am-5pm Mon-Sat) where you're staying.

CHOOSING THE AREA

To tour a selection of Dal Lake boats, engage a *shikara* (gondola-like boat) and drop into the options that take your fancy (the boatman will probably nudge you towards those that give him better commission).

PRICES

Officially prices are 'set', between ₹1100 (category D) and ₹4500 (deluxe) for a double room including all meals, but when occupancy is low you might be able to negotiate down to just a fraction of that.

ity's best place to indulge in top-quality Kashmiri delicacies. The better of the two separately managed dining rooms is upstairs above the bakery section.

ⓘ Information

Most banks, shops and offices shut for Muslim prayers around lunchtime on Friday: if you have urgent business, get it done by Thursday to be safe.

ATMs are widespread, especially on Residency Rd, but during prolonged curfews they might run out of funds. Beware of freelance moneychangers offering improbably good rates – you're likely to get forged banknotes.

Transcorp International (Boulevard; ⊙9.30am-6pm Mon-Sat) Half-hidden between hotels Sunshine and Dal View, this moneychanger offers good cash rates.

🛈 Getting There & Away

Air

Srinagar's sparkling new airport is 1.2km behind a high security barrier where there can be long queues for baggage and body screening.

Airport Arrival Scams

After arriving by air in Srinagar you'll have to fill out a form; one question asks you to name your hotel. Fill in anything believable but don't leave that section blank, or you may fall prey to a scam where you're 'obliged' to go to a commission-paying client hotel or houseboat. Also, be suspicious if an airport taxi won't take you to the hotel you request, on whatever pretext.

The following all fly to Delhi and/or Jammu. Air India also flies to Leh on Wednesdays.

Air India (☎2450247; www.airindia.in; Boulevard)

GoAir (www.goair.in)

IndiGo (www.goindigo.in)

Jet Airways (☎2480801; Residency Rd)

JetLite (www.jetlite.com)

Kingfisher (www.flykingfisher.com)

SpiceJet (www.spicejet.com)

🛈 Getting Around

Even when there's no official curfew, don't rely on being able to find an autorickshaw or boatman after 8pm, when Srinagar becomes eerily silent.
TO/FROM THE AIRPORT Prepaid, fixed-price taxis cost ₹350 to town.
AUTORICKSHAW From ₹25 for short hops, ₹50 across town, around ₹600 for a full-day tour including Mughal gardens, Old City and Hazratbal.
BOAT *Shikaras* charge ₹20 for short houseboat-to-shore hops. Posted per-hour rates (₹300) are very negotiable.

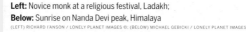

Left: Novice monk at a religious festival, Ladakh;
Below: Sunrise on Nanda Devi peak, Himalaya

(LEFT) RICHARD I'ANSON / LONELY PLANET IMAGES ©; (BELOW) MICHAEL GEBICKI / LONELY PLANET IMAGES ©

Leh

201982 / POP 28,640 / ELEV 3520M

Few places in India are at once so traveller-friendly and yet so enchanting and hassle-free as mountain-framed Leh, located in the Ladakh region. Dotted with stupas and crumbling mud-brick houses, the Old Town is dominated by a dagger of steep rocky ridge topped by an imposing Tibetan-style palace and fort. Beneath, the bustling bazaar area is draped in a thick veneer of tour agencies, souvenir shops and pizza restaurants but a web of lanes quickly fans out into a green suburban patchwork of irrigated barley fields. Leh's a place that's all too easy to fall in love with, but take things easy on arrival. The altitude means that most visitors initially suffer mild headaches and breathlessness. To prevent this becoming full-blown Acute Mountain Sickness (AMS), drink plenty of ginger tea and avoid strenuous exertion at first.

 Sights

Palace Ridge

Leh's major monuments are perched on the stark rocky ridge that forms the town's mesmerising visual focus.

LEH PALACE   Historic Building
(Indian/foreigner ₹5/100; ⊙dawn-dusk)
Bearing a passing similarity to the Potala Palace in Lhasa (Tibet), this nine-storey dun-coloured palace took shape under 17th-century king Sengge Namgyal. Essentially it has been unoccupied since the Ladakhi royals were stripped of power and shuffled off to Stok in 1846. Today the very sturdy walls are mostly unadorned and a few interior sections remain in a state of partial collapse; only the palace prayer room gives any sense of former grandeur. Carry a flashlight and watch out for holes in the floor.

PALACE GOMPAS   Buddhist Temples
A trio of photogenic religious structures guard the imposing palace entrance. The courtyard of the 1840 **Soma Gompa** is used in summer for **traditional dances** (admission ₹200; ☉5.30pm). Behind, the colourfully muralled **Chandazik Gompa** (Chenrezi Lhakhang; admission ₹20; ☉7am-6pm) celebrates the full pantheon of 1000 Buddhas (of which 996 have yet to be born). The main attractions of the red, 1430 **Chamba Lhakhang** (admission ₹20; ☉7am-6pm) are the medieval mural fragments between the inner and outer walls.

TSEMO FORT   Castle Ruin
(admission ₹20; ☉dawn-dusk) Visible from virtually everywhere in Leh, the 16th-century Tsemo (Victory) Fort is a defining landmark that crowns the top of Palace Ridge. Closer to, it's surprisingly small and the shattered walls contain little more than flapping prayer flags but scrambling around them provides a precarious frisson.

Other Central Sights

OLD TOWN   Area
Behind Leh's fanciful **Jama Masjid (Sunni men's mosque)**, the winding alleys and stairways of Old Town burrow between and beneath a series of eroded chortens (stupas) and traditional mud-brick Ladakhi houses. Belatedly, many finer structures are being restored and a new **Central Asian Museum** (www.tibetheritagefund.org/pages/projects/ladakh/central-asian-museum.php) is under construction, styled like a tapered fortress tower.

Informative small-group **walking tours** (per person ₹300; ☉9.30am & 3pm Tue, Thu & Sat) dawdle around the Old Town starting from Lala's Art Cafe (p384), where you should prebook. Although advertised as lasting two hours, sometimes they take double that.

Activities, Courses & Tours

CYCLING   Cycling
For an exhilarating yet effortless excursion take a jeep ride up to **Khardung La** (the 'world's highest road-pass') and let gravity bring you back down. Actually, given the potholes of the uppermost 15km you might prefer to start from South Pullu army camp, from which all 25km to Leh are well paved. The ₹700 to ₹900 per person fee includes bike hire, permit and support vehicle (minimum group-size four). Book through **Summer Holidays** (☏252651; Zangsti Rd) or **Himalayan Bikers** (☏250937; www.himalayan-biker.com; Changspa). Both also rent mountain bikes (per day ₹350 to ₹550).

Woman in traditional dress, Ladakh
RICHARD I'ANSON / LONELY PLANET IMAGES ©

MAHABODHI CENTRE
Yoga, Meditation

(☑251162; www.mahabodhi-ladakh.org; Chang-pa Lane; 90min yoga class ₹150-250) Daily except Sundays there's a meditation session (by donation) and several 1½-hour yoga classes in a variety of styles.

RAFTING & KAYAKING
Outdoor Adventure

In summer, numerous agencies offer daily rafting excursions through glorious canyon scenery. You can also follow in a kayak for around 50% extra. Prepare to get very wet. There are two main routes, **Phey to Nimmu** – grade II (beginners) from ₹1000; and **Chiling to Nimmu** – grade III, tougher, from ₹1400, kayakers must be experienced.

Useful contacts:

Rimo (☑253348; www.rimoriverexpeditions.com; Zangsti Rd) Very helpful staff.

Splash Adventures (☑254870; www.splashladakh.com) Central (Zangsti Rd) Changspa (Changspa Rd)

🛏 Sleeping

Leh has hundreds of guesthouses and around 60 hotels. Hot water is typically provided either morning or evening (sometimes both) using wood-fired boilers. Water can take up to 10 minutes to run warm, wasting a precious resource. An ecofriendly alternative is to request hot water by bucket or use it less often.

Most accommodation closes in winter. A few hotels and family guesthouses do stay open, the latter often charging ₹100 extra for heating and offering only bucket water since pipes freeze.

Old Town

PALACE VIEW GUEST HOUSE
Guesthouse $

(☑250773; palace.view@hotmail.com; d from ₹450, without bathroom ₹200-300) First opened in 1975, this upliftingly lived-in

family place has garden seating, two sitting rooms and a rooftop with brilliant views of the palace ridge. Rooms are simple with ageing but clean linen, the cheapest using camp-beds. Bathrooms have geysers. The owners are friendly and conscientious. Ladakhi dinners available if you order by 5pm. Open year-round.

Changspa
CHOW GUEST HOUSE
Guesthouse $

(☑252399; d ₹400, without bathroom ₹250) Sparkling clean, airy budget rooms with good mattresses and log ceilings in two new but unobtrusive buildings set in a beautiful flower-filled garden down a narrow path from Changspa Rd.

HOTEL GAWALING INTERNATIONAL
Hotel **$$**

(☏253252; www.hotelgawaling.com; s/d/deluxe ₹1980/2640/2970; @ 🛜) Rooms are better maintained than at most other Leh hotels with parquet floors and good bathrooms albeit offering minimal toiletries. Each has a balcony (huge in deluxe rooms) facing attractively rural scenery and the whole complex is serenaded by a flowing river.

Fort Road Area

Fort Rd is a major tourist street with heavy daytime traffic, but peaceful side alleys balance tranquillity with convenience.

🌿 PADMA HOTEL
Hotel **$$**

(☏252630; www.padmaladakh.net; d ₹1850-2200; @ 🛜) Hidden in a large garden, the eco-aware Padma has attractively appointed new 'hotel' rooms with fan, bed lamps, good linen and simple bathrooms using solar-heated water. The upstairs restaurant and common balconies enjoy fine mountain views, there's a library, ₹8 water refills and free wi-fi. The 'guesthouse' section (double ₹600) with shared bathrooms occupies the family's traditional Ladakhi house complete with traditional kitchen and chapel/meditation room.

🌿 INDUS GUEST HOUSE
Guesthouse **$**

(☏252502; masters_adv@yahoo.co.in; Malpak Alley; d ₹300-700; 🛜) All 16 rooms are en suite, the water heated all day by a furnace burning waste (cardboard, cow-dung etc). Little shared terraces have fortress views and the semi-enclosed courtyard is peacefully tree-shaded. Food served on request, is mostly sourced from the well-travelled family's organic farm. Original treks available.

🌿 POPLAR ECO-RESORT
Ecoresort **$$**

(☏253518; poplar_ecoresort@yahoo.com; Shenam Rd; s/d ₹1600/2200, full board ₹2450/3300) Lost in the birdsong of an overgrown apricot orchard are a series of two-room cottages, each pair sharing a verandah with wicker chairs. Rooms have good tile

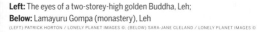

bathrooms with all-day hot water, though beds are soft and decor is mostly lacking. Most food and juice served is sourced from the organic garden.

Tukcha

GANGS-SHUN   Homestay **$**
(☏252603; morup_lee@yahoo.co.in; Upper Tukcha Rd; d ₹600-700, f ₹800) Five guest rooms above an attractive new family home have good beds, quality parquet flooring and bathrooms that are better quality than in most Leh hotels. Shared upper terrace.

NORZIN HOLIDAY HOME   Guesthouse **$**
(☏252022; norzinholidays@gmail.com; Upper Tukcha Rd; r ₹500-600, without bathroom s/d ₹200/300) Unusually well-kept local home with roof terrace, garden seating and a glassed-in verandah. Free drinking water refills, welcoming family.

Old Road Area

Many mid-range hotels here, some comparatively overpriced.

PANGONG HOTEL   Hotel **$$**
(☏254655; www.pangongladakh.com; Chulung Lane; s/d ₹2000/2210; @ 🛜) Despite a few signs of wear, the Pangong is comparatively stylish with attractive pine cladding in public areas. The best rooms are on the top floor with rooftop terraces. Wi-fi per hour/day costs ₹100/500.

HOTEL GRAND DRAGON   Hotel **$$$**
(☏250786; www.thegranddragonladakh.com; Old Rd, Shenam; s/d/ste ₹6050/7150/11,000; 🛜) Leh's only really international-standard hotel, the Grand Dragon is professionally appointed with functioning lift, fitting carpets and rooms approximating to business standards (safe and fridge in suites). However, it's away from shops down a busy road and there's an ugly foreground to the mountain views. Open year-round.

Eating

Traveller cafes abound, Israeli and Chinese options supplementing curries, banana pancakes, tandoori pizzas and Tibetan favourites, but curiously few restaurants offer true Ladakhi food (try Chopsticks or request it at family guesthouses). Many eateries, including Changspa's garden-restaurants, close from mid-September to July, their owners often decamping to Goa.

Town Centre

You won't need a guide to find the numerous rooftop and Tibetan/Chinese restaurants dotted all along Main Bazaar. Sadly, the food is rarely as good as the view in the former, while many of the latter are less than inviting.

NORLAKH　　　　　　　Tibetan $
(Main Bazaar; mains ₹40-100, momos ₹50-95, rice ₹30) The best of several town-centre options with mildly trendy decor touches and great pure-veg Tibetan food. Try the cheese-and-spinach *momos* or special *gyathuk* (a rich noodle soup). It's upstairs and easy to miss, hidden behind a willow tree almost opposite Ladakh Bookshop.

**Pumpernickel German
Bakery**　　　　　　　Bakery Cafe $
(Zangsti Rd; meals ₹70-180) Behind the simple bakery counter (good strudels) is a merrily ramshackle dining room with Ladakhi wooden columns and a full multicuisine menu.

Fort Road

Chopsticks　　　　　　Asian $$
(Fort Rd; mains ₹60-180, rice ₹55) This 3rd-floor pan-Asian restaurant is one of Leh's most stylish eateries. Their 'Wonderwok' stir-fries and Thai green curry are excellent and prices are very fair, given the high quality of service.

Gesmo　　　　　　Multicuisine $
(Fort Rd; curries ₹40-100, rice ₹35) Old-fashioned traveller haunt, with gingham tablecloths, checkerboard ceilings and and good-value meals from curries to yak-cheese pizza.

Tenzin Dickey　　　　　Tibetan $
(Fort Rd; mains ₹40-70) Cosy if unpretentious eatery serving generous portions of excellent vegetarian Tibetan and Chinese food at sensible prices. Try the delectable cheese *kothay* (like Japanese *gyoza*).

Summer Harvest　　Oriental, Indian $
(Fort Rd; mains ₹70-120, rice ₹30-90) Tourist favourite with pseudo-traditional lacquered-wood columns and dangling mod-Chinese lamps. Our *malai kofta* was divine but *momos* were bullet-proof. Service charge 10%.

Changspa

BON APPETIT　　　　Multicuisine $$
(📞251533; mains ₹180-350; ⏰11am-late) By far Leh's most imaginative restaurant is a stylish exercise in Ladakhi minimalist architecture and offers a wide panorama of the southern mountains. A limited but thoroughly scrumptious selection of artistically prepared dishes includes sublime cashew chicken in pesto sauce.

CALABRIA　　　　　Multicuisine $
(Changspa Rd; mains ₹45-90, rice ₹30, pastas ₹160-180) The decor wins no prizes and traffic outside can be annoying but the vegetarian Indian and Chinese fare is consistently excellent, sensibly priced and obligingly served.

CAFÉ JEEVAN　　　　Multicuisine $
(Booklovers Retreat; Changspa Rd; meals ₹70-140) Despite the comparatively sophisticated appearance, prices aren't significantly higher than most bog-standard and traveller pads. A glass-sided kitchen turns out high-quality vegetarian meals in a wide range of cuisines, including some of Leh's best pizza. There's also a two-case bookshop and a covered roof terrace.

Drinking

LALA'S ART CAFE　　　　Cafe
(Old Town; ⏰8.30am-7.30pm) A tiny, brilliantly restored mud-brick Old Town house with trip-you-up stone steps and an open roof terrace serving great Italian coffee and scrumptious cake-of-the-day. Read the newspapers then check out the ancient carved steles in the ground-floor shrine section.

Zoya Cafe   Cafe

Old Town; ⊙9am-7pm) Handy as a landmark
when climbing to the palace or as a tea-stop
when returning, entry is disconcertingly through
a typical local home but the 360-degree rooftop
views are unparalleled anywhere in Leh.

⭐ Entertainment

KC GARDEN
RESTAURANT   Cinema Restaurant

(Changspa Rd) A lively evening spot. Open-
air movies are projected and it's also the
pick-up point for all-night parties (₹400
including transport) on full-moon nights
May to August.

Traditional Ladakhi
Song & Dance Shows   Cultural Program

(admission R200; ⊙5.30pm) Tourist-oriented,
held on summer evenings outside Soma Gompa;
partly visible for free from the ridge behind.

ⓘ Information

There are numerous moneychangers on Changspa
Rd and Main Bazaar. Compare rates carefully. Leh's
two ATMs are the only ones in Ladakh and are often
over stretched. Keep back-up cash for emergencies.

J&K Forex (1st fl, Himalaya Complex, Main
Bazaar; ⊙8.30am-4pm Mon-Fri, to 1pm Sat)
Good exchange rates, better still for
travellers cheques. ATM on Ibex Rd.

Oxygen Bar (KC Garden Restaurant;
per min ₹20) Breathe pure oxygen
to relieve altitude sickness, or just
for the buzz.

SBI (Main Bazaar; ⊙10am-
4pm Mon-Fri, to 1pm Sat) The
upstairs exchange desk can
be chaotic and long queues
are common at the 24-hour
ATM outside.

Tourist office (☎253462;
www.ladakhtourism.in; Ibex
Rd; ⊙10am-4pm Mon-Sat)
General info, listings and very
rough maps.

ⓘ Getting There & Away

Air

Delhi-Leh flights rarely cost under ₹11,500 in
summer but in winter ₹4000 is possible.

Air India (☎252076; Fort Rd; ⊙10am-1pm &
2-4.30pm) Leh–Delhi (₹11,661), via Srinagar
(₹7354, Wednesday).

Jet Airways (☎250999; Main Bazaar; ⊙10am-
1pm & 2-5pm) Leh–Delhi daily in August. Frequency
drops gradually to twice weekly in February.

Kingfisher (www.flyingkingfisher.com) Leh–Delhi
daily in summer.

Taxi & Charter-Jeep

Published in a booklet (updated yearly), fares are
the same for taxis and charter-jeeps and include
stopping time en route for photos/visits; fares from
Leh include Manali (₹13,547/17,611 one-way/return)
and Srinagar (₹9773/12,700 one-way/return).
Longer waits cost ₹160/650/1251 per hour/half-
day/full day, extra overnight stops add ₹350 and
unplanned diversions from the agreed routing can
cause unexpected difficulties, so plan carefully.

Fresh juice stall, Amritsar p(387)
APRIL MACIBORKA / LONELY PLANET IMAGES ©

HUW JONES / LONELY PLANET IMAGES

Don't Miss Golden Temple

True to Sikhism's inclusive nature, everyone is welcome at the Sikhs' holiest shrine. The temple's architecture is a blend of Hindu and Islamic styles but with unique distinctions. The golden dome (said to be gilded with 750kg of gold) represents an inverted lotus flower a symbol of Sikh devotees' aim to live a pure life.

A causeway (Gurus' Bridge) leads to the two-storey marble temple, **Hari Mandir Sahib** (or Darbar Sahib). This stands in the middle of the sacred pool, **Amrit Sarovar** (Pool of Nectar), which gave the town its name.

Priests inside the temple keep up a continuous chant (in Gurmukhi) from the Sikh holy book, which is broadcast around the complex by loudspeakers. The original copy of this book, the **Guru Granth Sahib**, is kept under a shroud in the Hari Mandir Sahib during the day and returns ceremoniously to the Akal Takhat at night. Ceremony times are 5am and 9.40pm in winter, and 4am and 10.30pm in summer.

The **Akal Takht**, where the Shiromani Gurdwara Parbandhak Committee (SGPC), or Sikh Parliament, traditionally meets, was heavily damaged when it was stormed by the Indian army in 1984. The Indian government later repaired it, but the Sikhs, appalled by the army's actions in the first place, pulled it down and rebuilt it themselves.

Completed in 1784, the octagonal **Baba Atal Tower** commemorates Atal Rai, the son of the sixth Sikh guru, Har Gobind. After Atal performed a miracle, bringing back to life a playmate who had died of a snake bite, his father scolded him for interfering with the ways of God. The repentant youngster committed suicide on this spot in return for the life he had saved. The nine storeys each represent one year of Atal's short life.

THINGS YOU NEED TO KNOW

⊙ dawn-around 10pm

Getting Around

TO/FROM THE AIRPORT The airport's well-guarded terminal is at Km430 of the Leh-Spituk highway, 4km south of the centre. Taxi transfers cost ₹150/190 to central Leh/Changspa.

TAXI Leh's little micro-van taxis charge from ₹75 per hop. Flagging down rides rarely works; go to a taxi stand to make arrangements.

PUNJAB

Amritsar

☎0183 / POP 1.25 MILLION

Founded in 1577 by the fourth guru Ram Das, Amritsar is home to Sikhism's holiest shrine, the spectacular Golden Temple. The gold-plated gurdwara glitters in the middle of its sacred pool of placid water and draws millions of pilgrims from all over the world. A welcome escape from the frenetic bazaars, this gilded temple is rated by many tourists as a glowing high-light of their visit to India. Regrettably, the same can't be said for the hyperactive streets!

 Sights & Activities

JALLIANWALA BAGH   Historic Site
(⏰6am-9pm summer, 7am-8pm winter) Near the Golden Temple, this poignant park commemorates those Indians killed or wounded here by the British authorities in 1919.

Tours

Sanjay from the Grand Hotel runs reputable and good-value tours that include the Attari–Wagah border-closing ceremony, Mata Temple and a night visit to the Golden Temple from ₹500 per person. Day tours can also include the Golden Temple, Jallianwala Bagh and Sri Durgiana Temple.

 Sleeping

GRAND HOTEL   Hotel $$
(☎2562424; www.hotelgrand.in; Queen's Rd; s/d from ₹1000/1200; ❄@⏅) This three-star hotel, close to the train station, is deserved-ly popular. The rooms aren't exactly grand but are certainly comfortably appointed and well kept. They, along with a restaurant (mains ₹50 to ₹250), a pub and a breezy verandah with tables and chairs (perfect at beer o'clock), fringe a leafy garden.

MRS BHANDARI'S GUEST HOUSE   Guesthouse $$
(☎2228509; http://bhandari_guesthouse.tripod.com; 10 Cantonment; camping ₹200, s/d from ₹1500/1800; ❄@⏅) Legacy of the much-loved Mrs Bhandari (1906–2007), this earthy, ecoconscious guesthouse is set on spacious green grounds. The comfy rooms bring back memories of grandma's place and will appeal to those seeking a calm, uncommercial atmosphere.

ISTA HOTEL   Hotel $$$
(☎2708888; www.istahotels.com; GT Rd; s/d from ₹9000/9500; ❄@⏅⏅) Amritsar's only five-star sits beside a bright shop-ping mall, alphaOne, 3km east of the interstate bus terminus. Fans of five-stars may be a little underwhelmed by the smallish standard rooms, but will adore the pool and the pampering Ista Spa, which has quite a reputation.

HOTEL INDUS   Hotel $$
(☎2535900; www.hotelindus.com; Sri Hamandir Sahib Marg; r from ₹1550; ❄⏅) The dramatic million-dollar view of the Golden Temple from the rooftop is reason alone to stay at this modern-style hotel. Apart from being smallish, rooms are otherwise fine with two (303 and 304; ₹2116) boasting spectacular temple vistas – book ahead!

 Eating

Amritsar is famous for its *dhabas* (snack bars) such as **Punjab Dhaba** (Goal Hatti Chowk), **Kesar Da Dhaba** (Passian Chowk) and **Brothers' Dhaba** (Town Hall Chowk), all

with (mainly Indian) thali meals averaging ₹65 to ₹110, and open early to late. Brothers' is the current favourite. Hotels and restaurants in the (holy) Golden Temple locale don't serve alcohol; elsewhere your beer may be disguised in a napkin.

The city is also famous for its 'Amritsari' deep-fried fish with lemon, chilli, garlic and ginger; sniff out the stalls frying it up (especially prevalent in the old city).

MOTI MAHAL DELUXE
North Indian $$

(☏5069991; Hotel Grand Legacy, GT Rd, Model Town; mains ₹130-350; ⏰9am-11.30pm; ❄) Moti Mahal enjoys a well-deserved reputation for expertly prepared North Indian cuisine (especially tandoori). Consider the tasty *murgh makhani* (butter chicken) and *diwani handi* (mixed veggies in a roulette of fenugreek and mint). Icy cold Kingfisher beer is available.

CRYSTAL RESTAURANT
Multicuisine $$

(☏2225555; Cooper Rd; mains ₹140-250; ⏰11am-11.30pm; ❄) Rated by many as one of Amritsar's best restaurants, Crystal boasts all sorts of yummy global favourites, from lasagne to fish curry. Book ahead, especially on weekends. There are two 'Crystals' (one upstairs and one downstairs), apparently due to a family split...we're equally divided when it comes to which is best. You'll just have to try both

ASTORIA FOOD PAVILLION
Multicuisine $

(mains ₹140-325; ⏰noon-11pm; ❄) It sounds like a food court, but it is in fact a pleasant multicuisine restaurant near the MK Hotel cooking up a mishmash of dishes, from chicken Patiala and veg biryani to poached fish and spinach cannelloni. Head upstairs to the sister restaurant, Oka (mains ₹120 to ₹300) where pizza, pasta, stir-fry and burgers are cooked fresh right in front of you.

SAGAR RATNA
South Indian $

(Queen's Rd; mains ₹50-110; ⏰9am-11pm; ❄) An easygoing South Indian veg restaurant with fresh lime sodas that will quench the most savage summer thirst.

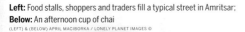

Left: Food stalls, shoppers and traders fill a typical street in Amritsar;
Below: An afternoon cup of chai
(LEFT) & (BELOW) APRIL MACIBORKA / LONELY PLANET IMAGES ©

xcellent southern speci-
lities (*idlis*, dosas, *uttapams*
tc) with a sprinkling of North
ndian and Chinese dishes.

❶ Information

Medical Services

ortis Escort Hospital (📞2573901; Majitha
erka Bypass)

Money

DFC (Golden Temple branch; 🕙9.30am-
.30pm Mon-Sat) Exchanges travellers cheques
nd currencies; has an ATM.

Tourist Information

ourist office (📞2402452; Railway Station
xit, Queen's Rd; 🕙9am-5pm Mon-Sat) Has
ood free maps covering Punjab and Amritsar.

❶ Getting There & Away

Air

Amritsar's Sri Guru Ram Dass Jee International
Airport services domestic and international
flights. One-way flights to Delhi/Mumbai cost
around ₹3200/7800.

Train

Apart from the train station, a less busy train
reservation office (🕙8am-8pm, to 2pm Sun) is
at the Golden Temple.

The fastest train to Delhi is the twice-daily
Shatabdi Express (5.10am service chair car/
executive ₹570/1095, 5pm service ₹675/1260,
5¾ hours).

❶ Getting Around

A cycle-rickshaw from the train station to
the Golden Temple costs around ₹30, an
autorickshaw ₹50 and a taxi (📞01835151515)
₹120. To the airport, an autorickshaw costs ₹200
and a taxi ₹500.

India

In Focus

A woman carries a pot of water, Pushkar
RICHARD I'ANSON / LONELY PLANET IMAGES ©

India Today

> *As India has become a leader in modern industries, a new, affluent middle class has emerged.*

Porters waiting for work on Chandni Chowk, Delhi

if India were 100 people

41 would speak Hindi

55 would speak one of 21 other official languages

4 would speak one of around 400 other languages

Note: 10 of these 100 will speak English as a second language

belief systems
(% of population)

80.5 Hindu

13.4 Muslim

2.3 Christian

1.9 Sikh

1.9 Other

population per sq km

♦ ≈ 30 people

India   China   USA

Politics

India is an important player in the international scene – influential culturally and politically, as well as a military and nuclear-armed power – and has enjoyed years of economic boom even as places elsewhere in the world have slid into recession. However, it's also the second-most populous country in the world, and faces a number of social and environmental problems of its own.

India is the world's largest democracy: 344 million people voted in the most recent election (2009). The method of rule in part reflects the nation's diversity – the central government rules in conjunction with the country's 28 states, and its ethos is determinedly secular.

In 2004, when the Indian National Congress (INC) party regained power after a period out of office, it was under the leadership of Sonia Gandhi, the Italian-born wife of the late Rajiv Gandhi, who had served as prime minister from 1984 to 1989 (after his mother, Prime Minister Indira Gandhi, was assassinated).

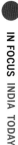

India's socialist-leaning economy was shaken up in 1991 when Manmohan Singh, then the finance minister, undertook the momentous step of partially floating the rupee against a basket of 'hard' currencies. State subsidies were phased out and the economy was opened up, with foreign multinationals drawn to India for its multitudes of educated professionals and relatively low wages.

Over the past few decades India has become a leader in modern industries, such as information technology, and a new, affluent middle class has emerged. However, the huge increase in wealth across the country and healthy annual growth rate of 9% have not had a notable impact on the problem of poverty nationwide, with the vast majority of the very poor remaining as such.

RICHARD l'ANSON / LONELY PLANET IMAGES ©

The other major political party, the Bharatiya Janata Party (BJP), found its planned national agitation campaign against Sonia Gandhi's foreign origins subverted when she stepped aside to allow Manmohan Singh to be sworn in as Prime Minister. With a reputation for transparency and intelligence, Singh is largely popular among Indians, though many believe that Gandhi wields considerable influence over his decisions.

Under Singh's leadership, India has carried out a program of economic liberalisation, along with a number of education, health and other social-reform initiatives.

Economy

Independent India's first prime minister, Jawaharlal Nehru, created a vast (and expensive) public infrastructure in line with his socialist ideals; it was much later that India began to encourage economic reform and foreign investment.

Conflict

India is made up of numerous different cultural and religious groups speaking a vast variety of local languages. With such religious and regional differences, communal tensions occasionally erupt, though there has been no major incident since the Hindu-Muslim riots (in Gujarat) of 2002.

Another flashpoint of unrest is the Kashmir Valley. Predominantly Muslim, it is claimed by both India and Pakistan – and now, Kashmiris – and the impasse has plagued relations between the two countries since Partition in 1947 (see p403). After three wars between the two nations and countless skirmishes, there's still no solution in sight.

History

A man holds an image of a Hindu goddess

LIZ THOMPSON / LONELY PLANET

Indian history has always been a work in progress, a constant process of reinvention and accumulation that makes grasping its essential essence difficult. Brahmanical empires and Hindu–Buddhist dynasties dominated for over a millennium before the arrival of the Islamic sultanates, which, along with the Mughals, established Muslim control for several hundred years; they were overtaken by the Europeans – especially the British, who managed to conquer the peninsula.

Indus Valley Civilisation

The Indus Valley, straddling the modern India–Pakistan border, is the cradle of civilisation on the Indian subcontinent. The first inhabitants of this region were nomadic tribes who cultivated land and kept domestic animals. Over thousands of years, an urban culture began to emerge from these tribes, particularly from 3500 BC. By 2500 BC large cities were well es-

10,000 BC

Stone Age paintings first made in the Bhimbetka rock shelters, in what is now Madhya Pradesh.

ablished, the focal points of what became known as the Harappan culture, which would flourish for more than 1000 years.

By the middle of the 3rd millennium BC the Indus Valley culture was arguably the equal of other great civilisations emerging at the time. Recovered relics, including models of bullock carts and jewellery, offer the earliest evidence of a distinctive Indian culture. Indeed, many elements of Harappan culture would later become assimilated into Hinduism: clay figurines found at these sites suggest worship of a Mother goddess (later personified as Kali) and a male three-faced god (believed to be the historic Shiva) sitting in the pose of a yogi attended by four animals. Black stone pillars (associated with phallic worship of Shiva) have also been discovered.

Early Invasions & the Rise of Religions

The Harappan civilisation fell into decline from the beginning of the 2nd millennium BC. Some historians attribute the end of the empire to floods or decreased rainfall, which threatened the Harappans' agricultural base. The more enduring, if contentious, theory is that an Aryan invasion put paid to the Harappans, despite little archaeological proof or written reports in the ancient Indian texts to that effect. As a result, some nationalist historians argue that the Aryans (from a Sanskrit word meaning 'noble') were in fact the original inhabitants of India and that the invasion theory was actually invented by self-serving foreign conquerors. Others say that the arrival of Aryans was more of a gentle migration that gradually subsumed Harappan culture.

Those who defend the invasion theory believe that from around 1500 BC Aryan tribes from Afghanistan and Central Asia began to filter into northwest India. Many of the original inhabitants of northern India, the Dravidians, were pushed south.

The Hindu sacred scriptures, the Vedas, were written during this period of transition (1500–1200 BC), and the caste system became formalised.

As the Aryan tribes spread across the Ganges plain in the late 7th century BC, many were absorbed into 16 major kingdoms, which were, in turn, amalgamated into four large states.

During this period, the Indian heartland narrowly avoided two invasions from the west which, if successful, could have significantly altered the path of Indian history. The first was by the Persian king Darius (521–486 BC), who annexed Punjab and Sindh (on either side of the modern India–Pakistan border). Alexander the Great advanced to India from Greece in 326 BC, but his troops refused to go beyond the Beas River in Himachal Pradesh. Alexander turned back without ever extending his power into India itself.

2600–1700 BC

The heyday of the Indus Valley civilisation, spanning parts of Rajasthan, Gujarat and the Sindh province in present-day Pakistan.

1000 BC

Indraprastha, Delhi's first incarnation, is founded. Archaeological excavations at the Purana Qila continue even today.

326 BC

Alexander the Great invades India, but a rebellion within his army keeps him from advancing beyond the Beas River.

The Mauryan Empire & its Aftermath

If the Harappan culture was the cradle of Indian civilisation, Chandragupta Maurya was the founder of the first great Indian empire. He came to power in 321 BC and soon expanded the empire to include the Indus Valley, previously conquered by Alexander.

From its capital at Pataliputra (modern-day Patna), the Mauryan empire encompassed much of North and South India. The empire reached its peak under the emperor Ashoka. Such was Ashoka's power to lead and unite that after his death in 232 BC the empire rapidly disintegrated, collapsing altogether in 184 BC.

None of the empires that immediately followed could match the stability or enduring historical legacy of the Mauryans. Despite the multiplicity of ruling powers, this was a period of intense development. Trade with the Roman Empire (overland, and by sea through the southern ports) became substantial during the 1st century AD; there was also overland trade with China.

The Best... Ancient Cities

1 Qutb Minar (p96)

2 Fatehpur Sikri (p105)

3 Old Delhi (p64)

The Golden Age of the Guptas

Throughout the subcontinent, small tribes and kingdoms effectively controlled territory and dominated local affairs. In AD 319 Chandragupta I, the third king of one of these tribes, the little-known Guptas, came to prominence. Poetry, literature and the arts flourished, with some of the finest work done at Ajanta (p139), Ellora (p137) and Sarnath (p329). Towards the end of the Gupta period, Hinduism became the dominant religious force, and its revival eclipsed Jainism and Buddhism; the latter in particular went into decline in India and would never again be India's dominant religion.

The invasions of the Huns at the beginning of the 6th century signalled the end of this era.

The Hindu South

Southern India has always laid claim to its own unique history. Insulated by distance from the political developments in the north, a separate set of powerful kingdoms emerged, among them the Satavahanas, who ruled over central India for about 400 years. But it was from the tribal territories on the fertile coastal plains that the greatest southern empires – the Cholas, Pandyas, Chalukyas, Cheras and Pallavas – came into their own.

The south's prosperity was based on long-established trading links with other civilisations, among them the Egyptians and Romans. In 850 the Cholas rose to power

321–185 BC

The pan-Indian Maurya empire briefly adopts Buddhism during the reign of Emperor Ashoka.

AD 52

St Thomas the Apostle thought to have arrived in Kerala to bring Christianity to India through his preaching.

nd superseded the Pallavas, who had ruled since the 4th century. They soon set about turning the south's ar-reaching trade influence into territorial conquest.

The Muslim North

While South India guarded its resolutely Hindu character, North India was convulsed by Muslim armies invading from the northwest.

At the vanguard of Islamic expansion was Mahmud of Ghazni. Today, Ghazni is a nondescript little town between Kabul and Kandahar in Afghanistan. But in the early years of the 11th century, Mahmud turned it into one of the world's most glorious capital cities, which he largely funded by plundering his neighbours' territories. From 1001 to 1025, Mahmud conducted 17 raids into India, effectively shifting the balance of power in North India.

Following Mahmud's death in 1033, Ghazni was seized by the Seljuqs and then fell to the Ghurs of western Afghanistan, who similarly had their eyes on the great Indian prize. The Ghur style of warfare was brutal: the Ghur general Ala-ud-din was known as 'Burner of the World'.

In 1191 Mohammed of Ghur advanced into India. Although defeated in a major battle against a confederacy of Hindu rulers, he returned the following year and routed his enemies. One of his generals, Qutb ud-din Aibak, captured Delhi and was appointed governor; it was during his reign that the great Delhi landmark, the Qutb Minar complex (p96), was built. A separate Islamic empire was established in Bengal and within a short time almost the whole of North India was under Muslim control.

North Meets South

Mohammed Tughlaq ascended the throne in 1324. In 1328 Tughlaq took the southern strongholds of the Hoysala empire. India was Tughlaq's for the taking.

However, while the empire of the pre-Mughal Muslims would achieve its greatest extent under Tughlaq's rule, his overreaching ambition also sowed the seeds of its disintegration.

After a series of successful campaigns, Tughlaq decided to move the capital from Delhi to a more central location. The new capital was called Daulatabad and was near Aurangabad in Maharashtra. Tughlaq sought to populate the new capital by forcefully marching the entire population of Delhi 1100km south, resulting in great loss of life. However, he soon realised that this left the north undefended and so the entire capital was moved north again.

The Best...
Colonial-era Architecture

1 New Delhi (p72)

2 Kolkata (p298)

3 Old Goa (p207)

4 Mumbai (p120)

5 Puducherry (p275)

IN FOCUS HISTORY

319–510

The golden era of the Gupta dynasty, marked by a creative surge in literature and the arts.

4th to 9th centuries

The Pallavas, known for their temple architecture, enter the shifting landscape of southern power centres.

7th century

The new religion of Islam spreads to India through Arab merchants and traders visiting the Keralan coast.

The days of the Ghur empire were numbered. The last of the great sultans of Delhi, Firoz Shah, died in 1388, and the fate of the sultanate was sealed when Timur (Tamerlane) made a devastating raid from Samarkand (in Central Asia) into India in 1398.

After Tughlaq's withdrawal from the south, several splinter kingdoms arose. The two most significant were the Islamic Bahmani sultanate, and the Hindu Vijayanagar empire, founded in 1336 with its capital at Hampi. The battles between the two were among the bloodiest communal violence in Indian history and ultimately resolved nothing in the two centuries before the Mughals rose to power.

The Mughals

Even as Vijayanagar was experiencing its last days, the next great Indian empire was being founded. The Mughal empire was massive, at its height covering almost the entire subcontinent. Its significance, however, lay not only in its size. Mughal emperors presided over a golden age of arts and literature and had a passion for building that resulted in some of the finest architecture in India.

The founder of the Mughal line, Babur, marched into Punjab in 1525 from his capital at Kabul. With technological superiority brought by firearms, and consummate skill in simultaneously employing artillery and cavalry, Babur defeated the numerically superior armies of the sultan of Delhi at the Battle of Panipat in 1526.

Despite this initial success, Babur's son Humayun (r 1530–56) was defeated by a powerful ruler of eastern India, Sher Shah, in 1539 and was forced to withdraw to Iran. Following Sher Shah's death in 1545, Humayun returned to claim his kingdom, eventually conquering Delhi in 1555. He was succeeded in power by his young son Akbar (r 1556–1605) who managed to extend and consolidate the empire until he ruled over a mammoth area.

Jehangir (r 1605–27) ascended to the throne following Akbar's death. Despite several challenges to the authority of Jehangir himself, the empire remained more or less intact. He was succeeded by his son, Shah Jahan (r 1627–58), who secured his position as emperor by executing all male relatives who stood in his way. During his reign, some of the most vivid and permanent reminders of the Mughals' glory were constructed, including the Taj Mahal (p99) and Delhi's Red Fort (p65).

The last of the great Mughals, Aurangzeb (r 1658–1707), imprisoned his father (Shah Jahan) and succeeded to the throne after a two-year struggle against his brothers. Aurangzeb devoted his resources to extending the empire's boundaries,

The Best... Mughal Sites

1 Taj Mahal (p99)

2 Fatehpur Sikri (p105)

3 Agra Fort (p103)

4 Red Fort (p65)

5 Humayun's tomb (p73)

1192
Prithviraj Chauhan loses Delhi to Mohammed of Ghur. The defeat effectively ends Hindu supremacy in the region.

1325
Mohammed bin Tughlaq becomes sultan of Delhi, moves the capital to Daulatabad and creates forgery-prone currency.

1336
Foundation of the mighty Vijayanagar empire, named after its capital city, the ruins of which can be seen today close to Hampi

and thus fell into much the same trap as that of Mohammed Tughlaq some 300 years earlier. He, too, tried moving his capital south (to Aurangabad) and imposed heavy taxes to fund his military. A combination of decaying court life and dissatisfaction among the Hindu population at inflated taxes and religious intolerance weakened the Mughal grip.

The empire was also facing serious challenges from the Marathas in central India and, more significantly, the British in Bengal. With Aurangzeb's death in 1707, the empire's fortunes rapidly declined.

The Rajputs & the Marathas

Throughout the Mughal period, there remained strong Hindu powers, most notably the Rajputs. Centred in Rajasthan, the Rajputs were a proud warrior caste with a passionate belief in the dictates of chivalry, both in battle and in state affairs. The Rajputs opposed every foreign incursion into their territory, but were never united or adequately organised to deal with stronger forces on a long-term basis. This eventually led to their territories becoming vassal states of the Mughal empire. Their prowess in battle,

Religious items for sale outside Jama Masjid (p65), India's largest mosque, Delhi
TIM MAKINS / LONELY PLANET IMAGES ©

1398
Timur (Tamerlane) invades Delhi with extreme violence, on the pretext that the Delhi sultans are too tolerant with their Hindu subjects.

1498
Vasco da Gama, a Portuguese voyager, discovers the sea route from Europe to India.

1510
Portuguese forces capture Goa under the command of Alfonso de Albuquerque.

however, was acknowledged, and some of the best military men in the Mughal armies were Rajputs.

The Marathas were less swashbuckling but ultimately more effective. They gradually took over more of the weakening Mughal empire's powers, first by supplying troops and then actually taking control of Mughal land, but this expansion came to an abrupt halt in 1761 at Panipat, when they were defeated by Ahmad Shah Durani from Afghanistan.

The Rise of European Power

The British weren't the first European power to arrive in India, nor were they the last to leave – both of those 'honours' go to the Portuguese. In 1498 Vasco da Gama arrived on the coast of modern-day Kerala, having sailed around the Cape of Good Hope. Pioneering this route gave the Portuguese a century-long monopoly over Indian and far-eastern trade with Europe. In 1510 they captured Goa, which they controlled until 1961.

In 1600 Queen Elizabeth I granted a charter to a London trading company that gave it a monopoly on British trade with India. In 1613 representatives of the East India Company established their first trading post in northwest India.

By 1672 the French had established themselves at Pondicherry (now Puducherry), an enclave they held even after the British departed and where architectural traces of French elegance remain. But serious French aspirations effectively ended in 1750 when the directors of the French East India Company decided that their representatives were playing too much politics and doing too little trading. Key representatives were sacked, and a settlement designed to end all ongoing political disputes was made with the British. The decision effectively removed France as a serious influence on the subcontinent.

Britain's Surge to Power

The transformation of the British from traders to governors began almost by accident. Having been granted a licence to trade in Bengal by the Mughals, and following the establishment of a new trading post at Calcutta (now Kolkata) in 1690, business began to expand rapidly. Under the apprehensive gaze of the nawab (local ruler), British trading activities became extensive and the 'factories' took on an increasingly permanent (and fortified) appearance.

Eventually the nawab decided that British power had grown large enough. In June 1756 he attacked Calcutta and, having taken the city, locked his British prisoners in a tiny cell. The space was so cramped and airless that many were dead by the following morning. The cell infamously became known as the 'Black Hole of Calcutta'.

Six months later, Robert Clive, an employee in the military service of the East India Company, led an expedition to retake Calcutta and entered into an agreement with one of the nawab's generals to overthrow the nawab himself. He did this in June 1757 at the Battle of Plassey (now called Palashi), and the general who had assisted him was placed on the throne.

1526

Babur becomes the first Mughal emperor after conquering Delhi. He stuns Rajasthan by routing its confederate force.

1540

The Sur dynasty briefly captures Delhi from the Mughals, after Sher Shah Suri's Battle of Kanauj victory over Humayun.

1542–45

St Francis Xavier's first mission to India. He preaches Catholicism in Goa, Tamil Nadu and Sri Lanka.

Enter the Portuguese

Just a few years after they arrived, the Portuguese were well on their way to establishing a firm foothold in Goa. On 20 May 1498 Vasco da Gama dropped anchor off the South Indian coast. It had taken him 23 days to sail from the east coast of Africa, guided by a pilot named Ibn Masjid, sent by the ruler of Malindi in Gujarat.

The Portuguese sought a sea route between Europe and the East so they could trade directly in spices. They also hoped they might find Christians cut off from Europe by the Muslim dominance of the Middle East, while at the same time searching for the legendary kingdom of Prester John, a powerful Christian ruler with whom they could unite against the Middle Eastern rulers. In India they found spices and the Syrian Orthodox community, but not Prester John.

In 1771 Warren Hastings was made governor in Bengal. During his tenure the company greatly expanded its influence.

British India

By the early 19th century, India was effectively under British control, although there remained a patchwork of states who administered their own territories. However, a system of central government was developed. British bureaucratic models were replicated in the Indian government and civil service – a legacy that still exists.

Trade and profit continued to be the main focus of British rule in India, with far-reaching effects. Iron and coal mining were developed, and tea, coffee and cotton became key crops. A start was made on the vast rail network that's still in use today, irrigation projects were undertaken, and the zamindar (landowner) system was encouraged. These absentee landlords eased the burden of administration and tax collection for the British but contributed to the development of an impoverished and landless peasantry.

The Road to Independence

The desire among many Indians to be free from foreign rule remained. Opposition to the British increased at the turn of the 20th century, spearheaded by the Indian National Congress, the country's oldest political party, also known as the Congress Party and Congress (I).

1556

Hemu, a Hindu general in Adil Shah Suri's army, seizes Delhi after Humayun's death.

RICHARD I'ANSON / LONELY PLANET IMAGES ©

1674

Shivaji establishes the Maratha kingdom, spanning western India and parts of the Deccan and North India.

It met for the first time in 1885 and soon began to push for participation in the government of India. A highly unpopular attempt by the British to partition Bengal in 1905 resulted in mass demonstrations and brought to light Hindu opposition to the division; the Muslim community formed its own league and campaigned for protected rights in any future political settlement.

With the outbreak of WWI, the political situation eased. India contributed hugely to the war (more than one million Indian volunteers were enlisted and sent overseas, suffering more than 100,000 casualties). The contribution was sanctioned by Congress leaders, largely with the expectation that it would be rewarded after the war. No such rewards transpired. Disturbances were particularly persistent in Punjab, and in April 1919, following riots in Amritsar, a British army contingent was sent to quell the unrest. Under direct orders of the officer in charge, they ruthlessly fired into a crowd of unarmed protesters. News of the massacre spread rapidly throughout India, turning huge numbers of otherwise apolitical Indians into Congress supporters.

At this time, the Congress movement found a new leader in Mohandas Gandhi. As political power-sharing began to look more likely, and the mass movement led by Gandhi gained momentum, the Muslim community's reaction was to consider its own

Carved marble pillars inside a Jain temple, Rajasthan (p143)
ORIEN HARVEY / LONELY PLANET IMAGES ©

1672

The Compagnie française des Indes Orientales, or the French East India Company, establishes an outpost at Pondicherry.

1707

Death of Aurangzeb, the last of the Mughal greats. His demise triggers the gradual collapse of the Mughal empire.

1747

Afghan ruler Ahmad Shah Durani sweeps across northern India, capturing Lahore and Kashmir, and sacking Delhi.

immediate future. The large Muslim minority realised that an independent India would be dominated by Hindus and that, while Gandhi's approach was fair-minded, others in the Congress Party might not be so willing to share power. By the 1930s Muslims were raising the possibility of a separate Islamic state.

Political events were partially disrupted by WWII, when large numbers of Congress supporters were jailed to prevent disruption to the war effort.

Independence & the Partition of India

The Labour Party victory in the British elections in July 1945 dramatically altered the political landscape. For the first time, Indian independence was accepted as a legitimate goal. This new goodwill did not, however, translate into any new wisdom as to how to reconcile the divergent wishes of the two major Indian parties. Mohammed Ali Jinnah, the leader of the Muslim League, championed a separate Islamic state, while the Congress Party, led by Jawaharlal Nehru, campaigned for an independent greater India.

In early 1946 a British mission failed to bring the two sides together, and the country slid closer towards civil war. In February 1947 the nervous British government made

The Kashmir Conflict

Kashmir is the most enduring symbol of the turbulent partition of India. In the lead-up to Independence, local rulers were asked which country they wished to belong to. Kashmir was a predominantly Muslim state with a Hindu maharaja, Hari Singh, who tried to delay his decision. A ragtag Pashtun (Pakistani) army crossed the border, intent on annexing Kashmir for Pakistan, whereupon the maharaja panicked and requested armed assistance from India. The Indian army arrived only just in time to prevent the fall of Srinagar, and the maharaja signed the Instrument of Accession, tying Kashmir to India, in October 1947. The legality of the document was immediately contested by Pakistan, and the two nations went to war, just two months after Independence.

In 1948 the fledgling UN Security Council called for a referendum to decide the status of Kashmir. A UN-brokered ceasefire in 1949 kept the countries on either side of a demarcation line, called the Cease-Fire Line (later to become the Line of Control, or LOC), with little else resolved. Two-thirds of Kashmir fell on the Indian side of the LOC, which remains the frontier, but neither side accepts this as the official border.

1757
The East India Company registers its first military victory on Indian soil in the Battle of Plassey.

1857
First War of Independence against the British; freedom fighters coerce the Mughal king to proclaim himself emperor of India.

1858
The British government assumes control over India, beginning the period known as the British Raj.

the momentous decision that independence would be effected by June 1948. In the meantime, the viceroy, Lord Wavell, was replaced by Lord Louis Mountbatten.

The new viceroy encouraged the rival factions to agree upon a united India, but to no avail. A decision was made to divide the country, with Gandhi the only staunch opponent. Faced with increasing civil violence, Mountbatten made the precipitous decision to bring forward Independence to 15 August 1947.

Dividing the country into separate Hindu and Muslim territories was immensely difficult; the dividing line proved almost impossible to draw. Some areas were clearly Hindu or Muslim, but others had evenly mixed populations, and there were 'islands' of communities in areas predominantly settled by other religions. Moreover, the two overwhelmingly Muslim regions were on opposite sides of the country and, therefore, Pakistan would inevitably have an eastern and western half, divided by India. The instability of this arrangement was self-evident, but it was 25 years before the split finally came and East Pakistan became Bangladesh.

The problem was worse in Punjab, where intercommunity antagonisms were already running at fever pitch. Punjab, one of the most fertile and affluent regions of the country, had large Muslim, Hindu and Sikh communities. The Sikhs had already

Young monks at a Buddhist temple
RICHARD I'ANSON / LONELY PLANET IMAGES ©

1869

Suez Canal opens; journey from England reduced from three months to three weeks. Bombay's economic importance skyrockets.

1919

On 13 April, unarmed Indian protesters are massacred at Jallianwala Bagh in Amritsar (Punjab).

1947

India gains independence on 15 August. Pakistan is formed a day earlier. Partition is followed by mass cross-border exodus.

campaigned unsuccessfully for their own state and now saw their homeland divided down the middle. The new border ran straight between Punjab's two major cities, Lahore and Amritsar.

Punjab contained all the ingredients for an epic disaster, but the resulting bloodshed was far worse than anticipated. Huge population exchanges took place. Trains full of Muslims, fleeing westward, were held up and slaughtered by Hindu and Sikh mobs. Hindus and Sikhs fleeing to the east suffered the same fate at Muslim hands. The army that was sent to maintain order proved inadequate and, at times, all too ready to join the sectarian carnage. By the time the Punjab chaos had run its course, more than 10 million people had changed sides and at least 500,000 had been killed.

India and Pakistan became sovereign nations under the British Commonwealth in August 1947 as planned, but the violence, migrations and the integration of a few states, especially Kashmir, continued. The Constitution of India was at last adopted in November 1949 and came into effect on 26 January 1950. After untold struggles, independent India had officially become a republic.

IN FOCUS HISTORY

1948

Mahatma Gandhi is assassinated in New Delhi by Nathuram Godse on 30 January.

26 January 1950

India becomes a republic. Date commemorates Declaration of Independence proposed by Congress in 1930.

WAYNE WALTON / LONELY PLANET IMAGES ©

Family Travel

A young Sikh boy at the Golden Temple (p386), Amritsar

SARA-JANE CLELAND / LONELY PLANET IMAG

Fascinating, frustrating, thrilling and fulfilling, India is as great an adventure for children as it is for parents. Though the sensory overload may be at times overwhelming for younger kids and even short journeys can prove rigorous for the entire family, the colours, scents, sights and sounds of India more than compensate by setting young imaginations ablaze.

A Warm Welcome

You'd be hard-pressed to find a country more accommodating than India when it comes to travelling with children. Hotels will almost always come up with an extra bed or two, and restaurants with a familiar meal; cooing domestic tourists may even ask to take a photograph of you and your adorable brood. But while all this is fabulous for outgoing children it may prove tiring or disconcerting for those of a more retiring disposition. The key as a parent is to stay alert to children's needs and to remain firm in fulfilling them.

Sleeping

India offers such an array of accommodation, from beach huts to five-star fantasies, that you're bound to be able to find something that will appeal. Most places won't mind cramming several children into a regular-sized double room along with their parents. If your budget can stretch a bit, a good way to maintain familial energy levels is to mix in a few top-end stays.

Health

The availability of decent health care in India makes keeping children healthy easier than you might think. It's usually easy to find a doctor at short notice (most hotels will be able to recommend a reliable one), and prescriptions are quickly and cheaply filled at pharmacies. The most common concerns include heat rash, skin complaints such as impetigo, insect bites or stings and tummy troubles, all of which can be treated swiftly and effectively with the help of a well-equipped first-aid kit.

Before You Go

Remember to visit your doctor to discuss vaccinations and other health-related issues involving your children well in advance of travel. For more tips and first-hand accounts of travels in the country, pick up Lonely Planet's *Travel with Children* and log on to the Travel with Children branch of Lonely Planet's online Thorn Tree forum.

The Best...
Best Places for Kids

1 Rajasthan (p144)

2 Leh (p379)

3 Himachal Pradesh (p359)

4 Goa (p193)

5 Kerala Backwaters (p230)

Need to Know

o **Changing facilities** Not usually available – take a portable changing mat and plenty of wipes.

o **Cots** Bring the lightest fold-up baby bed you can find.

o **Health** Bring a first-aid kit, plus insect repellent, sun lotion and – for those with younger children – nappy-rash (diaper-rash) cream. Calendula cream works well against heat rash, too.

o **Highchairs** Available in some upmarket restaurants.

o **Kids' menus** You'll find these at occasional big-city restaurants, but otherwise there's plenty of cuisine to please all palates.

o **Nappies (diapers)** Bring as many nappies as you can; they are available in India, but are often expensive and may not be your preferred brand.

o **Strollers** Pavements, if they exist, are usually rough, making these a bane rather than a boon.

o **Transport** Pack diversions – portable DVD players make good travel companions, as do the cheap books, toys and games available widely across India.

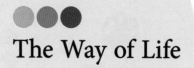

The Way of Life

A woman trying on bracelets, Delhi

PAUL BEINSSEN / LONELY PLANET IM

For travellers, one of the most enduring impressions of India is the way everyday life is intimately intertwined with the sacred. Examples abound, from the housewife who devoutly performs puja *(prayers) at home each morning, to the shopkeeper who – regardless of how many eager-to-buy tourists may be in the store – rarely commences business until blessings have been sought from the gods.*

Along with religion, family lies at the heart of Indian society. For most Indians, the idea of being unmarried and without children by one's mid-30s is unthinkable. Despite the rising number of nuclear families – primarily in larger cities such as Mumbai (Bombay), Bengaluru (Bangalore) and Delhi – the extended family remains a cornerstone in both urban and rural India; men, usually the breadwinners, are generally considered the head of the household.

Marriage, Birth & Death

Marriage is an exceptionally auspicious event for Indians and although 'love marriages' have spiralled upwards in recent times (mainly in urban hubs), most Hindu and many Muslim marriages are arranged.

Dowry, although illegal, is still a key issue in many arranged marriages (primarily in the more conservative communities), with some families plunging into debt to raise the required cash and merchandise (such as cars, computers, washing machines and TVs). Health workers claim that India's high rate of abortion of female foetuses (though sex-identification tests are banned in India, they still clandestinely occur in some clinics) is predominantly due to the financial burden of providing a daughter's dowry.

Divorce and remarriage is becoming more common (primarily in India's bigger cities), but divorce is still not granted by courts as a matter of routine and is generally not looked upon favourably by society.

The birth of a child is another momentous occasion, with its own set of special ceremonies that take place at various auspicious times during the early years of childhood. These include the casting of the child's first horoscope, name-giving, feeding the first solid food and the first hair-cutting.

Hindus cremate their dead, and Muslims bury them. Funeral ceremonies are designed to purify and console both the living and the deceased.

The Best... Places to Experience Indian Spirituality

1 Pushkar (p165)

2 Varanasi (p319)

3 Hazrat Nizam-ud-din Dargah (p77)

4 McLeod Ganj (p368)

The Caste System

Although the Indian constitution does not recognise the caste system, it still wields considerable influence, especially in rural India, where your family's caste largely determines your social standing in the community, and can influence one's vocational and marriage prospects. Traditionally, caste is the basic social structure of Hindu society. Living a righteous life and fulfilling your dharma (moral duty) raises your chances of being reborn into a higher caste and thus into better circumstances. Hindus are born into one of four varnas (castes): Brahmin (priests and scholars), Kshatriya (soldiers), Vaishya (merchants) and Shudra (labourers). The Brahmins were said to have emerged from the mouth of Lord Brahma at the moment of creation, Kshatriyas were said to have come from his arms, Vaishyas from his thighs and Shudras from his feet.

Beneath the four main castes are the Dalits (once known as Untouchables), who hold menial jobs such as latrine cleaners. At the bottom are the Denotified Tribes, known as the Criminal Tribes until 1952, when a reforming law officially recognised 198 tribes and castes. Many are nomadic or seminomadic, forced to eke out a living on society's fringes.

To improve the Dalits' position, the government reserves considerable numbers of public-sector jobs, parliamentary seats and university places for them. Today these quotas account for almost 25% of government jobs and university (student) positions.

Women in India

Women in India are entitled to vote and own property. While the percentage of women in politics has risen over the past decade, they're still notably underrepresented in the national parliament, accounting for around 10% of parliamentary members.

Professions are still male-dominated, but women are steadily making inroads, especially in urban centres. Kerala was India's first state to break societal norms by recruiting female police officers in 1938, and the first to establish an all-female police station (1973).

In low-income families, especially, girls can be regarded as a serious financial liability because at marriage a dowry must often be supplied.

For the urban middle-class woman, life is materially much more comfortable, but pressures still exist. Broadly speaking, she is far more likely to receive a tertiary

Hijras

India's most visible nonheterosexuals are *hijras,* a caste of transvestites and eunuchs. Some are gay, some are hermaphrodites and some were unfortunate enough to be kidnapped and castrated. Since it has traditionally been impossible to live openly as a gay man in India, *hijras* get around this by becoming in effect a 'third sex'. They work mainly as uninvited entertainers at weddings and celebrations of the birth of male children, and possibly as prostitutes.

Read more about *hijras* in *The Invisibles* by Zia Jaffrey and *Ardhanarishvara the Androgyne* by Dr Alka Pande.

education, but once married is still usually expected to 'fit in' with her in-laws and be a homemaker above all else. Like her village counterpart, if she fails to live up to expectations – even just not being able to produce a grandson – the consequences can sometimes be dire, as demonstrated by the horrifying practice of 'bride burning', wherein a man or his in-laws douse his wife with kerosene and set her alight. If convicted offenders can be punished by death, or up to life in prison, but the practice continues.

In October 2006, following women's civil rights campaigns, the Indian parliament passed a landmark bill (on top of existing legislation), which gives women who are suffering domestic violence increased protection and rights.

Sport

Cricket

Travellers who show even a slight interest in cricket can expect to strike up passionate conversations with people of all stripes, from taxi drivers to IT yuppies. Cutting across all echelons of society, cricket is not just a national sporting obsession but a matter of enormous patriotism, especially whenever India plays against Pakistan. Matches between these South Asian neighbours – which have had rocky relations since Independence – attract especially high-spirited support, and the players of both sides are under colossal pressure to do their respective countries proud.

Today cricket – especially the recently rolled out Twenty20 format (see www.cricket20.com) – is big business in India, attracting lucrative sponsorship deals and celebrity status for its players. The sport has not been without its murky side though, with Indian cricketers among those embroiled in match-fixing scandals over past years.

International games are played at various centres – see Indian newspapers and/or surf the net for details about matches that coincide with your visit.

Keep your finger on the cricketing pulse at www.espncricinfo.com (rated most highly by many cricket aficionados) and www.cricbuzz.com.

India's first recorded cricket match was in 1721. It won its first test series in 1952 in Chennai against England.

Tennis

Although nowhere near as popular as cricket, tennis is steadily generating greater interest in India. Perhaps the biggest success story for India is the doubles team of Leander Paes and Mahesh Bhupathi, who won Wimbledon's prestigious title in 1999, the first Indians ever to do so. At the 2005 Dubai Open, Indian wild card Sania Mirza first made international waves when she convincingly defeated 2004 US Open champion Svetlana Kuznetsova. Mirza, then ranked 97th, 90 spots behind Kuznetsova, became the first Indian woman to win a Women's Tennis Association Tour title. More recently, Mirza and Bhupathi won the Mixed Doubles title at the 2009 Australian Open, which secured Mirza a place in history as India's first woman to win a Grand Slam event.

The All India Tennis Association (AITA; www.aitatennis.com) has more information about the game in India.

Polo

Polo intermittently flourished in India (especially among the aristocracy) until Independence, after which patronage sharply declined due to a lack of sufficient funds. Today there's renewed interest in the game thanks to beefed-up sponsorship, although it still remains an elite sport and consequently fails to attract widespread public interest.

Travellers can catch a polo match and hobnob with high society during the winter months in cities such as Delhi, Jaipur, Kolkata and Mumbai (check local newspapers for dates and venues). Polo is also occasionally played in Ladakh and Manipur.

The origins of polo are unclear. Believed to have roots in Persia and China some 2000 years back, in the subcontinent it's thought to have first been played in Baltistan (in present-day Pakistan). Polo publications claim that Emperor Akbar (who reigned in India from 1556 to 1605) first introduced rules to the game, but that polo, as it's played today, was largely influenced by a British cavalry regiment stationed in India during the 1870s. A set of international rules was implemented after WWI. The world's oldest surviving polo club, established in 1862, is in Kolkata – see Calcutta Polo Club (www .calcuttapolo.com).

Men playing cricket, Kerala

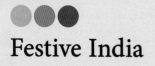

Festive India

Musicians play at the Gangaur festival, Jaipur

SARA-JANE CLELAND / LONELY PLANET IMA[...]

No other country can throw a festival quite like India. With its remarkable mix of religious groups – from Hindus, Sikhs and Jains to Muslims and Buddhists – the subcontinent is home to myriad wildly diverse celebrations, and every festival is a valuable thread when it comes to weaving the unique and colourful tapestry that is Festive India.

Pongal

Tamil Pongal is South India's major harvest festival, when gods are thanked for gifts of crops, nature, the cow and kinship. It takes place in the Hindu calendar period known as Magha (January/February). Many homes are decorated with *kolams* (see the boxed text). Families may prepare *pongal* (a mixture of rice, sugar, dhal and milk), symbolic of prosperity and abundance, then feed it to lovingly adorned cows.

Diwali

Diwali, the Festival of Lights, is the country's most widely celebrated Hindu event (primarily in North India), spanning five days in Kartika (October/November). Buildings are illuminated with twinkling lights, flickering candles are set afloat on rivers to guide Lord Rama home from exile, and there are masses of fireworks.

Holi

Fun-filled Holi, on the day of the full moon in the Hindu month of Phalguna (February/March), is India's most exuberant Hindu festival. Folks greet each other with bright colours – everything from a cheeky daub to a veritable deluge of multicoloured water from buckets. Wear old clothes and get ready to duck!

Dussehra

This Hindu festival honours Durga and Rama, who both valiantly conquered evil forces. It spans 10 joyous days in Asvina (September/October). People all over India spend Navratri (the first nine nights) in the worship of Durga, culminating in Dussehra on the 10th day.

Ganesh Chaturthi

Celebrating the jolly, much-loved, elephant-headed Hindu god, Ganesh Chaturthi takes place in Bhadra (August/September). The most spectacular celebrations occur in Mumbai (Bombay), with parades of giant idols.

Gangaur

One of Rajasthan's most widely celebrated festivals, Gangaur (March/April) honours the love between Shiva and his consort Parvati; celebrants make and worship small terracotta and/or wooden figures of the two deities. Parvati symbolises perfection in married life, so it is deemed wise for all women (married or single) to pay her tribute.

Janmastami

Celebrated in Bhadra (August/September), this festival commemorates the birth of Lord Krishna, notably with *ras-lila,* the re-enactment of Krishna's dances with the *gopis* (milkmaids).

Ramadan & Eid Al-Fitr

Ramadan (Ramazan) is the Islamic month of dawn-to-dusk fasting that falls in August, September or October (dates vary according to the Islamic lunar calendar). Muslims are enjoined to fast in daylight hours so they can understand the suffering of the poor. The final (30th) day is Eid al-Fitr, when feasts joyously mark the end of the fast.

The Best... Festivals

Colourful Kolams

Kolams (or *rangoli*), intricate rice-flour paste designs adorning thresholds, are traditionally drawn at sunrise for good luck, and to protect against the evil eye. They also symbolise a reverence for all living things as animals will often eat them. Deities are thought to be attracted to beautiful *kolams,* and they also serve as a signal to sadhus (holy people) that food may be offered at that house.

Delicious India

A mixed-course thali meal, Goa

GREG ELMS / LONELY PLANET IM

Brace yourself for the culinary trip of your life! Simmering, sizzling, kneading and flipping a deliciously diverse array of regional dishes, India's talented chefs ensure that you will feast your way through the subcontinent. India's many different cuisines reflect the fresh local produce available – from the desert vegetables of Rajasthan to the cardamom of Kerala – combined with an extraordinary amalgam of regional and global influences.

Land of Spices

Christopher Columbus was looking for the black pepper of Kerala's Malabar Coast when he stumbled upon America. The region still grows the world's finest pepper, and it's integral to most savoury Indian dishes. Turmeric and coriander seeds are other essentials, while most Indian 'wet' dishes begin with the crackle of cumin seeds in hot oil. The green cardamom of Kerala's Western Ghats scents and flavours savouries, desserts and chai (tea). Saffron, the dried stigmas of crocus flowers grown in Kashmir, is so light it takes more than 1500 hand-plucked flowers to yield just one gram.

Rice Paradise

Rice is a staple, especially in South India. Long-grain white rice varieties are the most popular, served with just about any 'wet' cooked dish. Rice is often cooked up in a pilau (or pilaf; spiced rice dish) or biryani.

Flippin' Fantastic Bread

While rice is paramount in the south, wheat is the mainstay in the north. Roti, the generic term for Indian-style bread, is a name used interchangeably with chapati to describe the most common variety, the unleavened round bread made with whole-wheat flour. It may be smothered with ghee (clarified butter) or oil.

Puri is deep-fried dough puffed up like a crispy balloon. Kachori is similar, but the dough has been pepped up with corn or dhal, which makes it considerably thicker. Flaky, unleavened *paratha* can be eaten as is or jazzed up with fillings such as paneer (soft, unfermented cheese). The thick, teardrop-shaped naan is cooked in a tandoor.

Dhal-icious!

While the staple of preference divides north and south, the whole of India is melodiously united in its love for dhal (curried lentils or pulses). You may encounter up to 60 different pulses: the most common are *channa,* a sweeter version of the yellow split pea; tiny yellow or green ovals called *moong* (mung beans); salmon-coloured *masoor* (red lentils); the ochre-coloured southern favourite, *tuvar* (yellow lentils; also known as *arhar*); *rajma* (kidney beans); *kabuli channa* (chickpeas); *urad* (black gram or lentils); and *lobhia* (black-eyed peas).

The Best... Dishes to Try

1 *Masala dosa* (curried-vegetables pancake), Chennai (p268)

2 *Bhelpuri* (fried dough with lentils and spices), Mumbai (p126)

3 *Rasgulla* (cream-cheese balls flavoured with rose-water), Kolkata (p303)

4 *Paratha* (stuffed bread), Delhi (p82)

5 Bebinca (coconut cake), Panaji (p205)

Street Food

Tucking into street food is one of the joys of travelling in India – here are some tips to help avoid tummy troubles.

○ Give yourself a few days to adjust to the local cuisine.

○ If the locals are avoiding a vendor, you should too.

○ Check how clean the stall looks, and don't be shy to make a hasty retreat if you think it looks unclean.

○ Don't be put off when you order some deep-fried snack and the cook throws it back into the wok. It's common practice to cook the snacks first and then finish them off once they've been ordered. Frying them hot again will kill any germs.

○ Unless a place is reputable (and busy), avoid eating meat from the street.

○ The hygiene standard at juice stalls is wildly variable, so exercise caution.

○ Don't be tempted by glistening pre-sliced fruit, which keeps its luscious veneer with the regular dousing of (often dubious) water.

Meaty Matters

India has an extensive repertoire of carnivorous fare. Chicken, lamb and mutton (sometimes goat) are the mainstays; religious taboos make beef forbidden to devout Hindus and pork to Muslims.

In northern India you'll come across meat-dominated Mughlai cuisine, which includes rich curries, kebabs, koftas and biryanis. This spicy cuisine traces its history back to the (Islamic) Mughal empire that once reigned supreme in India.

Tandoori meat dishes are another North Indian favourite. The name is derived from the clay oven, or tandoor, in which the marinated meat is cooked.

Feasting Indian-Style

Most people in India eat with their right hand – the left hand is reserved for unsanitary actions such as removing shoes. Before and after a meal, it's good manners to wash your hands.

Deep-Sea Delights

With around 7500km of coastline, it's no surprise that seafood is an important staple, especially from Mumbai (Bombay) down to Kerala. Kerala is the biggest fishing state, while Goa boasts particularly succulent prawns and fiery fish curries.

Fruit & Veg

Vegetables are usually served at every main meal across India, and *sabzi* (vegetables) is a word recognised in every Indian vernacular. They're generally cooked *sukhi* (dry) or *tari* (in a sauce).

Potatoes are ubiquitous, often cooked with various masalas and other vegetables, or mashed and fried for *aloo tikki* (potato patties), or cooked with cauliflower to make *aloo gobi* (potato-and-cauliflower curry). Fresh green peas are stir-fried with other vegetables in pilaus and biryanis and in the magnificent *mattar paneer* (unfermented cheese and pea curry). *Baigan* (eggplant/aubergine) can be curried or sliced and deep-fried. Also popular is *saag* (a generic term for leafy greens), which can include mustard, spinach and fenugreek. Something a little more unusual is the bumpy-skinned *karela* (bitter gourd) which, like the delectable *bhindi* (okra), is commonly prepared dry with spices.

India's fruit basket is a bountiful one. Along the southern coast are super-luscious tropical fruits such as pineapples and papayas. Mangoes abound during the summer months (especially April and May), with India boasting more than 500 varieties, the pick of which is the sweet Alphonso. Citrus fruit such as oranges (often yellow-green in India), tangerines, grapefruits, kumquats and sweet limes are widely grown.

Vegetarians & Vegans

India is king when it comes to vegetarian fare. However, there's little understanding of veganism (the term 'pure vegetarian' means without eggs), and animal products such as milk, butter, ghee and curd are included in most Indian dishes.

For further information, surf the web – good places to begin include Indian Vegan (www.indianvegan.com) and Vegan World Network (www.vegansworldnetwork.org).

Dear Dairy

Milk products make a staggering contribution to Indian cuisine: *dahi* (curd/yoghurt) is commonly served with meals and is great for subduing heat; paneer is a godsend for vegetarians; lassi is one in a host of sweet and savoury beverages; ghee is the traditional cooking medium; and some of the finest *mithai* (Indian sweets) are made with milk.

Sweet at Heart

India has an incredible kaleidoscope of *mithai* (Indian sweets), usually sinfully sugary. The main categories are *barfi* (a fudgelike milk-based sweet), soft *halwa* (made with vegetables, cereals, lentils, nuts or fruit), *ladoos* (sweet balls made of gram flour and semolina), and those made from *chhana* (unpressed paneer) such as *rasgullas* (cream-cheese balls flavoured with rose water). There are also simpler, but scrumptious, offerings such as *jalebi* (orange-coloured coils of deep-fried batter dunked in sugar syrup).

Kheer (called *payasam* in the south) is one of the most popular after-meal desserts. It's a delicate, creamy rice pudding, enhanced with cardamom, saffron, pistachios, almonds, cashews or dried fruit. Other favourites include *gulab jamun,* deep-fried balls of dough soaked in rose-flavoured syrup, and *kulfi,* a firm-textured ice cream made with reduced milk and flavoured with nuts (often pistachio), fruits and berries.

Each year, an estimated 14 tonnes of pure silver is converted into the edible foil that decorates many Indian sweets.

Daily Dining Habits

Three main meals a day is the norm in India. Breakfast is usually light, maybe *idlis* (spongy, round, fermented rice cakes) and *sambar* (soupy lentil dish with cubed vegetables) in the south, and *parathas* in the north. Lunch can be substantial (perhaps a thali) or light, especially for time-strapped office workers. Dinner is usually the main meal of the day. It's generally comprised of a few different preparations – several curried vegetable (maybe also meat) dishes and dhal, accompanied by rice and/or chapatis. Dishes are served all at once rather than as courses. Desserts are optional and most prevalent during special occasions.

Food stall selling traditional Indian dishes, Pushkar (p165)

Art & Architecture

Wall paintings, Sri Meenakshi Temple (p282), Madurai

ANDERS BLOMQVIST / LONELY PLANET IMA

Over the centuries India's many ethnic and religious groups have spawned a vivid artistic heritage that is both inventive and spiritually significant. Today, artistic beauty lies around almost every corner, whether it's the garishly painted trucks rattling down dusty country roads or the exquisite, spidery body art of mehndi (henna).

Painting

Around 1500 years ago artists covered the walls and ceilings of the Ajanta caves (p139) in western India with scenes from Buddha's life. The figures are endowed with an unusual freedom and grace, and contrast with the next major style that emerged from this part of India in the 11th century.

India's Jain community created some particularly lavish temple art. However, after the Muslim conquest of Gujarat in 1299, the Jains turned their attention to illustrated manuscripts, which could be hidden away. These manuscripts are the only known form of Indian painting that survived the Islamic conquest of North India.

The Indo-Persian style – characterised by geometric design coupled with flowing form – developed from Islamic royal courts.

The Persian influence blossomed when artisans fled to India following the 1507 Uzbek attack on Herat (in present-day Afghanistan), and with trade and gift-swapping between the Persian city of Shiraz, an established centre for miniature production, and Indian provincial sultans.

The 1526 victory by Babur at the Battle of Panipat ushered in the era of the Mughals in India. Although Babur and his son Humayun were both artistic patrons, it's Humayun's son Akbar who is generally credited with developing the characteristic Mughal style. This painting style, often in colourful miniature form, largely depicts court life, architecture, portraits, and battle and hunting scenes.

Akbar's son Jehangir also patronised painting, but he preferred portraiture, and his fascination with natural science resulted in a vibrant legacy of paintings of flowers and animals. Under Jehangir's son Shah Jahan, the Mughal style became less fluid.

Various schools of miniature painting (small paintings crammed with detail) emerged in Rajasthan from around the 17th century. The subject matter ranged from royal processions to *shikar* (hunting expeditions), with many artists influenced by Mughal styles. The intense colours, still evident today in miniatures and frescoes in some Indian palaces, were often derived from crushed semiprecious stones, while some paintings use finely pounded pure gold and silver leaf.

By the 19th century, painting in North India was notably influenced by Western styles (especially English watercolours), giving rise to what has been dubbed the Company School.

In 21st-century India, paintings by contemporary Indian artists have been selling at record numbers (and prices) around the world. One very successful online art auction house is the Mumbai-based Saffronart (www.saffronart.com).

The Best... Religious Architecture

1 Taj Mahal (p99)

2 Ellora (p137)

3 Ajanta (p139)

4 Sri Meenakshi Temple (p282)

5 Golden Temple (p386)

Sacred Architecture

Travellers will come across various forms of historic and contemporary temple architecture, India's most striking and revered form of construction. Although few of the early wooden (occasionally brick) temples have weathered the vagaries of time, by the advent of the Guptas (4th to 6th centuries AD) of North India, sacred structures of a new type were being constructed, and these largely set the standard for temples for several hundred years.

Complex rules govern the location, design and building of each Hindu temple, based on numerology, astrology, astronomy, religious principles and the concept of the square as a perfect shape. Essentially, a temple represents a map of the universe. At the centre is an unadorned space, the *garbhagriha* (inner sanctum), which is symbolic of the 'womb-cave' from which the universe is said to have emerged. This provides a residence for the deity to whom the temple is dedicated.

Above the shrine rises a superstructure known as a *vimana* in South India, and a *sikhara* in North India. The *sikhara* is curvilinear and topped with a grooved disk, on which sits a pot-shaped finial, while the *vimana* is stepped, with the grooved disk being replaced with a solid dome. Some temples have a *mandapa* (temple forechamber)

connected to the sanctum by vestibules. These *mandapas* may also contain *vimanas* or *sikharas*.

A *gopuram* is the soaring pyramidal gateway tower of a Dravidian temple. The towering *gopurams* of various South Indian temple complexes (eg Madurai's Sri Meenakshi Temple, p282) took ornamentation and monumentalism to new levels.

Commonly used for ritual bathing and religious ceremonies, as well as adding aesthetic appeal to places of worship, temple tanks have long been a focal point of temple activity. These often-vast, angular, engineered reservoirs of water, sometimes fed by rain, sometimes fed – via a complicated drainage system – by rivers, serve both sacred and secular purposes. The waters of some temple tanks are believed to have healing properties, while others are said to have the power to wash away sins. Devotees (as well as travellers) may be required to wash their feet in a temple tank before entering a place of worship.

From the outside, Jain temples can resemble Hindu ones, but inside they're often a riot of sculptural ornamentation, the very opposite of ascetic austerity. Meanwhile, gurdwaras (Sikh temples) can usually be identified by a *nishan sahib* (flagpole flying a triangular flag with the Sikh insignia). Amritsar's sublime Golden Temple (p386) is Sikhism's holiest shrine.

Stupas, which characterise Buddhist places of worship, essentially evolved from burial mounds. They served as repositories for relics of Buddha and, later, other venerated souls. A relatively recent innovation is the addition of a *chaitya* (hall) leading up to the stupa itself. The gompas (Buddhist monasteries) found in places such as Ladakh and Sikkim are characterised by distinctly Tibetan motifs.

India's Muslim rulers contributed their own architectural conventions, including arched cloisters and domes. The Mughals uniquely melded Persian, Indian and provincial styles. Examples include the tomb of Humayun in Delhi (p73), the fort at Agra (p103) and the city of Fatehpur Sikri (p105). Emperor Shah Jahan was

Humayun's tomb (p73), Delhi
HUW JONES / LONELY PLANET IMAGES

Magical Mehndi

Mehndi is the traditional art of painting a woman's hands (and sometimes feet) with intricate henna designs for auspicious ceremonies, such as marriage. If quality henna is used, the design, which is orange-brown, can last up to one month.

In touristy areas, *mehndi*-wallahs are adept at applying henna tattoo 'bands' on the arms, legs and lower back. If you're thinking about getting *mehndi* applied, allow at least a couple of hours for the design process and required drying time (during drying you can't use your hennaed hands). Once applied, henna usually fades faster the more you wash it and apply lotion.

It's always wise to request the artist to do a 'test' spot on your arm before proceeding, as nowadays some dyes contain chemicals that can cause allergies. If good-quality henna is used, you should not feel any pain during or after the procedure.

responsible for some of India's most spectacular architectural creations, most notably the milky-white Taj Mahal (p99).

One of the most striking differences between Hinduism and Islam is religious imagery. While Islamic art eschews any hint of idolatry or portrayal of God, it has evolved a rich heritage of calligraphic and decorative designs. In terms of mosque architecture, the basic design elements are similar worldwide. A large hall is dedicated to communal prayer and within the hall is a mihrab (niche) indicating the direction of Mecca. The faithful are called to prayer from minarets, placed at cardinal points. Delhi's formidable 17th-century Jama Masjid is India's biggest mosque, its courtyard able to hold 25,000 people.

Churches in India reflect the fashions and trends of typically European ecclesiastical architecture with many also incorporating Hindu decorative flourishes. The Portuguese, among others, made impressive attempts to replicate the great churches and cathedrals of their day – Goa (p209) has a particularly rich legacy of ornate examples.

Landscape & Wildlife

Indian elephant, Corbett Tiger Reserve (p357)

HIRA PUNJABI / LONELY PLANET IMAG

India is an incredibly diverse country, with landscapes encompassing everything from steamy jungles and tropical rainforest to arid deserts and the fierce peaks of the Himalaya. Such variety also supports an extraordinary array of wildlife, including elephants, tigers, lions, monkeys, leopards, antelope, rhinos, crocodiles, many different species of reptiles and a kaleidoscopic quantity of birdlife. National parks and wildlife reserves across the country allow you a closer look at many of these creatures.

THE LAND

At 3,287,263 sq km, India is the second-largest Asian country after China, and it forms the vast bulk of the South Asian subcontinent – an ancient block of earth crust that carried a wealth of unique plants and animals like a lifeboat across a prehistoric ocean before slamming into Asia about 40 million years ago.

Plants

Once upon a time India was almost entirely covered in forest; now India's total forest cover is estimated to be around 20%, although the Forest Survey of India has set an optimistic target of 33%. Despite widespread clearing of native habitats, the country still boasts 49,219 plant species, of which some 5200 are endemic. Species on the southern peninsula show Malaysian ancestry, while desert plants in Rajasthan are more clearly allied with the Middle East, and conifer forests of the Himalaya derive from European and Siberian origins.

Environmental Issues

With over a billion people, ever-expanding industrial and urban centres, and an expansive growth in chemical-intensive farming, India's environment is under tremendous threat. An estimated 65% of India's land is degraded in some way, and nearly all of that land is seriously degraded, with the government consistently falling short on most of its environmental protection goals due to lack of enforcement or will power.

ANIMALS

Big sprawling India harbours some of the richest biodiversity in the world, with 397 species of mammals, 1250 bird species, 460 reptile species, 240 species of amphibians and 2546 kinds of fish – among the highest counts for any country in the world. Understandably, wildlife-watching has become one of the country's prime tourist activities and there are hundreds of national parks and wildlife sanctuaries offering opportunities to spot rare and unusual creatures.

The Big Ones

If you had to pick India's top animals, the list would inevitably include tigers, elephants and rhinos, all of which are scarce and in need of stringent protection. It's fortunate that Asian elephants – a somewhat smaller version of the African elephant –

The Best...
Wildlife & Birdwatching Experiences

1 Ranthambhore National Park (p168)

2 Kerala Backwaters (p230)

3 Periyar Wildlife Sanctuary (p249)

4 Sunderbans Tiger Reserve (p311)

5 Jaisalmer Camel Safaris (p187)

IN FOCUS LANDSCAPE & WILDLIFE

Hooray for Project Tiger

When naturalist Jim Corbett first raised the alarm in the 1930s nobody believed that tigers would ever be threatened. At the time it was believed there were 40,000 tigers in India, although nobody had ever conducted a census. Then came Independence, which put guns into the hands of villagers who pushed into formerly off-limits hunting reserves to hunt for highly profitable tiger skins. By the time an official census was conducted in 1972, there were only 1800 tigers left and an international outcry prompted Indira Gandhi to make the tiger the national symbol of India and set up **Project Tiger** (http://projecttiger.nic.in). The project has since established 39 tiger reserves totalling over 32,000 sq km that not only protect this top predator but all animals that live in the same habitats. After an initial round of successes, tiger numbers have recently plummeted from 3600 in 2002 to a new low of 1500 due to relentless poaching, so another $153 million and high-tech equipment have been devoted to the effort to help stop this slide towards extinction.

are revered in Hindu custom or they would have been hunted to extinction long ago, as they were in neighbouring China.

Hoofed & Handed

By far the most abundant forms of wildlife you'll see in India are deer (nine species), antelope (six species), goats and sheep (10 species), and primates (15 species). In the open grasslands of many parks, look for the stocky nilgai, India's largest antelope, or elegantly horned blackbucks. If you're heading for the mountains, keep your eyes open in the Himalaya for blue sheep with their partially curled horns or the rare argali with its fully curled horns that can be found in Ladakh. The deserts of Rajasthan are home to desert-adapted species such as chinkaras (Indian gazelles).

India's primates range from the extremely rare hoolock gibbon and golden langur of the northeast, to species that are so common as to be a pest – most notably the stocky and aggressive rhesus macaque and the elegant grey langur.

Birds

With well over one thousand species of birds, India is a birdwatcher's dream. Winter can be a particularly good time because northern migrants arrive to kick back in the lush subtropical warmth of the Indian peninsula. In the breeding season look for colourful barbets, sunbirds, parakeets and magpies everywhere you travel.

A grey langur, Ranthambhore National Park (p168)
DANIEL BOAG / LONELY PLANET IMAGES ©

Survival
Guide

Vegetable seller at a street bazaar, Mumbai
HUW JONES / LONELY PLANET IMAGES ©

A-Z
Directory

Sample Accommodation Costs

CATEGORY	LEH	RAJASTHAN	TAMIL NADU
budget $	<₹800	<₹1000	<₹1000
midrange $$	₹800-2000	₹1000-5000	₹1000-3000
top end $$$	>₹2000	>₹5000	>₹3000

Accommodation

Accommodation in India ranges from grim hostels to opulent palaces fit for a maharaja. In this guide, we've not included anywhere grim, and listed reviews by author preference. See the Royal Retreats list on www.incredibleindia.org for a list of palaces and forts that offer accommodation for paying guests.

COSTS

Given that the cost of budget, midrange and top-end hotels varies so much across India, it would be misleading of us to provide a 'national' price strategy for each category. The best way to gauge accommodation costs is to go directly to the Fast Facts and the Sleeping sections of this book's regional chapters. Keep in mind that most establishments raise tariffs annually, so the prices may have risen by the time you read this.

PRICE ICONS

The price indicators in this book refer to the cost of a double room, including private bathroom, unless otherwise noted. The sample costs table is based on price indicators for Leh, Tamil Nadu and Rajasthan and gives an example of the difference in accommodation costs across India.

RESERVATIONS

◉ The majority of top-end and some midrange hotels require a deposit at the time of booking, which can usually be done with a credit card.

◉ Some midrange places may ask for a cheque or cash deposit into a bank account to secure a reservation. This is usually more hassle than it's worth.

◉ Some budget options won't take reservations as they don't know when people are going to check out; call ahead to check.

◉ Other places will want a deposit at check-in – ask for a receipt and be wary of any request to sign a blank impression of your credit card. If the hotel insists, consider going to the nearest ATM and paying cash.

◉ Reservations by phone without a deposit are usually fine, but call to confirm the booking the day before you arrive.

SEASONS

◉ Rates in this guide are full price in high season. High season usually coincides with the best weather for the area's sights and activities – normally summertime in the mountains (around June to October), and the cooler months in the plains (around October to mid-February).

◉ In areas popular with foreign tourists there's an additional peak period over Christmas and New Year; make reservations well in advance.

Book Your Stay Online

For more accommodation reviews by Lonely Planet authors, check out hotels.lonelyplanet.com/india. You'll find independent reviews, as well as recommendations on the best places to stay. Best of all, you can book online.

At other times you may find significant discounts; if the hotel seems quiet, ask for one.

Some hotels in places like Goa shut during the monsoon period.

Many temple towns have additional peak seasons around major festivals and pilgrimages; for festival details see the Month by Month chapter and festivals sections of regional chapters.

TAXES & SERVICE CHARGES

- State governments slap a variety of taxes on hotel accommodation (except at the cheaper hotels), and these are added to the cost of your room.

- Taxes vary from state to state and are detailed in the regional chapters.

- Many upmarket hotels also levy an additional 'service charge' (usually around 10%).

- Rates quoted in this book's regional chapters exclude taxes unless otherwise noted.

BUDGET & MIDRANGE HOTELS

- If you're planning on staying in budget places, bring your own sheet or sleeping-bag liner. Sheets and bedcovers at cheap hotels can be stained, well-worn and in need of a wash.

- Sound pollution can be irksome (especially in urban hubs); pack good-quality earplugs and request a room that doesn't face a busy road.

- It's wise to keep your door locked, as some staff (particularly in budget accommodation) may knock

Practicalities

- **Newspapers & Magazines** Major English-language dailies include the *Hindustan Times*, the *Times of India*, *Indian Express*, *Hindu*, *Statesman*, *Telegraph*, *Daily News & Analysis* (*DNA*) and *Economic Times*. Regional English-language and local-vernacular publications are found nationwide. Incisive current-affairs magazines include *Frontline*, *India Today*, the *Week*, *Tehelka* and *Outlook*.

- **Radio** Government-controlled All India Radio (AIR), India's national broadcaster, has over 220 stations broadcasting local and international news. Private FM channels broadcast music, current affairs, talkback and more.

- **Television** The national (government) TV broadcaster is Doordarshan. More people watch satellite and cable TV; English-language channels include BBC, CNN, Star World, HBO and Discovery.

- **Weights & Measures** Officially India is metric. Terms you're likely to hear are lakhs (one lakh = 100,000) and crores (one crore = 10 million).

and automatically walk in without awaiting your permission.

- Blackouts are common (especially during summer and the monsoon) so double-check that the hotel has a backup generator if you're paying for electric 'extras' such as air-conditioners and TVs.

- Note that some hotels lock their doors at night. Members of staff might sleep in the lobby but waking them up can be a challenge. Let the hotel know in advance if you'll be arriving or returning to your room late in the evening.

Activities

India covers every terrain imaginable, from sun-baked deserts and moist rainforests to snow-dusted mountains and plunging ravines. With all this to play with, the opportunities for outdoor activities are endless. Choose from trekking, paragliding, mountaineering, jungle safaris, scuba diving, surfing and elephant rides as well as yoga, meditation and much, much more. See individual listings in each chapter for more information.

Business Hours

- Official business hours are from 9.30am to 5.30pm Monday to Friday but many offices open later and close earlier.

- Most offices have an official lunch hour from around 1pm.

- Bank opening hours vary from town to town so check

Standard Hours

We've only listed business hours where they differ from the following standards.

BUSINESS	OPENING HOURS
Airline offices	9.30am-5.30pm Mon-Sat
Banks	9.30 or 10am-2pm or 4pm Mon-Fri, to noon or 1pm Sat
Government offices	9.30am-1pm & 2-5.30pm Mon-Fri, closed alternate Sat (usually 2nd and 4th)
Post offices	9am-6pm Mon-Fri, to noon Sat
Museums	10am-5pm Tue-Sun
Restaurants	lunch noon-2.30 or 3pm, dinner 7-10 or 11pm
Sights	10am-5pm
Shops	10am-7pm, some closed Sun

Climate

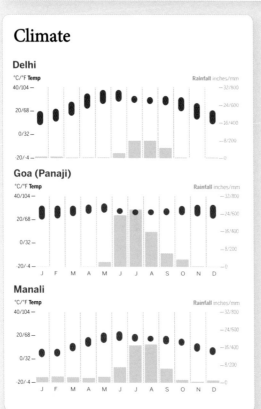

Delhi

Goa (Panaji)

Manali

locally; foreign-exchange offices may open longer and operate daily.

o Some larger post offices have a full day on Saturday and a half-day on Sunday.

o Curfews apply in some areas, notably Kashmir and the Northeast States.

o All timings vary regionally; exceptions are noted in the regional chapters.

Customs Regulations

o Travellers are supposed to declare any amount of cash/travellers cheques over US$5000/10,000 on arrival.

o Indian rupees shouldn't be taken out of India; however, this is rarely policed.

o Officials very occasionally ask tourists to enter expensive items such as video cameras and laptop computers on a 'Tourist Baggage Re-export' form to ensure they're taken out of India at the time of departure.

○ See p12 for information on prohibited exports.

●●●●
Electricity

220V/50Hz

220V/50Hz

220V/50Hz

●●●
Gay & Lesbian Travellers

In July 2009 Delhi's High Court overturned India's 148-year-old antihomosexuality law. Prior to this landmark ruling, homosexual relations for men were illegal, with penalties for transgression theoretically up to life imprisonment (there's no law against lesbian sexual relations).

However, the country remains largely conservative and public displays of affection are generally frowned upon for heterosexual couples as well as gay and lesbian couples.

There are low-key gay scenes in a number of cities including Mumbai, Delhi, Kolkata, Bengaluru and Chandigarh (Gay Pride marches have been held at some of these centres).

PUBLICATIONS

Bombay Dost (www.bombaydost.co.in) GLBTQ magazine in Mumbai.

Time Out Delhi (www.timeoutdelhi.net) Fortnightly listing of gay events in Delhi.

Time Out Mumbai (www.timeoutmumbai.net) Gay events in Mumbai.

WEBSITES

Delhi Frontrunners & Walkers (www.delhi frontrunners.org) Weekly running and walking club for Delhi's LGBT crowd.

Gay Bombay (www.gaybombay.org) Lists gay events as well as offering support and advice.

Gay Delhi (gaydelhi-subscribe@ yahoogroups.com) Send a blank email to join and tap into the capital's gay scene.

Indian Dost (www.indiandost.com/gay .php) News and information including contact groups in India.

Indja Pink (www.indjapink.co.in) India's first 'gay travel boutique' founded by a well-known Indian fashion designer. A number of Indian cities have support groups, including the following:

CHENNAI

Shakti Center (☏ 044-45587071; www.shakticenter .org) A collective of LGBT activists and artists, which holds workshops, exhibitions and other activities.

DELHI

Nigah (http://nigahdelhi .blogspot.com) Autonomous collective that holds monthly queer events and organises the annual **Nigah Queerfest** (www.thequeerfest.com).

KOLKATA

Counsel Club (counselclub93@hotmail .com) Support group for gays, lesbians, transgenders and bisexuals and arranges monthly meetings. The affiliated **Palm Avenue**

Integration Society offers health advice.

Sappho (www.sapphokolkata .org) operates as a support group for lesbian, bisexual and transgender women.

MUMBAI

Humsafar Trust (☎ 022-26673800; www.humsafar.org) Runs gay and transgender support groups and advocacy programs. The drop-in centre in Santa Cruz East hosts workshops and has a library – pick up a copy of the pioneering gay-and-lesbian magazine *Bombay Dost*. It's also one of the venues for 'Sunday High', a monthly screening of queer-interest films.

Health

India's huge geographical variation can present environmental issues that cause health problems, and hygiene is poor in most regions, so food and water-borne illnesses are common. Insect-borne diseases are present in tropical areas. Medical care is basic in many areas (especially beyond the larger cities) so it's essential to be well prepared.

Becoming ill in some way is very common, but fortunately most travellers' illnesses can be prevented with some common-sense behaviour or treated with a well-stocked medical kit. However, never hesitate to consult a doctor while on the road: self-diagnosis can be hazardous.

INSURANCE

Don't travel without health insurance. Emergency evacuation is expensive – bills of over US$100,000 are not uncommon. Consider the following when buying insurance:

o You may require extra cover for adventure activities such as rock climbing and scuba diving.

o In India, doctors usually require immediate payment in cash. If you do have to claim later, make sure you keep all relevant documentation.

MEDICAL CARE

Medical care is hugely variable in India. Some cities now have clinics catering specifically to travellers and expatriates; they're usually more expensive than local medical facilities and offer a higher standard of care. They also know the local system, including reputable local hospitals and specialists, and can liaise with insurance companies should you require evacuation. It's usually difficult to find reliable medical care in rural areas.

INFECTIOUS DISEASES
MALARIA

This is a serious and potentially deadly disease, caused by a parasite transmitted by the bite of an infected mosquito. Before you travel, seek expert advice according to your itinerary (rural areas are especially risky) and on medication and side effects.

The most important symptom of malaria is fever, but general symptoms, such as headache, diarrhoea,

cough or chills, may also occur. Diagnosis can only be properly made by taking a blood sample.

To prevent malaria, you need to avoid mosquito bites *and* take antimalarial medications. Most people who catch malaria are taking inadequate or no antimalaria medication.

To prevent mosquito bites

o Use a DEET-containing insect repellent on exposed skin. Wash this off at night, as long as you are sleeping under a mosquito net. Natural repellents such as citronella can be effective, but must be applied more frequently than products containing DEET.

o Sleep under a mosquito net impregnated with pyrethrin.

o Choose accommodation with proper screens and fans (if not air-conditioned).

o Impregnate clothing with pyrethrin in high-risk areas.

o Wear long sleeves and trousers in light colours.

o Use mosquito coils.

o Spray your room with insect repellent before going out for dinner.

OTHER DISEASES

Dengue Fever This mosquito-borne disease is becoming increasingly problematic, especially in cities. There's no vaccine available, so it can be prevented only by avoiding mosquito bites at all times. Symptoms include high fever, severe headache and body ache, and sometimes a rash and diarrhoea. Treatment is rest and paracetamol – do not take aspirin or ibuprofen

Vaccinations

The only vaccine required by international regulations is **yellow fever**. Proof of vaccination will only be required if you have visited a country in the yellow-fever zone within the six days prior to entering India.

The World Health Organization (WHO) recommends the following vaccinations for travellers going to India (as well as being up to date with measles, mumps and rubella vaccinations):

o **Adult diphtheria & tetanus** Single booster recommended if none in the previous 10 years. Side effects include sore arm and fever.

o **Hepatitis A** Provides almost 100% protection for up to a year; a booster after 12 months provides at least another 20 years' protection. Mild side effects such as headache and sore arm occur in 5% to 10% of people.

o **Hepatitis B** Now considered routine for most travellers. Given as three shots over six months. A rapid schedule is also available, as is a combined vaccination with Hepatitis A. Side effects are mild and uncommon, usually headache and sore arm. In 95% of people lifetime protection results.

o **Typhoid** Recommended for all travellers to India, even those only visiting urban areas. The vaccine offers around 70% protection, lasts for two to three years and comes as a single shot. Tablets are also available, but the injection is usually recommended as it has fewer side effects. Sore arm and fever may occur.

o **Varicella** If you haven't had chicken pox, discuss this vaccination with your doctor.

as it increases the likelihood of haemorrhaging. Make sure you see a doctor to be diagnosed and monitored.

Hepatitis A This food- and water-borne virus infects the liver, causing jaundice (yellow skin and eyes), nausea and lethargy. There is no specific treatment for hepatitis A; the liver simply needs time to heal. All travellers to India should be vaccinated against hepatitis A.

Hepatitis B This sexually transmitted disease is spread by body fluids and can be prevented by vaccination. The long-term consequences can include liver cancer and cirrhosis.

Hepatitis E Transmitted through contaminated food

and water, hepatitis E has similar symptoms to hepatitis A, but is far less common. It is a severe problem in pregnant women and can result in the death of both mother and baby. There is no commercially available vaccine, and prevention is by following safe eating and drinking guidelines.

OTHER HAZARDS

Traveller's Diarrhoea By far the most common problem affecting travellers in India. Treatment consists of staying well hydrated; rehydration solutions like Gastrolyte are the best for this. Antibiotics such as ciprofloxacin or azithromycin should kill the bacteria quickly. Seek medical attention quickly if you do not respond to

an appropriate antibiotic. Loperamide is just a 'stopper' and doesn't get to the cause of the problem. It can be helpful, though (eg for long bus rides). Don't take loperamide if you have a fever or blood in your stools.

Giardiasis Giardia is a parasite that is relatively common in travellers. Symptoms include nausea, bloating, excess gas, fatigue and intermittent diarrhoea. The parasite will eventually go away if left untreated but this can take months; the best advice is to seek medical treatment. The treatment of choice is tinidazole, with metronidazole being a second-line option.

FOOD

Eating in restaurants is a big risk for contracting diarrhoea. Ways to avoid it include:

- eat only freshly cooked food
- avoid shellfish and buffets
- peel fruit
- cook vegetables
- eat in busy restaurants with a high turnover of customers.

HEAT

Many parts of India, especially down south, are hot and humid throughout the year. For people not accustomed to this climate, swelling of the feet and ankles is common, as are muscle cramps caused by excessive sweating. Prevent these by avoiding dehydration and excessive activity in the heat. Don't eat salt tablets (they aggravate the gut); drinking rehydration solution or eating salty food helps. Treat cramps by resting, rehydrating with double-strength rehydration solution and gently stretching.

Dehydration is the main contributor to heat exhaustion. Recovery is usually rapid and it is common to feel weak for some days afterwards. Symptoms include:

- feeling weak
- headache
- irritability
- nausea or vomiting
- sweaty skin
- a fast, weak pulse
- normal or slightly elevated body temperature.

Treatment for dehydration:
- get out of the heat
- fan the sufferer
- apply cool, wet cloths to the skin
- lay the sufferer flat with their legs raised
- rehydrate with water containing one-quarter of a teaspoon of salt per litre.

Heat stroke is a serious medical emergency. Symptoms include:

- weakness
- nausea
- a hot dry body
- temperature of over 41°C
- dizziness
- confusion
- loss of coordination
- seizures
- eventual collapse.

Treatment for heat stroke:
- get out of the heat
- fan the sufferer
- apply cool, wet cloths to the skin or ice to the body, especially to the groin and armpits.

Prickly heat is a common skin rash in the tropics, caused by sweat trapped under the skin. Treat it by moving out of the heat for a few hours and by having cool showers. Creams and ointments clog the skin so they should be avoided. Locally bought prickly-heat powder can be helpful.

Insurance

- Comprehensive travel insurance to cover theft, loss and medical problems (as well as air evacuation) is strongly recommended.

- Some policies specifically exclude potentially dangerous activities such as scuba diving, skiing, motorcycling, paragliding and even trekking: read the fine print.

Drinking Water

- Never drink tap water.

- Bottled water is generally safe – check that the seal is intact at purchase.

- Avoid ice unless you know it has been safely made.

- Be particularly careful of fresh juices served at street stalls – they may have been watered down or be served in unhygienic jugs/glasses.

- Boiling water is usually the most efficient method of purifying it.

- The best chemical purifier is iodine. It should not be used by pregnant women or those with thyroid problems.

- Water filters should also filter out viruses. Ensure your filter has a chemical barrier such as iodine and a small pore size (less than four microns).

- Some trekking agents may only accept customers who have cover for emergency helicopter evacuation.

- If you plan to hire a motorcycle in India, make sure the rental policy includes at least third-party insurance.

- Check in advance whether your insurance policy will pay doctors and hospitals directly or reimburse you later for overseas health expenditure (keep all documentation for your claim).

- It's crucial to get a police report in India if you've had anything stolen; insurance companies may refuse to reimburse you without one.

- Worldwide travel insurance is available at www .lonelyplanet.com/travel_ services. You can buy, extend and claim online anytime – even if you're already on the road.

⚫⚫⚫

Internet Access

Internet cafes are widespread and connections are usually reasonably fast, except in more remote areas. Wireless (wi-fi) access is available in an increasing number of hotels and some coffee shops in larger cities. In this book, hotels offering internet access are marked by @.

PRACTICALITIES

- Internet charges vary by area (see regional chapters); charges fall anywhere between ₹15 and ₹90 per hour and often with a 15- to 30-minute minimum.

- Power cuts are not uncommon; avoid losing your email by writing and saving messages in a text application before pasting them into your browser.

- Bandwidth load tends to be lowest in the early morning and early afternoon.

- Some internet cafes may ask to see your passport; carrying photocopies of the relevant pages (information and visa) saves you having to dig your passport out each time.

- See the 'Need to Know' section of each destination chapter for useful India-specific web resources.

SECURITY

- Be wary of sending sensitive financial information from internet cafes; some places are able to use keystroke-capturing technology to access passwords and emails.

- Avoid sending credit-card details or other personal data over a wireless connection; using online banking on any nonsecure system is generally unwise.

LAPTOPS

- Many internet cafes can supply laptop users with internet access over a LAN Ethernet cable; alternatively join an international roaming service with an Indian dial-up number, or take out an account with a local Internet Service Provider (ISP).

- Make sure your modem is compatible with the telephone and dial-up system in India (an external global modem may be necessary).

- Companies including Reliance, Airtel and Vodafone offer 3G Data Cards, which can be plugged into the USB port of your laptop and will allow you to access the internet.

  - Tariffs start from ₹800 per month for 3 GB up to ₹1500 per month for 15 GB.

  - Make sure you check whether the area you're travelling to is covered by your service provider.

- Consider purchasing a fuse-protected universal AC adaptor to protect your circuit board from power surges.

- Plug adaptors are widely available throughout India, but bring spare plug fuses from home.

⚫⚫⚫

Legal Matters

If you're in a sticky legal situation, contact your embassy as quickly as possible. However, be aware that all your embassy may be able to do is monitor your treatment in custody and arrange a lawyer. In the Indian justice system, the burden of proof can often be on the accused and stints in prison before trial are not unheard of.

ANTISOCIAL BEHAVIOUR

- Smoking in public places is illegal throughout India but this is very rarely enforced; if caught you'll be fined ₹200.

- People can smoke inside their homes and in most open spaces such as streets (heed any signs stating otherwise).

o A number of Indian cities have banned spitting and littering, but this is also variably enforced.

DRUGS

o Indian law does not distinguish between 'hard' and 'soft' drugs; possession of any illegal drug is regarded as a criminal offence.

o If convicted, the *minimum* sentence is 10 years, with very little chance of remission or parole.

o Cases can take months, even several years, to appear before a court while the accused may have to wait in prison. There's also usually a hefty monetary fine on top of any custodial sentence.

o Marijuana grows wild in various parts of India, but consuming it is still an offence, except in towns where bhang is legally sold for religious rituals.

o Police are getting particularly tough on foreigners who use drugs, so you should take this risk very seriously.

POLICE

o You should always carry your passport; police are entitled to ask you for identification at any time.

o If you're arrested for an alleged offence and asked for a bribe, the prevailing wisdom is to pay it as the alternative may be a trumped-up charge; there are no 'rules' guiding how much you should pay.

o Corruption is rife so the less you have to do with local police the better; try to avoid all potentially risky situations.

Money

The Indian rupee (₹) is divided into 100 paise (p) coins, which are becoming increasingly rare. Coins come in denominations of ₹1, ₹2 and ₹5; notes come in ₹5, ₹10, ₹20, ₹50, ₹100, ₹500 and ₹1000 (this last is handy for paying large bills but can pose problems in getting change for small services). The Indian rupee is linked to a basket of currencies and has been subject to fluctuations in recent years; see p49 for exchange rates.

ATMS

o ATMs are found in most urban centres.

o Visa, MasterCard, Cirrus, Maestro and Plus are the most commonly accepted cards.

o The ATMs listed in this book's regional chapters accept foreign cards (but not necessarily all types of cards).

o Banks in India that accept foreign cards include Citibank, HDFC, ICICI, HSBC and the State Bank of India.

o Before your trip, check whether your card can reliably access banking networks in India and ask for details of charges.

o Notify your bank that you'll be using your card in India (provide dates) to avoid having your card blocked; take along your bank's phone number in case.

o Always keep the emergency lost-and-stolen numbers for your credit cards in a safe place, separate from your cards, and report any loss or theft immediately.

o Away from major towns, always carry cash or travellers cheques as back-up.

BLACK MARKET

o Black-market moneychangers exist but legal moneychangers are so common that there's no reason to use them, except perhaps to change small amounts of cash at land border crossings. If someone approaches you on the street and offers to change money, you're probably being set up for a scam.

CASH

o Major currencies such as US dollars, British pounds and euros are easy to change throughout India, although some bank branches insist on travellers cheques only.

o Some banks also accept other currencies such as Australian and Canadian dollars, and Swiss francs.

o Private moneychangers deal with a wider range of currencies, but Pakistani, Nepali and Bangladeshi currency can be harder to change away from the border.

o When travelling off the beaten track, always carry an adequate stock of rupees.

o Whenever changing money, check every note. Don't accept any filthy, ripped or disintegrating notes, as these may be difficult to use.

o It can be tough getting change in India so keep a stock of smaller currency; ₹10, ₹20 and ₹50 notes are helpful.

o Officially you cannot take rupees out of India, but this is laxly enforced. You can change ny leftover rupees back into foreign currency, most easily at the airport (some banks have ₹1000 minimum). You may have to present encashment certificates or credit-card/ATM receipts, and show your passport and airline ticket.

CREDIT CARDS

o Credit cards are accepted at a growing number of shops, upmarket restaurants, and midrange and top-end hotels, and they can usually be used to pay for flights and train tickets.

o Cash advances on major credit cards are also possible at some banks.

o MasterCard and Visa are the most widely accepted cards.

ENCASHMENT CERTIFICATES

o Indian law states that all foreign currency must be changed at official moneychangers or banks.

o For every (official) foreign-exchange transaction, you'll receive an encashment certificate (receipt), which will allow you to change rupees back into foreign currency when departing India.

o Encashment certificates should cover the amount of rupees you intend to change back to foreign currency.

o Printed receipts from ATMs are also accepted as evidence of an international transaction at most banks.

INTERNATIONAL TRANSFERS

o If you run out of money, someone back home can wire you cash via moneychangers affiliated with **Moneygram** (www.moneygram.com) or **Western Union** (www .westernunion.com). A fee is added to the transaction.

o To collect cash, bring your passport and the name and reference number of the person who sent the funds.

MONEYCHANGERS

o Private moneychangers are usually open for longer hours than banks, and are found almost everywhere (many also double as internet cafes and travel agents).

o Upmarket hotels may also change money, but their rates are usually not as competitive.

TIPPING, BAKSHEESH & BARGAINING

o In tourist restaurants or hotels, a service fee is usually already added to your bill and tipping is optional. Elsewhere, a tip is appreciated.

The Art of Haggling

Government emporiums, fair-trade cooperatives, department stores and modern shopping centres in India almost always charge fixed prices. Anywhere else, you'll need to bargain. Shopkeepers in tourist hubs are accustomed to travellers who have lots of money and little time to spend it, so you can often expect to be charged double or triple the 'real' price (souvenir shops are the most notorious for this).

The first rule of haggling is to never show too much interest in the item you've got your heart set upon. Also, resist buying the first thing that takes your fancy. Wander around and price items at different shops, but don't make it too obvious – if you return to the first shop the vendor will know it's because they're the cheapest, resulting in less haggling leeway for you.

Decide how much you'd be happy to pay, and then express a *casual* interest in buying. If you have absolutely no idea of what something should really cost, start by slashing the price by half. The vendor will (most likely) look utterly aghast, but you can now work up and down respectively in small increments until you reach a mutually agreeable price. You'll find that many shopkeepers will lower their 'final price' once you start to leave and say you'll 'think about it'. If a vendor seems to be charging an unreasonably high price, simply look elsewhere.

Haggling is a way of life in India and is usually taken in good spirit – it should never turn ugly. Remember to always keep in mind exactly how much a rupee is worth in your home currency to put things in perspective.

● Hotel bellboys and train/airport porters appreciate anything around ₹50; hotel staff should be given similar gratuities for services above and beyond the call of duty.

● It's not mandatory to tip taxi or rickshaw drivers, but it's good to tip drivers who are honest about the fare.

● If you hire a car with driver for more than a couple of days, a tip is recommended for good service (see p19).

● Baksheesh can loosely be defined as a 'tip'; it covers everything from alms for beggars to bribes.

● Many Indians implore tourists not to hand out sweets, pens or money to children, as it encourages them to beg. To make a lasting difference, donate to a reputable school or charitable organisation.

● Except in fixed-price shops (such as government emporiums and fair-trade cooperatives), bargaining is the norm.

TRAVELLERS CHEQUES

● All major brands are accepted, but some banks may only accept cheques from American Express (Amex) and Thomas Cook.

● Pounds sterling and US dollars are the safest currencies, especially in smaller towns.

● Keep a record of the cheques' serial numbers separate from your cheques, along with the proof-of-purchase slips, encashment vouchers and photocopied passport details. If you lose your cheques, contact the American Express or Thomas Cook office in Delhi.

● To replace lost travellers cheques, you need the proof-of-purchase slip and the numbers of the missing cheques (some places require a photocopy of the police report and a passport photo). If you don't have the numbers of your missing cheques, the issuing company (eg Amex) will contact the place where you bought them.

Public Holidays

There are officially three national public holidays. Every state celebrates its own officia holidays, which cover bank hol idays for government workers as well as major religious festi vals. Most businesses (offices, shops etc) and tourist sites close on public holidays, but transport is usually unaffected It's wise to make transport

Prohibited Exports

To protect India's cultural heritage, the export of certain **antiques** is prohibited. Many 'old' objects are fine, but the difficulties begin if something is verifiably more than 100 years old. Reputable antique dealers know the laws and can make arrangements for an export-clearance certificate for any old items that you're permitted to export. If in doubt, contact Delhi's **Archaeological Survey of India** (☏ 011-23010822; www.asi.nic.in; Janpath; ◷ 9.30am-1pm & 2-6pm Mon-Fri) next to the National Museum. The rules may seem stringent but the loss of artworks and traditional buildings in places such as Ladakh, Himachal Pradesh, Gujarat and Rajasthan, due to the international trade in antiques and carved windows and doorframes, has been alarming. Look for quality reproductions instead.

The Indian Wildlife Protection Act bans any form of **wildlife trade**. Don't buy any products that endanger threatened species and habitats – doing so can result in heavy fines and even imprisonment. This includes ivory, shahtoosh shawls (made from the down of chirus, rare Tibetan antelopes), and anything made from the fur, skin, horns or shell of any endangered species. Products made from certain rare plants are also banned.

Note that your home country may have additional laws forbidding the import of restricted items and wildlife parts. The penalties can be severe, so know the law before you buy.

...nd hotel reservations well in ...dvance if you intend visiting ...uring major festivals.

PUBLIC HOLIDAYS

Republic Day 26 January

Independence Day 15 August

Gandhi Jayanti 2 October

MAJOR RELIGIOUS FESTIVALS

Mahavir Jayanti (Jain) February

Holi (Hindu) March

Easter (Christian) March/ April

Buddha Jayanti (Buddhist) April/May

Eid al-Fitr (Muslim) August/ September

Dussehra (Hindu) October

Diwali (Hindu) October/ November

Nanak Jayanti (Sikh) November

Christmas (Christian) 25 December

● ● ●

Safe Travel

Travellers to India's major cities may fall prey to petty and opportunistic crime but most problems can be avoided with a bit of common sense and an appropriate amount of caution; see the text on p49, p89, p163, p322 and p378 for more information. Also have a look at the India branch of Lonely Planet's **Thorn Tree Travel**

Forum (www .lonelyplanet.com/thorntree), where travellers often post timely warnings about problems they've encountered on the road. Always check your government's travel advisory warnings.

REBEL VIOLENCE

India has a number of (sometimes armed) dissident groups championing various causes, who have employed the same tried-and-tested techniques of rebel groups everywhere: assassinations and bomb attacks on government infrastructure, public transport, religious centres, tourist sites and markets. For further information read p393.

● Certain areas, including Kashmir, are particularly prone to insurgent violence.

● Curfews and strikes can close the roads (as well as banks, shops etc) for days on end in sensitive regions like Kashmir.

● International terrorism is as much of a risk in Europe or America, so this is no reason not to go to India, but it makes sense to check the local security situation carefully before travelling (especially in high-risk areas).

● ● ●

Telephone

● There are few payphones in India (apart from in airports), but private PCO/STD/ISD call booths do the same job, offering inexpensive local, interstate and international calls at lower prices than calls made from hotel rooms.

● These booths are found around the country. A digital meter displays how much the call is costing and usually provides a printed receipt when the call is finished.

● Costs vary depending on the operator and destination but can be from ₹1 per minute for local calls and between ₹5 and ₹10 for international calls.

● Some booths also offer a 'call-back' service – you ring home, provide the phone number of the booth and wait for people at home to call you back, for a fee of around ₹10 on top of the cost of the preliminary call.

● Getting a line can be difficult in remote country and mountain areas – an engaged signal may just mean that the exchange is overloaded, so keep trying.

● Useful online resources include the **Yellow Pages** (www.indiayellowpages.com) and **Justdial** (www.justdial .com).

MOBILE PHONES

● Indian mobile phone numbers usually have 10 digits, typically beginning with ☎9.

● There's roaming coverage for international GSM phones in most cities and large towns.

● To avoid expensive roaming costs (often highest for incoming calls), get hooked up to the local mobile-phone network.

● Mobiles bought in some countries may be locked to a particular network; you'll have to get the phone unlocked, or buy a local phone (available from ₹2000) to use an Indian SIM card.

437

Important Numbers

From outside India, dial your international access code, India's country code then the number (minus '0', which is used when dialling domestically).

Country code	91
International access code	00
Ambulance	102
Fire	101
Police	100

GETTING CONNECTED

❍ Getting connected is inexpensive but increasingly complicated, owing to security concerns, and involves a lot of paperwork.

❍ Foreigners must supply between one and five passport photos, their passport, and photocopies of their passport identity and visa pages.

❍ You must also supply a residential address, which can be the address of the hotel where you're staying (ask the hotel to write a letter confirming this).

❍ Some phone companies send representatives to the listed address, or at the very least call to verify that you are actually staying there.

❍ Some travellers have reported their SIM card being suspended once the phone company realised that they had moved on from the hotel where they registered their phone. Others have been luckier and used the same SIM card throughout their travels.

❍ Another option is to get a friendly local to register the phone using their local ID.

❍ Prepaid mobile-phone kits (SIM card and phone number, plus an allocation of calls) are available in most Indian towns from around ₹200 from a phone shop or local PCO/STD/ISD booth, internet cafe or grocery store.

❍ You must then purchase new credits on that network, sold as scratch cards in shops and call centres.

❍ Credit must usually be used within a set time limit and costs vary with the amount of credit on the card.

❍ The amount you pay for a credit top-up is not the amount you get on your phone – state taxes and service charges come off first.

❍ For some networks, recharge cards are being replaced by direct credit: you pay the vendor and the credit is deposited straight to your phone. Ask which system is in use before you buy.

CHARGES

❍ Calls made within the state or city in which you bought the SIM card are cheap – ₹1 per minute – and you can call internationally for less than ₹10 per minute.

❍ SMS messaging is even cheaper – usually, the more credit you have on your phone, the cheaper the call rate.

❍ The most popular (and reliable) companies include Airtel, Vodafone and BSNL.

❍ Most SIM cards are state-specific; they can be used in other states, but you pay for calls at roaming rates and you'll be charged for incoming as well as outgoing calls.

❍ If you buy a SIM card in Delhi, calls to anywhere outside Delhi will be around ₹1.50 per minute, while the charge to receive a call from anywhere in India (outside of Delhi) is ₹1 per minute.

❍ Unreliable signals and problems with international texting (messages or replies being delayed or failing to get through) are not uncommon.

❍ As the mobile-phone industry continues to evolve, mobile rates, suppliers and coverage are all likely to develop during the life of this book.

JAMMU & KASHMIR

❍ Due to ongoing terrorist threats, mobile phone use in Jammu & Kashmir is more strictly controlled.

❍ Roaming on foreign mobiles won't work here, nor will pay-as-you-go SIM cards purchased elsewhere in India (post-paid ones will, if you're an Indian resident).

❍ To purchase a SIM card you'll need a photocopy of your passport and visa, four or five passport photos and a reference from a local who has known you for at least one month.

❍ You may be able to tip a local to apply for a SIM in their name and sell it on to you – although they will need all the photos and ID documents too.

o An additional stumbling block is that your ID is supposed to provide proof of your father's name – if this detail isn't in your passport (as is the case for many Western nationals) you might not get the SIM at all.

o During times of tension you will not be able to send or receive SMS text messages.

PHONE CODES

o Calling India from abroad: dial your country's international access code, then 📞91 (India's country code), then the area code (without the initial zero), then the local number.

o Calling internationally from India: dial 📞00 (the international access code), then the country code of the country you're calling, then the area code (without the initial zero if there is one) and the local number.

o Phone numbers have an area code followed by up to eight digits.

o Toll-free numbers begin with 📞1800.

o The government is slowly trying to bring all numbers in India onto the same system, so area codes may change and new digits may be added to numbers with limited warning.

Time

India uses the 12-hour clock and the local standard time is known as IST (Indian Standard Time). IST is 5½ hours ahead of GMT/UTC. The floating half-hour was added to maximise daylight hours over such a vast country.

CITY	NOON IN DELHI
Beijing	2.30pm
Dhaka	12.30pm
Islamabad	11.30am
Kathmandu	12.15pm
London	6.30am
New York	1.30am
San Francisco	10.30pm
Sydney	4.30pm
Tokyo	3.30pm

Tourist Information

In addition to the Government of India tourist offices (also known as 'India Tourism'), each state maintains its own network of tourist offices. These vary in their efficiency and usefulness – some are run by enthusiastic souls who go out of their way to help, others are little more than a means of drumming up business for State Tourism Development Corporation tours. Most of the tourist offices have free brochures and often a free (or inexpensive) local map.

The first stop for information should be the tourism website of the Government of India, **Incredible India** (www .incredibleindia.org); for details of its regional offices around India, click on the 'Help Desk' tab at the top of the homepage.

See regional chapters for contact details of relevant tourist offices.

Travellers with Disabilities

India's crowded public transport, crush of humanity and variable infrastructure can test even the hardiest able-bodied traveller. If you have a physical disability or you are vision impaired, these can pose even more of a challenge. If your mobility is considerably restricted you may like to ease the stress by travelling with an able-bodied companion.

Accommodation Wheelchair-friendly hotels are almost exclusively top end. Make pre-trip enquiries and book ground-floor rooms at hotels that lack adequate facilities.

Accessibility Some restaurants and offices have ramps but most tend to have at least one step. Staircases are often steep; lifts frequently stop at mezzanines between floors.

Footpaths Where pavements exist, they can be riddled with holes, littered with debris and packed with pedestrians. If using crutches, bring along spare rubber caps.

Transport Hiring a car with driver will make moving around a lot easier (see p19); if you use a wheelchair, make sure the car-hire company can provide an appropriate vehicle to carry it.

For further advice pertaining to your specific requirements, consult your doctor before heading to India.

The following organisations may be able to offer further information or at least point you in the right direction.

Mobility International USA (MIUSA; www.miusa.org)

Access-Able Travel Source (www.access-able.com)

Global Access News (www.globalaccessnews.com)

Royal Association for Disability & Rehabilitation (RADAR; www.radar.org.uk)

Accessible Journeys (www.disabilitytravel.com)

Visas

A pilot scheme is currently in place to provide visas on arrival to nationals of Japan, New Zealand, Singapore, Luxembourg and Finland at Mumbai, Chennai, Kolkata and New Delhi airports. This scheme has been introduced on a one year 'experimental' basis, so double-check before you fly. All other nationals – except those from Nepal and Bhutan – must get a visa *before* arriving in India. These are available at Indian missions worldwide. Note that your passport needs to be valid for at least six months beyond your intended stay in India, with at least two blank pages.

ENTRY REQUIREMENTS

○ In 2009 a large number of foreigners were found to be working in India on tourist visas, so regulations surrounding who can get a visa and for how long have been tightened. These rules are likely to change, however, so double-check with the Indian embassy in your country prior to travel.

○ Most people travel on the standard six-month tourist visa.

○ Student and business visas have strict conditions (consult the Indian embassy for details).

○ Tourist visas are valid from the date of issue, not the date you arrive in India. You can spend a total of 180 days in the country.

○ An onward travel ticket is a requirement for most visas, but this isn't always enforced (check in advance).

○ Additional restrictions apply to travellers from Bangladesh and Pakistan, as well as certain Eastern European, African and Central Asian countries. Check any special conditions for your nationality with the Indian embassy in your country.

○ Visas are priced in the local currency and may have an added service fee (contact your country's Indian embassy for current prices).

RE-ENTRY REQUIREMENTS

○ Current regulations dictate that, when you leave the country, you will receive a stamp in your passport indicating you may not re-enter India for two months, regardless of how much longer your visa is valid for.

○ If you wish to return to India before the two-month period has passed, you will have to visit the Indian High Commission or Consulate in the country you are in, or where you are a resident, and apply for a Permit to Re-enter. This permit is only granted in urgent or extreme cases.

○ If you're travelling to multiple countries, a permit is not needed as long as your trip follows an itinerary, which you can show at immigration (eg if you're transiting through India on your way home from Nepal).

○ If granted a permit, you must register with the Foreigners Registration Office (FRO) within 14 days.

Transport

Getting There & Away

Getting to India is increasingly easy, with plenty of international airlines servicing the country. Flights, tours and other tickets may also be booked online at www.lonely planet.com/bookings.

ENTERING INDIA

Entering India by air or land is relatively straightforward, with standard immigration and customs procedures (p3).

PASSPORT

To enter India you need a valid passport, visa (p16) and an onward/return ticket. Your assport should be valid for at least six months beyond our intended stay in India. If our passport is lost or stolen, immediately contact your country's embassy or consulate. Keep photocopies of your airline ticket and the identity and visa pages of your passport in case of emergency. Better yet, scan and email copies to yourself. Check with the Indian embassy in your home country for any special conditions that may exist for your nationality.

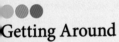

✈ AIR

AIRPORTS & AIRLINES

India's national carrier is **Air India** (www.airindia.com), of which the former state-owned domestic carrier, Indian Airlines, is now a part, following a merger deal. Air India has had a relatively decent air safety record in recent years.

Getting Around

✈ AIR

AIRLINES IN INDIA

India has a very competitive domestic airline industry. Some well-established players are Air India (which now includes Indian Airlines), Kingfisher and Jet Airways. Hosts of budget airlines offer discounted fares on various domestic sectors. Airline seats can be booked directly by telephone, through travel agencies or cheaply over the internet. Domestic airlines set rupee fares for Indian citizens, while foreigners may be charged US dollar fares (usually payable in rupees).

At the time of writing, the following airlines were operating across various destinations in India – see regional chapters for specifics about routes, fares and booking offices. Keep in mind, however, that the competitive nature of the aviation industry means that fares fluctuate dramatically. Holidays, festivals and seasons also have a serious effect on ticket prices so check for the latest fares online.

Air India (☎ 1800 1801407; www.airindia.com) India's national carrier operates many domestic and international flights.

GoAir (☎ 1800 222111; www.goair.in) Reliable low-cost carrier servicing Goa, Cochin, Jaipur, Delhi and Bagdogra among other destinations.

IndiGo (☎ 1800 1803838; www.goindigo.in) Good, reliable budget airline flying to numerous cities including Kolkata, Mumbai, Delhi and Chennai.

Jagson Airlines (☎ 011-23721593; www.jagsonairline.com) Among other destinations, it uses tiny Dornier planes to access small runways in Himachal Pradesh.

Jet Airways (☎ 011-39893333; www.jetairways.com) Rated by many as India's best airline, with growing domestic and international services.

JetLite (☎ 1800 223020; www.jetlite.com) Jet Airways' budget carrier flies to

numerous destinations including Amritsar, Dehradun, Chennai and Jodhpur.

Kingfisher Airlines (☎ 1800 2093030; www.flykingfisher.com) Domestic and international flights.

Kingfisher Red (☎ 1800 2093030; www.flykingfisher.com) Kingfisher Airlines' low-cost option.

Spicejet (☎ 1800 1803333; www.spicejet.com) Budget carrier whose destinations include Bengaluru (Bangalore), Varanasi, Srinagar, Colombo (Sri Lanka) and Kathmandu (Nepal).

Climate Change & Travel

Every form of transport that relies on carbon-based fuel generates CO2, the main cause of human-induced climate change. Modern travel is dependent on aeroplanes, which might use less fuel per kilometre per person than most cars but travel much greater distances. The altitude at which aircraft emit gases (including CO2) and particles also contributes to their climate change impact. Many websites offer 'carbon calculators' that allow people to estimate the carbon emissions generated by their journey and, for those who wish to do so, to offset the impact of the greenhouse gases emitted with contributions to portfolios of climate-friendly initiatives throughout the world. Lonely Planet offsets the carbon footprint of all staff and author travel.

Prepaid Taxis

Most Indian airports and many train stations have a prepaid-taxi booth, normally just outside the terminal building. Here, you can book a taxi for a fixed price (which will include baggage) and thus avoid commission scams. However, officials advise holding onto the payment coupon until you reach your chosen destination, in case the driver has any other ideas! Smaller airports and stations may have prepaid autorickshaw booths instead.

Security at airports is generally stringent. All hold baggage must be x-rayed prior to check-in and every item of cabin baggage needs a label, which must be stamped as part of the security check (don't forget to collect tags at the check-in counter). Flights to sensitive destinations, such as Kashmir and Ladakh, have extra security restrictions: cabin baggage may be completely prohibited and batteries usually need to be removed from all electronic items and placed in the hold. You may also need to identify your bags on the tarmac before they are loaded on the plane.

The recommended check-in time for domestic flights is one hour before departure.

The usual baggage allowance is 20kg (10kg for smaller aircraft) in economy class, and 30kg in business.

🚌 BUS

o Buses go almost everywhere in India and are the only way to get around many mountainous areas. They tend to be the cheapest way to travel; services are fast and frequent.

o Roads in curvaceous terrain can be especially perilous; buses are often driven with wilful abandon, and accidents are always a risk.

o Avoid night buses unless there's no alternative: driving conditions are more hazardous and drivers may be suffering from lack of sleep.

CLASSES

o State-owned and private bus companies both offer 'ordinary' and more expensive 'deluxe' buses. Many state tourist offices run their own reliable deluxe bus services.

o 'Ordinary' buses tend to be ageing rattletraps while 'deluxe' buses range from less decrepit versions of ordinary buses to flashy Volvo buses with AC and reclining two-by-two seating.

o Buses run by the state government are usually the more reliable option (if there's a breakdown, another bus will be sent to pick up passengers), and seats can usually be booked up to a month in advance.

o Private buses are either more expensive (but more comfortable), or cheaper but with kamikaze drivers and conductors who cram on as many passengers as possible to maximise profits.

o Travel agencies in many tourist towns offer relatively expensive private two-by-two buses, which tend to leave and terminate at conveniently central stops.

o Some agencies have been known to book people onto ordinary buses at super-deluxe prices – if possible, book directly with the bus company.

o Timetables and destinations may be displayed on signs or billboards at travel agencies and tourist offices.

COSTS

o The cheapest buses are 'ordinary' government buses, but prices vary from state to state (consult regional chapters).

o Add around 50% to the ordinary fare for deluxe services, double the fare for AC, and triple or quadruple the fare for a two-by-two service.

LUGGAGE

o Luggage is stored in compartments underneath the bus (sometimes for a small fee) or carried on the roof.

o Arrive at least an hour before departure time – some buses cover roof-stored bags with a canvas sheet, making last-minute additions inconvenient/impossible.

o If your bags go on the roof, make sure they're securely locked, and tied to the metal baggage rack – unsecured bags can fall off on rough roads.

○ Theft is a (minor) risk: watch your bags at snack and toilet stops; *never* leave day-packs or valuables unattended inside the bus.

RESERVATIONS

○ Most deluxe buses can be booked in advance – government buses usually a month ahead – at the bus station or local travel agencies.

○ Reservations are rarely possible on 'ordinary' buses; travellers can be left behind in the mad rush for a seat.

🚗 CAR

Few people bother with self-drive car hire – not only because of the hair-raising driving conditions, but also because hiring a car with driver is wonderfully afford-able in India, particularly if several people share the cost. Seatbelts are either nonexistent or of variable quality. International rental companies with representa-tives in India include **Budget** (www.budget.com) and **Hertz** (www.hertz.com).

HIRING A CAR & DRIVER

○ Most towns have taxi stands or car-hire companies where you can arrange short or long tours (see regional chapters).

○ Not all hire cars are licensed to travel beyond their home state. Those that are will pay extra state taxes, are added to the hire charge.

○ Ask for a driver who speaks some English and knows the region you intend visiting, and try to see the car and meet the driver before paying anything.

○ Ambassador cars look great but are rather slow and uncomfortable if travelling long distances – keep them for touring cities.

○ For multiday trips, the charge should cover the driver's meals and accommodation. Drivers should make their own sleeping and eating arrangements.

○ It is *essential* to set the ground rules from day one; politely but firmly let the driver know that you're boss in order to avoid anguish later.

COSTS

○ The price depends on the distance and the terrain (driving on mountain roads uses more petrol, hence the higher cost).

○ One-way trips usually cost the same as return ones (to cover the petrol and driver charges for getting back).

○ Hire charges vary from state to state. Some taxi unions set a time limit or a maximum kilometre distance for day trips – if you go over, you'll have to pay extra.

○ To avoid potential misunderstandings, get *in writing* what you've been promised (quotes should include petrol, sightseeing stops, all your chosen destinations, and meals and accommodation for the driver). If a driver asks you for money for petrol en route because he is short of cash, get receipts for reimbursement later.

○ For sightseeing day trips around a single city, expect to pay upwards of ₹800/1000 for a non-AC/AC car with an eight-hour, 80km limit per day (extra charges apply).

○ A tip is customary at the end of your journey; ₹125-150 per day is fair (more if you're really pleased with the driver's service).

LOCAL TRANSPORT

○ Buses, cycle-rickshaws, autorickshaws, taxis, boats and urban trains provide transport around India's cities.

○ Costs for public transport vary from town to town (consult regional chapters).

○ For any transport without a fixed fare, agree on the price *before* you start your journey and make sure that it covers your luggage and every passenger.

○ Even where meters exist, drivers may refuse to use them, demanding an elevated 'fixed' fare. Insist on the meter; if that fails, find another vehicle.

○ Fares usually increase at night (by up to 100%) and some drivers charge a few rupees extra for luggage.

○ Carry plenty of small bills for taxi and rickshaw fares as drivers rarely have change.

○ Some taxi/autorickshaw drivers are involved in the commission racket – see p90 and p378.

AUTORICKSHAW, TEMPO & VIKRAM

○ The Indian autorickshaw is a three-wheeled motorised contraption with tin or canvas roof and sides, with room for two passengers (although you'll often see many more squeezed in) and limited luggage.

- They are also referred to as autos, scooters, riks or tuk-tuks.

- They are mostly cheaper than taxis and usually have a meter, although getting it turned on can be a challenge.

- Travelling by auto is great fun but, thanks to the open windows, can be smelly, noisy and hot!

- Tempos and *vikrams* (large tempos) are outsized autorickshaws with room for more passengers, running on fixed routes for a fixed fare.

- In country areas, you may also see the fearsome-looking 'three-wheeler' – a crude tractorlike tempo with a front wheel on an articulated arm.

CYCLE-RICKSHAW

- A cycle-rickshaw is a pedal cycle with two rear wheels, supporting a bench seat for passengers. Most have a canopy that can be raised in wet weather, or lowered to provide extra space for luggage.

- Many of the big cities have phased out (or reduced) the number of cycle-rickshaws, but they are still a major means of local transport in many smaller towns.

- Fares must be agreed upon in advance – speak to locals to get an idea of what is a fair price for the distance you intend to travel. Tips are always appreciated, given the slog involved.

- Kolkata is the last bastion of the hand-pulled rickshaw, known as the tana rickshaw. This is a hand-cart on two wheels pulled directly by the rickshaw-wallah.

Manning the Meter

Getting a metered ride is only half the battle. Meters are almost always outdated, so fares are calculated using a combination of the meter reading and a complicated 'fare adjustment card'. Predictably, this system is open to abuse. If you spend a few days in any town, you'll soon get a feel for the difference between a reasonable fare and a blatant rip-off.

TAXI

- Most towns have taxis, and these are usually metered, however, getting drivers to use the meter can be a major hassle. If drivers refuse to use the meter for any reason, find another cab.

- To avoid fare-setting shenanigans, use prepaid taxis where possible (regional chapters contain details).

- Be aware that many taxi drivers supplement their earnings with commissions from hotels or shops that they may try to take you to.

OTHER LOCAL TRANSPORT

In some towns, tongas (horse-drawn two-wheelers) and victorias (horse-drawn carriages) still operate. Kolkata has a tram network, and both Delhi and Kolkata have efficient underground train systems. Mumbai, Delhi and Chennai, among other centres, have suburban trains that leave from ordinary train stations. See regional chapters for comprehensive details.

TOURS

Tours are available all over India, run by tourist offices, local transport companies and travel agencies. Organised tours can be an inexpensive way to see several places on one trip, although you rarely get much time at each place. If you arrange a tailor-made tour, you'll have more freedom about where you go and how long you stay.

Drivers may double as guides, or you can hire a qualified local guide for a fee. In tourist towns, be wary of touts claiming to be professional guides (see p89 and p322). See the Tours section in the regional chapters for details about local tours.

INTERNATIONAL TOUR AGENCIES

Many international companies offer tours to India, from straightforward sightseeing trips to adventure tours and activity-based holidays. To find current tours that match your interests, quiz travel agents and surf the web. Some good places to start your tour hunt:

Dragoman (www.dragoman .com) One of several reputable overland tour companies offering trips in customised vehicles.

Exodus (www.exodustravels .co.uk) A wide array of

specialist trips, including tours with a holistic, wildlife and adventure focus.

India Wildlife Tours (www .india-wildlife-tours.com) All sorts of wildlife tours, plus jeep, horse or camel safaris and birdwatching.

Indian Encounter (www. indianencounters.com) Special-interest tours that include wildlife spotting, river-rafting and ayurvedic treatments.

Intrepid Travel (www .intrepidtravel.com) Endless possibilities, from wildlife tours to sacred rambles.

Peregrine Adventures (www.peregrine.net.au) Popular cultural and trekking tours.

Sacred India Tours (www .sacredindiatours.com) Includes tours with a holistic focus such as yoga and ayurveda, as well as architectural and cultural tours.

Shanti Travel (www. shantitravel.com) A range of family and adventure tours run by a Franco-Indian team.

World Expeditions (www. worldexpeditions.com.au) An array of options, including trekking and cycling tours.

🚆 TRAIN

Travelling by train is a quintessential Indian experience. Trains offer a smoother ride than buses and are especially recommended for long journeys that include overnight travel. India's rail network is one of the largest and busiest in the world and Indian Railways is the largest utility employer on earth, with roughly 1.5 million workers. There are around 6900 train stations scattered across the country.

We've listed useful trains throughout this book but there are hundreds more services. The best way of sourcing updated railway information is to use relevant internet sites such as **Indian Railways** (www.indianrail .gov.in) and the useful www. seat61.com/India. There's also *Trains at a Glance* (₹35), available at many train station bookstands and better bookshops/newsstands, but it's published annually so it's not as up to date as websites. Nevertheless, it offers comprehensive timetables covering all the main lines.

TRAIN CLASSES

There is a range of classes on Indian trains, though not all are offered on all trains. Air-Conditioned 1st Class (1AC) is most expensive, with two- or four-berth compartments. The next level down is Air-Conditioned 2-Tier (2AC), with two-tier berths, while 3AC has three-tier berths. AC Executive Chair and AC Chair offer comfortable, reclining chairs and plenty of space. Sleeper Class features open plan carriages with three-tier bunks and no air-con (but the open windows afford great views). Unreserved 2nd Class is extremely cheap and involves wooden or plastic seats and a lot of people.

BOOKING TICKETS IN INDIA

You can either book tickets through a travel agency or hotel (for a commission) or in person at the train station. Big stations often have English-speaking staff who can help with choosing the best train. At smaller stations, midlevel officials such as the deputy stationmaster usually speak English. It's also worth approaching tourist-office staff if you need advice about booking tickets, deciding train classes etc. The nationwide railways enquiries number is 📞139.

At the Station

Get a reservation slip from the information window, fill in the name of the departure

Train Passes

The IndRail Pass permits unlimited rail travel for the period of its validity, but it offers limited savings and you must still make reservations. Passes are available for one to 90 days of travel. The easiest way to book these is through the IndRail Pass agency in your home country; they can also book any necessary train reservations for you. Overseas travel agencies and station ticket offices in major Indian cities also sell the pass – click on the Information/International Tourist link on www.indianrail.gov.in for further details, including prices. There's no refund for either lost or partially used tickets.

Express Train Fares in Rupees

DISTANCE (KM)	1AC	2AC	3AC	EXECUTIVE CHAIR	CHAIR CAR (CC)	SECOND (II)
100	541	322	267	424	212	65
200	814	480	363	594	297	90
300	1077	633	473	764	382	115
400	1313	770	572	918	459	135
500	1499	879	650	1040	520	150
1000	2451	1432	1048	NA	760	230
1500	3069	1791	1306	NA	825	224
2000	3316	1935	1410	NA	893	243

station, destination station, the class you want to travel and the name and number of the train. Join the long queue for the ticket window where your ticket will be printed. Women should take advantage of the separate women's queue – if there isn't one, go to the front of the regular queue.

Tourist Reservation Bureau

Larger cities and major tourist centres have an International Tourist Bureau, which allows you to book tickets in relative peace – check www.indianrail.gov.in for a list of these stations.

RESERVATIONS

o Bookings open 90 days before departure and you must make a reservation for all chair-car, sleeper, and 1AC, 2AC and 3AC carriages. No reservations are required for general (2nd class) compartments.

o Trains are always busy so it's wise to book as far in advance as possible, especially for overnight trains. There may be additional services to certain destinations during major festivals but it's still worth booking well in advance.

o Reserved tickets show your seat/berth and carriage number. Carriage numbers are written on the side of the train (station staff and porters can point you in the right direction). A list of names and berths is posted on the side of each reserved carriage.

o Refunds are available on any ticket, even after departure, with a penalty – rules are complicated, check when you book.

o Trains can be delayed at any stage of the journey; to avoid stress, factor some leeway into your plans.

o Be mindful of potential drugging and theft – don't accept food or drink from strangers on trains.

If the train you want to travel on is sold out, make sure to enquire about the following.

Tourist Quota

A special (albeit small) tourist quota is set aside for foreign tourists travelling between popular stations. These seats can only be booked at dedicated reservation offices in major cities (see regional chapters for details), and you need to show your passport and visa as ID. Tickets can be paid for in rupees (some offices may ask to see foreign exchange certificates – ATM receipts will suffice), British pounds, US dollars or euros, in cash or Thomas Cook and American Express travellers cheques.

Taktal Tickets

Indian Railways holds back a (very) small number of tickets on key trains and releases them at 8am two days before the train is due to depart. A charge of ₹10–300 is added to each ticket price. First AC and Executive Chair tickets are excluded from the scheme.

Waitlist (WL)

Trains are frequently overbooked, but many passengers cancel and there are regular no-shows. So if you buy a ticket on the waiting list, you're quite likely to get a seat, even if there are a number of people ahead of you on the list. Check your booking status at www.indianrail.gov.in/pnr_stat.html by entering your ticket's PNR number. A refund is available if you fail to get a seat – ask the ticket office about your chances.

Reservation Against Cancellation (RAC)

Even when a train is fully booked, Indian Railways sells a handful of seats in each class as 'Reservation Against Cancellation' (RAC). This means that if you have an RAC ticket and someone cancels before the departure date, you will get his or her seat (or berth). You'll have to check the reservation list at the station on the day of travel to see where you've been allocated to sit. Even if no one cancels, as an RAC ticket holder you can still board the train and, even if you don't get a seat, you can still travel.

COSTS

Fares are calculated by distance and class of travel; Rajdhani and Shatabdi trains are slightly more expensive, but the price includes meals. Most air-conditioned carriages have a catering service (meals are brought to your seat). In unreserved classes it's a good idea to carry portable snacks. Seniors (those over 60) get 30% off all fares in all classes on all types of train. Children below the age of five travel free, those aged between five and 12 are charged half price.

A-Z

Language

HINDI

Hindi has about 180 million speakers in India, and it has official status along with English and 21 other languages.

If you read our pronunciation guides as if they were English, you'll be understood. The length of vowels is important (eg 'a' and 'aa'), and 'ng' after a vowel indicates nasalisation (ie the vowel is pronounced 'through the nose'). The stressed syllables are marked with italics. The abbreviations 'm' and 'f' indicate the options for male and female speakers respectively.

BASICS

Hello./Goodbye.
नमस्ते ।   na·ma·*ste*
Yes.
जी हाँ ।   jee haang
No.
जी नहीं ।   jee na·*heeng*
Excuse me.
सुनिये ।   su·ni·*ye*
Sorry.
माफ़ कीजिये ।   maaf *kee*·ji·ye
Please ...
कृपया ...   kri·pa·*yaa* ...
Thank you.
थैंक्यू ।   *thayn*·kyoo
How are you?
आप कैसे/कैसी   aap *kay*·se/*kay*·see
हैं?   hayng (m/f)
Fine. And you?
मैं ठीक हूँ ।   mayng teek hoong
आप सुनाइये ।   aap su·*naa*·i·ye
Do you speak English?
क्या आपको अंग्रेज़ी   kyaa aap ko an·*gre*·zee
आती है?   *aa*·tee hay
How much is this?
कितने का है?   *kit*·ne kaa hay

I don't understand.
मैं नहीं समझा/   mayng na·*heeng* sam·jaa/
समझी ।   *sam*·jee (m/f)

ACCOMMODATION

Do you have a single/double room?
क्या सिंगल/डबल   kyaa *sin*·gal/da·*bal*
कमरा है?   *kam*·raa hay
How much is it (per night/per person)?
(एक रात/हर व्यक्ति) (ek raat/har *vyak*·ti)
के लिय कितने   ke li·*ye kit*·ne
पैसे लगते हैं?   *pay*·se *lag*·te hayng

EATING & DRINKING

I'd like ..., please.
मुझे ... दीजिये ।   mu·*je* ... *dee*·ji·ye
That was delicious.
बहुत मज़ेदार हुआ ।   ba·*hut* ma·ze·*daar* hu·*aa*
Please bring the menu/bill.
मेन्यू/बिल लाइये ।   *men*·yoo/bil *laa*·i·ye

I don't eat ...
मैं ... नहीं   mayng ... na·*heeng*
खाता/खाती ।   *kaa*·taa/*kaa*·tee (m/f)
  fish   मछली   *mach*·lee
  meat   गोश्त   gosht
  poultry   मुर्गी   *mur*·gee

EMERGENCIES

I'm ill.
मैं बीमार हूँ ।   mayng *bee*·maar hoong
Help!
मदद कीजिये!   ma·*dad kee*·ji·ye
Call the doctor/police!
डॉक्टर/पुलिस   *daak*·tar/pu·*lis*
को बुलाओ!   ko bu·*laa*·o

DIRECTIONS

Where's a/the ...?
... कहाँ है?   ... ka·*haang* hay
  bank
  बैंक   baynk
  market
  बाज़ार   *baa*·zaar
  post office
  डाक ख़ाना   daak *kaa*·naa
  restaurant
  रेस्टोरेंट   *res*·to·rent
  toilet
  टॉइलेट   *taa*·i·let
  tourist office
  पर्यटन ऑफ़िस   *par*·ya·tan *aa*·fis

TAMIL

Tamil is the official language in the state of Tamil Nadu and one of the major languages of South India, with about 62 million speakers.

Note that in our pronunciation guides, the symbol 'aw' is pronounced as in 'law' and 'ow' as in 'how'.

BASICS

Hello.
வணக்கம். va·*nak*·kam

Goodbye.
போய் வருகிறேன். *po*·i va·*ru*·ki·reyn

Yes./No.
ஆமாம்./இல்லை. *aa*·maam/*il*·lai

Excuse me.
தயவு செய்து. ta·ya·*vu* sei·*du*

Sorry.
மன்னிக்கவும். *man*·nik·ka·vum

Please ...
தயவு செய்து ... ta·ya·*vu* chey·*tu* ...

Thank you.
நன்றி. *nan*·dri

How are you?
நீங்கள் நலமா? *neeng*·kal na·*la*·maa

Fine, thanks. And you?
நலம், நன்றி. na·*lam nan*·dri
நீங்கள்? *neeng*·kal

Do you speak English?
நீங்கள் ஆங்கிலம் *neeng*·kal *aang*·ki·lam
பேசுவீர்களா? *pey*·chu·*veer*·ka·la

How much is this?
இது என்ன விலை? i·*tu* en·na vi·*lai*

I don't understand.
எனக்கு e·*nak*·ku
விளங்கவில்லை. vi·*lang*·ka·vil·*lai*

ACCOMMODATION

Do you have a single/double room?
உங்களிடம் ஓர் *ung*·ka·li·tam awr
தன/இரட்டை ta·*ni/i*·rat·*tai*
அறை உள்ளதா? a·*rai* ul·la·taa

How much is it per night/person?
ஓர் இரவுக்கு/ awr i·ra·*vuk*·ku/
ஒருவருக்கு o·ru·va·*ruk*·ku
என்னவிலை? *en*·na·vi·lai

EATING & DRINKING

I'd like the ..., please.
எனக்கு தயவு e·*nak*·ku ta·ya·*vu*
செய்து ... chey·*tu* ...
கொடுங்கள். ko·*tung*·kal

bill	விலைச்சீட்டு	vi·*laich*·cheet·tu
menu	உணவுப் –	u·na·*vup*·
	பட்டியல	pat·ti·yal

I'm allergic to ...
எனக்கு ... உணவு e·*nak*·ku ... u·na·*vu*
சேராது. chey·*raa*·tu

dairy	பால்	paal
products	சார்ந்த	*chaarn*·ta
meat	இறைச்சி	i·*raich*·chi
stock	வகை	va·*kai*
nuts	பருப்பு வகை	pa·*rup*·pu va·*kai*
seafood	கடல்	ka·*tal*
	சார்ந்த	*chaarn*·ta

EMERGENCIES

Help!
உதவி! u·ta·*vi*

Call a doctor!
ஐ அழைக்கவும் i a·*zai*·ka·vum
ஒரு மருத்துவர்! o·*ru* ma·*rut*·tu·var

Call the police!
ஐ அழைக்கவும் i a·*zai*·ka·vum
போலீஸ்! pow·*lees*

DIRECTIONS

Where's a/the ...?
... எங்கே ... *eng*·key
இருக்கிறது ? i·*ruk*·ki·ra·tu

bank		
	வங்கி	*vang*·ki
market		
	சந்தை	*chan*·tai
post office		
	தபால் நிலையம்	ta·*paal* ni·*lai*·yam
restaurant		
	உணவகம	u·na·va·*kam*
toilet		
	கழிவறை	ka·*zi*·va·rai
tourist office		
	சுற்றுப்பயண	chut·*rup*·pa·ya·na
	அலுவலகம்	a·*lu*·va·la·*kam*

Behind the Scenes

Author Thanks

ABIGAIL HOLE

Many thanks to all at LP, especially to commissioning editors Suzannah Shwer and Kate Morgan, to Ali Lemer for her calm and efficiency, and to Alex Leung for his cartography skills and patience. Special thanks to Sarina Singh and my coauthors for all their remarkable work on this book, as well as to the many local helpers on the road, without whom none of this would be possible, and to the many travellers who wrote in with advice and updates.

Acknowledgments

Climate map data adapted from Peel MC, Finlayson BL & McMahon TA (2007) 'Updated World Map of the Köppen-Geiger Climate Classification', *Hydrology and Earth System Sciences*, 11, 163344.

Illustrations pp66-7, pp100-1 and pp332-3 by Javier Zarracina.

Cover photographs: Front: The Taj Mahal at dawn, Agra, Uttar Pradesh, Dallas Stribley / Lonely Planet Images; Back: Tea plantation workers in the high ranges of Munnar, Kerala, Lindsay Brown / Lonely Planet Images. Many of the images in this guide are available for licensing from Lonely Planet Images: www.lonelyplanetimages.com.

This Book

This 1st edition of Lonely Planet's *Discover India* v written by Abigail Hole, based on her research and that of Michael Benanav, Lindsay Brown, Mark Ellic Katja Gaskell, Kate James, Amy Karafin, Anirban Mahapatra, Bradley Mayhew, Daniel McCrohan, Joh Noble, Kevin Raub and Sarina Singh. David Lukas wrote the Landscape & Wildlife chapter, Amelia Thomas cowrote the Family Travel chapter and Dr Trish Batchelor wrote the Health section. This guidebook was commissioned in Lonely Planet's Melbourne off and produced by the following:

Commissioning Editors Suzannah Shwer, Kate Morgan
Coordinating Editor Ali Lemer
Coordinating Cartographer Alex Leung
Coordinating Layout Designer Jessica Rose
Managing Editors Brigitte Ellemor, Bruce Evans
Managing Cartographer Adrian Persoglia
Managing Layout Designers Chris Girdler, Jane Hart
Assisting Editors Kate James, Craig Kilburn, Anne Mulvaney, Catherine Naghten, Jeanette Wall, Helen Yeates
Assisting Cartographer Anita Banh
Assisting Layout Designer Paul Iacono
Cover Research Naomi Parker
Internal Image Research Rebecca Skinner
Language Content Branislava Vladisavljevic
Thanks to Shahara Ahmed, Nigel Chin, Helen Christini Ryan Evans, Gerard Walker

SEND US YOUR FEEDBACK

We love to hear from travellers – your comments ke us on our toes and help make our books better. Our well-travelled team reads every word on what you loved or loathed about this book. Although we cann reply individually to postal submissions, we always guarantee that your feedback goes straight to the a propriate authors, in time for the next edition. Each person who sends us information is thanked in the next edition, and the most useful submissions are rewarded with a free book.

Visit **lonelyplanet.com/contact** to submit you updates and suggestions or to ask for help. Our award-winning website also features inspirational travel stories, news and discussions.

Note: We may edit, reproduce and incorporate your comments in Lonely Planet products such a: guidebooks, websites and digital products, so let know if you don't want your comments reproduc or your name acknowledged. For a copy of our privacy policy visit lonelyplanet.com/privacy.

Index

000 Map pages

000 Map pages

000 Map pages

How to Use This Book

These symbols will help you find the listings you want:

- ⊙ Sights
- ✈ Activities
- ⊖ Courses
- ⊕ Tours
- ★ Festivals & Events
- ⊟ Sleeping
- ✗ Eating
- ⊖ Drinking
- ★ Entertainment
- ⊕ Shopping
- ⊕ Information/ Transport

Look out for these icons:

FREE No payment required

🌿 A green or sustainable option

Our authors have nominated these places as demonstrating a strong commitment to sustainability – for example by supporting local communities and producers, operating in an environmentally friendly way, or supporting conservation projects.

These symbols give you the vital information for each listing:

- ♪ Telephone Numbers
- ☉ Opening Hours
- P Parking
- ⊖ Nonsmoking
- ✳ Air-Conditioning
- @ Internet Access
- ☎ Wi-Fi Access
- ☒ Swimming Pool
- ✔ Vegetarian Selection
- ⊡ English-Language Menu
- ♦ Family-Friendly
- ☺ Pet-Friendly
- ⊟ Bus
- ⊛ Ferry
- Ⓜ Metro
- Ⓢ Subway
- ⊖ London Tube
- ⊟ Tram
- ⊟ Train

Reviews are organised by author preference.

Map Legend

Sights
- ⊙ Beach
- ⊙ Buddhist
- ⊙ Castle
- ⊙ Christian
- ⊙ Hindu
- ⊙ Islamic
- ⊙ Jewish
- ⊙ Monument
- ⊜ Museum/Gallery
- ⊙ Ruin
- ⊙ Winery/Vineyard
- ⊗ Zoo
- ⊙ Other Sight

Activities, Courses & Tours
- ⊛ Diving/Snorkelling
- ⊙ Canoeing/Kayaking
- ⊙ Skiing
- ⊙ Surfing
- ⊙ Swimming/Pool
- ⊙ Walking
- ⊙ Windsurfing
- ⊙ Other Activity/ Course/Tour

Sleeping
- ⊙ Sleeping
- ⊙ Camping

Eating
- ⊗ Eating

Drinking
- ⊙ Drinking
- ⊙ Cafe

Entertainment
- ⊙ Entertainment

Shopping
- ⊕ Shopping

Information
- ⊟ Bank
- ⊙ Embassy/ Consulate
- ⊕ Hospital/Medical
- ⊚ Internet
- ⊙ Police
- ⊙ Post Office
- ⊙ Telephone
- ⊙ Toilet
- ⊙ Tourist Information
- • Other Information

Transport
- ⊙ Airport
- ⊗ Border Crossing
- ⊛ Bus
- ⊕ Cable Car/ Funicular
- ⊙ Cycling
- ⊙ Ferry
- Ⓜ Metro
- ⊙ Monorail
- ⊙ Parking
- ⊙ Petrol Station
- ⊙ Taxi
- ⊙ Train/Railway
- ⊙ Tram
- • Other Transport

Routes
- Tollway
- Freeway
- Primary
- Secondary
- Tertiary
- Lane
- Unsealed Road
- Plaza/Mall
- Steps
- Tunnel
- Pedestrian Overpass
- Walking Tour
- Walking Tour Detour
- Path

Geographic
- ⊙ Hut/Shelter
- ⊙ Lighthouse
- ⊙ Lookout
- ▲ Mountain/Volcano
- ⊙ Oasis
- ⊙ Park
-)(Pass
- ⊙ Picnic Area
- ⊙ Waterfall

Population
- ⊙ Capital (National)
- ⊙ Capital (State/Province)
- ⊙ City/Large Town
- ⊙ Town/Village

Boundaries
- — — — International
- — — State/Province
- — — — Disputed
- — — Regional/Suburb
- Marine Park
- Cliff
- Wall

Hydrography
- River/Creek
- Intermittent River
- Swamp/Mangrove
- Reef
- Canal
- Water
- Dry/Salt/ Intermittent Lake
- Glacier

Areas
- Beach/Desert
- Cemetery (Christian)
- Cemetery (Other)
- Park/Forest
- Sportsground
- Sight (Building)
- Top Sight (Building)

KATE JAMES

Kerala & South India Melbourne-born Kate grew up in Ooty, where her parents taught at an international school. Her family holidayed across India for eight years and used the very first edition of Lonely Planet's *India*; Kate has returned with almost every one since. Journalism in Australia led to an editing job at Lonely Planet and then into freelance writing and editing. Kate has worked on two editions of Lonely Planet's *India* and also wrote *Women of the Gobi* (Pluto Press, 2006).

AMY KARAFIN

Plan Your Trip, Goa & Around, History Amy headed straight to India after university and spent the next few years alternating between New York and faraway lands until, fed up with being a travel editor in a Manhattan cubicle, she relinquished her MetroCard to make a living on the road. She has been freelancing seminomadically ever since, spending time in Senegal, Ghana, Guinea and India and writing for Lonely Planet, *Condé Nast Traveler, National Geographic Traveler* and the *Boston Globe*. Amy has worked on four editions of Lonely Planet's *India*.

ANIRBAN MAHAPATRA

Darjeeling, Varanasi & the Northeast, Mumbai (Bombay) & Around, Goa & Around After obtaining a degree in literature, Anirban worked as a travel writer in Delhi for seven years. Since 2007 he has contributed to subcontinent-specific Lonely Planet guidebooks, as well as regularly writing for widely circulated Indian broadsheets. He is also a published and exhibited photographer. When not living out of a rucksack, he cools his heels in Kolkata and Delhi.

BRADLEY MAYHEW

Darjeeling, Varanasi & the Northeast Bradley has been visiting the Himalaya for 20 years now, and has also been the co-ordinating author of Lonely Planet guides to *Bhutan, Nepal* and *Trekking in the Nepal Himalaya*. He was recently the subject of a five-part Arte/SWR documentary retracing the route of Marco Polo from Venice to Xanadu through Iran, Afghanistan and Central Asia. See what he's currently up to at www.bradleymayhew.blogspot.com.

DANIEL McCROHAN

Delhi & the Taj Mahal, Darjeeling, Varanasi & the Northeast Daniel has been travelling to India on and off for almost 20 years. His writing career began in London in the late 1990s, where he worked as a news and sports reporter for seven years before switching to travel. He now specialises in India and China, and has cowritten six Lonely Planet guidebooks, including *India, China* and *Tibet*. He now lives in China, but never tires of returning to India thanks to the gems it throws up each visit.

JOHN NOBLE

Rajasthan John, from England, lives in Spain and has written on 20 or so countries for Lonely Planet. He first experienced India in the days of Rajiv Gandhi but has never written about it until now. Best on-the-road decision: a predawn safari where he saw not one but four young lions strolling casually through the bushes in the early morning light.

Read more about John at:
lonelyplanet.com/members/ewoodrover

KEVIN RAUB

Mumbai (Bombay) & Around Kevin grew up in Atlanta, USA and started his career working for *Men's Journal* and *Rolling Stone* magazines in New York before taking up travel writing. During a decade of trips to India, he's ogled the Taj Mahal, tracked tigers in Madhya Pradesh and navigated Keralan backwaters. He contributes to a wealth of travel and entertainment magazines and has worked on 10 Lonely Planet guides. You can find him at www.kevinraub.net.

SARINA SINGH

Plan Your Trip, India In Focus After finishing a business degree in Melbourne, Sarina worked as a freelance journalist and foreign correspondent in India. After returning to Australia and pursuing a postgraduate journalism degree she coauthored Lonely Planet's very first edition of *Rajasthan*, and has since worked on about 30 Lonely Planet books. Her extensive publication portfolio includes *National Geographic Traveler* (USA), the *Sunday Times* (UK) and a monthly column for *Lonely Planet Magazine* (India). Further details at www.sarinasingh.com.

Read more about Sarina at:
lonelyplanet.com/members/sarinasingh

CONTRIBUTING AUTHORS

DAVID LUKAS lives on the edge of Yosemite National Park, where he studies and writes about the natural world. He has contributed environment chapters to almost 30 Lonely Planet guides and is the author of *A Year of Watching Wildlife*. David wrote the Landscape & Wildlife chapter.

AMELIA THOMAS is a writer and journalist working throughout India and the Middle East. Her four small children have travelled extensively throughout India and beyond, and particularly enjoy *masala dosas,* mango lassis and hurtling through the streets of Old Delhi on autorickshaws. Amelia cowrote the Family Travel chapter.

Our Story

A beat-up old car, a few dollars in the pocket and a sense of adventure. In 1972 that's all Tony and Maureen Wheeler needed for the trip of a lifetime – across Europe and Asia overland to Australia. It took several months, and at the end – broke but inspired – they sat at their kitchen table writing and stapling together their first travel guide, *Across Asia on the Cheap*. Within a week they'd sold 1500 copies. Lonely Planet was born.

Today, Lonely Planet has offices in Melbourne, London and Oakland, with more than 600 staff and writers. We share Tony's belief that 'a great guidebook should do three things: inform, educate and amuse'.

Our Writers

ABIGAIL HOLE

Coordinating Author, Plan Your Trip, India in Focus, Delhi & the Taj Mahal, Kerala & South India Abigail was first bewitched by India around 15 years ago, when she travelled around the north on a hot and bewildering summer trip. She's returned at least every couple of years with increasing regularity, and has worked on Lonely Planet's *India* guide four times. She also cowrote the first edition of *Rajasthan, Delhi & Agra* and has written about India for various newspapers and magazines, including *Lonely Planet Magazine*. Authoring this edition gave her the welcome opportunity of covering Kerala and Delhi, two of her favourite places.

MICHAEL BENANAV

Northern Mountains & Amritsar Michael has been to North India four times but still hasn't visited the Taj Mahal. He'd like to, really, but maybe he's too busy migrating through Uttarakhand with a family of nomadic water-buffalo herders, or attaining spiritual enlightenment by riding buses over the mountain roads of Himachal Pradesh. Michael freelances for the *New York Times, Geographical* and other publications. His website is www.michaelbenanav.com.

LINDSAY BROWN

Rajasthan, Northern Mountains & Amritsar After completing a PhD on evolutionary genetics and a stint as a science editor, Lindsay started working for Lonely Planet. Formerly the publishing manager of outdoor activity guides at Lonely Planet, Lindsay returns to the subcontinent to trek, write and photograph whenever possible. He has also contributed to Lonely Planet's *South India, Nepal, Bhutan, Rajasthan, Delhi & Agra* and *Pakistan & the Karakoram Highway* guides, among others.

MARK ELLIOTT

Northern Mountains & Amritsar, Darjeeling, Varanasi & the Northeast Mark has been making forays to the subcontinent since a 1984 trip that lined his stomach for all eventualities. For this edition an eventful summer saw him dodging landslides in Ladakh, curfews in Srinagar and stone-throwing mobs around Kashmir. When not researching travel guides Mark lives a blissfully quiet suburban life with his beloved Belgian bride, Danielle, who found him at a Turkmen camel market.

KATJA GASKELL

Survival Guide More than 16 years ago Katja arrived in India on a six-week, ill-planned trip convinced that Rajasthan couldn't be that hot (it was) or the Goa monsoon rains that heavy (they were). She still fell in love with the country and vowed to return. Today she calls Delhi home and regularly escapes the city to explore India with her husband and two kids.

More Writers ....

Published by Lonely Planet Publications Pty Ltd
ABN 36 005 607 983
1st edition – Nov 2011
ISBN 978 1 74220 291 4
© Lonely Planet 2011   Photographs © as indicated 2011
10 9 8 7 6 5 4 3 2 1
Printed in Singapore